PRAIS

APPALACHIAN ZEN

"Amazing and intense. A unique, entertaining, and valuable contribution to the Dharma literature, *Appalachian Zen* addresses a part of the Western Dharma world that hasn't received much attention: class."

— Rev. Sumi Loundon Kim, Buddhist chaplain, Yale University, author of *Blue Jean Buddha* and *Sitting Together*

"Zen is becoming native to America and the West, and there's no better place to see what this looks like than with Steve Kanji Ruhl's *Appalachian Zen*. It's an intimate memoir; you can taste and smell and feel his journey into the depths. At the same time, it's a very good invitation into the details of a contemporary Zen life. I strongly recommend it."

— James Ishmael Ford, author of *Introduction to Zen Koans: Learning the Language of Dragons*

"*Appalachian Zen* is the record of the journey of a restless soul in search of home, who finds it, finally, in the dynamic silence of Zen. Steve Kanji Ruhl's poetic descriptions of his birthplace in hardscrabble Appalachian Pennsylvania, his wanderings through Japan, his education in elite universities, and of the often harrowing incidents of his life, make this book an engrossing read. What is life, what is death, why are we here? No one avoids such questions, here explored with honesty and depth."

— Norman Fischer, Zen priest and poet, author of *When You Greet Me I Bow: Reflections from a Life in Zen* and *Selected Poems 1980-2013*

"This beautifully written memoir traces the author's pilgrim's progress from the conservative American heartland to the depths of the Buddhist dharma, mirroring Martin Buber's claim that every journey has a 'secret destination of which the traveler is unaware.' Insightful, accessible, and emotionally transparent, this epic spiritual journey from West to East and back again will open your mind and widen your heart. I recommend it highly."

"A wise, wonderful, and fierce book."

JOURNEYS IN SEARCH OF TRUE HOME,
FROM THE AMERICAN HEARTLAND TO THE BUDDHA DHARMA

APPALACHIAN
ZEN

STEVE KANJI RUHL

Monkfish Book Publishing Company
Rhinebeck, New York

Paperback ISBN: 978-1-948626-80-4
eBook ISBN: 978-1-948626-81-1

Library of Congress Cataloging-in-Publication Data

Names: Kanji Ruhl, Steve, author.
Title: Appalachian Zen : journeys in search of true home, from the American
    heartland to the Buddha dharma / Steve Kanji Ruhl.
Description: Rhinebeck : Monkfish Book Publishing Company, 2022. | Includes
    bibliographical references.
Identifiers: LCCN 2022017885 (print) | LCCN 2022017886 (ebook) | ISBN
    9781948626804 (paperback) | ISBN 9781948626811 (ebook)
Subjects: LCSH: Kanji Ruhl, Steve. | Buddhist converts--United
    States--Biography. | Buddhism--United States.
Classification: LCC BQ968.A455 A3 2022 (print) | LCC BQ968.A455 (ebook) |
    DDC 294.30973--dc23/eng/20220609
LC record available at https://lccn.loc.gov/2022017885
LC ebook record available at https://lccn.loc.gov/2022017886

Book and cover design by Colin Rolfe

Monkfish Book Publishing Company
22 East Market Street, Suite 304
Rhinebeck, NY 12572
(845) 876-4861
monkfishpublishing.com

CONTENTS

Introduction   Practice as if Your Head Is on Fire (1997)   vii

Part One   In Penn's Woods:
               On the Search for True Home (1992)   1

Part Two   Narrow Road to the Rising Sun:
               On Beginning to Practice (1997–1999)   87

Part Three   All Is Lost, Be of Good Cheer:
               On the Death of the Self (2003)   157

Part Four   Errant Pilgrim:
               On Zen Buddhist Ministry (2005–2011)   229

Part Five   Gone Beyond:
               On the Path of Heartland (2012–2022)   263

Notes   327
Acknowledgments   333

INTRODUCTION

PRACTICE AS IF
YOUR HEAD IS ON FIRE

1997

LIGHT GRAZES peaks of the Kitakami Highlands.

Light burnishes the rice flats.

A Zen priest, Watanabe, climbs the stairs of Taiyo-ji's bell tower. Land of the rising sun.

He chortles to himself, round-faced *rōshi* with shaven scalp. Clad in robes of indigo. Drape of khaki across his shoulder. His eyes are lit, as always, with imperturbable private mirth. I follow him. We stand on the belfry, its plank flooring littered with yellow fans of ginkgo leaves.

I rose at five-thirty in a room brittle with cold. Dressed, then moved outdoors into fading darkness. Incipient radiance seeped the air. Fog lifted off the Kitakami River.

I rode a bicycle past cherry and persimmon trees. Rode past tile-roofed houses, azaleas, chestnuts, past vegetable gardens and sentry pines, the six-foot protective walls of bristled hedges, streets of the former samurai district. I saw no one.

Chuffing squawk of a raven.

Sunshine gathering now in the east. Sky is the blue gaseous heart of fire.

Watanabe chants orisons, bent stiffly, hands palm-to-palm. I reach for the log suspended in its rope harness. I pull back and then, in an uninterrupted glide, strike the massive iron bell. The sound—a shaped sonic pulse in the air, stately, ferrous, with a bass underhum—ripples over canted rooftops and cedars and the Buddhist cemetery of Kanegasaki, Japan. I bow. During the past month I've learned what to do: I make a steeple of my pressed hands. Watanabe chants. When the bell's vibrato begins to dim, when it nearly subsides, I reach and pull and strike again. Eight times.

Inside Taiyo-ji Temple, I sit, knees to the floor, astride a black *zafu*.

Stare at mesh of *tatami* mat.

Stillness. Breath.

A monk materializes behind me, unseen, noiseless as the thoughts I quell minute by minute, and he presses the stick, *kyōsaku*, to my spine to straighten my posture; he vanishes. Now breathing. Now stillness.

Stillnessbreathing.

I am the first foreigner to sit *zazen* at Taiyo-ji in the temple's four-hundred-year history.

◯

THIS VISIT marks my first venture into Japan. In 1997, the end of the century, I've done what vagabond Americans always do: I've lit out for the West. I've flown from Boston into Chicago and then across the prairies and Canadian Rockies and over the unpeopled limitless sweep of Alaska to the Pacific. But I haven't paused there. I've continued westward into fulgent, perpetual sun. I've gone so far west I've wound up in the "Mysterious East."

I've landed here at forty-three, newly emerging from a baffled life, having lost much of what felt familiar and having experienced through many contested nights and days my own foreignness, the rawness and novelty of a world I scarcely recognize any longer as my own.

Perhaps living one season in Japan—the irreducible oddity of it; the dislocation and jetlag; the jeopardy of loneliness; the unreliability of language, of custom—will help me understand some of this.

I'm not sure. I live now with few expectations, and certainly without hope. Which is to say, I seem to live increasingly for this very instant, imparadised, abundant, and live in moods of quiet, unreasoning happiness. Perhaps this is good Zen.

But it's difficult. Still a novice at practicing Zen, after only three years, I relapse often into meanness and mistaken habit. Nor is that all: a novice

at practicing middle age, I seem to totter between mastery and buffoonery, last chance and reformation.

*I can only guess what my father dreamed for us as he drove through early
morning darkness of fading stars, or through a blizzard or through rain, humming his favorite Kingston Trio songs. On his way to work he shared lonely
stretches of asphalt with an occasional highballing Mac diesel rig. Watching
for deer that might step gingerly from pine groves into his headlights on the
long straightaways between Lock Haven and Bellefonte he'd drive into the
dawn. He worked as a drafting engineer at the Titan Metal factory. My dad
toted his lunch bucket and drove his gas-reeking Ford clunker eighty miles
roundtrip every day, Monday through Friday, to glean for us paychecks total-
ing eleven thousand dollars a year. We lived in a trailer. Our trailer sat among
other trailers at the edge of scrub woods, off a two-lane blacktop called Route
220 in Clinton County.*

*My dad and my uncles had survived shell bursts and machine guns in
the South Pacific and in lethal fields of Italy. The uncles and buddies: noisy,
profane guys with cock-of-the-walk grins, their hair bristle-cut, their shirtsleeves rolled up past their biceps, men who shadow-punched and hollered
at the TV—"Attaboy, jab, jab, goddammit, hit him with yer left!"—when
the fights were on, men who bluffed and wheeler-dealed through five-card-
stud in kitchens on Saturday afternoons, smoking Luckies, pouring libations
of Carling Black Label while the wives gibbered over coffeecake. They were
the first men I knew. Guffawing. Backslapping. "Gimme 'nother one a them
goddamn cards there, okay boys, read 'em an' weep, now beat that sonofa-
bitch." Most of them worked the pulp tubs and cutters at Hammermill in
Lock Haven. All-night eleven-to-seven shift. You could watch specters of mist
hazard the river at sunrise.*

*My mom pinned our wash to the wind and she planted marigolds, she
blared* South Pacific *and* My Fair Lady *on the hi-fi, testament—I realize
only now—to unplumbed yearnings. When she was a little girl during the
Depression she lived with her mother and sisters and her besotted stepfather a
few miles beyond the outpost of White Pine, on a little husk of a farm alone
in the woods.*

In our trailer when I was a kid we watched Walt Disney's Wonderful

World of Color *on a boxy black-and-white TV. We heard hound dogs moaning
at the Penn Central freight trains that racketed out through the Appalachian
Mountains at night—out past the barns with "Mail Pouch Tobacco" painted
on wood long abused by weather, out past the truck farms and junk lots,
the neglected bridges of trestled iron, past boneyards, the cow-flop pastures
and the forests, the Susquehanna. On winter nights we heard high school
wrestling matches on the radio, sweaty farm boys from Bald Eagle-Nittany
and Warriors Run on the mat, angling for half-nelsons in a gym full of roaring millhands. We scrimped for school clothes ordered from the Sears catalog.
Three times a week we shared bathwater. Every May we saw fly fishermen
troll Bald Eagle Creek. Every November Clinton County honored the first day
of buck season and doe season—official school holidays, like Thanksgiving or
Christmas. Men stopped shaving and grew their buck-beards. They wore black
and red Woolrich parkas, hunting licenses safety-pinned to the backs. Men
disappeared into woods around Swissdale or Tangascootac in rattletrap cars
and pickups, Remington thirty-ought-sixes in the gun racks. They swigged bottles of Old Granddad in hunting shanties called Ponderosa and Shangri-La.
They munched fried-baloney sandwiches and scrapple and sticky-buns. Men
hung parkas outside on tree limbs so the wool could lose its human scent.
Mornings before setting out they rubbed deer piss on their boots. They checked
ammo and honed their gutting knives. When they returned, driving through
Lock Haven, they had big fulvous six-point whitetails lashed to their hoods
and fenders, the deers' white bellies flecked with blood, heads dangling under
weight of antlers, each deer's eye a black marble.*

*Clinton County, Pennsylvania. Heart of the Keystone State, fifty miles
east of the anthracite fields, land of backwoods factory towns, tough-luck
Appalachian farms and skid-row country motels, land of cinderblock bars
with "Genesee" in red neon and Johnny Cash on nickel jukeboxes.*

Since arriving in Japan, I've sought Zen.

In Tokyo—amid cubbyholes of groceries and directly opposite a
Sumitomo bank—broods the imposing Thunder Gate of Asakusa
Kannon. Hiroshige depicted it in falling snow in his series of woodblock
prints, "One Hundred Famous Views of Edo." Not affiliated with Zen,
the temple of Asakusa Kannon features elements of Shingon and Tendai

Buddhist sects. Its gate displays, locked in screened cages as if they might burst free, statues of belligerent tutelary gods: Fūjin, the muscular *kami* of wind; Raijin, the scowling thunder kami. I roamed with mounting dismay, accompanied by a woman who in Kanegasaki would serve briefly as my advisor. We slipstreamed into the Buddhist temple's market bazaar of Nakamise-dori, an Atlantic City arcade of garish plastic trinkets and windup toys, of gimcrack geisha combs and postcards and King Kong masks, flea market *yukata*, rice-cracker stalls and discount Hokusai T-shirts. The aisles flooded with shoppers and tourists.

In the main temple compound people mobbed a kettle of "curative" incense smoke. Superstitious pilgrims bought talismans. Grandmothers pressed hands in prayer. They tossed fifty-yen coins at shrines. Pigeons with cravats of green and lavender huffed askant the cobblestone. When the birds airlifted among pagodas, people tracked them with cameras. Men in business suits knotted Shinto prayer offerings to lattices.

Escaping to secluded pine gardens I watched pools of carp—orange, black-sprinkled, as if daylilies had submerged and transmuted by sorcery into fish.

Then I returned to the hubbub. Inside the temples people gaped at Buddhist Baroque, at fussbudgety golden altars, at vaulted ceilings, gaudy with ersatz Indian murals of bodhisattvas. The faithful pitched their coins. They prayed to Kannon, goddess of compassion, for miracles. Is there any world religion, I wondered, not tainted by quackery and hucksterism?

A week later I stood inside Eitoku-ji. This remote Zen temple abides the centuries far from Tokyo, concealed among a bosk of evergreens in mountains outside Kanegasaki. To reach it, I stepped along a path of moss and wet pebbles. The sky was rinsing out with light after quick showers.

Silence so thick I could breathe it, could take the silence directly into my lungs.

Inside the *zendo*: walls of creviced white plasterboard. Roof supported by logs adorned with enchased scrollwork so elementary it looked gouged out of the wood by a blunted pocketknife. Bat dung peppered one corner of the concrete floor. An unshielded lightbulb hung by its wire from the ceiling. At the altar, modest bodhisattvas—one of compassion, astride an elephant; one of wisdom, astride a rotund, fanciful lion; one snug within a throne of blossoms—rested on calices of wooden lotus petals. A single Zen monk tended Eitoku-ji. Young, strong-jawed, he wore steel-rimmed glasses and his black robes flurried. I noted his ease. His attentive, bright-gazed composure. In the adjoining temple he knelt on tatami and he unwrapped sheets of ancient rice paper to reveal their inked sutras to a contingent of visiting Kanegasaki elders. I toured the small room, admiring its paintings of exquisitely gracile white cranes and its somersaulting lions rendered in *sumi-e* brushstrokes. I admired a polished *taiko* drum.

Outdoors I paused between the toilet and the temple bell. I discovered something in the grass that looked like a crinkled strip of plasticine. Membranous, translucent silver, I knew it instantly. Shed snakeskin. Auspicious omen: casting-off of an old self.

We suppose we build our homes. But in fact our homes build us, memory by memory:

Riding the Coudersport road with my parents, my brother and sister, woozy summer evenings when we escaped the trailer's heat by riding mountain roads with our car windows down. My father braking to admire a trio of whitetails. The doe and buck hesitant. Watchful. Their fawn inquisitive. Until a sudden noise made them dart like Nijinskys out of the apple orchard and vanish....

Kneeling on the curb on Main Street in Lock Haven, Memorial Day 1962, sipping an orange Nehi and watching fire trucks from Black Moshannon rumble past the crowd....

My father and I riding in the station wagon through June's mugginess, the air like a wet washcloth. We'd step into the ice factory near Piper. Workmen in its archaic, refrigerated brick warehouse grappled with ice blocks the size of suitcases. They slid the ice off pallets and across the sawdust floor with huge metal tongs. We'd pay for our block, then wrestle it onto newspapers in the trunk of the Ford, speeding home before it melted....

In our kitchen, sharding that block with an ice pick. Dumping chips into the bottom of a tub. Adding rock salt, sugar, vanilla, thick milk, eggs, churning it to ice cream. Dulcet, granular, numbing on the tongue....

Saturday morning. A radio grinding out noise, Pops Stover and the

Trailblazers live from the Country Tavern on WBPZ, sharp Appalachian twang, their yodels and frisky mandolin runs on "Carry Me Back to Ol' Virginny...."

Wading knee-deep river shallows to Boom Island with my dad and my brother, an August morning when I was nine years old, a morning that seemed poured from a bucket of light....

Trekking a cliffside path up Peter's Steps, seeing all Lock Haven from the ledges: smokestacks of the paper mill; rooftops and church spires and City Hall; buff-colored pylons and concrete arches of a viaduct called the Constitution Bridge; beyond, the wooded mountain with its cicatrix of rockpile; and the Susquehanna, gray anaconda....

Memory functions as human chronometer. The body has its clock, set to circadian rhythms, to mensal cycles. Memory is the clock of consciousness:

I remember an afternoon in May. My mother driving back to our trailer. An impulse: she veered off the highway. She parked our car beside a weed-filled ditch, then hurried up the slope to a derelict woodshed, to a lilac bush. She gathered an armful of lilacs. Another; another. She festooned our front seat with lilacs, back in the days when she was younger than I am now, and she liked to hum "The Blue Danube."

My high school Humanities classroom. My teacher and friend, Bruce Bechdel: "Pay attention, people! A thousand 'A's to the person who can tell me the basis of the conflict between Antigone and Creon!" Kids squirming. Me as a teenager in 1971, hair draping my shoulders, clad in my faded Army jacket with the peace symbol, answering him: "Fundamental conflict between individual conscience and the authority of the state." I could do this without seeming like a teacher's pet, because, as the school rebel, I had impeccable outlaw credentials. Bruce: "Right! A thousand 'A's for Ruhl!" A crewcut farmboy from Beech Creek tips back in his chair, arms folded, demanding, "Whatta we gotta read all this Sophocles crap for, Bruce?" A Mill Hall girl pops bubblegum: "Yeah, Bruce, it's boring." Bruce, an anomaly in that small country-bumpkin school, an urbane sophisticate with tousled hair and turtlenecks and sly grin, prepossessing in his late thirties, connoisseur of opera and Victoriana, of Bergman films and Eliot's "Four Quartets." His voice, its unique cadences and intonations:

"You read Sophocles, people, who is ONLY one of the greatest writers who ever LIVED, to enrich your TAWDRY– little—existence! So you won't be a bunch of pathetic little—APPALACHIAN—HILLBILLIES—your entire—GODDAMN—LIVES!" Leering with glee as he shouts.

Years after his alleged suicide, Bruce Bechdel will gain national notoriety in the acclaimed bestselling graphic memoir, written by his daughter Alison, called Fun Home: A Family Tragicomic. *Chosen as* Time *magazine's "Book of the Year." Finalist for the National Book Critics Circle Award. Even more implausibly, this book about my high school teacher in our unknown Appalachian hills and farm valleys will become the Tony Award-winning musical* Fun Home *on Broadway, where, astoundingly, an actor starring as Bruce will dance and sing onstage. Then Hollywood will greenlight a movie version with Jake Gyllenhaal slated to play Bruce. All of this far into the future.*

Improbable, too, is what awaits me in that future: I will become the first person in seven generations of my Pennsylvania clan of indentured servants, farmers, soldiers, and factory workers to graduate from college; will continue to Harvard University for a Master of Divinity degree in Buddhism and teach class sessions at Yale; publish books; travel the world; ordain as a Zen Buddhist minister and teach the dharma to Zen students. Decades away from that classroom in Mill Hall....

Now, though, I'm remembering Bruce's voice:

"And you're going to READ Sophocles and learn to APPRECIATE it. If. It's. The. Last. GOD. Damn. Thing. I. Ever. DO!" Playful. An earnest show-man. Jabbing chalk at the blackboard. Pacing. His eyes fevered with the joy of someone in full aliveness of his gift. Bruce's gift was teaching. Kids chiming in mock protest, "Hey, who you callin' a hillbilly there, Bruce?" And "Hey, what's that word 'tawdry' mean, Bruce? We don't know all them big fancy words." Bruce: "'Tawdry'! What's it mean! Johnsonbaugh! Dictionary! Look it up! Read it! Out loud!" Bruce tossing his head back in laughter, then gazing conspiratorially at me, his prized pupil: "I love it!" Then to the class: "Okay, people! Let's go! A thousand 'A's to anyone who can tell me what makes this young girl Antigone such a hero!"

Bruce, who served as my confidante and mentor.

—

"To study the Buddha Way is to study the self," said Dōgen, an extraordinary philosopher and poet who lived as a contemporary of Saint Francis of Assisi. He established Sōtō Zen in Japan. "To study the self is to forget the self. To forget the self is to be enlightened by the ten thousand things."

"Ma ka han nya ha ra mi ta shin gyo...."

After we sit zazen at dawn in Taiyo-ji Temple near downtown Kanegasaki on Mondays, priest Watanabe, his wife, and a monk and I chant the Heart Sutra in Japanese. I've come to Japan for the same reason explorers sought headwaters of the Nile: to sit at the source. This is it. *"Kan ji zai bo sa gyo jin han nya ha...."*

Completing the sutra I kneel behind the Zen priest, prayer book between thumbs and forefingers. Watanabe always plumps himself onto the floor in a mound of dark blue robes, his shaven head laureled with incense smoke. He looks like a benign little Vesuvius.

The monk kneels in a far corner by the altar. He taps a four-four cadence on the drum. Both men sing prayers in a humming monotone, nasal, deeply bombinating, their voices ascending, tumbling, then blending in vibratos of wondrous harmonic resonance—imagine bees inside a didgeridoo—then diverging again. I'm the first foreigner in Kanegasaki privileged to hear this.

North of Kanegasaki—I know, because I've traveled there en route to the Pacific seacoast with my friend Eishi—the crumpled mountain wilderness of Iwate endures. A legendary forbidden realm of boreal demons, it's accessible nowadays via precipitous two-lane highways and switchbacks that hug forested cliff faces and river gorges. The gorges run freshets unstopped and headlong. Mist among the pines resembles trailing hems of ghost brides.

Northern Japan is terrain of waterfalls and volcanic basalt peaks, their high cones sheathed in kudzu and cedar, in *mizunara* oak forests of damp entangled green. I've seen doughty little farm compounds there, tucked into mountain notches: timeless cabins of wood and corrugated tin, with winged roofs and eaves, with arched door lintels. Wicker fences thatched with bundled rice stalks enclose gardens of *daikon* and sunflowers. Women in visored hoods, their floral jackets heavily quilted, stoop in rice fields to hack grain as they would have two millennia ago.

Excepting the island of Hokkaidō, this northern prefecture of Japan remains the country's most sparsely populated. Zen poet Miyazawa Kenji, who lived in nearby Morioka, loved this region. To him, it seemed a utopia, and he named it "Ihatov." But sophisticated Japanese in Kyoto and Tokyo long disavowed it as northern barbaric waste, an uninviting mountain fastness haunted by impoverished rubes. This was Japan's Appalachia.

The distance traversed. Beyond the scope of statute or nautical miles, beyond the map's imposed meridians.... Distance traveled from forebears who strove in daunted hills, in pine hollows....

"The purpose of *angya*, or pilgrimage, is to convince the monk of the fact that his whole life is a search, in exile, for his true home." —Thomas Merton.

Distance traversed. Find the self to lose the self. Find home to leave home.

My passport fails to divulge my place of origin, terrain of recollection, landscape that intersplices through nerves and marrow. Generations of ancestors.

When I was nine years old I acquired as a Cub Scout project a pen pal from Japan, a boy who wrote letters to me from Kanazawa on carefully inked rice paper. He wrote of balloon carp flying on Boys' Day; the Grand Shrine of Ise, dedicated to the Sun goddess Amaterasu-Ōmikami; the custom of shobuyu, the iris bath. He wrote on paper weightless and frail. The paper white as August milkweed in our wasted Appalachian fields....

Here in Kanegasaki, I recall those fields. I remember how I drove back to them five years ago. How I drove to the insolvent towns. How I drove to the mountains enclosing them. There had been seasons in my life when I avoided each mountain of Clinton County, Pennsylvania, as if it were a spring-trap. Mountains of tensed blue steel.

Five years ago, in the summer of 1992, I did not yet practice Zen. There was no reason to imagine I ever would.

The stereotypical view of American Buddhism: a privileged indulgence of affluent white upper-class suburbanites and city people, seeking inner bliss by pampering themselves at posh meditation retreats.

I move congenially among these people. But I share a different origin story.

Increasingly, so do other Buddhists in the United States—Blacks, Latinos, and of course Asian communities, here for more than a century.

And working-class folks.

I belong to the latter group. We come to Buddhism in earnest.

A traditional maxim:

What is the correct way to practice Zen meditation?

Practice as if your head is on fire.

PART
ONE

IN PENN'S WOODS:
ON THE SEARCH
FOR TRUE HOME

1992

◖

"The scribe of Pennsylvania casts his pen upon the earth."
— **William Blake, "America: A Prophecy"**

ONE

Zen Buddhists extol a life of alert composure, of transparent presence in the here-and-now. This life they call "the true home." It exists for each of us if we will only awaken to it.

An unlikely prospect for Zen, I once knew as little of the phrase "true home," or its frequent mention in Buddhist literature, as I knew of "treasure in poverty" or the spiritual kinship of Zen masters. "What is the meaning of 'true home'?" asked Thich Nhat Hanh, a Vietnamese monk and teacher whose words I would not discover until long after my foray into Pennsylvania, when my life had changed and I'd begun to sit zazen. "Sometimes we have a feeling of alienation.... We have been a wanderer and tried hard but have never been able to reach our true home. However, we all have a home, and this is our practice, the practice of going home."

Distance traversed, beyond the map's imposed meridians....

In the heat-ridden summer of 1992 I returned home in the most literal sense, driving to the inordinately difficult land of my birth and childhood and broken adolescence. For many years I thought I could evade this place by adopting a home elsewhere: living in New Mexico, I thought my love for renegade juniper deserts, for pine-stubbled peaks outside Santa Fe, might transform them into home. Dwelling in New England, I've often supposed the intimate Berkshire foothills, the woodlots, the stone-bound pastures of western Massachusetts might become home.

These stratagems of evasion and exile could not succeed forever. When they began to falter I admitted, finally, the need to go back. Back to Pennsylvania's rubbled mountains and dead factory towns, my place of origin.

*What I could not understand until much later: my quest for "true home"
in the Buddhist sense could never begin until I'd completed this other, primal
quest, equally important, equally pressing.*

And my journey began.

◯

EIGHT HOURS from the boutiques and espresso bars of my most recent
address, Northampton, Massachusetts—eight hours from my studio apartment with its *futon*, its glossed hardwood floor and its book-
shelves—I'm driving headlong through Pennsylvania forest. Deer habitat.
Remote backcountry. It's late July and the woods look febrile, look steamy
and inhospitable.

Close to sunset, cruising a bend of the interstate, I see wooded mountains of central Appalachia recede a mile to the horizon. A valley appears
to my left. Stretches of sweet corn, entire fields waving like those flags
borne by girls in Chinese operas, banners of emerald silk.

The valley disappears. I'm in serried hills again, homing in, getting
closer, closer, the smell of woods—damp leaf-rot, loam, heat—rushing
the open car windows.

A British map of 1755 depicts the region I'm approaching as virtually unmarked wilderness, bordered to the north by "A Pine Swamp" and
"Endless Mountains." To an eighteenth-century cartographer in London,
this must have seemed the farthest, most godforsaken tract of wasteland,
the very rim of the planet.

Interestingly, my 1992 Rand McNally road map of Pennsylvania looks
similar. Almost smack in the middle, an area immediately adjacent to a
little town called Lock Haven—much of northern Clinton County, in
fact—is denoted by a blank expanse of white and green. No roads. No
villages. No anything.

Three centuries ago this land I'm driving toward in central
Pennsylvania belonged to women and men who called themselves

Munsees of the Leni-Lenape: the Wolf Clan of the Original People. Mountain dwellers. English settlers referred to them as Delaware Indians.

Men shaved sides of their heads. They left scalp locks hanging behind. They tattooed spidery blue arabesques on their chins and foreheads, resembling a kind of facial scrimshaw. They wore breechclouts and claw necklaces. They donned, in spring feasts and dance ceremonies honoring the Corn Mother, gorgeous mantles of turkey feathers. Women wore fringed deerskin dresses stained with walnuts, elaborately festooned with colored porcupine quills.

These people spoke Algonquian—a thick porridge of language, guttural, fricative, harrumphing with consonants. The river near here, which they paddled in canoes of birch bark or in dugout logs of tulip tree, they called *Quenis-cha-cha-chyek-hanna*. If you whisper that word you can hear the liquid in it, the gurgle of water over stones. From that word derives the one I grew up speaking: "Susquehanna."

Mountain forests covered this region. Chestnut and oak. Pine. Giant hemlock. Trees, never grazed by an ax, had developed trunks of massive girth and towered high as a modern ten-story office building—sometimes the lowest branches started forty-five feet above a woman's or a man's head. When a Munsee warrior strode forest paths in central Pennsylvania, he moved through a hushed basilica of trees, trees that rose in colossal pillars beneath a vaulted dome of foliage.

Elk bugled across Pennsylvania woodlands. Whitetail deer nuzzled thickets of laurel and mountain azalea, ears flicked and alert. Panthers stalked high crags. Rattlers denned on sunstruck ledges. In lower forests, otters and beaver plashed in spring-fed ponds among cattails, home to Canadian geese. Passenger pigeons and Carolina paroquets shadowed the skies. Broad-winged hawks. Bald eagles. Buffalo traversed Pennsylvania's riverine grasslands. Black bears ruled the dark interior forests, and packs of gray wolves—cousins of the Munsee clan.

The Leni-Lenape people discerned something electrifying, something otherworldly, in each of these animals. They believed every bird and mammal, every fish, moved in its own nimbus of spiritual fire, in a sort of halo; every creature an energy field; each mallard, each salmon, each bobcat an emblem of infinite power in the cosmos, power manifest in living fur, in living fin and feather. The Leni-Lenape could chat with these animals. They could ask questions and receive answers. A man hunted these creatures with handmade arrow and bow, using beasts as provender, gratefully, while venerating them in prayer. It was an intricate relationship of utility and worship, founded in convictions of a sacred, pervasive, and abiding kinship.

In Northampton I've been living off the bankroll of a lavish grant, awarded by a private foundation, while I toil fulltime on a novel. During the last ten years I've published poems in nationally respected magazines, plucked a few prizes and participated in a group reading at Harvard, wrested some local acclaim as a journalist and editor. I'm healthy. I enjoy the convivial banter and the camaraderie of generous, stalwart, interesting friends. My new girlfriend Corinna is sexy and smart. Sometimes, if I'm not mistaken, she adores me.

Yet increasingly in this summer of 1992 my moods go under, submerge in confusion and dread. I seem to live in mourning. I don't even know what I've lost. Time races. Two years ago, when I was still married, my wife and I stood on the deck of a small, chartered boat as it plowed through swells during a whale-watching cruise, ten miles off the coast of southern California. Mammoth gray whales breached, upending flukes in cascading tumults of whitewater, then sank, full tonnage, beneath the ocean, water closing smooth as a lid above them. Not even a ripple.

"That's my life," I've been musing lately. That's my life: sinking without a trace.

Interstate 80 charges flat and straight between roadcut embankments. I pass a semi. Over the mountain, lazing arcs against the sky, a lone red-tailed hawk.

Graffito on a bridge: "One Way Jesus."

Just west and north of here rises the steep, fifteen-hundred-foot escarpment of the Allegheny Front, imposing mountains that form the edge of the Appalachian Plateau. The plateau, comprising much of Pennsylvania, is high tableland: forbidding summits, the chasms between them chiseled by mountain brooks. Farming becomes nearly impossible up there. That's back-forest country, realm of anglers and nimrods. That's Appalachian coal mining territory.

Another bridge: "Trust Jesus."

Before crews built the interstate in 1970, mountains and lost valleys of Clinton County seemed inaccessible as the Rub' al Khali desert, as Patagonia or Kazakhstan.

Rounding a bend I speed past the familiar cut at Long Run.

My breath snags a moment. There's the trough-shaped East End, fields and farmsteads I know by heart.

This is my valley.

Land of affliction, land of mortal injury....

Nittany Mountain borders its southern rim, and Bald Eagle Mountain to the northwest. Heavily timbered.

Names of villages through my native region: Beech Creek. Chatham Run. Haneyville. Logan's Mills. Booneville. Mountain Spring. Mill Hall. Lizardville. Greenburr.

"Literature," said Jean Cocteau, "is the force of memory we have not yet understood."

Hammersley's Fork. Rauch's Gap. Pine Station. Swissdale. Loganton. North Bend. Castanea.

Force of memory. Voices of Clinton County:

"They git thet damn interstate built, first thing comin' through here's gonna be buncha damn city slickers. Goddamn cars with New York plates. Hell, ain't nothin' good gonna come of it."

It mimics a West Virginia accent, the central Pennsylvania drawl. Back-of-the-throat molasses. The drawl coats a slur of lackadaisical syllables, words full of aw-shucks lethargy. Spaced by silence. Or it can be sly and mocking, concealing a wry smile. Or it can inflect to something nasal, jangly, abruptly manic: words doing banjo riffs. Then down again: clipped with menace.

Growing up I said "crick" instead of "creek." I pronounced the word "mile" as "mal." I said "you'uns": "Hey, you'uns all wanna go in town after bit?"

Force of memory: Big Rock. Shintown. Tamarack. State Camp. Cedar Springs. Mackeyville. Avis. Lamar. Renovo. Lock Haven.

Force of memory, not yet understood.

Pillow talk. Afterheat of sex.

"Maybe you should go ahead, hon. You know. Make that trip." We lay entwined, still covetous of touch. "Maybe you should go on down to Pennsylvania." Fleet kiss. My lovemate, Corinna, spider-walked her fingers across my chest. Kiss. Kiss again. "Put all those bad things behind you."

I used to think a person could simply adopt a home.

Returning for the ritual of my high school reunion after two decades of sporadic exile—thirty-eight years old, divorced, failing valiantly, it seems, at manly enterprises of earning money and sustaining love—I recognize the contours of this place:

Knobbed mountains, sunlight deepening the napped plush of conifers and hardwoods an hour before dusk. Farms voluptuous with sweet corn. Coppice of maples. Meadow fallow with clover. Windrow trees. Lusciously verdant, triple-canopied, hundred-acre forests watered by mountain runoffs, trout streams called Fishing Creek and Lick Run and Roaring Brook....

A minute later I speed through another curve and wonder, not for the first time, and not, perhaps, unlike a million other guys my age, how I could be approaching forty years old with nothing to show for it but ignominy and psychic bruises, utter confusion, botched plans. In magazine articles it's called a midlife problem. I call it skin-diving in a whirlpool.

$$\supset$$

"PAST IS preserved as memories of vanished time recovered artistically."

My high school teacher Bruce Bechdel penciled those words, in precise cursive, atop the first page of "The Wasteland" in his copy of T. S. Eliot's *Complete Poems*. Bruce died in 1980 at the age of forty-four. He'd stepped in front of an onrushing truck, apparently with lethal intent. Months later, during one of my sporadic forays to our Appalachian valleys of

Pennsylvania, I stopped to see his widow, Helen. We sat in the library of their Gothic Revival homestead with its flocked Victorian wallpaper, its Tiffany lamps and massive caparisons of velvet swags and drapery. Near the end of our conversation she said, "I'd like you to have one of Bruce's books. Take anything you want." I scanned the collection in the imposing walnut bookcase, with its carved finials and glass panes, and selected the Eliot. Bruce had taught me not only "The Wasteland" but "Prufrock" and "The Hollow Men," "Ash Wednesday" and "Four Quartets." It seemed a fitting choice.

Taking the book home, I found within its covers even greater bounty: Bruce's marginalia. On the opening page of "Four Quartets," among other voluminous notes, he'd written, "Time as real simultaneity…. The poems are a process of exploration, both *along* the movements of time, and *inward* into the stillness of 'consciousness.'"

$$\supset$$

EXPLORATION ALONG the movements of time.

Memory. Cyclical pattern. Flux. Revelation of history….

Seeking a lineage.

On a morning in spring a venturesome man named Georg Friedrich forsook his German village in low mountains of the Palantine Region along the Rhine. Bidding farewell to friends, unburdening himself of the failures and constraints and sorrows of his youth, with his wife Catherine and two small sons he left home forever.

He was a peasant farmer. He probably was stocky, ruddy faced, his hair loosely tied back. He probably wore a coarse woven shirt, a leather waistcoat, breeches, wooden shoes.

It was late May of 1771. Georg Friedrich and Catherine and their young boys probably boarded near Heilbronn. They scrunched in the dark, creaking hold of a packet boat with scores of other passengers. Traveling the Rhine they may have peeked through hatches and portholes, snatching glimpses of the land they were leaving behind. Their boat was towed past woodlots. Past bluffs and hilltop medieval castles. Past stone cottages. Plowed fields. Men with ox carts. Past riverside towns of wharves and narrow, gabled houses, storks' nests in the high chimneys. The trip up the Rhine lasted a month-and-a-half.

Often they sat in the hold for days, listening to the lap of water while the boat swayed at anchor. The boat docked at twenty-six customs houses in cities along the river. At each lengthy stop Georg Friedrich and other male passengers were led up a ladder and gathered on deck. Officials forced the men to open their purses and hand over scarce coins to buy food and pay exorbitant customs fees. Soon they became destitute.

At the end of August, Georg Friedrich and Catherine, their small family, and their companions—people with surnames such as Zimmerman, Lautenschläger, Grunwald, and Eberhardt, according to official records—at last boarded an English ship called the *Tyger*. They sailed out of Rotterdam. The ship dropped anchor at the British port of Cowes on the Isle of Wight. I've seen an etching of it—if Georg Friedrich peered out at this foreign place he'd have found whitewashed houses, trees, wooded hills and sheep meadows, three-masted schooners. The ship was delayed another fortnight. In mid-September of 1771 the *Tyger* finally began its voyage across the Atlantic to the New World.

The trip would have been hellish. Contemporary accounts suggest that Georg Friedrich, his wife and sons and more than a hundred other German peasants would have crammed below decks in the foul, damp, shadowy hulk, tossing with the ship, day after night, night after day, sleeping in brine puddles, munching weevil-infested biscuit and rancid salt pork, seasick, retching, bundled against cold. Often on these voyages people moaned with dysentery. They lay feverish in their own filth. Others, wracked with scurvy, spat blood. On many of these ships—perhaps on the *Tyger* as well—parents hugged children blistered with smallpox and watched helplessly as the children perished; then the parents died. Bodies were dumped into the ocean.

Georg Friedrich must have held his boys fretfully and clung to his wife and prayed. What burned in him? What did he demand, in those fierce, agonized moments, from God and from his dream of America? What did he hope to claim from the unknown paradise called Penn's Woods? What valor, what love, what yearning sustained him? What would he have whispered to his sons?

Often, according to testimonies I've read, winter storms hit the Atlantic voyages. Three-day gales lashed the ships, hurling them against towering sea waves. The *Tyger* probably endured such gales. People must have wept aloud. When storms passed the *Tyger* shoved on, seeking fresh winds.

This ordeal lasted two months.

The *Tyger* finally landed in the colony of Pennsylvania, sailing up the Delaware River and docking in Philadelphia in mid-November. A health officer boarded the ship and inspected the survivors. Sickened passengers were quarantined at Province Island. The others—Georg Friedrich among them—were led off the wharves through frozen dirt streets and cobbled thoroughfares of Philadelphia, among bewigged men in ruffled coats and tricorne hats and women in bone-hoop skirts and calashes, among surreys and shays and coaches. They were taken past trim brick row houses to City Hall, where they swore allegiance to the British Crown. Then they were marched back to the ship.

Georg Friedrich, like most of the German peasants, had been pushed deeper and deeper into debt throughout the half-year's journey. He owed piles of crowns and shillings for the trip across the Atlantic and even more for customs charges and provisions. This happened in an era when debtor's prisons flourished. The ship's merchants had a legal method for resolving the debt. They sold Georg Friedrich.

We don't speak much in the United States about our eighteenth-century practice of indentured servitude. On November 19, 1771, buyers strode aboard the *Tyger* and chose people to purchase, as if bidding for horses or cattle.

Georg Friedrich was one of 130 men sold. The buyer paid Georg Friedrich's debts, and in return Georg Friedrich became the legal property of Philadelphia store owners Willing and Morris, toiling in warehouses for them over the next several years until he'd worked off his debt.

This indentured servant, Georg Friedrich, must have wondered about his new home. He spoke no English. Did he realize that only a year before, the Boston Massacre had exploded in the Massachusetts colony, and that Philadelphia coffeehouses were now a din of revolutionary fervor? Did he know that north of Philadelphia and the tenuously farmed river valleys a wilderness began, a world of copious hardwood forests and pines and daunting mountains, lorded by eagles and panthers and painted men and women called Delaware and Iroquois? Did he know the challenges he faced?

I wonder myself.

Georg Friedrich had a last name.

It was Rühle.

He was my great-great-great-great-great-grandfather.

In Zen we find lineage, a connection with forebears—with Hakuin, with Dōgen, with Lin-chi or Huineng—linking us through centuries.

Returning to Appalachia I had no Zen practice yet, no living connection to an ancient line of succession. But in 1992 I yearned to know my family's ancestry. My father and I had searched my genealogy in libraries, paging through ships' logs and church records. Like many people, I hungered for kinship.

In Japan, in Mexico, in Israel, in China, people light candles for their ancestors. But we bury our dead too deeply. Our children grow up ignorant of the women and men whose intricate lives shaped their own, whose DNA they carry in their own genes, whose spirits doggedly insist on revelation. We don't know where we come from. We don't know who we are. It's our national amnesia. Most Americans couldn't tell you the names of their great-grandparents.

Until recently, I couldn't either.

Many Black Americans, of course, face special difficulties in tracing a lineage of ancestors, because of the brutal legacies of slavery. It obliterated names; it split and cruelly displaced families.

I'm fortunate to know my roots.

Because of Georg Friedrich and Catherine Rühle, I am an eighth-generation Pennsylvanian. Yet even those deep roots never held me to the native soil. Born in 1954 in the last-gasp mill town of Lock Haven, I fled this land briefly the summer I turned eighteen. I cadged my father's car, an aptly named Rambler American, and with my fifteen-year-old brother in the passenger seat—two long-haired hippie kids—I floored it due west, eager for prairie and open sky and mesas. I had scarcely ventured out of

Clinton County before. Five years after returning I fled again. This time, expatriating myself, I sought to create another home in New England. Memories of my birthplace and my neighbors and these Pennsylvania hick towns churned with hatred.

I'm visiting now to enact the odd American custom of the high school reunion.

Reunion: as I drive headlong into middle age I'm not sure what I'm seeking to reunify. Myself, obviously. But what else?

At heart I'm coming here, maybe, to do what we all must: to craft my truce with the future. To sign my armistice with the past.

TWO

LAND OF mortal affliction.

An April night. A dance in the high school gym. Shouts: "There's a fight outside!" A bunch of us ran to see.

Illuminated by a streetlight, two senior boys slugged each other.

Volts of excitement. "Git him!"

"Yeah! Attaway!"

"Go on!"

The pair flung off their shirts. They wore jeans and boots. Though early spring, the night had a glint of ice to it. You could see breath. Each fighter's naked torso shone with sweat.

It was 1968, but they wore their hair in a common local style, greased back in 1950s ducktails. I recognized one of the fighters. A tough-mouth pug, he hailed from a Mill Hall clan living in a shack up in the woods. The other, a rangy guy, was said to be from Lock Haven. They were fighting about a girl.

They hunched as if leaning into a gale. Fists rolling on air. Eyeing each other. The Mill Hall fighter swayed in close. After a quick tussle he pulled the Lock Haven guy to the ground. He knelt on top of him, almost tenderly. Very methodically he began using his fists to knock the bones of the young man's face apart.

While disassembling the face, he paused to study it, like a car mechanic taking apart an engine. Deciding where to hit next. Then he'd take care to raise his fist high. He was powerfully muscled, and each time he struck the young man's cheekbones, or the fragile cartilage of the nose, he hit full force.

We all hushed by then.

The young man getting his face stoved-in became hushed.

The sister of the Mill Hall tough stood nearby. She screamed. Grinning, she screamed, "Kill him! Do it! Kill him!"

How could I accept this place as home? And how could I let go?
Years of misguided effort....
How might a person live without regret? Without encumbrance of lasting
blame or rancor? How does a person fit a writhing history into the present?
Years passed before I started to realize: these questions are Zen questions.

I used to love riding through summer days—days such as this—watching the valley open. I loved the dells of farmland, the distant silos, meticulous clusters of dairy barns; the specks of cattle, motionless, a mile over the karst; vaporous bluish curve of the mountains.

I'm cruising north on Route 64 along a ridge crest. Acres of corn extend along the highway, each stalk tasseled as if wearing a fez. Heatwaves turn distant barns to mirages of liquefying glass. From the cornfield blows a dense wind of moist sugar. It's almost cloying, like frangipani, like an odalisque's perfume.

Light traffic two hours after suppertime. I pass a Lutheran church, cemetery shadowed by pines. Then Dotterer's Farm Equipment, with its Allis Chalmers combines and manure spreaders, its New Holland tractors. An auction barn along the highway offers "Guns and Ammo." Two Amish buggies approach, their harnessed trotters high-stepping the macadam.

A mile outside Cedar Springs a pickup revs past me. Gun rack. Bumper sticker: "This vehicle protected by Smith & Wesson."

Driving, I'm thinking about that fight on the high school lawn twenty-four years ago. Thinking about the sound a fist makes on a young man's face.

Driving, I'm looking for clues.

Endemic violence.

On a spring afternoon in 1972 my cousin Kathy and her friend, ninth graders at Lock Haven Junior High, walked past houses on East Water

Street, chatting, giggly. They held math books and tablets like shields against their chests, as schoolgirls used to do. They were a few blocks from home.

A car passed. Then it came by again. It braked at the curb. A man got out. He glanced up and down the street. He approached the girls; said something. Then he flashed the knife.

He ordered Kathy into the car. He directed the other girl at knifepoint into the backseat beside her. He locked the doors and sped away.

He drove them into densely wooded mountains along a road called the Bucktail Trail, northwest of Lock Haven, pulling off somewhere past Tangascootac, the car dust-deviling and sidewinding over dirt logging roads.

The sun went down. He parked in the forest. He put pillowcases over the girls' heads. He tied their hands. The man with the knife informed them that he planned to kill them.

By flashlight he led the hooded girls up a ridge in the dark. He uncoiled a length of rope. He strapped the girls to a tree.

Men throughout Lock Haven and Mill Hall formed search parties, grabbing their lanterns and hunting rifles and their dogs and fanning out with police squads through miles of wooded hills. My dad, though he owned no guns, joined the searchers. They found nothing.

Through the night, repeatedly, the man raped the girls.

Eventually he began gulping whiskey, and he dozed off. My cousin Kathy chewed through her ropes. Wriggling free, she untied her friend. They ran scraping blindly down the mountain, half-naked and bleeding, dumbfounded with shock. They hid in the brush till dawn.

They made their way back toward the Bucktail Trail. They heard a diesel rig approaching. They limped out, shivering and crying, and they flagged it down.

Five years before my journey to Kanegasaki, Japan, when I visited Pennsylvania, I knew only vaguely the definition of kōan, the Zen conundrum, the Zen challenge to a reasoning mind. Yet I see now that my efforts to reclaim an American homeland that defies reclamation, my struggle to understand it, functioned as my elusive and maddening kōan.

The question: Where do you find the true place you are born?

Lock Haven, Pennsylvania—population: 8,900—is a mill town. Hammermill Paper Company employs most of the men who've been able to scrounge a job in Clinton County. They trudge in their undershirts and work jeans, clutching black "dinner-pails." They punch in for the all-night eleven-to-seven shift. Or they arrive for the morning shift, when fog blows in tattered wisps over the sludge basin and the company smokestacks belch fumes into the gray sky over Bald Eagle Ridge.

In the factory these men stand over sloshing tubs of pulp, the odor of white, pasty wood creamy and sweet. Or they monitor production runs farther down the line. Megalithic, roaring machines stretch the paper to dry and send it clattering in long pale strips over spools big as wheels on a locomotive. The paper is clipped by flashing blades. My father worked at the mill for a while, and most of my uncles spent entire lives there. One of my uncles caught his sleeve accidentally in the machinery and it chomped his arm off at the elbow. A fly fisherman, he died soon after, perhaps of sorrow.

Clinton County—of which Lock Haven is the county seat—remains one of the poorest places in Pennsylvania, with an unemployment rate of about fifteen percent. In some Clinton County towns like Renovo, stuck way up in the boonies along a discontinued rail spur, nearly everybody's out of work. People pass hard luck and destitution from generation to generation like a battered heirloom.

The county extends about forty miles north to south, from the mountainous hemlock wilderness of Beech Bottom down to the farms of Sugar Valley. It stretches about thirty miles at the widest point west to east, from Lower Jerry Run across the hills out toward Miller Run. Lock Haven hugs the Susquehanna along the county's lower border.

Despite the county's unemployment rate, fortunate people in the area live cozily, with SUVs and ATVs in their garages, swimming pools and grills in their backyard gardens, and flat-screen TVs in their living rooms; they vacation at the Grange Fair or at their hunting camps or at Penn State football tailgating parties; their kids play Little League and patrol the mall, like kids everywhere. But up in the mountains it remains possible to find, unchanged, the country slums of central Appalachia. (Poverty is like salt. It preserves things.)

When I was young I saw families off the Bucktail Trail living in tin-roof hovels, their rust-heap Pontiacs and junked refrigerators piled behind shacks. In a dirt yard confettied with trash, rank with weeds and pricklebushes, kids with tousled hair and unwashed cheeks and no shoes taunted a snapping hound dog chained to a stake. Fathers and older brothers of these kids endured as ridge-runners. They wandered the forest peaks behind their shanties. They shot deer, illegally, all year long. Broods named Shirk and Conway and Rauman—angry clans who made their own rules and hated strangers. Rumors floated of dark violence, moonshine, incest. Sometimes the kids showed up briefly in school, runty and faded-looking, smelly. I know that some of those tarpaper shacks in Sugar Run and Tangascootac had no plumbing and people pissed in a hole in the floor.

"My God," friends in Amherst have said. "It sounds like *Deliverance*."

"Yeah, well. You know that kid at the beginning of the movie, the one with the big head who's playing the banjo? He was in my class. He was our class treasurer."

"Very funny."

Farmers were poor, too. The woebegone, half-mortgaged Clinton County farms of my youth, with their mud slops, their tumbledown barns, their rat-scavenged silos and pens of doleful cattle, were maintained by sunburned, laconic men who knew they were beaten from the start. Their wives knew it, too. Their kids—shy, beefy girls who wore shapeless, antiquated dresses and styled their hair in Tammy Wynette beehives; boys with grease under their fingernails who wore flannel shirts and sack-trousers and shitkickers, who carried sets of keys on their belts and tins of Red Man chew-tobacco in their pockets, who wore 4-H pins in lapels of their suitcoats on school dress-up days, who obtained special driving licenses at age fourteen to operate tractors and missed a week of classes at harvest time—these kids might not have known it, but they soon found out.

The Lock Haven I knew was a small riverside city. Worn-out, three-story commercial row houses dating from the era of Boss Tweed. Brick buildings with corner quoins and elaborate lintels and ornate, bracketed cornices. Dress shops. Some banks. A Woolworth's. A marble-façade drugstore. A plethora of bars, where out-of-work men and women hunched in smoky corners to bitch and pick fights. There were two seedy art deco movie houses, the Roxy and the Garden. A silver-spired courthouse, vaguely Moorish. A Civil War monument. The Ross Library. An elm-darkened esplanade along the Susquehanna, where people watched Fourth of July boat races. The Jay Street Bridge, quarter-mile truss spans of arched steel and crossbeams and lacy strutwork atop stone pilings, connecting Lock Haven with the village of Lockport. There was a chair factory beside railroad tracks. A silk mill, ancient bastion of chipped paint, with closed, barred windows and gasping steam vents, a muffled roar of machines from within the walls. There was the paper mill. There were Catholic churches for descendants of Irish lumbermen and for all the Italian families who somehow ended up in those godforsaken Pennsylvania hills. There was a synagogue. There were Baptist and Presbyterian churches for everyone else. And of course the encroaching mountains, barriers against the world.

Out near Great Island, where farmers grew potatoes and leaf tobacco on the dusty floodplain of the Susquehanna, stood Lock Haven's premier industry, the Piper airplane factory. At the air field small planes stood in the grass like brightly colored wasps. My brother Larry, sister Sherry and I enjoyed scrambling onto the wings, peering in cockpits. If we waited long enough, if our luck held, we might see a Piper Comanche test the runway, hop to the air, then skitter over treetops to vanish in clouds over the Susquehanna. Now those planes have gone forever. The factory closed, leaving hundreds of families behind. They subsist in bleak grids of low-income housing—neighborhoods of beige pillboxes and wire fencing and kids' tricycles, houses clustered around Piper like rusting tugboats around a scuttled battleship.

Sectors of middle-class prosperity remain. What realtors term "quality family homes" enhance Sunset Pines and Susquehanna Avenue across from Price Park, and in outlying neighborhoods of Fifties-era ranch houses and split-levels. Relics of Lock Haven's nineteenth-century heyday persist, too. On streets near the river, languishing among oak trees, a pass-erby can admire Second Empire manses with balustrades and pilasters and pavilions, porches fussy with gingerbread, mansard roofs steeply pitched against the sun. There are Italianate villas with arched windows. Chaste Federal homes. Greek Revivals with ivied walls and Doric columns on West Church and West Main. Georgian townhouses of brick or yellow stucco, highlighted with pink-blossoming rhododendron.

Many of these homes, former abodes of Victorian river merchants and lumber magnates, provide lodging now for faculty members and their families, for Lock Haven is, at least technically, a college town. Twenty years ago the "teacher's college" existed as an anomaly, a kind of sanctum on the edge of Lock Haven. Professors and students kept their distance from townsfolk. The townspeople, with their native distrust of "egg-heads" and "stuck-ups who use big fancy words," tolerated the school but remained suspicious. Lock Haven had none of the trappings of a college town. No student bars. No bookstores. No classy little cafés or hangouts. There was only the Texas Diner, where gruff men, hair slickly Brylcreemed, their shirtsleeves rolled to display a flag-and-dagger tattoo, took their scrapple and home fries with ketchup before prowling bars for the next free beer.

☽

SUNNY-HAIRED AND ebullient, twenty-one years old, Diana majored in pre-law at Hampshire College in Massachusetts, known at that time as the priciest school in the United States. We shared an Amherst apartment during the mid-'80s while I worked as a newspaper reporter and she fin-ished her studies. Diana belonged to a sportively enterprising clan from Connecticut. Her mother kept a house on Long Island Sound. Wicker deck chairs adorning the living room once belonged to Commodore Vanderbilt. Diana's father worked as a venture capitalist, which is to say, he made three telephone calls from his study each morning. Mostly he pottered about a summer home on Fisher's Island, off the southern New England coast. There his parcel of real estate offered views of ersatz

Tudor mansions owned by notables such as the DuPonts, visible like little "Monopoly" hotels across the saltwater bay.

Weekending on the island, freshened by breezes off the Sound, Diana and I would pad barefoot across her father's dock. "What do you feel like doing, Steve-arino?" Brimming with eagerness. "Badminton? A bike ride? We could take the boat out—" The boat was a beauty, a classic little Italian Riva Aquarama, vintage 1940s, the type of craft a man in a polo sweater might navigate, a man holding a brandy snifter. The hull was honey-shellacked mahogany. Growing up in the central Appalachians of Pennsylvania I'd never dreamed I might one day be privy to a girlfriend who said things like, "We could take the boat out—"

"I know!" Diana suggested one afternoon. "Let's take my father's car and go exploring. I can show you everything!"

As we twined among screens of sawgrass and wild plum on the island's sandy back roads, past phone poles crowned with osprey nests, I glimpsed hidden oceanfront estates. Summer places with names like "Windfall" and "The Breakers." We encountered a Mercedes bouncing over the sand path, driven by a housemaid on her daily errand into the village to fetch sweet corn and melons newly arrived from the mainland and prime lobsters hauled in that very morning by local trawlers. I noted an enormous yacht anchored in the cove. It belonged to a Hollywood star. Patinaed and sleek: a boat such as Brancusi might have designed. Trimmed in nautical blue, its topsails glowing, its brass virtually ringing aloud in the sun.

Some weekends, instead of sojourning on the island, we rendezvoused with Diana's friends in Manhattan. Diana had friends who looked like they'd been designed by a Swedish engineering team: blond, gleaming girls, with triumphant smiles and faultless skin, athletic, chirpy, insouciant. They were accustomed to ski chalets. To BMWs. To those new status symbols of the early Reagan years, their own platinum Visa cards. One of these friends, Annette, had received, as a gift upon graduating from Vassar, a Park Avenue apartment. Jacqueline had just returned from a three-month jaunt in Europe. To mark her own graduation from Hampshire in 1984 my girlfriend accepted from her father a six-week holiday in Paris, the Riviera, Rome, and Berlin. Diana's raffish younger brother,

Walter Schimmerhorn Hallman III, nicknamed (of course) "Skipper," had flunked prep school and, when he wasn't raiding the Glenlivet, or out hauling sail in cup races off Newport, adhered to Fitzgeraldian stereotype by scuffing about in open-throated shirts and chinos, awaiting his twenty-first birthday and his trust fund.

During the two years of our lovefest, my gorgeous blue-chip girl—who is now a lawyer, espoused to another attorney and presumably residing in Connecticut—ushered me to private beaches at Fisher's Island, beaches of profligate rose bushes and strewn cobbles, beaches talced with white, white sand. She ushered me to beaches of lolling waves reserved exclusively for the gambols of lithe, fine-boned, pedigreed kids on summer vacation from Smith and Dartmouth and Yale, kids whose laughter sounded to me freshly struck from purest sterling. Diana escorted me to a wedding bash at a Long Island yacht club. She escorted me to a party near Stowe where I heard a man with shaved head, wearing Gucci sunglasses, remark to a justice of the state Supreme Court that he had a friendly little wager riding on the morrow's Super Bowl, a wager to the tune of twenty thousand dollars. I began to understand that I was a guest from a remote serfdom.

One Saturday Diana and I drove north of Amherst and happened upon Turner's Falls, a beat-up, orphaned mill town in western Massachusetts, on the upper banks of the Connecticut River.

Diana had never seen it before. She looked at storefronts, plywood sheathing nailed across the windows. Leftover Christmas lights, tinsel from six months before. A closed Shell station. Cracked sidewalks. As we drove she glanced furtively at neglected brick tenements.

"Maybe it's good to see places like this sometimes," she said as we rode past. "It's important to remember that places like this exist. We need to be reminded."

I steered the corner. Diana and I were still getting to know each other.

"I don't need to be reminded," I told her. "I came from a town like this, back in Pennsylvania. I've been trying to escape from it my whole life. I'm trying to *forget* places like this."

The distance traversed. Beyond the scope of statute or nautical miles, the map's imposed meridians…. Distance traveled from forebears who strove in

daunted hills, in pine hollows.... My passport fails to divulge my place of
origin, terrain of recollection....

"*The purpose of angya, or pilgrimage, is to convince the monk of the fact*
that his whole life is a search, in exile, for his true home...."

Through the strait at Ax Factory Gap, where Fishing Creek chutes
a notch between forested mountains, I leave Nittany Valley and enter
the one known as Bald Eagle. Moments later I'm driving into Mill Hall.
Typical Appalachian rust-belt town; population: 1,744. This is where I
attended high school. The creek, miserly, amber-hued, gurgles between
concrete retaining walls.

Bridges connect the borough. A street of shabbily nailed-up stores,
a bank, a bar, a C&T food market stagnates on the east side. Grayish-
green maple trees look like they could use a good dusting. On Mill Hall's
west side, crammed against the mountain, are Depression era houses with
knock-kneed porches. Paint is chipping off the windowsills. Many have
walls of aluminum siding; others, gritty asbestos shingles the color of
Spam. Or cat vomit.

A beer-bellied guy in a red muscle shirt slobs around an open screen
door, TV visible behind him. A few doors down, an obese woman with
hair of string plops in a lawn chair. She winces at a cigarette. Kids stam-
pede through dirt.

I downshift and go past a water tank near the Penn Central track, then
past the deserted Northeast Rebuilders factory, its glass panes smashed
like windows in a Halloween mansion, the yard mangy with thistle and
ragweed, the chain-link fence topped with barbed wire.

Exactly the same as always. And now I'm remembering:

Rained-out Saturday afternoons. These ashen houses. Living rooms
awash in a gray chatter of television. Sullen men in undershirts, laid-off at
the mill, snoring on their La-Z-Boys. On couches, the sour, pinch-lipped
women, hair in curlers. Teenage boys would escape these living rooms,
ride streets of Mill Hall or streets of Lock Haven—five miles away—looking for fights. They'd spot a stranger walking the sidewalk: "Hey, ask this
here guy! Ask him!" Slowing their Dodge Charger or souped-up Camaro
they'd crank down the window: "Hey, wanna fight? Come on, pussy!"

—

I'm driving by a few blocks of tract houses with heat-blistered lawns. Twilight's approaching. A man sudsing his car stops to watch me drive by. Apparently he's noticed my Massachusetts plates, because he watches me all the way down the street.

The high school hasn't changed. Bordered on two sides by cornfields, someone designed its rambling L-shape of brick and glass to look modern during the Eisenhower era. Inside, this building was distinguished by a maze of dark penal corridors.

Nine hundred kids from rural villages came here. Grades seven through twelve. Because these far-flung communities were scattered through woods and farmlands of the Bald Eagle and Nittany valleys, people named this junior-senior high school Bald Eagle-Nittany, or B.E.N. For school colors they chose black and white. Nullity and void. The school mascot was the panther, a creature shot and trapped to extinction in these hills a century-and-a-half ago.

In 1967 a balding, bespectacled man named Leo Held strode into the paper mill in Lock Haven carrying a rifle.

He moved briskly and purposefully, a man with important errands. His first errand consisted of opening the door of the payroll office, walking inside, and shooting a manager. That errand accomplished, he proceeded with his "things to do" list.

The next item, apparently, was to walk through the noisy plant, down long aisles between tubs and pulp processors and huge, shaking belt-driven machines, aiming his rifle at people he recognized and firing. People screamed. People ducked for cover. A wounded man crumpled behind a steel-plated cutter. Blood trickled the concrete. Leo Held reloaded and kept walking. He noticed a man taking a break near the coffee machine. Held blew half the man's skull off. A woman fled down a side corridor. Held shot her. He entered the finishing department and again he began shooting. He walked to the plant's main generator and put a bullet through the power assembly, pitching the entire factory into darkness.

He walked outside and got in his car.

That done, he drove several miles to the other side of Lock Haven and parked at the Piper Aircraft factory. It was a busy morning for Leo Held. His next errand was to enter the management offices toting his rifle, where he began picking off people at their desks. Then he returned to his car and zoomed off into the mountains.

I was in study hall—right there, in that high school cafeteria, where those windows are—sitting with classmates at a long table. A drizzling morning in October. Sodden orange and rust-colored leaves on the mountains. An English teacher sprinted into the cafeteria. He conferred anxiously with some other teachers and they began bolting windows shut, drawing the venetian blinds, turning off lights.

"Everyone stay away from the windows!"

Kids from other classes began streaming into the cafeteria.

"Someone shot a buncha people at the paper mill!"

In a small town, calamity hits everybody at once. Kids' fathers and mothers worked at the mill. My uncles—Uncle Ralph, Uncle Dick, Uncle Pat—worked there.

A janitor rushed in. "Some kook shot a whole buncha people at the mill an' he's on the loose, no one knows *where* the hell he's at, the state boys think the sumbitch might be on his way over here to the school, stay down, I'm goin' for a rifle."

Teachers dashed outside to this lot, right here where I'm parked. They flipped open their car trunks and they began passing out firearms. In Mill Hall and Lock Haven nearly every family owns a cache of deer-hunting and target-shooting weapons; our teachers kept arsenals in their homes and in their cars, like everyone else. Nevertheless I was surprised to see enough guns pop out of those cars to equip a platoon. Our teachers were deploying through the halls with loaded 30-30 caliber Winchesters and pump-action 12-gauge shotguns, taking guard posts at the doors. Ancient white-haired Mr. Renninger, the eighth-grade science teacher, leaned against that glass door near the cafeteria, cradling a thirty-ought-six bolt action rifle with a scope.

We waited for Held to arrive. He outfoxed everyone. He roared past our high school, through Salona, through Rote, up rugged pine mountains on a sinuous road following the watercourse of Long Run. Then he drove out of the mountains into farmlands of Sugar Valley, into the village of Loganton, where he lived. He pulled into the driveway of his brick home. He walked across the street to the unpainted woodframe house of his neighbors, the Quiggles. No one kept doors locked in Loganton. Held entered their living room, walked up the stairs to their bedroom, and shot twenty-seven-year-old Donna Quiggle and her husband Floyd as they savored a lazy morning in bed. Mrs. Quiggle was critically wounded; Floyd Quiggle died instantly. A Loganton constable later found their five-year-old daughter Jody Lynn downstairs, crying into the telephone: "Help me, somebody shot my daddy and mama."

Leo Held finished his visit to the Quiggles and walked outside to his backyard, pausing at his tool shed to retrieve more ammo.

The police caught up with him. A shootout exploded. Guns blasted in those prim backyards, bullets clipping rosebushes. Cops crouched and pell-melled past the garages for cover.

A bullet nicked Leo Held in the ankle. Then police shot him dead.

At suppertime we watched CBS News. "And in Lock Haven, Pennsylvania," intoned Walter Cronkite, "a man went on a two-and-a-half-hour rampage, shooting twelve people and killing seven before being shot by police himself." And we saw it all on videotape: the Piper plant; the paper mill, its floor pooled with blood; state troopers talking solemnly; the Leo Held residence; the numb survivors.

That night, for a few hours in living rooms across America, "Lock Haven" became a household phrase.

Our violence had finally put us on the map.

⊃

THIS MORNING before leaving the motel I phoned my girlfriend Corinna in Massachusetts. "I miss you, too, sweetheart. Hey, listen. This reunion thing. I'm not sure it's a good idea. I might not go. I start to remember that damn Clinton County, it churns up a lot of uncomfortable memories. A lot of pain and anger actually. Maybe this is a mistake. I don't know if I'm ready for this."

Words I dared not speak aloud:

I crave something. I'm not sure what. Other people must feel similar yearnings. I'm searching but have no idea what's needed. No idea where to turn, where to begin. I only know I feel homesick. I feel homesick for a place I can't seem to locate.

"In the longing that starts one on the way of Zen is a kind of homesickness, and some way, on this journey, I have started home...." Recently, five *years after my trip to Pennsylvania, I've discovered this passage from Peter Matthiessen's* Nine-Headed Dragon River: Zen Journals. *"Homegoing," he writes, "is the purpose of my practice, of my mountain meditation...."*

"Home" meaning: rediscovery of what in Zen is called "original nature."

I think of *Appalachian Spring* sometimes when I drive the land where I was born. Copland's score, penned for Martha Graham's ballet, sets to music the optimism of a young woman and her pioneer husband as they celebrate their newly built home in rural Pennsylvania.

Driving in Clinton County I've recalled strains of that music: guarded tenderness and restrained hope of solo woodwinds; tentative impishness of the strings; a grave, dignified heartiness in the brief fanfares. Their lightsome beauty is punctuated by hints, staccato sixteenth notes, of sadness, of diffidence then stoic resolve. The music evokes the halting, ambivalent joy that marks my own response to this backwoods farm country.

Copland included the melody "'Tis a Gift to Be Simple," the Shaker hymn, in his Appalachian suite. In truth, no Shaker settlements existed in Pennsylvania.

But Amish abound. Now, in this Appalachian summer, as I leave Mill Hall and pass Cedar Springs, I hear a crisp strike of horseshoes on pavement. Rattle of harness; the iron-rim wheels. Soon I'm approached in the opposite lane by a roan trotter pulling a black surrey, woman in gray dress and bonnet at the reins. A load of little girls in similar dresses and bonnets squirms and waves hello.

Amish arrived in Nittany Valley in the early 1970s, about the time Interstate 80 opened—simultaneous events at opposing ends of a vast cultural scale.

These are Old Order Amish. The Plain People.

When the Amish arrived in this region the mood began to change. If I travel through the hinterlands of southern Clinton County I no longer run afoul of grim, semi-literate clodhoppers and dumb-ass, hardscrabble dirt farmers with hair-trigger tempers. Instead I meet Amish—these godly, innocuous people. My whole body relaxes. My soul can breathe here again.

It's the crucial reason I feel comfortable enough to return to these valleys at all.

Growing up working-class makes you a Platonist; from daily life you deduce that two worlds exist, Ideal and Actual. As a kid thumbing through the Sears Christmas catalog ("The Wish Book") when I curled in one of our trailer's living room chairs, I knew the bejeweled Raleigh bicycles, the electric race car sets, belonged to the Ideal realm, and other, more modest things must serve to adorn my Actual world. That conditioning shaped me. Years would pass before I could walk as an adult into a bookstore, peruse a volume, and before automatically returning it to the shelf realize, dumbfounded, "Hey, wait a minute—I actually could buy this."

Another impoverishment stunted us in Clinton County: impoverishment of experience. In the late 1960s a rabble of teenagers from our drama club piled into a school bus. We sputtered out of Mill Hall, out of the mountains and down the highway to a college two hours distant. There we sat in a real theater—some of us for the first time—as if bewitched and gaped at *The Glass Menagerie*. On the way back, our bus parked at a Howard Johnson's for dinner.

I'd seen Howard Johnson's advertised in *Life* magazine. Therefore I considered it very posh, very exclusive; I remember thinking movie stars ate at Howard Johnson's.

We Clinton County kids moved stiffly as a waitress escorted us to booths near a window.

Whispering: "Which those forks we s'posed ta use?"

As I remember this, a slipknot begins to tighten inside my throat.

At home, in addition to standard American fare that we saw Ward, June, Wally, and the Beave enjoy on TV—meatloaf, potatoes, string beans,

Jello for dessert—we ate working-class meals. Pork and beans. Chicken legs and creamed corn. And, like our neighbors, we ate Pennsylvania Dutch: shoo-fly pie. Pickled eggs in beet juice. Pot pie. Strudel. Biscuits smeared with apple butter. Scrapple. Creamed egg noodles. Pigs-in-a-blanket. Chow-chow. Sticky buns. On New Year's Day, sauerkraut with steamed hot dogs. Once a woman in a neighboring trailer at Pine Acres brought us bear meat she'd shot during hunting season—like a piquant, gamy version of roast beef, fulsome and tough.

Living outside town on a Rural Free Delivery route, we bought loaves of Holsum bread from a man who delivered them weekly in a panel truck. A milkman brought our milk in clattering glass bottles that he left in our milk box on the porch in the predawn hush.

We cooked with margarine, which we called "oleo." As a rare treat, my dad surprised me once when I was eight or nine with breakfast at a diner during our regular Sunday morning drive to fetch the *Grit* newspaper in Lock Haven (in *To Kill a Mockingbird*, Scout comments acerbically that the backwoods Alabama kids who bring clippings from "the *Grit* paper" to her school for current events class croon "sweetly sings the donkey" and pronounce it "dunkey.") That morning I savored flapjacks drenched in oleo that tasted extraordinary. For weeks afterward I pleaded with my mother to find that oleo of the miraculous flavor at our local A&P supermarket. Each brand she brought home to the trailer flunked my taste test. Years later, as a young adult, I found it. The moment it touched my tongue, a sort of Proustian memory awoke—aha! *There* was the elusive, long-sought ambrosia of my youth.

Butter.

Until I left high school, I never recognized the taste of butter.

Impoverishment of experience. Things my current friends in Northampton and Amherst take for granted as simple immutable facts of daily life were alien to working-class people in Clinton County half a century ago.

We almost never saw a dentist. We relegated visits for dental cleanings or six-month checkups to the category of luxuries. We brushed and hoped for the best. I did need to have a molar pulled once at the age of ten, and a dentist in Lock Haven assaulted my mouth with a device resembling a pair of pliers; jamming his foot against my chair he leaned back and, with grunting exertion, yanked and twisted the pliers till the tooth jerked free at the root. That's how it was done decades ago in rural backwater towns.

Low-income, blue-collar working families where I grew up eschewed non-essential medical care. Middle-class people in Lock Haven and Mill Hall fared better, but those on the lower rungs of the socio-economic ladder, with skimpy insurance, fended medically for themselves. A kid in my high school class had a harelip. Another had a clubfoot. One had a decayed black incisor, visible when he smiled. Another, a sophomore, had collapsed on a sweltering day of football practice, after the coach denied him permission to get a drink of water; the kid never emerged from a coma, and groups of us volunteered to leave school during study halls to drive out to his family's small trailer, in stubbled fields beyond the village of Salona, and move his rigid arms and legs in patterning exercises as he lay comatose in a large crib.

We commonly saw evidence of mishaps. A kid in my class had a glass eye from a farming accident. When my junior varsity wrestling team scrimmaged with a squad from the mountain hamlet of Renovo, one of our wrestlers grabbed his opponent's leg and it came off in his hand—it was artificial, legacy of another farm calamity. A kid in my class had a long scar on his cheek from falling on an ax. I bore a scar on my chin from a car wreck in fifth grade; the doctor recommended plastic surgery, but we couldn't afford it, so I managed, unfazed, without it—as I had learned to do in countless situations, countless times before.

Managing without things.

A genetically ingrained habit of working-class people.

Obviously they shunned any form of psychotherapy as well—assuming they might have found any in Clinton County during those Eisenhower-to-Nixon years. They considered therapy a scandalous voodoo, devised for weaklings unable to face life and tough it out; or for pitiable losers who lacked a supportive clan to aid them; or for shameless egotists who would divulge sordid private matters to a stranger; or for spendthrifts who would waste money hard-earned at the mill; or, most drastically, for "nut-jobs" on their way to the "loony-bin." Thus psychological debilities remained hidden, unattended except by shots of whiskey, and festered behind curtained windows.

☾

EVERYONE KNEW the code of manhood. Boys learned it like their A-B-C's or their times tables, drilling in it, acquiring knowledge on Clinton County playgrounds, in backyards and kitchens and classrooms. Boys and men tested each other in the code daily. Girls and women helped enforce it, flirting with guys who lived by the code, mocking and rejecting guys who failed.

The code functioned as a Ten Commandments of masculinity. We knew them by heart:

Never back down from a fight. Never cry. Never show pain. If someone taunts you or issues a challenge, defend yourself ruthlessly, fight without mercy, and win. Never betray your buddies. Never ask for help. Mind your own goddamn business. Don't be a quitter. If someone wrongs you, get even. Be tough; take your licks.

For those who shirked the code of manhood, people in Clinton County maintained a catalog of names:

Chickenshit. No Hair. Powderpuff. Pansy. No Dick. Candy Ass. Yella. Hairless. Creampuff. Dickless. Pantywaist. No Balls. Gutless. Pussy. Sissy.

Piercing whistle.

"Faster! Faster! Come on, you look like a buncha girls out there—Gingrich, what the hell you doin', you gotta take him DOWN, look, like THIS! FASTER! Watson, what the hell you call THAT, huh? Go for the leg, go for the leg, I wanna see you slap him on that mat, you HEAR me? Go!"

I wrestled in junior high. Winter evenings after school. First the locker room ritual: towel-snapping, grab-ass, guys pulling jockstraps, shouting insults and wisecracks. Greeting each other with boxing feints, mock punches, challenges, grins. Lacing my sneakers I'd overhear them:

"Hey, sis!"

"Yer the sis, not me!"

"I'll put you right through that wall, boy!"

"You ain't got the hair!"

"You wanna try me?"

"I'll git you, nigger!" (The omnipresent and disgusting word. Clinton County, incidentally, was all-white in those days. Black people wisely avoided the region; during my grandparents' era, several villages hosted rallies featuring local chapters of the Ku Klux Klan.)

Then into the gym. Our tattered warm-up jerseys were rank with sweat and mildew. We smelled like a chain gang.

Across the varnished wood floor we unrolled enormous rubber cushions, and atop these we unrolled dusty, thick-padded gray mats.

"Okay, let's go, get out there! Gimme a hundred jumpin' jacks!"

Situps. Pushups. Squats. Neck bends and shoulder rolls. Windmills. I wrestled at 148 pounds. As I stood upright a partner in my weight class would wrap his legs around my hips, embrace me with his arms around my neck, then cling to me like the dead weight of all my misgivings while I performed fifty toe-touches.

Coaches pacing and bellowing: "Okay, OTHER guy! Let's go, I wanna see SWEAT here tonight, we're goin' up against Montoursville next week, we gotta kick their ASSES, let's GO here!"

The gym echoing. Noise bouncing off girders, empty vaults of the high ceiling, sound ping-ponging off walls and backboards.

Shrill whistle.

Grueling hours of practicing moves: sit-out; take-down; fireman's carry.

"C'mon, what the hell you doin' there, switch him! Switch him! Cross-face! Cross-face him, Bennett! No, Ruhl, the other way, Jesus Christ, whadaya call that, huh? HUH?" Whistle. Guys yelling: "Chicken-wing him! Chicken-wing him!" Crunch of muscle, skin rasping across the mat, grunts, thuds, slam of a shoulder. "Shit!"

Endless repetition. Ache. Fatigue. An hour, then another hour, darkness and frost settling in the windows.

Guys half-famished from trying to make weight, popping their salt pills. Jungle-rot stench. Bodies steaming, jerseys sopping wet as if we'd hosed each other down in a cellblock riot. Everyone panting. Red-faced. Grimaces of pain and loathing and exhaustion.

Men in training, Mill Hall style.

"Hit him harder! HIT HIM NOW, damn it!"

I quit wrestling when I turned fourteen, in 1968; I'd been growing dizzy from Day-Glo posters, from the Beatles, and then the next year swept me irresistibly away into the heady emergence of something miraculous called Woodstock Nation—all delivered urgently and irresistibly into my primitive town by those great subversives, AM radio and *Life* magazine and television.

Few in my school seemed aware of these things. But they made me stir-crazy.

In quitting wrestling I also began to quit Clinton County.

Future Plans: Work.... Future Plans: Housewife.... Future Plans: Winner's Meatpacking Plant....

A flip through our yearbook's back pages offers clues to the destinies of Bald Eagle-Nittany High School's Class of '72:

Future Plans: Work or Army.... Future Plans: Job.... Future Plans: Stay in this area for a while.... Future Plans: None.

"Enjoy these school years while you still have them," teachers would admonish us. Dour, mush-faced men and women smelling of nicotine, sagging heavily into middle age, warned us repeatedly: "These are the best years of your life."

Future Plans: Switchboard operator.... Future Plans: Housewife.... Future Plans: None.... Future Plans: Navy.... Future Plans: Bloomsburg State College.... Future Plans: Secretarial position.... Future Plans: Work.... Future Plans: Williamsport Area Community College.... Future Plans: Farmer.... Future Plans: Marriage and job.

I find my own yearbook listing. School activities: Class President. Class Vice-President. Student Council. Drama Club.

I craved so much when I left these hills. When I departed Appalachia fifteen years ago for Amherst I dwelled "in Possibility," as that town's poet, Emily Dickinson, claimed of herself.

Future Plans: Travel. Writing. College.

I too believed I might spread wide my narrow hands and gather Paradise.

○

"HI, PAL! Welcome! You're lookin' good!"

I've seen photos of my parents before they married. I keep xeroxes of black-and-white snapshots taken in 1952, during a picnic in the mountains at Hyner Run, two years before my birth. Girlfriends who see these photos always exclaim, "Wow! Your dad was a total hunk! God, your mom was beautiful!" My father at twenty-nine: trim and brushcut, with a confident smile, wearing Bermudas, the sleeves of his T-shirt rolled to reveal the powerful arms of an ex-middleweight boxer. My mother at nineteen: willowy, with pronounced cheekbones and eyes unsettlingly large and comely. She wore madras short-shorts and a halter top. Her tresses—chevelure of thick brunette ringlets and tendrils—tossed at her bare shoulders. She looked like a backlot MGM starlet. Their sexiness was candid and unabashed. In one photo they're hugging, standing forehead to forehead, nuzzling like puppies.

As I wheel my car into the driveway this evening they emerge from the house to greet me.

"Lookin' good, Pal!" My dad, stocky, white-haired and smiling, extends his hand as I step out, then bear hugs me.

"How're you doin', Steve R?" My mother, frosty-haired, pretty, a little portly now, beams at me and blinks back tears. We're an emotional family. I come down here once or twice a year to see my parents, and every time it's the same tumult of weepy gratitude and elation. "I'm so glad you're here, honey!" She wraps her arms around me.

Beyond a stand of poplars in the fading daylight I see Amish hayfields, three mountain ridges, Lick Run Gap, miles of farmland in the sheltered eastern rim of Nittany Valley.

Later: nearly midnight. Across the street, a window flickers with blue phosphor of television.

Amish farmers have been asleep for hours.

Moving to the back door I step into my parents' yard. Noise of crickets. Barefoot in wet grass, I scan heaven for the Great Bear.

I'm listening for ghosts of the Leni-Lenape. I hear, out on the interstate, steady whoosh of tractor-trailers.

Four hundred miles north, in my adopted home of Massachusetts, lies the woman I hope to marry, Corinna, asleep in the bed we've shared in our lovemaking. So often I've sought home in the body of my beloved. The hearth of her. Comforting warmth of skin. Her safe and welcoming heartbeat. Tonight I miss her.

Black sky. Above a crest of southern mountains, diamond brooch of Libra.

Down the valley to the east, bright wings of Cygnus the swan.

Lots of random glister through the Milky Way.

And directly overhead, near the segmented tail of a huge twinkling dragon—the constellation Draco—there it is, lurking:

The Indians' sacred Great Bear, Ursa Major, aglow.

Whatever may come in these next two days—whatever apprehension, whatever indignation or lament, whatever surprise—let it come.

THREE

How to pacify memory?

How to honor the past yet be free of it?

If anyone had hinted that venerable rites of Zen might prove beneficial, I'd have balked. Zen Buddhism? That's so pointless, so passionless. So colorless. So nihilistic and grim; so alien. Sit on a cushion and stare blankly at a wall? You must be joking.

Years after my journey to Pennsylvania I discovered these sentences by the great twelfth-century teacher of Ch'an—the Chinese precursor of Zen—named Yuan-Wu:

"It is like coming across a light in thick darkness; it is like receiving treasure in poverty.... You gain an illuminating insight into the very nature of things.... Here is shown bare the most beautiful landscape of your birthplace."

☽

THE AUTHENTIC journey, always, cuts its trail inward. Details of outward travels must differ vastly, but inner journeys, the numinous ones, the sacred adventures, remain universally the same. A solo plunge into chasms. A harrowed struggle. The emergence into brightness and renewal.

A journey to find unique truths not only requires seeking the Great Jewel of the soul, as mystics call it. You also must confront the stench of everything that shames you, that scares you.

Bruce Bechdel gave me a different Great Jewel, one of the mind. Before I met him I was a kid with blond surfer bangs whose intellectual life consisted of *Zap Comix* and Tolkien and *Mad* magazine and watching *Laugh-In* on TV. Bruce gave me James Joyce, he gave me Virginia Woolf and Bloomsbury, he gave me Chartres Cathedral and Giotto and Stravinsky. During the worst years of my teenage estrangement and despair Bruce offered me sanctuary in his homeroom—a hubbub of Shakespeare and Jimi Hendrix, of Stanley Kubrick and psychedelia and Abbie Hoffman posters, coffee cups, vocabulary cards, stacks of poetry books, and the *Philadelphia Inquirer*. Each day at lunch we bantered at his desk.

Students laughed and chattered in his junior and senior "Humanities" survey of the Western canon, but they read the books that Bruce insisted they read and learned to read them well. They watched Kenneth Clark rhapsodize about Bernini's swooning St. Theresa in the PBS *Civilisation* series when Bruce wheeled out the TV. They closed their eyes, as demanded, and listened to Dylan Thomas intone "Fern Hill" when Bruce wheeled out the stereo. They copied into notebooks his exacting genealogies of the Bundrens and Snopes in Faulkner's Yoknapatawpha. And they rewarded him, most of them, with bemused affection. Bruce Bechdel ranked as one of the supremely popular teachers in that hayseed school.

He combined breeziness and casual mirth with the dictates of a taskmaster. Kids could lounge as if their desks were divans, snap gum, pass notes, gossip and murmur, but they also needed to pay on-the-spot attention and answer his relentless barrage of queries. "Prufrock says he has heard the mermaids singing each to each—is he just some demented old man, people? What's he saying? Schweitzer! Answer!…. Time's up! Ruhl!"

He gave us not only Stephen Dedalus and the Sistine Chapel and Pissarro; he and his wife Helen gave us our only living models of alternate possibilities, of liberality, of cosmopolitan flair in that land of chaw-tobacco and clodhoppers. Helen (featured, like Bruce, years later in their daughter Alison's books *Fun Home* and *Are You My Mother?*) was sharp, excitable, chic in her early-'70s midi-skirts and paisley scarves. A skillful pianist, an actress trained in Manhattan, a devotee of *Vogue*, she coached me through novels by Philip Roth and James Baldwin as my stern but patient, ever-nurturing eleventh-grade English teacher, and she offered Appalachian teenagers a hint of glamour. So did Bruce. He sported modish Bobby Kennedy hair and tailored jackets and knitted ties. He demonstrated for us that a man could be at ease while stylish and poised. His gushing young female student-teachers from Lock Haven State adored him. Even we could see that.

He introduced us to novelty. For lunch he ate yogurt, a food I'd never heard of. God knows where he found it. Certainly not in Clinton County. It must have come from one of his and Helen's excursions to Oz, into New York City itself—something nobody else did. They'd also been to Paris and Berlin—no one did that. They skied—no one did that, either. Bruce pushed us. "*Women in Love*—name the author, people, a thousand 'A's! Right: D.H. Lawrence! The movie's playing in State College this weekend. Ten thousand 'A's to anyone who goes to see the movie *Women in Love!*" And we went, my bold friends Dolores and Jeannine and I, driving forty miles at night to a tiny art-house cinema near the Penn State campus—where we basked in flickered screenlight, astounded by sensual lushness of English meads, vast stone manors with alluring hearths, and abrupt shifts from genteel drawing-room palaver to naked grappling and grunts of desire.

The courage of the man. To venture into that high school each day and assert himself, in all his gloried idiosyncrasies. To do it facing the mockery and contempt of his yokel colleagues, the snickering math teachers and skinhead football coaches in their Woolworth's shirts and brogans, their pot-guts looming over belts of shapeless trousers. The words "queer" and "homo" and "faggot" never far from their lips. To face six classes a day of heedless, rambunctious teens from dismal farms and villages of Nowhere, Pennsylvania, and inspire them to care about Gatsby's yearning gaze toward Daisy's green light across that impossible distance of water....

By turns grave, exasperated, jaunty, delighted: Bruce dared us. He offered always to our withering Appalachian lives a Great Jewel of artistic culture that sustained him, a treasure he shared with zealous love and generosity: Here! Take this! It's priceless and can change you forever!

How would Bruce have felt, in that besieged classroom where he jousted so long and so valiantly, if he'd foreseen that decades later critics who knew him merely from the book *Fun Home* and its Broadway show would describe him, in their articles for *Time* magazine, the *Village Voice,*

the *New Yorker*, the *Los Angeles Times*, the *New York Times*, as petty, tyrannical, cold, and closeted?

He could be manic in his enthusiasms; he could be sullen in his
frustrations; with me he relaxed. We gabbed for hours. Me with my
sandaled feet propped on his desk, renegade hippie kid with patched
bellbottoms and shoulder-length troubadour hair like Lennon's in the
White Album photo. Bruce attired as dashingly as Dick Cavett. Eighteen
years my senior, he could have impersonated an older cousin. He saw my
intellectual hunger. "We need to get you out of here, Ruhl. Out of goddamn Clinton County. You need to go to college. You need to find a way."

Bruce Bechdel, who saved lives.

Who saved mine.

At sixteen a young woman of vexatious—of arresting—voluptuous-
ness, Jeannine Antonio had perfected a technique, when speaking, of
brandishing her cigarette with precocious aplomb, as if impersonating
the mistress of an Italian *padrone*. She charmed me. When speaking, she
punctuated her sentences with dashes and commas of laughter. She'd turn
to me and ask, "Steve, what do you think?" I thought she was right,
always. Always. Her eyes were like the eyes of women in Pompeiian fres-
coes. She read Emily Brontë novels. She babysat for little Alison Bechdel
and the two young brothers when Bruce and Helen breezed out to parties. She was my age. She inspired in me crushes—not so secret, and not
reciprocated. Crushes unspeakable between us.

Each school night we'd cruise Mill Hall roads for hours.

Jeannine, newly arrived from Philadelphia, lived off Lusk Run Road
in the "hippie house." This handmade Big Sur fantasy of tilted walls and
towers and glass portholes was built of scraps and leaky, castoff lumber
by her stepfather, a bearded art major at Lock Haven State. Set incongru-
ously amid trees near Bald Eagle Creek, the house served as headquarters
for Lock Haven's beleaguered little counterculture. Each night when I
rendezvoused with Jeannine I'd step inside her house's multileveled maze
of lofts, skylights, exposed wooden beams and hear music unfamiliar to
me: Miles Davis or Nina Simone, recent Bob Dylan songs, Laura Nyro.
I'd catch whiffs of food I'd never imagined, such as lentil soup or bagels.

I'd see mop-haired college guys, beatnik college women in wool sweaters at the kitchen table with a bottle of Chianti, stubbing cigarettes, animatedly deploring Nixon's latest crimes in Indochina. Within minutes Jeannine and I were out the door, away in the car to pick up our classmate Dolores.

Dolores Chevalier lived with her parents and nine brothers and sisters in a farmhouse on a rain-gutted dirt road. They lived near Sugar Run, in Bald Eagle Valley. To get there each night I'd turn left where hulks of scrapped cars strewed a weed-infested hillside. Then I'd drive the mountain, its waste meadows and woods, the car churning fumes of dust like cavalry in an old Western, throwing gravel on the sharp turns. Dolores was a new arrival also, from Detroit. Sardonic, headstrong, theatrical, she wore horn rims and loved Streisand albums, late-night Judy Garland on TV.

The three of us navigated unmarked roads. Every night. The girls laughing. Leaning forward to switch a radio station. Blowing cigarette smoke from car windows.

Headlights carved out quick, bright swaths of fields, houses, trees from Clinton County's darkness....

"I don't understand this peculiar high-school-reunion-thing you have in the States," a British friend has told me. "In England, you leave secondary school—goodbye, nice to've met you—and you never see most of those people again; you move on to university, and that's that."

Perhaps a sprawling continent, a land of transient, hurried people, compels our desire for reunions. Americans always seem to rush away from each other while vowing to keep in touch. Reunions serve as communal homecoming for a nation of individualists, nation of busy vagabonds. "See you later," the standard American farewell—what is that but a promise of reunion?

At the time of our first high school reunion, in 1977, I groaned when an envelope postmarked "Mill Hall, PA" arrived at my Amherst apartment. A letter bearing the salutation "Dear Classmate" invited me to the gala event and urged me to buy raffle tickets to help finance it. One of the items to be raffled was a shotgun. Another was a bushel basket of "cheer"—that is, whiskey.

I declined. In fact I've declined each subsequent invitation mailed at five-year intervals.

Now, in late July of '92, they've scheduled our twentieth-year reunion at picnic grounds hidden somewhere along the Susquehanna, six miles northwest of Lock Haven in those broken-back mountains off the Bucktail Trail. The featured event: an outdoor pig roast. My friends in Amherst and Northampton find this hysterical.

Early light scalds the fog off Lick Run Gap. Hills are refulgent with summer. Descant of finches, of mourning doves and robins counterpoints a steady clipping noise.

The "clacket-click" comes from spinning blades of a horse-drawn thresher.

An Amish man is cutting hay. Just beyond the poplars at the edge of my parents' back lawn, he's standing—bearded, straw-hatted, suspendered—atop a rig, reins in hand, guiding a six-harness team of big, tawny draft horses.

Seeking lineage, a place among the ancestors....

In forlorn backwoods Appalachian mountains of central Pennsylvania, ten miles from here, my paternal great-great-great-grandmother—her name was Elizabeth Heckman Ruhl—might have stood on the porch and watched her husband cross the fields in this same way, behind his team of Clydesdales, geeing and hawing his horses through the summer cutting, spice of fresh mown hay, of heat and dusty sunshine.

It would have been the late 1840s. Years when Thoreau puttered at Walden Pond and the Mexican War was at full boil, years of revolt in Europe and famine in Ireland, years when Balzac indited his *La Comédie humaine* and Chopin's mazurkas sparkled in the salon of George Sand....

Elizabeth Ruhl would have baked cobblers in her Dutch oven. Dipped tallow candles. Weeded the corn patch. Fretted through droughts and frosts. Shuffled to the barn through snow drifts to milk a herd of impatient, lowing Holsteins and Guernseys. She may have rocked alone late at night, humming to soothe a wailing baby, looking out the crack of a shuttered window at swatches of cloud, a frozen moon. Or she might have lain on the corn-shuck mattress with her husband John, listening to barred owls as he touched her, whispered to her, maybe called her Libby, his darling Libby....

She must have harbored a secret wildness. Something in her that loved these hills and their seasons.

...The Amish man rattles his thresher through sifting, knee-high grass, a mown swath trailing behind. The horses' heads bob as they nudge forward. Clack, clicket, clack....

For socializing, the Ruhl family might have joined in corn huskings with their Brush Valley neighbors, or flax skutchings, or barn raisings. They'd have ridden dutifully to church on Sundays to hear about hellfire. A little clan sequestered among those green enfolding mountain slopes, those silences....

Clack. Clickety-ty-ty-ty, click. Clack. Clack.

The Amish farmer reaps another row of hay.

Simple lives.

Simple lives, with lasting consequences: Elizabeth and John set my family's lineage among these hills. They clinched our destinies.

They bequeathed me—a century later, when I was born here—my troubled homeland.

☽

IN AMHERST a half-dozen winters ago I stepped into the tavern of the Lord Jeffery Inn on a late afternoon, ordered a beer, spread a book on the table, and glancing around the room noticed that the only other customer was James Baldwin.

Visiting professor at the local Five Colleges, he sat at a table near a far window. Baldwin, unassumingly regal, wore a coat over his shoulders like a cape and sipped cognac while composing letters. In *Notes of a Native Son* James Baldwin wrote, "I imagine one of the reasons people cling to their hates so stubbornly is because they sense, once hate is gone, that they will be forced to deal with pain."

I borrow his words as epigraph for the recollections that follow.

Ten years after leaving Bald Eagle-Nittany High School I sat in a carpeted, gently lit room in the Amherst Resource Center and confessed to a therapist, "I never fought back."

She looked at me. She waited.

I studied the floor.

("Hey! Goddamn hippie!")

"I guess…." I looked at the therapist; looked again at the floor. "See, in high school I thought I was a pacifist. A peace-and-love flower child of the Sixties. Make love not war, the whole thing…."

"Wait a moment. Let's back up first. You referred last week to your notoriety in the very conservative area where you lived as a teenager," she said, occasionally checking a notebook on her lap. "How everyone in the little town in Pennsylvania where your high school was located—what was the name of the town?"

"Mill Hall."

"That's right, I remember now. How everyone in Mill Hall knew you by reputation, how you stood out. How isolated and alone you felt as a teenager. You were 'the hippie.' You were the only boy with long hair. The only one to wear bell bottoms and psychedelic shirts and Army jackets with peace symbols."

"Well, not the only one—there were also my younger brother Larry and eventually a few others. But I was the first. I was the most extreme, the most visible. And being the very first one to do all those things made me the obvious target."

The therapist's name was Laura. Attractive, with Mediterranean eyes and poufed auburn hair, attired in bulky turtlenecks, she was a patient listener, a woman who radiated so much warmheartedness that, were my hands frostbitten, and not merely my psyche, I could probably have held them before her and they would have thawed and healed. "Okay. And you told me how teachers threatened you with expulsion unless you obeyed the dress code and cut your hair. You said that when you were fourteen, you challenged the school board all by yourself at one of their meetings, stood up and made a speech to them about how the length of your hair was a form of freedom of expression, and protected by the First

Amendment. They ignored you. When you were fifteen, you and five 'hippie' boys from another school in a nearby town called, let me see, Lock Haven?"

"Uh-huh."

"—phoned a lawyer from the American Civil Liberties Union. None of you had money but he took the case anyway."

"That's right."

"All of you confronted the local school board again. This time they listened. Your lawyer told them the school's dress code was unconstitutional, and you forced the board to repeal it."

"Right."

"After that you grew your hair halfway to your waist, which, by the way, I think is great. Bravo! Good for you!" She smiled. "And you became very outspoken publicly in your opposition to the Vietnam War. You wrote a full-page letter to the editor published in your local newspaper explaining why you would refuse to be drafted."

"Right. The *Lock Haven Express.*" I opposed the war and said so in classrooms; I said so in that full-page letter, a morally indignant manifesto printed as an oddity among the newspaper's gridiron reports, "Li'l Abner" comics, and snapshots of bow hunters. Mill Hall was "America, Love It or Leave It" country. In homeroom I refused to mouth the Pledge of Allegiance, refused to salute the flag. On the day of the nationwide Vietnam moratorium I set up a table in the lobby outside the gym and handed out anti-war leaflets, which most teachers and students either ignored or crumpled and threw away.

I opposed the war because I no longer could reconcile the napalmed corpses I saw on TV with "Thou shalt not kill," a Biblical imperative learned during one of my rare but impressionable visits to a church in Lock Haven, years earlier. The moment I graduated from high school my government intended to pack me across the Pacific to maim and murder Vietnamese boys my own age. And for what? An undeclared war premised on lies. I decided that when my eighteenth birthday arrived I would argue my case before the draft board in Williamsport as a conscientious objector.

"And you told me that your local 'infamy'—that was your word—increased. And you said it became very difficult. That people shunned you, that adults in your town began to make threats, and that it felt very dangerous to you. I want to ask you more about that. You said that one of your neighbors threatened to shoot you if you stepped on his property."

"Yeah. He was the local commander of the National Guard. After Kent State happened, you know, it felt even more dangerous."

"And you said that your favorite teacher, let me see"—she glanced at her notebook—"his name was Bruce Bechdel, betrayed you once. I want to talk to you more about that, too. You said you were going around to various English classes, presenting a scene you were in from an upcoming student play, and when you got to his class it was full of kids older than you—'redneck kids,' you called them."

"Right." I stiffened at the memory.

"And you told Mr. Bechdel you'd do the scene if he promised not to leave the room. But midway he left to get coffee. And immediately the older 'redneck' boys began shouting, 'Kill him! Kill him!' And you said that the only way to escape was to pass through a gauntlet of them while they punched you."

I looked at the floor.

"You were bullied. You were bullied outrageously. Wasn't there anyone to help you?"

The abandonment. The sense of being culled from the herd and marked as prey. "I never told my parents. It would have upset them. I didn't want to worry them. Also they would have intervened at school. That would have embarrassed me. It would've made things worse. I felt it was important to stand up for myself, to stand on my own two feet."

"It sounds like you did. You were very brave. You say you were a pacifist and never fought back, but remember, you also never backed down. You never did. You remained true to yourself. Bravo for that, too! What about your friends?"

"Well, kids in my own grade knew me and liked me—you know, I think they felt mystified by the changes I'd gone through, all of my hippie transformations, but they respected me. One of them told me, 'Everything we only dream about doing, you actually do.' They even elected me class president, class vice-president, things like that. It helped to protect me, this support from my classmates."

"How did it protect you?"

"Well, if I'd been more isolated the older jocks and the redneck teachers would have felt completely free to destroy me. But I never talked to my friends Jeannine and Dolores or my buddy T.J. or my other friends about what was happening. I thought they could see it for themselves— wasn't it obvious? And I felt too depressed. You know, you feel so vulnerable as a teenager. And all your emotions are so heightened, so hormonal. And you just want to be accepted."

Rituals of social behavior govern small American towns like Mill Hall and Lock Haven, rituals of demeanor and conduct, traditions that hold the force of law and may not be transgressed lightly. I hadn't known this. It's shocking how quickly, how brutally, your neighbors will disown you.

Glowering waitresses ignored me if I tried to order a Coke at the lunch counter in Woolworth's. "Hey Dottie, what's thet settin' in yer booth, thet a girl or a boy?" "I don' know, but I ain't servin' it." I rode my bicycle along Fishing Creek Road; men in a pickup truck winged beer bottles at me. As I pedaled my bike another time outside Mackeyville a farmer unpenned his German shepherds yelling, "Git thet damn hippie! Sic 'im, boy!" Mothers of my sister's friends forbade their daughters to enter our house. Our high school football coach, "Chaz" Dole, a crewcut, lard-bellied rube who swaggered like Patton, called me "Stephanie" and devoted entire health classes to informing students why they must avoid me with the same pains they might take to shun a Satanist.

"You said last week that at age seventeen you 'felt so crippled by depression and fear' that you 'could barely function.' That's where we stopped. Is that a fair review? Have I covered everything?"

I said, "Yeah. But there's more."

In Amherst around 1978, six years after graduation, I had started plunging into nightmares: I'd enter the doors of Bald Eagle-Nittany High School gripping a black submachine gun. I dreamed of walking the halls as Leo Held had walked through the Lock Haven paper mill.

Annihilating everyone—teachers, students, all of them—in spitfire gales of blood and gore.

"They used to gang up on me in the lavatories, they'd ambush me in the hallways," I told the therapist, as I sat in that tranquil room in Amherst. "I felt tense and nervous all the time. I cut school a lot. Or I'd get there early and sneak to the auditorium and climb up a ladder to the catwalks hidden above the ceiling and spend the day up there, reading. On days when I had no choice but to go to classes, the football players, the older ones, would yell, 'Get a goddamn haircut!' in the halls. They'd surround me. Throw my books. Punch me."

"So they'd hit you even in the halls? In public?"

"They'd punch me in the mouth." Taste of blood, taste of saliva tinctured with iron, teeth piercing my lip. Eyes stinging. "Or punch me so hard in the chest that I couldn't breathe." At a high school dance a football player suddenly hit me. Gasping suffocation, pain drumming beneath my breastbone. I was unsure if my heart still beat. "I thought I was dying. In eleventh grade I lived in terror. At school I never knew when it would happen, never felt safe. An ambush could happen at any moment. At my locker. At the water fountain." Predatory, they approached with sniffing-the-air intensity. Hard stares. Fists ready. "Walking down the hall alone I'd see a line of older football players form a barrier ahead so I couldn't pass. And I knew what was coming. But I walked right up to them anyway. And looked them in the eye with this kind of defiance, you know. Actually, in a strange way I think they respected that. I never ran. Ever. And then they'd start punching me: 'Hippie son of a bitch!'"

Entering the lavatory: leering farmboys from the senior classes, rough-housing near sinks and urinals. Too late for me to turn and leave. "What the hell *you* doin' in here?" Gulping my fear I stood before a mirror. Slowly, miming nonchalance, I'd remove a comb from my jeans pocket. Snorting with derision they'd file past. Shoulder me with football blocks. Ram me against the sink. Slug me in the back. "Goddamn queer."

"The reason I never fought back is I prided myself on that Woodstock vibe of peace and 'turn the other cheek.' I felt self-righteous about it. And I admired Martin Luther King and nonviolence, you know, and wanted to emulate him. I thought of myself as very noble. But I'm beginning to realize that I wasn't a pacifist at all," I told her. "What I was really doing, every time they hit me, was choking down a tremendous amount of rage."

"Tell me about that."

"I was choking down all this rage, tremendous pain, so much fear and anger and the desire to hit back. I was...I...I mean, I feel...God, I feel so much anger now, I *hate* them, I want to kill them, you know, and—it feels explosive, I—I'm not sure what to do with it, it's like this volcano in me, everything I choked down and repressed all those years—"

"You need to feel these things," the therapist said.

I'd been stabbing the anger inward. Slashing in self-loathing. Making myself sick and suicidal. I had read of an epidemic in Africa, how larvae in water invade a human body, hatch to worms, gnaw their way excruciatingly through the skin. That's what my anger from high school threatened to do.

In Amherst in the late 1970s, early '80s, I cropped my hair. Razor-scraped the sides of my head to bare skin. I'd pull on a tattered Sex Pistols T-shirt. Sweatpants. Pair of Nikes. And I'd run. Not jog. Run: a three-mile frenzy. I needed to feel these things? I missiled through the streets. Liquid oxygen of rage. Swinging fists at road signs. Scowling at people in cars: You wanna fuck with me? Huh? Come on! I'll rip your throats out—

I hoisted barbells. No one would ever, *ever* hit me again. Tightened my body into one-hundred-and-ninety tensile pounds of muscle. Shoved past pool tables, past beer-chugging, bad-ass rowdies in a crummy rathskeller, practically throwing off sparks, daring anyone to challenge me, man, I felt homicidal, the hell with nonviolence.... Punk arrived at the perfect moment. Slamming to chainsaw-guitar bands like Deep Wound and Eighth Route Army in smoky Northampton rock clubs, caroming off sweatslick bodies in oblivious rage, raging in my apartment, enraged I cranked the Clash to a thousand wall-pulverizing megatons, hit pillows, kickboxed screaming across my room flailing fists at the air, raging on the street wore a studded motorcycle jacket of death-black leather, it was no fucking fashion statement, man, I meant it: You wanna fuck with me? Huh? Yeah, you! I'll take your head off at your knees, motherfucker—

"It's kind of frightening," I'd tell my therapist. "I worry—you know, if somebody would ever shove me, even accidentally, like in a checkout line at the supermarket—I can't stand the thought of someone shoving me. God, I think I'd go berserk. I will not be pushed around ever again. By anyone. I will not be disrespected or violated physically in any way. And I'm so full of anger—"

"You need to feel this. You were traumatized. You need to let it come out."

I've driven back to the high school this afternoon.

Breeze rattles the halyard on the flagpole. Distant hum of a lawnmower. One crow at the far edge of the parking lot.

Teachers at Bald Eagle-Nittany would beat us.

They'd stalk corridors of this high school carrying thick wooden paddles. Half the length of baseball bats, broad and flat, these special paddles featured holes augered into the wood, holes to make them bite.

"You could always tell when a teacher had just paddled someone," my brother has said. "They sort of strutted. Like, 'I'm a real tough guy.' You could tell just by looking at them. Like seeing a dog with blood on its muzzle."

Nearly every day, school halls echoed with the "wham! wham! wham!" of a paddle. Boys judged as miscreants and paddled would hobble afterward to their chairs, grinning. The code of manhood required a grin. In a cafeteria study hall I witnessed a gym teacher break a paddle over a kid's head. The split pieces whirligigged high into the air.

I got paddled. Ten whacks with a paddle left a branding mark, a wide paddle-shape, red like a sunburn. This damage lasted for days.

When I tell this to people in Amherst they're aghast. "My God, you mean there was corporal punishment in your school? I didn't think that happened anymore! What school was that? You mean they actually hit you? It sounds so—Dickensian, so nineteenth century, so—barbaric!" When my girlfriend Diana and I lived together I mentioned it one evening, off-the-cuff, and she grew somber. She touched my shoulder. She looked at me with concern. She murmured, "God, Steve-arino"—her pet name for me—"you were physically abused as a child. God, no, I mean it—you really were. You're a survivor of physical abuse."

"Really?" A pause. A revelation. "I never thought of it in those specific words."

Mill Hall people took it for granted. Parents expected teachers to hit kids. (I even saw Bruce Bechdel, who could have a temper like a hand grenade, lunge at a belligerent student and wrestle him to the floor: "Goddamn it, don't talk back to *me*, you little shit!") Parents thrashed their kids at home. "You keep thet up, yer gonna git a whippin'!" I heard parents say that to children in laundromats, on Main Street, in the Weis Supermarket, heard it from open windows of houses in summer. Fathers removed leather belts from their trousers, wrapped the buckled end of the belt around a fist, then used the other end like a bullwhip to flog a son or daughter. Sometimes I heard the resounding "wap! wap!" of the belt and some man yelling, "I'm gonna teach you to mind me good!" and, above the din of television, a child screaming.

But not in my household, and not in my elementary school. My dad spanked me with the palm of his hand, lightly, almost apologetically, perhaps twice throughout my childhood. At Akeley Elementary in Lock Haven, an experimental lab school on the campus of the teacher's college, I thrived from third through sixth grades in a wonderland of learning and rejoicing, of open classrooms, "new math," art and music projects, and color-coded SRA reading books. Our teachers, stout ladies named Miss Waterbury and Miss Holmes, clement and encouraging, wore wire spectacles and dressed like Eleanor Roosevelt. They never hit us.

By the time I reached sixteen I began to lie awake at night.

It seemed to me those Mill Hall teachers, dumped into their middle-aged bodies as if into sacks, their blood gone alkaline, found merry relief in bashing teenagers. Trying to bash the bright new personalities out of us. Trying to bash our zest, our frisky sexuality, our penchant for freedom. Teachers trying to bash the daylights out of unfettered, optimistic teenagers in spiteful retribution for their own blunted lives.

Several nights I contemplated this. Head on my pillow. Staring through darkness.

Why do they hit us? And then my epiphany: Why do we allow them?

Two days later, in homeroom, a teacher summoned me to get paddled. My felony: I'd talked to a girl as morning announcements blabbed over the P.A. speaker.

"Okay, Ruhl! Up front! Ten whacks!"

His name was Spitzer. A math teacher, slightly balding, with black-rimmed glasses, a devotee of plaid sports jackets. He half-smiled, reaching for the paddle. He looked forward to it. "You heard me, Ruhl! Up front!"

"No."

He remained smiling. But for a moment his face shifted. He looked like a man in a dentist's office hearing bad news about his X-rays. Then he recovered. He said, "Up here now, Ruhl, and get your whacks!"

"No. I won't allow you to hit me."

Chatter in the room subsided.

The teacher stopped smiling.

"I've made a decision. No teacher is ever going to paddle me again. I won't allow it."

Perfect quiet.

"If you try to hit me"—I said this calmly—"I'm going to grab the paddle, and I'm going to take it away from you."

This roused him.

"If—if you strike a teacher," he stammered, "you'll be expelled from school!"

"I didn't say anything about striking you. I said I won't let you hit me. I'll take the paddle out of your hand if I have to. But I won't strike you. And I won't allow you to hit me." For the first time since arriving at this school I felt no panic. "I've made a decision," I repeated. Perhaps for the thrill of hearing myself say it. "No teacher will hit me, ever again. I will not allow it."

After that morning, no teacher at Bald Eagle-Nittany dared to paddle me.

No teacher even tried.

My girlfriend Diana, twenty-one years old. Sitting on our disheveled mattress in Amherst.

She sat naked. Lit by a source I can't distinguish: morning sunlight, maybe, or winter afternoon, pale wash from the lamp, I don't know any-more. Whatever hour, it had grown very late for us.

Sheets and blankets at her waist. Her breasts terribly exposed, terrible because so matter-of-fact, so unerotic, terrible because eroticism was no longer part of a shared life between us.

Her arms braced, supporting her weight on her hands. Her hands pressed against the pillows on the bed.

Her face moistened with tears. This is what she said to me:

"You're so—you're so angry—at the whole world—"

And then, urgently, her eyes searching the room, she said, "I don't know what to do anymore—"

The silence in our bedroom filled with her crying. As Diana sobbed her voice almost fought to the surface. Then it sank beneath her crying. Her voice struggled up again, and what she finally said to me was this:

"You're so angry, and you won't let me love you."

She said: "I try and try, Steve. I try everything I can think of. But"—the words cracked and splintered—"you won't… let me… love… you…."

So angry at the whole world.

I look, one final time, at this high school.

When I gun the engine I'm gone.

FOUR

I'M DRIVING across an ocean floor.

Four hundred million years ago, during the Devonian Period of the Paleozoic, when crude mosses and ferns debuted on land, and the earliest amphibians, the region now known as Clinton County lay submerged beneath a balmy tropical sea. As a kid playing in our backyard I often discovered fossils from the Devonian: scallop shells intaglioed in rocks, marine trilobites in bas-relief.

Thus as I drive across this primordial seabed my car is a combination of time machine and bathysphere.

Air through my window sounds like a breaking surf, tidal ebb and flow of centuries.

I'm moving past clover, past clumps of weeds called dock and sorrel, redtop, yellow mullein, where butterflies—"dusty millers"—rumpus over the wild grass. Hot wind blowing across these fields smells like a bakery, honeyed and spiced.

A groundhog pokes from scrub thistle, noses the air.

I'm creeping at less than ten miles an hour, Amish buggy speed, the right velocity for traveling *in* this landscape, rather than through it. All my windows are rolled down. I hear the rattle and click of cicadas, like somebody shaking a maraca. To my left, behind a barbed fence, stands a ruminant milk-herd. One piebald Guernsey approaches, munching cud, her eye skeptical, her nose pebble-grained like a black leather wallet. "Howdy, cow!" No "moo" in reply. But redwing blackbirds fuss in a wind-row stand of hawthorns.

I swing past an Amish farm, past its cattle pens and cornrows, its teth-ered horses, a trio of grass-munching sheep. The unadorned white houses look simple as houses in a child's drawing. Buggies and wagons are parked near the barns. A hand-lettered sign advertises Amish "eye-dazzler" quilts ("No Sunday sales"). Women in white poke-bonnets, black aprons, long clean dresses of lavender, quietly hoe cabbage and weed marigolds. Their roadside greenhouse offers geraniums. Someone in the Amish family has posted a small sign by the greenhouse door. I ignore it. Then impulsively I put the car in reverse and stop to read it:

"It is best to be honest and truthful. To make the most of what we have, to be happy with simple pleasures, and to be cheerful, and have courage when things go wrong."

I read it again. Then again. These two sentences are the sanest I've encountered in months. Once I would have dismissed them as platitudes. But these words describe the life I want. The life I've begun to think about lately with vague, unfocused longing. "To be happy with simple pleasures. To have courage when things go wrong."

How can I create that life? I certainly can't become Amish. Where can I find it? Is it even possible?

Ten minutes later I park the car and hotfoot up a small embankment, through underbrush. I enter a narrow copse of forest at the periphery of a meadow.

Memories start flickering. They start to flicker like the foxfire that I dis-covered when I tented in these woods one moonless night, years ago, when the damp trees were luminous with a pale, spooky green phosphorescence.

I'm behind Cedar Heights. This was a ritzy neighborhood by Mill Hall's reckoning. We lived here during my embattled teenage years. This forest and meadow bordered our backyard. My family's house, one of the most distinctive, an imposing modern chalet, crowned a small hill. My parents could scarcely afford that house. It symbolized my father's white-collar promotion to a supervisor's position at the Titan Metal fac-tory and our ascension to the lower middle class; it rewarded us for five years cramped in our trailer. It compensated my parents' lifelong scrab-bling at the edges of Appalachian poverty. When we moved in 1966 to

Cedar Heights' collection of ranches and Capes and suburban split-levels among the hayfields, when we settled into our new showplace (which we barely could manage to furnish), my parents were grasping beyond their small bank account. Investing. Daring. Hoping. And without knowing it, acting on urges like those that prompted the first Ruhls to forgo their peasant hut in Germany, launching toward the New World.

We adored that house. It seemed palatial. We prided ourselves on its floor-to-ceiling fireplaces of mountain stone in the living room and family room, its latticed bay window and Dutch door, its swanky multi-storied spaciousness. We added books and our cheap hi-fi and our trailer furniture and made it our own. My mother perfumed the kitchen with wafting aromas of homemade bread. If high school meant hell, home meant sanctuary.

Down in those grassy swards when I was fourteen my buddies and I played tackle football—at the snap I'd pell-mell off the line, feint, charge for the long bomb. We played softball. The clean, pulpy swat of a bat—"Louisville Slugger"—against a ball, the ball soaring to its apogee against cloud and sun....

I'm here, yet it feels elusive. Again I feel homesick for a place I can't seem to find.

Cedar Heights offered a cross-section of postwar blue-collar and lower-echelon white-collar America: Hammermill factory workers, Piper aircraft engineers, a Bell Telephone lineman, an owner of a car dealership, some schoolteachers, and all the wives, those homemaker moms raising the next wave of Baby Boomers, young boys popping wheelies on banana bikes, their sisters swooning to the Monkees. Those memories suspend in a haze of sunshine. Beyond the meadow, past our house, in the heart of the neighborhood, we shot hoops on a fenced-in asphalt court, rambunctious in sweaty pickup games. Next to the basketball court, teenage Cedar Heights girls in bikinis and guys in trunks celebrated eternal summer at the Warner family's swimming pool. There, innocent of time, we cannonballed each other in tremendous spumes of sun-dazzled chlorine.

Read the best books first, advised Thoreau. Otherwise you may not get the chance to read them at all....

Stepping through these woods I locate a burled maple. Nailed in its trunk I find a few half-rotted planks. Above them, perched high in the leaves: three boards, a joist, some decayed sheathing. It's all that remains of the tree fort. Up there, the summer I turned nineteen, I discovered Proust.

The tree fort resembled a lookout post on the mizzenmast of a windjammer. Instead of topsails and staysails, however, foliage surrounded it. As junior high kids, when we weren't playing baseball, or football, or basketball, when we weren't hiking or swimming or bicycling, my friends and I had nailed the fort together. A secret getaway. A place to smoke cigars and swap *Playboy* mags. The year after my liberation from high school I rediscovered it. I commandeered the tree fort as an arboreal hideout, my scholar's retreat, my sanitarium. During that summer I'd amble through the meadow and into these woods, the Moncrieff/Mayor translation of *Remembrance of Things Past* tucked beneath my arm. I'd haul myself into splayed branches of this maple, then up to the fort, where leaves of the maple's upper boughs provided canopy.

Reading Proust felt transgressive. *Remembrance of Things Past* exemplified the type of exalted, canonical literature deemed too rarefied for a person of my humble origins. Defiantly, I claimed it as my own.

Morning light segued to afternoon light, faded to shadows at suppertime, day after day, week after week, as I hunkered in this aerie, working my way across Proust's seven volumes, all 2,280 pages: enraptured by complex passions of Marcel and Gilbertte and Albertine, rages of the magisterial Baron de Charlus, the doomed thralldom of that endearing popinjay, Swann, and the coquetries of his beloved Odette. I smiled at the inane pretensions of the Verdurins, admired the chivalries of Robert St. Loup. In my tree fort in Appalachia—a lonesome, fierce teenager, neglected, fed by unlikely yearnings—Proust gave me Paris, gave me a cosmos of human love and suffering and intoxicating grandeur.

Kept in memory: the sunlight. Stenciled leaf shadows on the books' pages. Sparrows. Faint underhum of bees. A fly fisherman's car door banging shut, down on the road. Winds brooming up the cliffside. Swaying of the tree's limbs as I'd read; purl of Fishing Creek's lambent waters. I remember always how I'd pause at the end of a page to look through tree-tops to the open meadow, its frippery of black-eyed Susans, chicory and milkweed, and its darting butterflies—powder-pinks and saffrons and blue pastels—alight in high, waving grass. Roof of my family's big house at the crest of the hill, banked against cumulus....

Walking back to the car I hear a mourning dove. The bird oboes its plangent, glissading high note, then three sustained lows: "Hey, hoo!... hoo... hoo... hoooo."

The way a spirit talks.

Now, twenty years after my sojourn with Proust, in the late summer of 1992, a couple of miles from the house in Cedar Heights, past a forested cliff, at a bend marked by willows and arching sycamores, Duck Run broadens to a still pool. Chambers of light diffuse through summer-hazed foliage. Brisk "rat-tat": Morse code of a woodpecker. Downstream at the rapids Duck Run makes a noise like silver coins tumbling in a glass. I cut the ignition. Step out of the car.

A mallard drake's trawling the riffles. Squirrels do their anxious run-stop-run through bracken. I smell familiar must of vegetation, dank mud. Flowers called celandine mob the roadside. When I snap one, yellow droplets ooze the stalk. Leni-Lenape Indians daubed this on their cheeks for battle. Today, though, I feel like making peace.

A heron swoops the water. A princely, primitive bird, each of its enormous slate-blue wings unfolds effortlessly as a chaise longue. The heron foot-drags the stream. Then it sails aloft and, turning, reveals the silhouette of a pteranodon.

I like to divine the lasting essence of this place.

I like to feel intimations of something akin to those tutelary spirits—near at hand, beyond spectrum of the visible—to whom Celts built menhirs and dolmens; spirits the pagan Romans called *genii loci*. Thracian shepherds would have known Duck Run inhabited by potamids, nymphs of rivers and streams. Shinto worshippers in Japan paid homage to divine spirits of leaves, to sacred life coursing through roots and bodies of trees, the kami spirits of wind and water.

I like to feel what they felt. I like to hear what they heard: the land improvising always—in zephyr, in freshet—its oracular speech, its earth-jazz, its wild glossolalia.

Seined light of late afternoon. Warblers and vireos launch from overhung boughs of sycamores, of cottonwoods. They blitz across Fishing Creek to cornfields. Then back again. Rusty-hinge sounds of a white-throated sparrow. Water, shatters, constantly, in, whitecaps, over, stones…. This creek living precisely as it lived a quarter-century ago in my boyhood….

My friends and I found a bee tree along this road. Walking one August we heard, humming above our heads, something like an electric shaver. We saw atop a dead oak the shape-shifting corona of honeybees. "Look!" A branch twenty feet above us. In the crevice lay a golden resin. It was the only bee tree we ever found.

Describing poets, Rilke said, "We are the bees of the invisible."

Trying to find my inner latitude and longitude…measuring landscape against memory….

I've stopped my car at Cedar Springs Cemetery. Meadows of clover and dandelion extend south to forested bluffs high above the creek. Fields to the east incline to a ridge cresting against the sky. Until I traveled across the Mississippi and onto the Great Plains when I was eighteen this sky, right here, was the boldest I knew.

The cemetery at Cedar Springs rolls across ascending hummocks. It's a park-like setting of tulip trees and spruces and these beautiful, eponymous cedars, many over a century old.

Intimations of mortality. An elaborate cast-iron statue of a Victorian angel kneels in flowing robes, wings outspread as if she's just alighted. As kids we spooked ourselves with stories about this angel. We insisted that her head swiveled at night and that her eyes, feline, shone like those of a witch's Graymalkin.

I used to wander a tractor lane out in those meadows beyond the cemetery. It led to the Horsepath Woods, a ten-acre tract of sugar maples and ferns, dogwood and oaks. Summers of my eighteenth and nineteenth birthdays I camped alone there. I'd pitch my tent on moss and leaves.

Night among those trees grew absolutely black. Fireflies appeared: zillions of live embers, little rafts set ablaze, adrift on eddies of air. I sat on a log to observe them. It felt like reclining in God's easy chair, watching galaxies wink on and off.

☽

"Every day is a journey," wrote the Japanese Zen poet Bashō, "and the journey itself is home."

In November of 1945 a US naval boat, LST 743, churned through waters of Sasebo, Japan. A dramatic harbor: sheer escarpments plunging straight into the sea. Wrecked Japanese aircraft carriers still lay blackened above ocean swells. The 743 cruised past other American occupation ships, all the sailors waving their caps, and it docked at the city wharves. The men took shore leave. My father was among them.

"All we'd been hearing for years was how terrible the Japs were," my dad has said. "But we went into Sasebo and, my God, the kids were so cute and the people so friendly, and you'd think, 'This is the enemy?'" He always chuckles when he relates this, wagging his head in disbelief. "It made you realize, people are just people, all over the world."

He strolled the streets with his buddies, giving away Hershey bars, taking photos of beaming children and of Shinto shrines.

He had spent two years as gunner's mate on the LST 743, witnessing death and dive-bombers and screeching shell-bursts in the South Pacific. His battles must have been horrifying. The invasion of New Guinea. The Admiralty Islands. Weeks of unceasing combat in the Philippines, fighting to wrest sweltering, mosquito-ridden islands from the Japanese. D-Day on the jungle beaches of Borneo. A very young Gene Ruhl screaming orders at his very young crews as they sighted their twin 40-millimeter guns and fired, swabbed the barrels, fired again, air slit with shrapnel and flares, beaches exploding....

Excerpt from an LST's ship log during the Tarakan landings: "The noise is deafening as round after round roars overhead from the large ships, the bomb and strafing blasts from aircraft set up a concussion felt by all.... The LSTs head for the beach carrying pontoons strapped on the sides. LST 584 is the first to hit the beach, followed by LST 743"—the boat on which Gene Ruhl commands the guns—"and 171. Beaching takes a skillful hand to avoid the concrete abutments placed there by the Japanese. Mortar and artillery shells fall in the area.... Rifle and machine gun fire are heard ashore...."

Fifty years later, he rarely talks of combat. This man who has refused all his civilian life to own or handle guns. What he loves to talk about—now, in fact, as we glide softly on the porch swing here in Pennsylvania, this summer of 1992, as we gaze across the backyard to the Amish hayfield and the mountains and Lick Run Gap—are the lulls. Moments of dazzlement and wonder:

Full moon spangling a thousand miles of open sea. Glimpses of destroyers and battleships in a far-flung convoy, phantoms in muted light. Red sun at daybreak. Frolicking splash of dolphins at the bow. One day, a waterspout a hundred miles to starboard. Another day, tropical atolls lain like a jade necklace across the horizon....

I've seen snapshots of my father at nineteen: grinning on deck, hard-muscled, suntanned, dog tags at his bare chest, sailor's cap perched rakishly, hands on hips of his denim Navy bell bottoms. A rural kid far from home for the first and only time in his life, worlds removed from Lock Haven, from the cloistered hills of Appalachia.

Ashore in New Guinea he and his crew saw Sepik headhunters patrolling the beach. They saw jungle festooned with orchids and birds-of-paradise. They saw clouded mountain carapace. Palm-fronded lagoons. Wreckage of crash-landed Japanese Zeros.

In January of 1945, when weeks of barbarous fighting finally won the Philippine Islands from the Japanese, Gene and sailors from the battle-gouged LST 743, anchored off Luzon, crowded the rail. They watched General MacArthur in his khakis and sunglasses and braided cap wade ashore with staff officers to claim victory.

The next stop was Japan. American troops dreaded the invasion, expecting unparalleled slaughter. My father shared that dread. "We thought it would be a bloodbath. Our fleet was off the coast of Japan, getting ready to go in."

On an evening in August 1945, rumors spread through the LST. Then news came over Armed Forces radio. A few days later newspapers arrived in the ship's small library. Gene took one to his bunk, where he learned the United States had detonated a futuristic science-fiction bomb. Its target, the Japanese industrial city of Hiroshima, had simply vanished. A few days later, another of the new bombs dropped on Nagasaki. Abruptly, the war in the Pacific ended.

The day after walking through Sasebo, handing Hershey bars to kids, my father and a friend hopped an Army jeep and hitched a ride to Nagasaki.

When they arrived my father gaped disbelievingly at a miles-wide plain of charred and flattened rubble. The city and its people had been swept away, clear to the cinder-gray horizon, as if by a mop.

Years later my dad told me, "Every politician, every one of these damn loudmouth congressmen and every president who rattles on about winning a nuclear war should be made to go out and look at what one of those bombs can actually do. The destruction—it's practically incomprehensible. And hell, the one they dropped on Nagasaki was just a little pop-gun compared to what they have now. It's just unbelievable."

Here at my parents' house we sit quietly on the swing.

Daylight starts to diminish, pulling itself in, as when a kerosene flame turns down slowly in a lantern.

Falsetto trill of a white-throated sparrow, somewhere in pine hedges.

A moist chill. First stars over Lick Run Gap. Out toward the west, across the ridge, burn of russet in sky where the sun's gone down.

"Red sky at night," I tell my dad. "Sailor's delight."

He smiles.

Seeking lineage, a connection with forebears....

When young, my father must have looked like one of those urchins in grainy WPA documentaries, walking rapidly along planked fence rows, back lots and alleys in that wan light of the 1930s, through stark shadows of Depression and need and hunger. A child in a cap and bib dungarees, warming his hands at a brick kiln.

Youngest boy of eleven children, Gene Ruhl grew up in Lockport, a crowded row of workers' tenements and clapboard houses shoved against the cliffs, directly across the river from Lock Haven. Summers he ran barefoot with a scruffy, tow-headed bunch of friends. They huddled round the lit dial of the Philco to hear "Gangbusters" and "Red Ryder" and prize fights of the famed Black boxing champ Joe Louis. Outdoors they kneeled under elm trees to shoot marbles, flicking aggies and cat's-eyes in carefully smoothed dirt. With pocket knives they played mumblety-peg. They followed the iceman or the horse-drawn milk wagon through Lockport's unpaved street, past the flophouses where tramps snored, past the brick hulk of the brewing company. Pigeons circled the Susquehanna, roosted on the Jay Street Bridge.

Winter evenings after school he and other kids hurried to the river, where teams of bays, duns, dappled grays and sorrels drew revelers in sleighs soaring over the ice, whips kerracking, bells jangling on harnesses. Children clamped skate-blades to their boots and Hans Brinkered lickety-split up the frozen Susquehanna for a mile or more. Trucks full of lumber drove warily over the ice, carting loads to Lockport. People built bonfires on the river. In crackling orange light of the flames men and women stood bundled in mackinaws and woolens, stomping warmth into numb feet, sipping cocoa and roasting chestnuts.

In high school Gene captained the basketball team and played first-string on the Bobcat football team; he rode in the rumble seat of a friend's DeSoto, listened to Tommy Dorsey records, went to pep rallies, to movies and sock hops. He showed talent academically, enjoying literature and history, publishing a poem in the yearbook, excelling at math. In classrooms he and other hayseed kids occupied seats in back rows, ignored by teachers who concentrated on prepping two or three local doctors' or lawyers' kids for college.

The summer before graduating, Gene and some football buddies took jobs on the New York Central Railroad as gandy-dancers. They banged spikes into wooden crossties with sledgehammers, eight hours a day. When he returned to Lock Haven in the fall of 1941, senior photos were taken: Gene Ruhl, rawboned and handsome, confronts the world, and posterity, in a dark suit jacket that he'd borrowed from the photographer, because he couldn't afford a jacket of his own.

The graduation photo marks a special triumph. Gene became the first person in the Ruhl family to get beyond eighth grade.

Tales of the ancestors.

Oldest of four girls, Janet Lee English was raised in a broken-luck hillbilly family that struggled alone in the forgotten woods several miles beyond a hamlet called White Pine, Pennsylvania. Even today White Pine is so inconsequential and so off-the-beaten-path that it fails to appear on most road maps. To get there you drive north on crumbling blacktop through the mountains, following Pine Creek, then climb through wilderness dotted sparsely with hunting camps. Keep an eye out for black bears and pheasants and foraging herds of whitetails, and don't attempt the trip if forecasts call for winter storms.

Her grandmother, Carrie Bryan, had ventured to America from Ireland, probably from County Clare, half a century after the famine. Carrie Bryan and her husband, a trolley car conductor named Divinia Fernberg, lived on a small hilltop in Lizardville, just outside Mill Hall, overlooking the dammed-up lake and marsh flats of Fishing Creek near the ax factory, with the mountain looming behind it. She taught piano lessons. Janet, who visited there as a blonde moppet with Shirley Temple ringlets, remembered my maternal great-grandmother as a stern, formidable presence.

Janet was a schoolkid during World War Two. By the '40s the Depression had begun to ease in much of America, but during her youth it still clenched the tiny farms in those Appalachian hills of central Pennsylvania. Jobs were rare. A skinny, barefoot girl in a hand-me-down gingham dress, her hair clipped with a barrette, Jan fed the cow and stuffed the family's mattresses with corn-shucks and weeded a tenacious vegetable patch. Sometimes she had to help with a hog butchering, which she hated. Life in the sticks was lonesome. Once in a while a jalopy flivvered by in the dust. Once in a while a farmer headed for Green Mountain stomped past with a team of mules. Sometimes a bindlestiff happened by and he'd plead for a handout. Jan and her three sisters fashioned dolls of hollyhocks. They scrubbed shirts on a nickel washboard or shelled snap-peas, sitting on the front porch of the two-story frame house. To help feed the family Jan and her sister Alice sold an ointment called White Cloverine Salve door-to-door at farmhouses. "It seemed like we walked a hundred miles and made two dollars." The four girls shared one bicycle, which they took turns pushing up the dirt road through woods to Larry's Creek, where they played, careful of rattlers. At night they heard bobcats scream.

"That book *The Grapes of Wrath*—I've read it so many times I practically know it by heart—sometimes I pick it up and just open to any page, sometimes I *have* to read it because I *saw* those things, I *heard* those things. Even in our little niche of the planet. I saw people coming by asking for handouts, and the most god-almighty awful—even then I thought they were awful—cars; when you read nowadays that those cars were held together with baling wire, well they really *were*."

Mostly her family fended for itself. Sometimes the girls got so hungry they ate Crisco from the can. When flour or bacon could be afforded they purchased it at Mecum's general store in White Pine, where goods were stocked in bins and cracker barrels. Jan survived as best she could. "An orange was something you only saw at Christmastime," she's told me. "And a banana—my God! I was in my twenties before I ate a whole banana."

Each morning, still a small girl, Jan walked alone for two miles. She walked the dirt lane through pine forest, hugging her books and the molasses bucket in which she toted her lunch. She walked to a one-room schoolhouse tucked back in the hollow along Wolf Run. "It was a long, long walk. Walking home after school in winter it was always cold, and so dark out," she said. "I was just a little thing. It was so scary."

It wasn't the only frightening thing. Her stepfather was shiftless, drunken, indifferent. He beat the girls. Sometimes Jan slept out in the fields to escape him. The brute stepfather "was an ignorant old mountain-man, a real Jed Clampett type. Before he moved in with us, he lived in a shack way up in the woods. He made moonshine." An Appalachian story: On a frigid January night in 1943 when my mother was a ten-year-old girl, alone with my grandmother Mary and that explosive man, he rampaged in one of his whiskey furies. Shaking a loaded Colt revolver he shouted, "T'night come hell-'er-high-water yer both gonna die!" My grandmother, a tiny woman, bundled her young daughter and they fled into the night. They ran on a snow-drifted road through the forest. When they reached the sheriff's house, he refused to help, fearing the stepfather's vicious reputation. My grandmother and that small girl who would become my own mother fled again into the frozen night. If they saw car headlights they hid in the snowbanks. They hiked fourteen miles, shivering with cold and fear, to the village of Salladaysburg. "I'll never forget that night," my mother has told me. "I know what it's like to be hunted with a gun."

School became her refuge. And books. (Even today Jan—my mom—reads Tolstoy for pleasure.) The schoolhouse's one-room cabin held a potbellied iron stove, on which the teacher cooked butternut squash for the scrawny Appalachian schoolchildren. Kids of all ages sat at six rows of wooden desks scribbling their history assignments or clamored at the blackboard as they tackled arithmetic problems. At recess they spilled into the yard. They free-for-alled over the steep hillside meadow behind the schoolhouse, or jump-roped, or plucked nosegays of asters at the forest's edge. At the end of the school day one of the older girls—sometimes Jan—swept the plank floor.

She proved herself a gifted child. Jan learned so readily that she skipped two grades in that elementary school. Her teacher, an amicable woman whose only son died in the war, insisted that somehow, some way, this bright, talented girl must find the means to attend high school.

There's a little thing I do lately when I'm with my parents.

Sometimes I close my eyes and imagine they've died. I imagine their absence, immutable and lasting, imagine the darkness of how much I miss them, the pang, the soreness deeper than where I breathe, anguish of knowing they're gone forever. Through long minutes I imagine how won-derful—how wonderful beyond all valuation—it would feel if I might request the impossible and see them, if only a fraction of one hour, alive again.

Then I open my eyes. Here they are, my parents, near me. Smiling. Speaking.

And the moment, otherwise nondescript, comes to me gift-wrapped, comes beribboned, and my whole being swells with thanks.

The miracle—the *miracle*!—of our time together! I improvise a sort of prayer to whatever guiding Consciousness might pervade the cosmos: Thank you. Thank you. Thank you for letting it not be too late. For letting them be alive with me still.

Right now on the porch swing, sitting beside my white-haired father as he reflects in silence—as he visits again, perhaps, vanished decades, Sasebo harbor, streets of Japan—and sitting beside my white-haired mother who has come to join us, I do this thing.

I close my eyes.

I open them.

FIVE

*"When we practice looking deeply, we realize that our home is everywhere,"
wrote Thich Nhat Hanh. "We have to be able to see that the trees are our
home and the blue sky is our home. It looks like a difficult practice, but it's
really easy. You only need to stop being a wanderer in order to be at home.
'Listen, listen. This wonderful sound brings me back to my true home.' The
voice of the Buddha, the sound of the bell, the sunshine, everything is calling
us back to our true home. Once you are back in your true home, you'll feel the
peace and the joy you deserve."*

You only need to stop being a wanderer....
   *Even if I'd heard those words as I crisscrossed the highways of Clinton
County, I would not have known how to stop. I no longer wandered in order
to escape; I wandered to engage, to engage old anger, old pain, to confront
memory. But I needed to keep moving, keep moving. Stop wandering? How
could I find the one road I now sought leading back into my homeland, the
road of reconciliation, if I stopped wandering? Stopped searching? If I sat still?
   Unfamiliar with Buddhism, I had no clue.*

☽

I'M FOLLOWING the Warrior's Path. This highway retraces sections of an
ancient trail used by Delaware Indians, the Leni-Lenape. During the
1700s the Warrior's Path wound from Great Island to the mountain
stronghold of war chief Bald Eagle, leader of the Munsee clans.
   I watch for deer on straightaways. The evening is humid and still.

A boy of the Leni-Lenape, at puberty, would roam mountains to starve himself and to beseech the spirits. He hoped to meet a numinous phantom animal—his *manito*—to serve as potent advisor and protector. Someone seeking a vision might pilgrimage across ravines of Nittany Mountain or Bald Eagle Ridge, the very hills I'm passing now in my car.

Mists suspend through laden air. Altonimbus over scumbled mountains. I check my rearview mirror. I see whorls of a dark storm cloud over Lick Run Gap.

Rain's holding at bay. Barometric pressure adds heft to light, to landscape.

My younger sister Sherry phoned this morning from her trailer in the boondocks out toward Coalport, a town hidden in mountains of the northwestern Appalachian Plateau. Her husband Ron, a long-haul truck driver, was making his overnight run and she felt like chatting.

"Hey, guess what?" I announced. "Guess where I might go today? My Bald Eagle-Nittany High School reunion."

She hesitated. "This is a joke, right? You're not really going to go back there, are you?"

◜

"Every day is a journey," wrote the Zen poet Bashō. *"The journey itself is home."*

When I was still an infant my parents rented the upstairs apartment in Lockport's old canal house, beside the Susquehanna. My first nights on earth I must have fallen asleep listening to riparian birds and the faint sough of that vast, flowing river, echoes of Lock Haven drifting over the water.

My mother looks slim and fetching in old photos; twenty-six when I started kindergarten, she wore Capri pants and loose blouses and she smoked L&Ms, which she left crumpled in ashtrays, imprinted with red lipstick.

A measure of wealth:

My mother finger-painted with me and, remembering this, I smell the paints—a smell like leaves of poplars in October—and feel the paper, wet squish of colors gooping between my fingers. She threw birthday parties. She hovered near me when I lay on the living room couch, incandescent as a Chinese lantern, delirious in the misery of chickenpox or measles. At Christmastime she showed me how to stencil our windows, and she took me to pay homage to Santa Claus, blithesome Jehovah in his hut beside the First National Bank in Lock Haven. At noon we lunched on TV dinners and watched *I Love Lucy*. On bedrizzled April days she led me to the window, showing me robins in our backyard as they paused, cocking their heads like audiophiles in a concert hall, "listening" for the subterranean murmur of earthworms. My mother read stories with me from Little Golden Books, her lacquered fingernail pointing to syllables, helping me sound them aloud. When she rinsed dishes I squatted in a corner of the kitchen with my child-size record player and listened to the equine tale of *Black Beauty*. Gruff voices of men, angry sibilance of the horsewhip, clopping hooves on a stony road, bursts of storm and thunder, shouts that the bridge was out; the poor, misunderstood, mistreated, marvelous black stallion, whinnying and rearing back, all of this I remember…. My mother walked me to Widmann's drugstore in Lock Haven for cherry Cokes. She surprised me with excursions to the Garden Theater and the Roxy, dimly lit, palatial, where I sat beside her, agog, introduced at the age of five to sublimities of motion pictures: *Ol' Yeller*, Disney's film of a pioneer boy and his beloved dog, and *Huckleberry Finn*, its unforgettable vignettes of a boy like me and his big Black friend, black as *Black Beauty*, commanding their raft down the luminous river, a river like the Susquehanna I knew so well….

I'm mystified when people confess how little they recall of their childhood.

Especially granted the ease of imbibing the Proustian lime-flower tea, of nibbling the morsel of madeleine cake:

House of pale-yellow stucco on Hill Street, my address until I turned seven, with dogwood near our front door and forsythia and the woods. The woods were magic. A woman, gnomic, withered, dwelled alone in those woods. She lived in a shack without electricity. Smoke scribbled from her chimney. An Appalachian mountain woman, she wore a shawl, poking the forest path with her stick. I'd hide behind a laurel bush to spy on her. She reminded me of a crone in my picture book of folk tales, the Russian witch Baba Yaga, living in her house of chicken bones.

I remember our cellar, iron behemoth of the coal furnace roaring. Remember the coal bin, my dad shoveling heaps of smoky black bituminous into the fire. Odor of soot. Remember the hand-cranked wringer washer. Remember the screened-in back porch, where my five-year-old friends and I cocooned inside sleeping bags on summer nights.

I whispered the frightening prayer: "If I should die before I wake, I pray the Lord my soul to take." I pondered this Deity who might grab my soul before dawn, a God who could eavesdrop on every thought as if my mind were linked to a telephone party-line; an occult, all-pervading busybody who demanded my love and devotion yet seemed unaccountably helpless in protecting me against wiles of His mischief-making rival, the Devil, that horned schemer who wore a goatee like a beatnik and dwelled in an underground barbecue pit. These musings were prompted by infrequent visits to Sunday school in Lock Haven, and by summer attendance at Bible Camp, where we belted out "Onward, Christian Soldiers" and pasted drawings of young blue-eyed Jesus to frames of popsicle sticks.

Heaven: I remember sitting with my dad on the front lawn after supper, waiting for Telstar to skiff the cirrus high above our house. "Look, Pal, there it goes!" A hurried speck, lit in its trajectory by the falling sun.

My dad had reached his mid-thirties in those years—close to the age I am now. He liked to sing. In sonorous baritone he sang, "I peeked in to say goodnight / and then I saw my child asleep." He sang, "Oh Danny boy, oh Danny boy, I love you so." Helping me lace my Buster Browns he sang, "Let's go where they keep on wearin' those frills an' flowers an' buttons an' bows," and when he tucked me into bed he sang, "The stars at night / are big and bright / (clap clap clap clap) deep in the heart of Texas." Driving the car he sang, "Her eyes are bright as diamonds, they sparkle like the dew." When he sang, "Oh Shenandoah, I long to see you, / far away, you rollin' river," that longing made his voice tremulous on the high notes, and he sang it *andante*, slowing its lilt to a lullaby.

He scented his skin with Old Spice, emollient of cream and nutmeg with a tang of acidic lime. When he returned from work in the evenings, his chin stubbled, I'd clamber on him and hug him and cub around on the floor with him, giggling, growling, and his chin rubbed my cheek like a pumice stone and I could smell the factory on him, smell the machine oil, pungency of forged brass, of copper. (Much later when I read of Blake's dark satanic mills I envisioned that factory. I envisioned Titan Metal's rod mill with its chain-link fence and blacked-out windows and, barely constrained within the walls, a pounding violence. I recalled its avalanche of noise, its slamming, percussive, floor-shaking rhythm of manufacture, blizzards of sparks, shriek of raw-forged metal.)

My generation often laments the absence of fathers from our late-1950s childhoods. We regret fathers lost to commuting and jobs, retreating at night to their dens and TVs. But I lucked out. My dad quizzed me jovially from my *How-and-Why Wonderbooks* and, kissing my forehead, said, "I love ya, Pal." On Parents' Day when I was in first grade my dad skipped work and missed a day's pay to sit proudly and attentively in my classroom, wearing his Sunday shirt and tie. No other parent showed up.

Measure of wealth:

At the kitchen table my dad would draw with me. We'd use pink drafting erasers and mechanical pencils, the kind engineers prefer. He would hike with me up the hill into Sunset Pines, where we might see a pileated woodpecker, a bird wearing the vermilion cap of a Jacobin. When the circus arrived in Lock Haven he treated me to its striped Bedouin tents on the grass at Piper airfield, near Great Island; I remember farmers and mill families on the midway, beer-belly guys with stogies, kids like me with balloons. Hurdy-gurdy music. Teenage Lock Haven toughs with greased pompadours swung a huge ball-peen hammer at the "He-Man" contest, whanging a bell to win teddy bears for their in-a-hurry, gum-popping girlfriends. I remember the Big Top, remember sitting delightedly with my dad and watching greasepaint clowns and svelte, fearsome jungle cats and rhinestoned aeronauts of the trapeze, swandiving through illumined arcs of space....

Measure of wealth.

This is my trust fund. This is my inheritance.

⊃

MUCH LATER, when I was eighteen, Bruce Bechdel would invite me to his restored manse in Beech Creek for iced tea. Nearby he moonlighted as a mortician at the Bechdel Funeral Home, an inherited family business. "It's something I have to do. I can't afford to buy antiques and renovate the house or go skiing or go to museums in Manhattan on a goddamn Clinton County schoolteacher's salary," he grumbled. Bruce invited me, too, into an empty house in Lock Haven to sip Chablis and listen to Verdi and Puccini. One summer afternoon he led me to an upstairs bedroom. I was naïve. We sat on a coverlet.

In the acclaimed book *Fun Home* and in the hit play of that title, Bruce Bechdel—a complex person, sometimes imperious, often funny, genial, brilliant; an inspiring teacher beloved by his many students and friends—is depicted as a two-dimensional caricature, morose, isolated, and hostile, a closeted gay man who preyed on male students.

It was more complicated than that. As we sat on the bed Bruce confided his passions. He flung his arms around me in a shy, lascivious hug, a gentlemanly seduction which I, incorrigibly girl-crazy, rebuffed.

He never made a sexual overture to me again. I was too young and inexperienced to fully understand what had happened. Mostly it confused me: What was *that* about? Homosexuality didn't bother me, in Bruce or anyone else. But no man had ever tried to seduce me before. How could he have misread me so drastically? Was I responsible in some way?

We got past it. The last time I saw him alive, we sat together in the audience of a musty barn, the Millbrook Playhouse, on an August evening to watch Helen perform in *A Little Night Music*—the same theater in which I'd appeared in *West Side Story* a decade earlier as one of the finger-snapping, teenaged members of the Sharks street gang. Bruce looked happy.

I kept his secret for thirty years and never betrayed him, respecting the man, the exceptional teacher he was, and his privacy, until his daughter publicly outed him in *Fun Home*. That book and its spinoff Broadway musical gratified Bruce's detractors in Mill Hall—people who'd never taken one of his classes, but who resented his bookishness, his handsome flair, his urbanity, his arrogant charm. Because of *Fun Home* they had a chance to snicker again: "See, what'd I tell ya? I always knew that weirdo creep Bruce Bechdel was nothin' but a faggoty pervert." Bruce, long dead, had no one to defend him.

It reminded me of Gatsby, forsaken at his funeral. The owl-eyed man in spectacles, arriving late at the cemetery and informed by Nick that no one had shown up at Gatsby's house for the memorial service, exclaims, "Why, my God! They used to go there by the hundreds."

Then he adds, "The poor son-of-a-bitch."

I also remembered words that are the last spoken by Nick to Gatsby as they say goodbye, words I offered now to Bruce:

"'They're a rotten crowd,' I shouted across the lawn. 'You're worth the whole damn bunch put together.'"

☽

THE VILLAGE of Beech Creek passes by quickly. Summer grass is brilliant as Astro-Turf, dotted like a Seurat with wild daisies and milkweed. With my car window down I hear robins in wooded swales rehearsing coloratura solos. Brief snatches of bird-melody rise and vanish in a white noise of tires and wind rush and engine.

I pass a bar called "Jimmy's," deer head painted above its door.

I pass the Bechdel Funeral Home. The "Fun Home."

I pass a Little League game, boys in red uniforms ranging the diamond, boys in white uniforms in the bullpen, each kid observant as if on jury duty. Jeeps and pickups are corralled near the backstop.

I'm crossing farms and cornfields of Bald Eagle Valley. The two-lane highway of the Warrior's Path leads me past antebellum houses of brick or mortared stone with central chimneys and recessed porticoes. It leads past cattle sheds and silos, past the big double-door red barns with louvered ventilation windows and weather vanes, drabbled cow yards malodorous with heat-fermented grain and straw and manure. On a wire fence sit grackles with their greasy black feathers.

I see the rim of mountains. Above Ax Factory Gap and hills to the east, hundreds of miles removed from the sea, the sky looks oceanic, clouds turning inside out, dissolved in halogen brightness.

◯

IF THEY'D wadded cotton and stuffed my throat with it, I couldn't have felt more suffocated.

When we were sixteen, school administrators decreed that each member of our class take a standardized IQ test. Feeling bored, resentful, and uncooperative I goofed my way through it. When the results came back a few months later I'd managed to hit enough correct answers to score well. The high school principal, swarthy and bejowled, and the guidance counselor, a genial incompetent in a porridge-brown suit, ushered me into an anteroom connected to the school office. They closed the door.

I slumped in a chair, arms folded, my long hair tumbling over my shoulders. Face locked shut with hatred.

"We have your IQ score here," they told me. "Why are you failing most of your classes?"

I wanted to bludgeon them. I refused to speak, my gaze blowtorching the wall.

I thought: I'm not failing, goddamn it. You're the ones who are failing.

I boycotted my high school graduation, and a few weeks later I stashed clothes and food in my dad's '68 Rambler American—a temperamental car with a busted speedometer—and when my fifteen-year-old brother Larry hopped in the front seat with his guitar, I drove straight for where the sun sets.

Leaving the Appalachians, two days later we crossed the Midwestern plains, miles of cornfields flattening out to the horizon's spinnakers of clouds.

We slept in highway pullovers. Slept in truck stops. The big diesel rigs humming all night. By day we swept past Chicago, our first view—ever— of skyscrapers, of six-lane freeways.

We crossed the Mississippi River, pushed through Iowa into the rust grass desert of Nebraska, the buttes and sere rim-rock country of Wyoming.

One night, west of Flaming Gorge, the wind woke us. Wind and silence. I drove a ribbon of pavement across miles of empty range at three in the morning. Braking for jackrabbits. Herds of antelope. Their eyes flared like miners' headlamps in my high beams. Distant canyons shone beneath the Moon When All Things Ripen, as the Lakota called it. Later the car broke down and a rancher towed us back to Laramie, snow predicted that August in the high country....

When we returned to Pennsylvania I began cobbling together my self-education program.

Born male in Clinton County, the path of my life pointed unerringly toward the Lock Haven paper mill, as it had for other men in my family. The sole expectation Clinton County held of me was that I take my assigned work shift on the factory floor. But I had pledged myself to a different vocation. I'd chosen the writing trade. Nurturing my vocation would require that I accumulate not only experiences but erudition. For six years our rural high school had cheated me. No guarantees existed for college. I would need to devise an education myself.

The Ruhl household esteemed learning. I knew my good fortune. I grew up, like everyone else I knew, on *The Man from U.N.C.L.E.* and *Gilligan's Island* and *The Dating Game* and *Bonanza*, but for each birthday my parents blessed us with a microscope or chemistry set from the Sears catalog, a stamp-collecting kit or a watercolor set and brushes, or a biology kit—and books. The homes of our neighbors in Cedar Heights lacked books; dominating each living room, next to the TV, stood the family gun cabinet, stocked with rifles and shotguns. Our home displayed precisely the opposite. No guns, but a living room with a bookcase full of novels and Time-Life volumes on science and mathematics, on ancient Greece, on the Egypt of pharaohs and pyramids, on Roman history, and—an extravagant splurge of my parents when we still lived in our trailer—a set of *World Book Encyclopedias*, through which I'd rummaged happily since childhood. Moreover, our mother and father sent the three of us to elementary school at Akeley, the lab school on the Lock Haven State College campus, where farm kids and mill workers' kids, merchants' kids and professors' kids mingled in classrooms and aspiring teachers received their training. We published our own newsletter, *The*

Campus Flash, solved math puzzles, performed in Gilbert and Sullivan's *H.M.S. Pinafore* (I swaggered onstage as Captain Corcoran and belted out my solos), made a papier-mâché volcano to commemorate the new state of Hawai'i, doggy-paddled weekly in the college pool, trooped across campus each Friday to the kids' annex of the collegiate library and borrowed books.

The reading habit stayed with me into adolescence. "I remember how hard you were working when you were eighteen, nineteen years old," my mother has told me. "My God, every day, down in that room, all those books."

I quit socializing. Each day from the autumn of 1972 until the spring of '74 I trained with ideas, with words, disciplined and devoted as an Olympian. The books I needed cost a fortune. When possible I requested books for Christmas; I hoarded my scant savings to buy books at Penn State University shops, forty miles distant; I borrowed books from the library or purchased them, dog-eared, a dime apiece, at sales. Books I could not afford I obtained through petty crime. I stole them. I took them from store shelves and slipped them beneath my coat. With savage logic I told myself I needed those books and I fucking deserved them. I was trying to find my way into a canon I barely knew existed, inventing a syllabus for my jerry-rigged, illicit, one-man university.

Joyously—I remember even today the power of that joy—I woke daily at eight o'clock, sunlight misting through the Nittany Mountains, and got started. My self-improvement project was of the type once undertaken by industrious working-class youths and which seems so quaint today. Or preposterous. Or maybe pretentious.

I wanted the world. On Sunday mornings before anyone woke I'd dress stealthily in dawn light and drive to the windowless bunker of the cinderblock porn shop in Mill Hall that sold—along with its shelves of raunchy skin mags and X-rated comics—newspapers. I'd buy a copy of the *New York Times*. I'd rush home. In the kitchen I made breakfast, and then across the table I'd spread the pages before me. And there it was: the world. For a precious hour before anyone rose from bed I basked in the world beyond Appalachia and gloried in Manhattan and the splendors of its cognoscenti, whom I hoped to join someday. I started each Sunday morning reverentially with the *Book Review*, my favorite section, then moved to the *Arts and Leisure* section and the magazine and *The Week in Review*, parceling the Sunday *Times* through the rest of my week, like doling out scant food rations in a disaster zone, reading some of it daily, nibbling at everything.

I craved ideas, the intellectual tradition of a Western culture that I was only beginning to claim as my own. I wanted it all. I read history and drew timelines of world events. In the hermitage of my bedroom I tutored myself in geometry using my father's old textbooks. I'd reviled math in high school and flunked it year after year but now, approaching it aesthetically, I enjoyed it. I grew enamored of Euclid's graceful proofs, the pleasing simplicity of forms, the circle, the line, the right angle. Tools for constructing an elegant universe. I read with a vengeance—literally. I avenged myself for everything the high school had withheld from me or ruined for me.

I read with that uniquely serendipitous, haphazard spirit of the autodidact. I paged through introductory texts, sometimes puzzling and intimidating, about particle physics and astrophysics and discovered Heisenberg's realm, the luminous, vast ambiguities within the subatomic; I discovered Einstein's realm, the curved immensities of time and distances, the breadth of their shimmering energies, mathematically calculable yet mysterious to the core. Realms never disclosed to me in high school science courses. I listened to albums of classical music. I wended through library tomes on European and American art, memorizing color plates, from Caravaggio's dramatic tableaux to Georgia O' Keefe's swanky, sybaritic orchids.

How to convey the ferocity of it? The pistoning force of it? The monomania? The needle-in-the-danger-zone intensity? Every book I absorbed: "Mine! No one can ever take it away from me, damn it!" Pushing. Pushing: "Stay the hell out of my way. I'll never give up. Never." I sought mastery, I sought power, the power of intellect, power of knowing. The only power I would ever have. I intended to use that power to escape Clinton County and create for myself a peerless future.

I dared myself. I dared myself to venture paragraph by paragraph through *A History of Western Philosophy* by Bertrand Russell, discovering—in pulses of excitement—that with assistance from Russell's witty, pellucid text I might begin faintly to comprehend outlines of Aristotle's doctrine of First Proof and Aquinas's scholastic inquiries into the existence of God, Descartes' imperious *cogito ergo sum*, Kant's categorical imperative, Hume's cantankerous skepticism. Russell's book led me into the Ross Library for original sources. I quickened when I found Plato's *Republic*, his *Parmenides* and *The Symposium*, wily Socrates entrapping the gentry of Athens with his nagging questions.

In a homeland of wretched farms and factories I strove awkwardly to invent myself as that most improbable of things, a man of letters. Recalling now the frisson, the shiver of wonderment.... My devouring, omnivorous curiosity.... I became my own Balboa. My own Magellan, exploring maris incognita, mapping my own routes.

Eating lunch I red-penciled my way through chapters in a volume of classic psychology texts. I scarcely knew where to begin. I started with Freud, whose name I recognized. He was still intellectually fashionable in those days. I tried to absorb his wry insights into dynamics of human personality, constant tussle of ego and id and superego for supremacy, pitfalls of cathexis and projection, the playfully enigmatic symbolism of jokes and dreams. Freud led to Jung, my guide on spelunking forays down into the psyche, where I encountered, in new guises, minotaur, mandala, mermaid, anima and animus, the archetypal fire, alchemist's gold, eternal serpent of the uroboros. I encountered, too, Jung's concept of Shadow, a foul thing with fangs hiding under the persona; this I recognized. This I knew well. Jung led me to Campbell's *The Hero With a Thousand Faces*, where I began to see how the soul's mission might lie encoded in universal tales of vagabonds, tricksters and searchers, their names "Raven," "Odysseus," "Parsifal."

I read poetry. I'd shoplifted some Norton anthologies at a Penn State bookstore and for me, in Mill Hall, they seemed brigand's plunder, casks of doubloons. I discovered Sylvia Plath's demonic, self-annihilating brilliance. Gary Snyder's rip-sawed Zen sagacity. Dylan Thomas's mellifluous Welsh arias. The luscious rococo, the sensuous, robust cerebralism, of Wallace Stevens. Theodore Roethke's brave, heartbroken meditations. Emily Dickinson's mystical, explosive little cryptograms, each a locket primed with dynamite. William Blake's revelations, besotted with the holy and profane. James Wright's sorrowful, wrathful, dirty-knuckled love songs to Ohio rivers, angelic horses, West Virginia steel mills. Gwendolyn Brooks's snappy Harlem jazz. John Berryman's boozy anguish, his appalling, beauteous tap-dances on the doormats of hell. Robert Frost's crabby Yankee aphorisms. Walt Whitman's chummy exhortations and his braggadocio, his rhapsodic derring-do. Elizabeth Bishop's keen, objective eye and Denise Levertov's lush restraint. Allen Ginsberg's zippy, freeform bebop solos, his apocalyptic chants.

I'd been lucky to acquire during my final years of formal education in Mill Hall those two remarkable teachers, the Bechdels, who prevented me from quitting school altogether. Bruce had earned my lasting affection and gratitude by urging me to read Hemingway and Fitzgerald and Joyce's *A Portrait of the Artist as a Young Man*. Now, two years later, on my own initiative I undertook *Ulysses*, which flabbergasted me. I launched an expedition through it using the authorized Stuart Gilbert reader's guide, following Bloom and Dedalus through Dublin's whirlpools and isle of the lotus-eaters, city of myth and language. Joyce's wondrous, beguiling novel changed forever my notions of what literature can attempt and the human mind assay.

Wanting so much….

I reserved each Friday night for our PBS television station, which aired films I'd never known existed, films that seemed to reveal in flickered black and white, in French, in Swedish, German, Italian, humanity's common travail and celebration: Truffaut's *Jules and Jim*; *Potemkin*, by Eisenstein; Renoir's *Rules of the Game* and Bergman's *Wild Strawberries*. I studied nearly a dozen of these indelible films, which captivated me (and helped prepare me, years later, to work briefly as a movie critic). Antonioni's sundazed, enigmatic *L'Avventura*. Fellini's romping and melancholic *La Dolce Vita*. Cocteau's *Beauty and the Beast*, the corridor of handheld torches in the magical lair of la Bête….

During those years my body seemed strung with high-voltage electric wires. It seemed I could feel, physically, the buzz of synapses, a trillion neurons long neglected and starting to flash, a tingling under the scalp as my brain began to rouse, to reawaken.

—

From perusing Beat poets I learned a little about Buddhist meditative practice. My first exposure to Buddhism had been through television at age nine. A monk sat on a Saigon street, wrapped in robes, hairless as a doll. He'd soaked himself in gasoline. He sat amid turbulent, lapping waves of fire. Utterly still. No black smoke. Yet his robe was in flames, the side of his head in flames.

It scared and confused me. Now, as a young man reading Ginsberg and Kerouac, I tried to make sense of this religion. I'd saunter along Fishing Creek, trying to empty my mind of the brabble of conscious thought.

Since childhood I'd known how to stand for long moments, transfixed by light in trees. Their numinous inner fire. The mystic, sacred glow. I'd known how to say *speak to me* and see maples and meadow asters flare into radiance, disclosing their true, hidden spirits, their secret names. I'd known how to discover timelessness in silence. I could sense the divine.

Now, walking, I tried to focus on breath, tried to allow squawks of blue jays, or plaited noises of water, to pass through me. I tuned myself to higher pitches of alertness.

Buddhism stirred me, but I couldn't understand it. One thing I did learn, however: you can purchase the world.

What do you pay?

You pay attention.

In the two hundred years since my paternal great-great-great-great-great-grandfather Georg Friedrich Rühle arrived in America from Germany with his wife and children and was sold onboard the *Tyger* as an indentured servant, not a single member of the Ruhl family had gone to college.

Twelve months after leaving Bald Eagle-Nittany High School I walked into the cafeteria on a weekend morning. I sat at a lunch table, near the milk machine, to take my College Board exams.

No one had coached me for SATs. None of the kids in Mill Hall had any preparation. The few of us who thought we might want to go to college simply took the test cold.

I achieved a high score. My parents had no money for sending me to a university. But now I began to wonder if perhaps I should try to figure out how to go.

A working-class person's pathetic badge of honor comes stamped, in tin, with the word "self-reliance."

I prided myself on needing help from no one. After a single academic year in Penn State University's elite English Honors Program—*mirabilis annum*; my year of fireworks; year of colloquies and straight "A" semesters (despite my penchant for hanging out in bars, dancing at parties, and inviting girls back to my cellar apartment for the night); year of scholarly triumph, of accolades from professors; year of wearing my arrogance like a sharp cologne—after this happy, auspicious year I dropped out of college and never returned until many years later.

Haughty. Intemperate. Mooncalf. Maverick. "I don't need any teachers. I don't need anybody for anything. I can go it alone. I always have." My family lacked funds for university study anyway. So the hell with it. Professors tried to dissuade me. "We need to get you into grad school at Yale or Harvard." I had no context for understanding what this meant. I refused to listen. I quit and moved northeast to Massachusetts, a culture so foreign to Clinton County I'm surprised I didn't need a visa to travel there.

Had I known the obstacles, foreseen the odds, I'd have done it regardless. It's what makes me a bad poker player. Headstrong and impractical, always bluffing myself, always betting high on a losing hand.

I decided, naturally, to become a poet.

Deserting academia, I also decided I needed to help people.

People botched by genetic catastrophes. People whose brains spasmed and malfunctioned, people abysmally deficient in capabilities most of us take for granted. People abandoned by their families at birth. They were not the adorable poster children seen in magazine ads for the Special Olympics or United Way agencies—they were the ones hidden away, seldom glimpsed by the public, with misshapen heads and flaccid bodies, adults who functioned as toddlers. People labeled, in earlier times, "mongoloid idiots" or "imbeciles." They occupied the dimmest end of the human spectrum; they inhabited a realm of ultraviolet. Indisputable evidence, they seemed to me at the time, of a universe coldly indifferent to human suffering.

While writing poems in Amherst I paid rent by caring for these people, now known as "developmentally disabled." Working for eight years as a direct-care provider in a state institution and in a community home I brushed these peoples' teeth. Some had teeth resembling stubs of charcoal. I bathed people. Some had skin cross-webbed with scars from floggings. I assisted people in buttoning shirts, knotting shoelaces. Cooked oatmeal for them at six-thirty in the morning before they left for jobs sorting bolts and lugs into plastic bags in "sheltered workshops." Dispensed heart medications and, for the most violent, Haldol. Devised "Individual Service Plans" in consultation with staff psychologists. Stuffed piss-drenched pajamas in the washer. Talked by miming with my fingers to people who could only grunt. Watched people slur crayons over paper, or sway *larghetto* like metronomes on the sofa, tuned to some ineffable music echoing within their skulls.

Such people grow and learn according to vastly calibrated, and hence slower, scales of time. For eight years I recorded their meager progress.

Other staff members and I took them shopping. Took them to movies. To restaurants. Sometimes they grinned. Thick-tongued. Sometimes they babbled, or chortled, or slobbered. Often they seemed oblivious. These people who were not curious about the world, who esteemed consistency and routine above everything, who remembered—what? What did they remember? What language ghostwrote their thoughts? Did they have thoughts? Sometimes the stronger, higher-functioning ones tried to rape the weaker ones. Sometimes they bit the staff people. Sometimes they ripped our hair. Sometimes they smashed bedroom windows with their fists or pounded their heads against walls. As if to punish themselves for the dull, daily headache of mental impairment. Very often they smiled and hugged me and with their hands formed a sign, finger hooked on finger, meaning "friend."

I grew fond of them. In attempting to help these people—their names were David, and Kathy, and Charlie, and Lisa and Randy and Paul; there were dozens of them—I discerned clues to what constitutes a human being. It's not intellect. It's not the ability to read *Ulysses*, or a chapter on Kant by Bertrand Russell, or an essay on quantum physics, as I had tried to do so earnestly in my self-schooling. The essence of being human is, instead, our distinctive pulse of consciousness and the ability—shared with equally conscious nonhuman creatures but expressed in our own signature style—to love, to hate and fear, to mourn and rejoice. That's all.

Six years after suffocating in the classrooms of Bald Eagle-Nittany High School, and two years after leaving Penn State, I stood as an invited guest with two other poets in a small auditorium in Widener Library at Harvard University. I read my poems, including several intimate ones about working with my mentally impaired clients, to an appreciative audience. A state council had awarded me its prestigious Massachusetts Artists Fellowship in poetry. One distinguished author, a future US poet laureate, wrote, "There is no word more accurate for these poems than 'beautiful.'"

Decades later I would return to Harvard for my Master of Divinity degree.

And still I could not quell the voices of Clinton County.

◯

"Every day is a journey." These words of ancient Zen poet Bashō come wafting back to me as a refrain. "And the journey itself is home."

If, in 1992, in my thirty-eighth year, I have begun to lose my way, at least these roads I know by heart.

Approaching Mill Hall, I veer left at the fork onto Lusk Run Road, the identical route my father drove home each night from the Titan Metal factory; the same rural lane I drove, a decade behind him, as a hippie teenager with my friends Jeannine and Dolores…. My other lifetime. Emblems of the lost world….

Yet so little has changed: tatty meadows of horseweed. Tussocks of sorrel. The same trailers. The same houses of faded pastels with their propane tanks. Same knockabout hills. Same acres of junked cars; hundreds of cars, exoskeletons, hulks decayed beneath fathoms of this heavy, heavy air. Same honey locusts and sumac. Deeper than memory, it's a terrain spliced into neural circuitry of my brain, circuitry of veins and capillaries, into that mystic whatever-it-is we name the soul.

After four miles I top a sylvan ridge at Sunset Pines. New houses look dressy and expensive. Descending, I pass my childhood home on Hill Street, the one we rented before moving to the trailer park and then to Cedar Heights. Tap the brakes: there's the sidewalk and cement steps my dad built after dinner on extended summer evenings when I, at five years old, helped clutch the measuring tape, helped steady the spirit-level. So easy, in that world, to find equilibrium….

(I arrive here sometimes by air. Not by plane, but in dreams: Gliding over Hill Street I lift my arms and rise, without effort, like a peregrine, like a kestrel in storm; below I see Lock Haven's leaf-crowns of maples, its chimneys and roof shingles.)

I've paused at a stop sign. Susquehanna Avenue is crowded with exhausted looking houses, like a stage-set for a one-act drama entitled "Who the Hell Cares." Or "Don't Even Bother." Or called—adapting that famous motto of Clinton County, recited over and over to us by high school teachers—"You Can't Do What You Want in Life." They're utilitarian houses, places to watch the Phillies on TV, drink Schlitz, eat beans and hotdogs heaped on mashed potatoes; places to sleep before returning to the mill. Houses squeezed between the ridge of Sunset Pines and the woods. The woods overlook discontinued railroad tracks, the floodplain tobacco farms, the mountains—"verdure-capped sentinels," as the *History of Clinton County* refers to them—and the widening West Branch of the river.

(When I dream of the river, I enter by a different means of flight. Fanning my arms, I sink beneath the surface of the oneiric river, the timeless river. I swim deeper, swim deeper. Openmouthed. Transubstantiating water to oxygen—fish, man, fetus—I breathe. Suspiring water, slipstream of bubbles. Land and air forgotten. Waters of that dream Susquehanna feed my lungs, become my native element.)

Lock: turn of the key; to confine or exclude. Imprisonment.

Haven: source of comfort and ease.

This place that is not-here and here. Gone yet enduring.

As light is particle, is wave.

I'm driving the Bucktail Trail.

These riverine woods, so emphatically green. So steaming. So moistened with green, so Amazonian, it scarcely would surprise me to see a toucan.

But these are Penn's Woods. Eighth-generation Pennsylvanian, hometown boy, I'm starting to drive into Appalachia's unsubduable mountain country.

The past is a world spinning through orbits that intersect our own. A world where the dimension of time subsumes dimensions of space, where people, landscapes, cities suspend eternally. The past is a planet of denser gravity.

Georg Friedrich Rühle sailed into the New World aboard the *Tyger* to escape the past, to wring himself free from history. Tyger, Tyger, burning bright....

Seven generations later I am come to claim that history. Driving through Penn's Woods upriver along the Susquehanna, river of lumberjacks and keelboat men, of Indians in dugouts, lynx and terrapin, salmon and cougar and the wild flocks beating wings at the moon....

Seven generations later, in the Appalachian Mountains of Clinton County, I am seeking—I am always seeking—my birthright and my blessing, wondering what, if anything, my great-grandfathers and my great-grandmothers through all the decades may have dreamed for me, their progeny and namesake, their muddling, despairing kinsman.

Maybe this. Maybe just this:

Four hundred miles from my Northampton, Massachusetts, apartment, pulling off the Bucktail Trail onto a mud lane uncoiling through oak forest and birch, I brake in a clearing filled with almost a hundred parked cars. Smoke from the pig roast. Balloons, pink and burgundy. Hand-lettered signs tacked to trees: "Welcome Class of '72!".... "It's Been a Long Time!"...."We're Glad You're Here!"

Milling, convivial chatter. Crowds of striped shirts, casual slacks, tennis shorts.

Approaching the picnic tables where middle-aged people stand holding plastic cups, people with unfamiliar faces, I feel quick spurts of doubt and indecision.

Then the faces turn to me. Smiling faces.

I hear my name.

And two or three people—my people?—four people, five, surge toward me, a hug, another hug, a handshake, more smiles.

We welcome each other.

And I see it, the Susquehanna.

It's a haze of liquid twilight, flowing through twilight of summer foliage.

An American hymn: *Shall we gather by the river, the beautiful, the beautiful river....*

And we shall.

We shall.

PART
TWO

NARROW ROAD TO THE
RISING SUN:
ON BEGINNING
TO PRACTICE

1997–1999

⊃

"When you first seek dharma, you imagine you are far away from its environs. But dharma is already correctly transmitted; you are immediately your original self."

– **Dōgen, "Genjōkōan,"** *Shōbōgenzō*

"In the utter silence
Of a temple,
A cicada's voice alone
Penetrates the rocks."

– **Bashō,** *The Narrow Road to the Deep North*

SIX

THE FINEST city in Japan for dharma bumming—even better than Nara, with its deer parks, its Tōdai-ji Temple and forest shrines—remains Kyoto. Kyoto functioned as Japan's capital for one thousand years. A walker in Kyoto moves through the city's strata of history, through a millennium of impacted layers, fifty generations of lives, densities of human drama retrograding through time scales barely conceivable to Americans.

This week I'm a dharma bum. Footloose, beatific, exploratory, spur-of-the-moment and alert I wander Kyoto, a daypack cinched at my shoulders. I roam this city of a million-and-a-half people daily. I roam until long past dusk, through alleys of lacquerware shops and red-lantern soba houses in the Higashiyama district, along canals draped by willow boughs.

I wander streets where traditional *machiya* buildings predominate, narrow "eel bedding places," tiled eave abutting tiled eave, entrances canopied and curtained, matchbox facades screened by wood latticework called *degoshi*, sidewalk planters of amaryllis or camellias or miniature plum trees at the doorsteps.

I sleep near the Heian Shrine at a small *ryokan*, my futon spread on tatami mats. I breakfast, usually, at a nook off the Higashi-Oji, where local salarymen smoke unfiltered Larks and where, from my front booth, I observe high school students in black Nehru jackets and black trousers pedaling bikes to class through October's drift of yellow leaves. My waitress, a gorgeous young African-Japanese woman in dreadlocks, glides to the New York acid jazz and funky club music she serves us continuously, fresh from the stereo.

"*Ongaku-wa totemo subarashii desu,*" I remarked yesterday when she placed hotcakes and sweet red-bean paste at my table—"The music is very wonderful"—and she paused in jolted surprise, then beamed her smile at me.

I roam the parks. I roam Nijō Castle, four-hundred-year-old demesne of Tokugawa shoguns, its plank "nightingale floor" warbling and chirping at every footfall.

I roam broad gravel avenues outside the Forbidden Gate of the Imperial Palace.

I roam the slopes of Sannen-zaka and Ninen-zaka, their doglegged streets of cobblestone barely wide enough for a compact sedan, their shop windows arrayed with Kiyomizu-yaki displays: beautifully uncomplicated Zen teacups; cleanly articulated bowls. I look at pastel-boxed *yatsuhashi* sweets. At scallop-edged folding fans. Richly gowned display dolls with faces of white shell paste. Bamboo baskets. Silk scarves. Parasols and awnings shade the shop portals, their alcoves dense with potted Asian foliage and red jungle flowers, their second-story casements shielded by wickerwork. Visible above tiled roofs and electric wires, the landmark, antenna-like spire of Yasaka pagoda. Many of these shops have remained in the same devoted families for hundreds of years.

Nearby, roaming markets of Kiyomizu-zaka, I'm surprised by four nocturnal creatures—*maiko*s, young apprentice geishas—strolling in daylight. Faces mime-white, coiffures garlanded with pale florets, their layered and bound kimonos envelop secret, untouchable flesh in bright mists of fabric.

I roam for hours. Pilgrim, not tourist. In the plaza of Kyoto's National Museum I find Rodin's *Thinker*—self-absorbed, fist on chin, frowning with the stern effort of analytical thought, of subdividing and categorizing the universe. Indoors I find a monumental Buddha. Gazing. Composed. Emblissed in undisturbed Awareness.

Roaming the museum's incongruous Italianate halls and chambers I stop, transfixed, before screen paintings of the sixteenth-century Momoyama period: joyously decorative, sublimely balanced confections of blossoms and meticulous, wafting birds, painted in gold pigments and whites and scarlets and blues on triptychs and sliding door panels by the master of the genre, Kanō Eitoku, and his acolytes, under the patronage of warlords whose brief, truculent lives were sweetened by these visual hymns to earthly pleasures.

I marvel, too, at a National Treasure: Hasegawa Tōhaku's large, four-hundred-year-old "Standing Screens of Pine Trees," borrowed from the Chishaku-in Shingon Temple. Stunning effects of snow and fog in conifer forest, implied through the merest, most delicate wisps of sumi-e brushwork on blank panels. This accomplishment would have required unflagging Zen wakefulness and presence with every brushstroke. Later, upstairs, I sit for a half-hour examining *Crows on Plum Tree* by Unkoku Togan. Finally I remove the notebook from my backpack. To answer the painting I draft a little Zen poem:

> Space…. Black birds
> on limb…. Golden haze.
> Now! Now!   No birds.

⊃

ZEN TRACES its unbroken lineage 2,500 years, to a flower and a smile.

On a morning in the kingdom of Magadha in northeastern India, land of Brahmin sects, throngs gathered outdoors to hear an address by an emphatically non-Brahmanic sage. They called the man *Buddha*, meaning "The Awakened One." Formerly a rajah of the Shakya clan, he'd renounced throne and palace to subsist as a wandering teacher. This Buddha had been altered by a spiritual illumination so searingly intense that it scorched away all personal dross, all impurities of the thing called *atman*, or self, and left him cleansed, bright in his essential being, and preternaturally clear.

The Buddha sat before his audience on a large boulder. He gazed across thousands of faces. The crowd waited expectantly. What wise and lengthy treatises would this famed teacher impart? What new scriptures would he bequeath them? The Buddha continued to gaze across the crowd. Then he plucked a flower. He held it aloft. End of sermon. A man named Kāśyapa looked upon the flower and smiled.

Zen's lineage began the instant Kāśyapa smiled—the instant he realized the Buddha's teaching—and thus he became the first dharma heir, the spiritual ancestor of all who practice zazen.

Zen concocts its unique elixir by blending India's Mahāyāna Buddhism with Chinese Confucianism and Taoism.

A spiritual practice with bite.

Bodhidharma, the pugnacious Indian master who, according to legend, founded the Ch'an (Zen) lineage in China, reputedly arrived in that country in the sixth century. He met the grand Emperor Wu. The emperor said, "I have embraced Buddhism and I have ordered many monasteries and temples built. I have read many sutras and performed numberless good deeds. I have helped to spread Buddhism throughout China by virtue of my generous patronage. Tell me," commanded the proud emperor, "how much merit have I earned?"

Bodhidharma snapped, "None."

A spiritual practice founded on improbability and paradox.

"Things are not what they seem," the Buddha said. "Nor are they otherwise."

A practice demanding quiet, unremarkable daily heroism. Selfless heroism. Existential heroism, taking full responsibility for life. This heroism means persevering with sincerity and with determination even if the effort seems futile. The Four Great Vows: "Sentient beings are numberless; I vow to save them. Desires are inexhaustible; I vow to put an end to them. The Dharmas are boundless; I vow to master them. The Buddha way is unattainable; I vow to attain it."

A Zen parable: a man pursued by a ravenous tiger reached a precipice and, looking over the edge, saw a tree branch extending below. He leaped in desperation.

He grabbed the branch. Hanging there, he looked at the tiger snarling above him. Glancing at the rocks a hundred feet below he saw more tigers prowling.

The man noticed a strawberry growing on the cliffside.

With one free hand he popped the fruit into his mouth. "Ah," he said. "How sweet! How delicious!"

Centuries ago, a sixteen-year-old girl named Satsu dwelled as a monastic at Shoin-ji Temple. She lived most of each day in full awareness. One evening, as the girl sat in zazen meditation atop a wooden altar box, her father approached and said, "What are you doing? Get down from there! Don't you know a sacred statue of the Buddha is in that box?"

She replied, "If there is any place where Buddha does not exist, show it to me."

A samurai learned that a Zen teacher had arrived in the city. The samurai, overweening and bellicose, found the wizened little master seated beneath a tree.

"Tell me," the samurai demanded, "is there such a thing as heaven and hell?"

The Zen master chuckled. "Look at you! You call yourself a samurai! You look like a ridiculous weakling to me! I'll bet you'd run from a dog! What a pathetic excuse for a samurai!"

Shocked and enraged, the samurai drew his sword and raised it to hack the Zen teacher to pieces.

"That," said the teacher quietly, "is hell."

The samurai froze. Awareness of what the teacher had said dawned within him, and he lowered his sword. He bowed to the master in humble gratitude.

"And that," said the Zen teacher, "is heaven."

Hell and heaven. By now, autumn of '97, I'm a beginning Zen practitioner, a novice of three years.

Throughout the Eighties I skittered through life as a poet and arts journalist, activist for the Nuclear Weapons Freeze, drummer in a post-punk band, founder of the postmodern literary zine *Jukebox Terrorists*, renegade aesthete in ripped jeans and motorcycle jacket, living in western Massachusetts and networking with the hipster underground scene in LA and New York. Everything I knew about Zen in those days could have been cribbed on the blank edge of a bookmark. This didn't prevent me from holding opinions on the matter:

"Why would I want to meditate? Why would I want to sit?" I'd scoff during rare moments when the subject of Eastern religion arose in conversations. "Why would I want to just be a zombie? I'm not interested in serenity. I want passion. I *want* to ride that roller coaster. I *want* to feel deeply, I *want* to suffer and rejoice—that's what it means to be an artist. That's what it means to be *alive*. If I want to just sit and be empty I can get a lobotomy."

As often happens with Zen, the lessons would soon arrive.

Lessons in ephemera; in dissolution and loss. Lessons in the blind despotism of the self. Lessons in corrading effects of wanting, of wanting someone, her voice, her body, lessons in wanting someone like air when a strangler's fingers shut the throat. Lessons in the anguish of desire.

My girlfriend Corrina and I had seemed to mesmerize each other sexually, had seemed to sleepwalk around each other's bodies in a heavy erotic haze. We made love in a blind heat, an Elysium of sex. It vanished when she left the relationship. The pain felt as if I lay drawn on a table and filleted, my heart yanked out, tossed in the garbage like so much offal.

I yearned for her. I didn't know if spirits of the dead haunt the living, didn't know if they can assail us, thumping at walls, chain-rattling, bewailing their earthly grievances. But I knew absolutely that spirits of the living haunt the living. In her sudden absence I felt her everywhere.

Lessons in relinquishing.

I could not understand those lessons, those teachings in Buddhism's Second Noble Truth: the cause of life's suffering is craving.

"My experience," writes Alice Walker, "is that almost everyone I've met who has turned to Buddha did so because they have suffered the end of a love affair. They have lost someone they loved…. Very often, people turn to the Buddha because they have been carried so deeply into their suffering by the loss of a loved one that without major help they fear they will never recover…. This is what happened to me. I had lost my own beloved. The pain of this experience seemed bottomless and endless."

I started practicing Zen because everything in my life had failed and at least I could sit on a cushion. I started because my life had become a dirge of piercing, daily grief. But at least I could sit on a cushion, and at least the Four Noble Truths and the Eightfold Path of Buddhism suggested possibilities of winning reprieve from suffering, escape from an ego shackled, by lifetime of habit, to its own recurrent agonies. I started because it seemed the only way out. I started because I'd turned forty and something needed to change. Because something needed to change profoundly and forever. And it needed to start changing immediately or it would be too late. I started because I faced an emergency. Because my life had become one unending plane crash. Because of the loneliness. The mourning. The breakup. The failures. Because for twenty years I had believed I could suture the raw injuries sustained in my homeland of Clinton County, Pennsylvania, if I lived in service to art, and art failed; if I could win the saving and essential love of the right woman, and love failed.

And yet at least I can sit on a cushion. At least I can breathe. I can breathe, and I can sit on a cushion: and whenever I do those two things, I feel that I've found my home at last.

☽

IN KYOTO I wander unrestrainedly as the *ronin*, masterless samurai who centuries ago knocked around these same streets. Walking, I savor fleet infatuations. Thousands of Japanese women black-haired or hennaed. Their dark eyes, incomparably arresting. Their courtesan smiles; their lithe, girlish small-breastedness. Their faces perfected by nature, skin the color of vellum, skin seemingly ladled over cheekbones like smoothest buttermilk. This one: descending from a bus she scans the arcade of Shin-Kyogoku. That one: imperturbably erotic and unhurried in her pigeon-gray sweater, her black sheath skirt. This shop girl arranging pyramids of mandarin oranges with deft, delicate fingers. This woman on Shijō-dori laughing discreetly with her friend. Their beauty clement but impenetrable to me as they lean confidentially over tea and pastries, and I gaze across the chasm of my foreignness.

I get lost. It doesn't matter. Vespertine rambles: evenings I'm often spin-drifting west on Higashiyama, past closet-size noodle shops, past fruit and vegetable stalls, past restaurants where ingenious polyethylene replicas of food—shrimp tempura; *soba* with raw egg; sashimi—lie enticingly in windows, perking appetites of passersby. One night I pop into an art gallery's exhibition opening, where a Kyoto University student in a bomber jacket displays bolted abstract sculptures of polished aluminum. No one speaks English. I'm hospitably served red wine and a salted scab, which turns out to be desiccated fishtail.

Often I roam toward central Kyoto, a sector of the city burned to ashes by fifteenth-century armies of Yamana and Hosokawa during the Ōnin Civil War. Now central Kyoto is a transnational urban spectacle of glass high-rise, where posh specialty boutiques and hotels vie with three-story video screens flashing Calvin Klein ads, while hyperkinetic *kanji* billboards flicker controlled visual riots a hundred feet above thronged streets.

One evening I straggle past the Higashiyama subway station. Impassive college students in a streetside plaza watch a young Japanese R & B band deliver its polite, laboriously note-perfect rendition of "Kansas City." I sally past a Seven-Eleven's window racks of Japanese porn comics. Past a CD shop's ubiquitous promo displays of Thee Michelle Gun Elephant, number-one Japanese neo-punk rock group; its members dress like mid-Sixties British mods on the cover of their latest recording, *Chicken Zombies.* Past four-lane city avenues manic with cars, motor scooters, cars, cars, taxicabs, cars. It's the quietest, most courteous traffic I've ever encountered. Rarely, in all this metropolitan bustle, do I hear a car horn.

Instead: birdlike cheeps of the street-crossing signals. Instead: happy surf-like roar of human voices, thousands of night-adoring fun seekers out on the town, enjoying a true cosmopolis, city of loveliness and civilized tradition, of spiritual rigor and refined pleasures, a city devoid of street thuggery, free of menace.

City of a thousand years.

Sounds of revelry increase when I maneuver through crowds jamming the bridge across the Kamo River. Below, lovers walk the strand. They toss morsels to cranes, to cormorants. Hundreds of kids hang out near public bathing huts. They chatter, caress guitars, lean against bicycles. Above us, in exclusive restaurants overlooking the river, shadows of diners and silhouetted waiters float behind pastel lantern-glow of plate glass. And the October full moon reigns over Kyoto.

Crossing the bridge I enter the Pontochō, fabled district of geisha. Red-lantern alleys—labyrinths of hedonism—each lane so narrow that two people barely pass abreast. As if through catacombs, black tunnels between buildings, I emerge in a smoky seepage of light. Doorway; a secret bar. Translucent silkscreen curtain. Women, a cluster of wobbling men, guffaw and raise their *sake* cups. Another alley: geisha in kimono penguin-shuffles to her next appointment. Another alley: guys in white shirts and skinny black ties bait young Japanese businessmen into the downstairs strip clubs, the soaplands, the boozy, hole-in-the-wall, pleasure-girl dives.

Sometimes I return to the main shopping thoroughfares, joining countless shag-hair university kids in their leather and shades and Levis, after-work midlevel execs in funereal business suits and the after-work secretaries, the few dazed European tourists and the few blond American youth hostelers and everyone else who blitzes the arcades to swap bundles of yen for lacquered tea trays, for calfskin Parisian handbags, for jade rings, for "floating world" block prints or Noh masks, perfumes imported from Madrid. *Titanic* is playing in the second-floor movie theaters. Japanese teenagers in backwards baseball caps flock a corner McDonald's.

Sometimes I recross the river. I walk three blocks south into the centuries-old Gion district, Kyoto's most famous geisha neighborhood and nighttime playland. In the Gion's mazes of back passageways, lit by trinket shops, by neon, by beer dens and *fugu* eateries and love hotels, their constricted lanes choked by limos and Mercedes and luxury Toyota sedans, I pass dozens of disconcertingly luscious, top-dollar Indonesian, Filipino and Japanese hostess girls. Expensively tailored, they confer brusquely with their cell phones. Then they disappear into one of the members-only, private entertainment clubs stacked atop each other in eight-story buildings, clubs with names like Lucky Strike and Hot Diamond.

◠

IN DAYLIGHT I roam the temples. Kyoto serves as home address to 1,600 Buddhist temples and more than four hundred Shinto shrines.

In Sanjūsangen-dō, a Tendai Buddhist temple, I move through the almost stupefying vastness of the Great Hall, air cloying from seven hundred years of incense. I steer through its candle-sputtered dimness. (An absorbing essay by the great novelist Jun'ichirō Tanizaki, entitled "In Praise of Shadows," describes the Japanese aesthetic of darkness and fireglow, a carefully nuanced, carefully manipulated chiaroscuro.) In Sanjūsangen-dō's dark recesses sits the enormous Kannon Bodhisattva statue, enthroned in Buddhist splendor, its face benignant, its hands clasped in *gasshō*. One thousand many-armed Kannon figures flank the statue. They align in tiers like choristers. Each figure of carved cypress is japanned in gold-leaf, protected by statues of choleric-looking, muscular kami deities. Again I long for Zen simplicity.

It evades me at half-a-dozen Tendai and Pure Land Buddhist temples, their halls oppressively weighty and opulent, their plazas swarmed by shutterbugs. It evades me most discouragingly at Kiyomizudera, the Hossō Buddhist temple built in 1633 atop a mountainside in southeastern Kyoto. Its breath-stopping Main Hall perches on more than a hundred Brobdingnagian wood pillars. I'm eager to visit. But this temple turns out to resemble a Buddhist carnival. (Today many Buddhist temples in Japan are mom-and-pop businesses, passed from parents to oldest son.) A favored destination for chartered buses, Kiyomizudera's crowds of Americanized Japanese sightseers and souvenir zealots banter amid the temple's gewgaw booths and Fuji film kiosks. They jostle the Suntory vending machines that dispense sweet tea and cans of Pocari Sweat or Coffee Boss. People click-snap photos. They slurp dippers of "holy water," or mumble their brief supplications to Kannon. Loud, oblivious schoolkids in navy-blue uniforms follow smiling teachers hoisting class pennants. I flee as if from a New Year's party.

I feel closer to what I seek—call it involucrum of silence; call it sanctuary—when I find Hōnen-in.

Coppice of bamboo. Their trunks green like a grasshopper's thorax; trunks immaculate as vinyl tubing. Beyond this bamboo grove, the modest woodland temple of Hōnen-in lies hidden at the base of Kyoto's Zenkizan Mountain.

Finding it requires snooping through alleys branching off the Philosopher's Path. The path borders a canal of teahouses, its arched footbridges and gardens interspersed with cherry trees, red maples and persimmons in Kyoto's northeastern Shishigatani district. Contemplatives have strolled the canal path for six hundred years.

Hōnen-in's entrance gate offers discreetly pointed commentary on the gargantuan, vainglorious edifices of other Buddhist temples. It is no larger than a one-car garage. Its roof of thatched rice-straw, plain as that of a dormouse home in a storybook, features no garniture save moss and fallen leaves.

The temple dates from 1680. Hōnen-in is not a Zen temple. Like many, it belongs to the Pure Land sect. Pure Land Buddhists, whose doctrines migrated to Japan via India and China, believe they may experience awakening to the "Pure Land" of eternal enlightenment by chanting the name of Amida Buddha, the Buddha of Light, and entrusting themselves to his salvific vow.

For centuries this notion appealed powerfully to unlettered farmers for whom the practice of Zen seemed too exacting, too recondite, too reliant on *jiriki*, or self-power. The twelfth-century Japanese priest Hōnen understood this. He spread Jōdo-shū, Pure Land Buddhism, among thousands of drudging, despairing peasants. Hōnen also taught that everyone—merchants and common laborers as well as noble samurai and royalty—walked as equals in the eyes of Amida. Because he espoused this, the emperor banished him. Five hundred years after Hōnen died, his followers built Hōnen-in Temple to honor him.

Narrow bridge. Its walkway curving up like the spine of a stretching cat. Lily pads. Temple pond deepening through spectra of green into blackness, pool of liquid jasper, undisturbed.

Outdoor statue of Hōnen, its face and robe of lambent black stone. The statue blesses a grotto sanctified with incense, with candles and camellias, four grapefruit on a wrought iron stand.

Exquisite courtesies of silence.

A woman's slow glissade in white kimono.

Twin mounds of sand, mounds tapered and rectangular as catafalques, each planed upper surface chamfered in patterns of leaves and swirls.

Stone basin velured with moss. Persimmon leaf tucked in the rim. The leaf guides excess rainwater in a spill of braiding silver to the trough below.

Impromptu ariettas of sylvan birds.

Sitting in the arbor of Hōnen-in's cemetery I've yanked my journal from the knapsack. I labor to describe the sound of a Buddhist funeral while it occurs behind trees, down the hillside. The priest's mesmerizing, eerie litany of monosyllables, his voice thwanging like a zither. I try to identify the scents of Japanese autumn. I note the cemetery walls, terraced stacks of river cobble, damp from last night's shower.... Bronze vases, froth of gold chrysanthemums.... A young Japanese woman appears, a university student, shoving her bicycle. I noticed her early this morning, pedaling on Imadegawa Street, round the corner from my ryokan, as I perched on a bus-stop bench tweezering up my breakfast of cold soba noodles with chopsticks. Here she is again. One of those random conjunctures of two disparate lives....

A half-hour later I'm tractioning up the wooded slope of Mount Zenkizan. Near a pavilion that houses the temple bell I've spied a path. The path narrows. It becomes mudslick, root-clogged, stony. I ascend through maples and pines. Underbrush. It looks like a New England forest. Yet because it's Japanese it feels immoderately mysterious, exotic. Some of Kyoto's forests harbor wild macaque monkeys. Perhaps this is one.

I halt at a sign in kanji—indecipherable to me. "No Trespassing" sign? Cocksure American, I figure what the hell, man, go for it; what're they gonna do, deport me? I resume my climb. The trail becomes very steep. It's like a mudslide on a broken escalator. Soon I'm dripping in humid forest. I remove my sweatshirt; I knot it around my hips. Noisy raiding party of mosquitoes. To my right, an entangled wooded gorge and beyond it, bluntly insuperable, a forested hill. I resume climbing, knapsack in hand. Ten minutes later I've lost the trail in a woodcut, mishmash of leafy brush and chain-sawed timber. I skedaddle back down the slope. I discover the trail veers to the left.

Glade of beech-like trees. Overhead, their leaves a green tarp. Unseen birds warn each other of my approach. The trail rises steadily. A switchback. More turns. I'm soaked; I roll my wet T-shirt above my midriff and keep climbing. Here the trail becomes sheer, assaulting the mountain directly. Open sky winks through trees at the ridge crest. Climbing, the exertion tensing my calves, I mop sweat from my face, breathe in strained spurts. Soon I attain a summit.

Hundreds of feet above the city of Kyoto I rest on a ledge. Peering down through foliage I see miniature white buildings and cars. How many Hōnen-in monks have stood here on this shelf of rock during the past three hundred years, looking toward nearby mountain peaks? I wonder if this trail, this forest, Zenkizan Mountain itself, has been employed by the monks during ritual pilgrimages, during sacred retreats.

I continue hiking, eager to claim the mountaintop. The trail dips into a small ravine. It inclines to bushy vert and cedar forest and levels out. I peel off my T-shirt. I'm walking without effort, naked to the waist. Air feels cooler up here. Moving among wild Japanese evergreens and wild Japanese hardwoods I begin to think I've reached my goal. I'm at the top!

Then I make a visor of my hands. Squinting through pines and yellow scraps of leaves I glimpse the truth: ahead waits another summit, a mile-and-a-half farther up the trail.

I haven't found the peak at all. I'm merely on one of the higher elevations.

The true peak—if it even *is* the true peak; there may remain another, hidden behind it—requires an additional hour of climbing.

Lesson for the aspirant: reach the top and there's always another mountain.

☽

THAT HUSH in which the world discourses.

Sunlight breaching high clouds.

Before me: raked sand. White like pulverized coral.

Ambient light: shadows cut rock.

Inhale.

Scent: pine wood. October air.

Exhale.

Sun-tepid stone. Ellipse of moss.

Isshidan Garden. Ryōgen-in Zen Temple. Kyoto. Five hundred years.

Black pebbles.

Inhale.

At my back: oldest meditation hall in Japan. Altar with oblation of fruit and flowers. Broom-swept tatami. Three panels, graced by mustachioed dragon emerging from a whirled nimbus of sumi-e ink.

Here, the authentic place.

Immaculate combed wavelets of sand. Raked by monks at dawn.

Here. Is.

What.

(Exhale.)

(No sound.)

I've.

(Emptiness. Plenitude.)

Sought.

Sunflood moss and boulders.

Ryōgen-in, a closeted dollhouse of a temple, ranks as one of twenty-three *tatchu*, or subtemples, of Daitoku-ji, the vast fourteenth-century compound in Kyoto's northwestern Murasakino neighborhood which functions as a headquarters for Rinzai Zen in Japan. "Daitoku-ji" means "Great Virtue Temple." No golden Buddhas on public display. Domain of humble service. Domain of hard, cleansing daily toil. Daitoku-ji became one of the places where Zen created its pared aesthetic, a place of harmonies severely and pleasingly refined. These temples were sanctums for Zen poets and painters, for masters of *chadō*, Zen tea ceremonies fastidiously enacted.

I sit unaccompanied. Behind adobe-like walls I study this rock and sand garden's almost maniacal order, a garden seemingly designed without human intervention, solely by straightedge and calipers. Silence becomes a medium with specific density. Silence becomes one of nature's primal forces: electromagnetic; gravitational.

Folding my hands, I begin to sit zazen.

Nearly four hundred years ago, during the Western era of Michelangelo and *King Lear* and Spanish plunder of the New World, horticulture masters designed the azalea garden of Chishaku-in Temple. They arranged its sequestered lair of rocky pathways, its pond and manicured shrubbery, its upright, clustered boulders to mimic terrain of Mount Rozan in China.

This garden in Kyoto's southeastern quadrant remains protected from city concerns, from city noise. In its pond, carp knot and disperse, reform in gliding underwater forays, tangerine, speckled white. Guggle of a cascade spills off the wooded hillside. Morning light decants to rain-haze. The world of striving seems very far away.

Around the corner, banners of purple, of emerald, of gold, banners of vermilion, of white silk. Over the pond, to create the effect called *izumi-dono*, extends a narrow wooden mezzanine. Translucent *shōji* door panels of tissued rice paper have been slid open to reduce distinctions of exit and ingress, of private interior, public daylight. Clean sweet-straw perfume of tatami mats. Stone basin, *tetsubachi*; a bamboo water dipper.

Wind rouses the hillside maples. Their foliage, like sails of a vast regatta, begins to swell, then puffs and rides the wind. Autumn colors— hues of carp—sift the lingering summer green. Air feels denser, moisture laden. Black birds congregate in topmost branches. I hear their loud scuttlebutt. These regal scavengers, these lordly ragpickers of birds. A light rain begins.

Opening my notebook I write a haiku:

Ravens. Faint shower
on carp pool, on waterfall.
Nothing more to say.

◯

AS AN American practicing within an Asian religion, both here and in the States, I try to stay vigilant concerning issues related to cultural appropriation—especially the purloining of spiritual traditions from foreign nations, indulging Romantic fantasies about "exotic" spiritualities of the "Other," arrogantly claiming for ourselves an array of cultural traditions that have never belonged to us. Such issues have validity. So do issues relating to spiritual dilettantism, the shallow, selfish dabbling in religious beliefs and practices of other people.

In Kyoto I'm mulling this as I rest on a futon spread on rice-straw mats in the small cubby of my ryokan. Serenaded by patter of an evening rainfall, it occurs to me that I need to distinguish between appropriation and assimilation. In any specific instance of cross-cultural encounter, what actually is transpiring?

To know this in regard to Buddhism, context helps. Since at least the era of Emperor Ashoka, ruling his Indian kingdom of the third century BCE, Buddhism has thrived as a missionary religion. Ashoka sent Indian missionaries packing in all directions to spread the Buddha's teachings. They flourished in Sri Lanka and southeast Asia, and so did their latter-generation disciples in China and Tibet. Eventually Buddhist teachers in China trained students who hailed from Korea and Japan, and those students took Buddhism back to their home countries. Did those cultures—Japan, in particular, where I've been dwelling these recent months—appropriate a foreign religion from India? Or did Japan assimilate it? Clearly, I reflect, it was the latter. This has been true of Buddhism's expansion throughout its history, including its recent exporting to America, brought to us by Asian teachers such as Nyogen Senzaki, Shunryu Suzuki, and many others. In the United States we're assimilating this Indian religion of Buddhism and adapting it to our own purposes, as the Japanese and Chinese and other non-Indian cultures have done for centuries.

Civilizations have interacted this way throughout millennia. When not warring against each other or colonizing or enslaving each other, they assimilate foreign cuisines, customs, sciences, arts, clothing—and religions—in mutual borrowings and adaptations. It's how humanity grows.

Moreover, fundamental Buddhist principles of clear mind and

beneficence do not exist exclusively in Asian cultures, ripe for appropriation by the West; they exist universally in people, innately, as part of our birthright, needing only to awaken through spiritual training. Buddha nature is human, and so is the Buddhism that allows us to realize it. Nobody "owns" Buddhism. It belongs freely to everyone. In Dōgen's words: "How could practice-realization be within any boundary?"

Still, we must remain scrupulous in paying attention to how we use forms and practices specific to religions that come to us from foreign cultures, Buddhist or otherwise. What criteria might we use, then, to establish whether intercultural contact represents an egregious case of appropriation or a healthy one of assimilation? As I ponder this, listening to the rain in Kyoto, two standards occur to me.

The first: Is there a current or historical power differential in the relationship of the cultures involved, due to colonialism or conquest? And does it result in the dominant power seizing religious elements from the colonized or conquered people for its own purposes? Back in the States, when non-Native American people sport with the spiritual practices of, say, Lakota or Navaho people, without training or permission, and flaunt elements of Native American clothing, ceremonies, or customs, we can consider it a possible instance of appropriation because of the enormous power differential between dominant white culture and oppressed Native American culture. Is it the same situation when Americans like me practice Japan's Zen Buddhism? Are we appropriating it? But I recall immediately that Japanese teachers *came to us*, seeking to share the dharma, seeking converts, and we responded. Moreover, in 1997 the power relationship between Japan and America, despite mid-century travails of World War II, doesn't manifest as colonizing or conquest. Today a rough socio-economic parity exists, and the cultural exchanges play out mutually—as I'm seeing constantly here in Kyoto, where Western fashions, music, and technologies abound. And finally, when we Americans sit zazen and wear *rakusus* and take Japanese dharma names, we're not appropriating traditional forms; we're paying homage to them, honoring what our Japanese teachers have given us, what they've authorized us to employ and what they've asked us to perpetuate on our own soil. We're expressing our gratitude. Not to do so, it seems to me, would constitute the real act of appropriation, by erasing Zen's Japanese roots and pretending that Zen belongs solely to us.

This implies the second standard in distinguishing between appropriation and assimilation: What is the intention? Is it to honor a foreign religious tradition or merely to profit from it through commercial exploitation? In the States, we might find an example of cultural appropriation in the spectacle of Hindu yoga being turned into a pop feel-good exercise program for predominantly white people in gyms and at resort spas. But is that what we see in American Buddhism, too, among non-Asian people in the US? Certainly some of that exists. Mostly, however, we see a process of sincere conversion—a process of assimilating, not appropriating.

For me, exploring Japan while living here for three months isn't the Orientalism of a besotted Westerner, infatuated by the enigma and fabled exoticism of the East. (Okay, maybe it is a little bit of that.) It's not sentimental nostalgia for the imagined splendors of a bygone era. (Okay, maybe it's a little bit of that, too.) At heart, it feels much more like the expression of an authentic, intimate act of connecting—karmic, predestined, at levels both psychic and cellular.

Though I'm an agnostic about reincarnation, I certainly consider it feasible. Here in Japan I'm considering it more earnestly. The possibility of reincarnation hugely expands ways of understanding personal identity as well as issues of cultural appropriation. In this lifetime I'm a twentieth-century white male in America who's practicing Zen Buddhism, but in another lifetime I may be a thirteenth-century Japanese woman living as a Buddhist nun. In this current existence, therefore, I'm not appropriating the spiritual tradition of another culture; I'm returning to something I know intimately. For me, absorbing a foreign religion on its own turf, here in Japan, or adopting that religion back in Amherst, Massachusetts, doesn't feel like an act of appropriation; it feels like an act of recovering something precious: "I know this place. This way of life. I've been here before." In Kyoto I wander among temples and streets previously unknown to me in this current "Steve Ruhl" existence, yet I do so in perpetual recognition. This subtle déjà vu of rediscovery, this familiarity and ease, suggests a primal bond sourced, very possibly, in past-life experience. It doesn't feel like appropriating a foreign culture. It feels like returning home.

HOME FOR Tachibana no Kachiko existed here in Kyoto. A ninth-century empress of Japan, she became the first person in the country to practice Zen. Having invited a Ch'an monk from China to instruct her, she built a temple for him, then became a nun.

Four centuries later, Dōgen's life also began in Kyoto and ended in Kyoto. This brilliant pioneering Zen teacher, descended from Japanese imperial royalty, traveled extensively in China then returned to his homeland and established the school of Sōtō Zen. He built his Temple of Eternal Peace in a remote mountain wilderness of northern Japan. Dōgen's writings, now vastly esteemed, lay forgotten through more than half a millennium. It recalls an item I saw on a science program: botanists recently discovered an ancient orchid bulb at a temple near Tokyo, dormant for centuries. They planted the bulb and miraculously it bloomed. Something similar has occurred with Dōgen's reputation. After 750 years the creator of Sōtō Zen in Japan has flowered into belated fame, apprized increasingly as a discerning philosopher, a poet of exceptional sophistication, and a meritorious spiritual teacher; one of the finest, in fact, the world has known. He returned here from his wilderness temple in 1253 to die in his native city. In one of his final poems he wrote:

> Just when my longing to see
> The moon over Kyoto
> One last time grows deepest,
> The image I behold this autumn night
> Leaves me sleepless for its beauty.

TWO NIGHTS ago I saw the spot-lit Temple of the Golden Pavilion, Kinkaku-ji. Its reflection hovered on black water of the "mirror pond" like a moth of winged fire. Early the next morning at Ginkaku-ji, Kyoto's Silver Temple, I inspected eighteenth-century screens of birds, of hemp palms and tranquil sages daubed by the haiku poet Buson in the small *hondō*. I admired sulcate beds of raked sand. Water gardens, ponds the green of slivered quince. Islands of ferns and lichened rock. Plum trees and spurge. Peninsulas of sculpted pines.

I've returned now to Kyoto's Ryōgen-in Zen temple at Daitoku-ji. Subsiding racket of language in my head. Settle into no-thinking. Breathe. Look.

Mind and body: a skiff becalmed at windless latitude.

In my notebook I write: "October 28, 1997, sitting alone at Isshidan Garden, Ryōgen-in Zen Temple. This raked sand is Temple of *Sunyata*, of emptiness. Yet in this emptiness inheres everything: all life and all worlds. Suzuki noted Buddhism is only religion which can be expressed as mathematical equation: zero equals infinity. Infinity equals zero. To connect with this emptiness, this fullness, feels to me like reattaching psychic equivalent of lost umbilical. Of swimming—right here—in great empty womb of the Cosmos, where all is interconnected. Feels so perfect. So right."

Turning a corner I reach the moss garden, Ryugintei. Intimate, enclosed, a moquette of rumpled green, the moss garden looks like the surface of a billiard table abandoned for decades to the rain.

When I return to the Isshidan garden of raked sand, a Japanese couple sits pensively on its wooden deck. Near four o'clock, the sun edges below a tiled rooftop.

Opening my notebook again, I write: "Odd to realize this Zen temple coeval with Western Renaissance. Hard to believe. And while Renaissance extolled individual self, Zen sought to negate it. Western mind chose to scale natural world to human dimensions—'man is measure of all things' etc.—while Japanese in gardens like this one sought to accommodate human proportions to nature. Amazing. Also ironic, what Renaissance sages valued as knowledge—intellectual products resulting from discriminatory, analytical powers of mind—Japanese sages derided as ignorance."

A temple bell strikes.

—

Ikkyū Sōjun, who called himself "Crazy Wind Person," may have heard the same bell when he charged about these grounds of Daitoku-ji in the 1400's, serving as abbot and overseeing temple construction. The bastard son of Emperor Gokomatsu, ordained a monk at the age of six, he wandered from home as a young man to live as a tramp. "Having no destination," he said, "I am never lost." One day he opened into *satori*—flash of enlightenment—upon hearing the loud squawk of a crow. This "Crazy Wind Person" became an influential Rinzai Zen instructor, master of tea ceremony, of *shakuhachi* flute, of calligraphy, and an exceptional poet.

Ikkyū revolted against Buddhism's sacerdotal elite, the priests who quoted scriptures in their gold and purple robes, corrupted by avarice and privilege. In the process he extended the grand tradition of rowdy Zen masters. A fiercely jolly and unencumbered Falstaffian bad-ass, he delighted in sake-guzzling and whoring in the Gion quarter of Kyoto, the same pleasure districts I roam at night; the best place for Zen, declared Ikkyū, is in a brothel. Zen has never been sullied by puritanism. Ikkyū wrote sexy poems inspired by his young lover, Mori, ribald verses praising her lips, her breasts, her thighs, and the bliss therein. Ikkyū's Zen argues powerfully for becoming a zesty human being who glories in life. As always, the secret lies in not becoming slavishly *fixated* on pleasure: enjoy, then relinquish. Think William Blake here: "He who binds himself to a joy / Doth the winged life destroy / But he who kisses the joy as it flies / Lives in Eternity's sunrise."

Ikkyū kept his teachings straightforward. "Don't waste time reading the Buddhist sutras," he counseled. "Read love letters sent by snow, by wind, by rain."

A visitor to these temples at Daitoku-ji asked Ikkyū, "Master, I have been told you are enlightened. Will you please share with me your highest wisdom?"

Ikkyū wielded his ink brush. He dashed one word: "Attention."

"But surely this cannot be all," the man protested. "Can you not share with me the secret of enlightenment?"

Ikkyū wrote again: "Attention."

"Well, this certainly does not seem like wisdom," the man harrumphed. "Where is the depth to this? Where is the learned subtlety? There is nothing profound."

Ikkyū then wrote three times: "Attention. Attention. Attention."

Very annoyed, the man protested, "Attention? What do you mean by this word 'attention'?"

"Attention means attention," said Ikkyū.

Another time Ikkyū visited a dying student here at Daitoku-ji. "Do you require my help?" Ikkyū asked.

"No, I don't require anything. I will simply be crossing over into the changeless."

"If you still think you're a 'somebody' who's going 'somewhere,' then you require my help," said Ikkyū.

Just before his own death Ikkyū told students, "Some of you will become hermits in the mountains of Kyoto, living in forests and devoting yourselves to meditation. On the other hand, some of you will devote yourselves to wine and to pleasure girls in the whorehouses of the Gion. Either way is excellent Zen practice. Just don't become a professional priest and walk pompously around a temple in your robes spouting nonsense about 'the way of Zen.' If you do that, you're not my student. You're my enemy."

Not until I'm leaving the temples of Daitoku-ji do I remember that Takuan also walked here. Three-hundred-and-fifty years ago Takuan Sōhō served as abbot, integrating neo-Confucian principles and Shintōism with Zen. Takuan composed poems, he painted, he mastered arts of tea ceremony and flower arranging. Most important, he taught the Way of the Sword.

⊃

WE GLIDE in unison, our *katanas*—our swords—hissing on the downslice. We glide barefoot. Six men and two women in white wraparound *haoris*, our black full-skirted *hakemas* ballooning as we kneel and pivot. We choke-up on the sword handles, *tsuka-ito*, with both fists as we lunge. Our blades make the air gasp.

"The sword is mind. Right minded is right sword."

Iai-dō, "the way of drawing the sword," developed four hundred years ago as a means for samurai and for *sōhei*—warrior monks—to disable attackers in a single fluent unsheathing of the blade. *Iai* transforms the act of removing sword from scabbard into lethal choreography. Performed correctly it's like a hybrid of ceremonial dance and Errol Flynn.

We resume our positions. Sweeping our hakemas imperiously behind our legs we kneel on the wooden floor. Positioning hands on our upper thighs we gaze toward the mirror. Our sword master, Sato-*sensei*, claps twice. Each woman and man breathes into the *hara*, the mind-body locus beneath the navel. Exhales. Breathes again. Now: left hand floats to scabbard, right hand to the sword hilt; we rise on our knees. Deadly pause. Flash: swords emerge. Iced sizzle of light on steel. We glide in unison....

"The opponent is Emptiness, I am Emptiness." Those words, written by Takuan, appear in his classic manual on Zen swordsmanship, *The Unfettered Mind*. "The hand that holds the sword, the sword itself, is Emptiness."

Zen and swordsmanship merged in Japan during the thirteenth century, when meditation practice joined the *bushidō* tradition of professional warriors. Feudal lords sent their samurai to Zen monasteries to gain spiritual instruction in overcoming fear of death; Zen monks trained in martial arts, including the Way of the Bow, the Way of Fighting with Empty Hand, the Way of the Sword. Japanese sabers, three feet long with a mild curvature at the cutting edge, were forged by Tendai Buddhist monastics who adorned them with sacred kanji. The blades, of refined low-carbon steel, excel even the legendary Damascus blades wielded by Muslims during the Crusades, believed by Europeans of the era to have had no equal in the world. An early Japanese swordsmith, quoted in a book called *Zen and the Way of the Sword* by Winston L. King, described his weapon-making technique: "Heat the steel at final forging until it turns to the color of the moon about to set out on its journey across the heavens on a June or July evening...."

Our own swords, though modern reproductions, cost thousands of yen and their annealed slashing-edges, rivaling a surgeon's scalpel, could open flesh as if it's muskmelon. Every part of the sword bears a name. These names have persisted for centuries. The sword point: *kissaki*. The ridgeline: *shinogi*. Hardened edge: *yakiba*. Its pattern: *hamon*. Blade surface above ridgeline: *shinogi-ji*. Measure of curvature: *sori*. After each session we wipe our blades reverentially with oiled cloth before we swaddle them with indigo felt and slipcase them in leather. Prior to each session we lay our swords upon the floor and thread the tasseled *sageo* between our fingers then prostrate ourselves. We murmur thanksgiving.

"The mind is not detained by the hand that brandishes the sword. Completely oblivious to the hand that wields the sword, one strikes."

Slay the ego.

We practice a full hour, then another hour, then another hour, each Monday evening in the Moriyama Community Center near downtown Kanegasaki in northern Japan, where I'm living. I, of course, am the only non-Japanese. As we glide, as we sweep our swords in bright arcs and shout "*Ei!*" and cleave the air before us, hour upon hour, we examine judiciously in the mirror every footfall, every hip turn and arm thrust, every acute angle of elbow and sword.

We study a type of *iai* called *Musō Jikiden Eishin-ryū*. Of the dozens of movements a sword master must accomplish—slow escadrilles of the body and its keen responsive blade—we concentrate on seven: *mae*; *migi*; *hidari*; *ushiro*; *yaegaki*; *ukenagi-shi*; *kaiswaku*. A Zen-trained samurai of four centuries ago could perform these blindfolded. They were peerless combat techniques. Today they serve as kinetic mind-body training, a spiritual regimen of active, focused meditation.

Takuan, in essays written between his two terms as abbot of Daitoku-ji Zen Temple in Kyoto, instructed sword students to cultivate an alert, weightless mind and allow it to flow through tendons, through bone and muscle, the entire physique. The swordsman, nimble and decisive in each lucid moment of combat—now! now! now!—could let hand and saber perform instinctively. Parry. Deflect. Attack. No conscious strategy: pure action. Takuan named this the doctrine of "No Mind."

The human body: fired and hammered steel.

The human body: a whetted knife-edge.

The sword: heartbeat, sinew, live breathing tissue.

Our teacher, Mr. Sato, has eyes like an impala's. He chain-smokes. During practice he drills us reflexively in mae, the basic starting form. We steady our concentration. Throughout each procedure we must observe fine minutiae when positioning fingers, wrists, elbows, feet. Every motion of the sword requires dexterous sequences of micro-adjustments to ensure flawless execution. It all must happen uninterruptedly. And not slug-gishly, but with the most beauteous and deliberate and unassuming haste.

Throughout the first month's practice Mr. Sato grabbed my arm. "No!" One of two English words familiar to him; the other was "watch." "Watch!" he'd command, opposite me. He'd demonstrate, one time only, the intricate movement sequences of mae or migi or hidari, then nod curtly, a signal for me to mimic what I'd just observed. I'd try. Immediately: "No!" Grabbing my forearm. "No! No!" Stinging reprimands, his hand rebuking my every attempt. He spoke as if to a dog pissing on a carpet. "No! No! No!" Try again. "No!" He'd brusquely force my wrist to the proper angle. "No!" Apparently my finger placement was botched. I tried to please him. "No!" He'd jerk my arm disgustedly to the proper height. Again, try; again. "No! No!" Three hours. "No! No! No!"

Chafing with frustration and embarrassment, I vowed to quit: This is unbearable; this is awful; I can't learn this way…. Then I'd make another attempt.

"No!"

After five weeks of scolding, he changed.

Now he smiles with placid forbearance. He patiently scrutinizes my progress. He has adopted a new English word. "Good." When I demon-strate mae, Sato-sensei bestows on me his smile. "Good," he says. It occurs to me that by persevering through the first terrible month I've unwittingly passed a private test, a gate of initiation.

…We're gliding barefoot. Two women, six men, swords hissing on the down slice….

The famed nineteenth-century sword master and Rinzai Zen practi-tioner Yamaoka Tesshū wrestled ten years with a kōan: "Originally not one thing exists." Then he received a classic three-line warrior kōan that began, "When two flashing swords meet there is no place to escape." Two flashing swords meeting in no place: Relative and Absolute. Tesshū grappled three years with that kōan. When finally he awoke to its meaning, he bested his teacher in a duel of wooden swords and left to establish his own school of *kendō*. Tesshū named his Zen method "the Sword of No-Sword." His school, Shumpukan, or Spring Breeze Hall, trained students in a vehement, uncompromising discipline—thousands of hours of sparring practice; marathon daylong fencing exams—designed to shove them past all physical barriers into selfless, spontaneous mastery.

Quotes from Tesshū's writings offer the flavor of his Zen sword instruction:

"Swordsmanship should lead to the heart of things where one can directly confront life and death." And this: "There is victory and defeat in swordsmanship, but forging the spirit is far more important. What is the secret? The mind has no limits." And this: "Since I am a swordsman I best express my understanding of Rinzai's Zen teaching through the Way of the Sword. No matter how great your intellectual comprehension, if you mimic someone else, your Zen is dead." And this: "If there is self, there is an enemy; if there is no self, there is no enemy."

No self, no enemy.

"Softer. Less power. You understand? Yes." Yukie, a fellow student, corrects me when I try to muscle-through my sword patterns during *hidari*. "Less power. Very simple, you see? Yes. Yes. Good."

I've become friends with Yukie, an extremely pretty woman, her hair tinted that rich, lustrous cinnamon favored by modish Japanese. It enhances the blazed umber of Asian eyes. Her smile is worth gold, literally; among spotless teeth she sports a metallic one, a decorator touch, not unusual in northern Japan. Yukie has practiced *iai-dō* for only a year and already shows admirable suppleness and control. She manipulates her sword like Zorro. When not working as a "beauty planner" in her downtown cosmetics and hairstyling salon, called Silver Graces, she instructs Tai Chi classes. She also speaks some English, a rarity here. On first acquaintance she told me she'd studied Tai Chi in China with "a great teacher. Yes, he is very great. He is my master." Then she smiled. "Master only in Tai Chi, not in other ways," and we shared a moment's laughter.

Her demeanor shifts from earnest natural dignity to insouciance and sprightly charm. Though she looks a decade younger, Yukie is my age, married twenty years; she's mother of three teenagers. I bask in her attentiveness. Yukie encourages me in her faltering English. I interject my clumsy Japanese. We achieve rapport with impressive celerity. It helps when she underscores her points non-verbally, feathering her fingertips across my bare arm. She touches me often. She touches me, in fact, very often, particularly for a Japanese woman. Her hands feel cooled on my skin, alluring, faintly moistened. It helps when she underscores her points by leaning close to me, then closer; by laughing; by electrostatically charging the air between my body and her own; by provoking little stirs of erotic turbulence with her gaze. This I do not attempt to ignore. Tonight, as she guides my sword arm, she offers me instruction, half-whispering in English, "*Iai* is very much about...." She rummages for the word. "Concentration –?"

"Yes, concentration." I offer synonyms. "Focus. Awareness."

"Yes. Is very important. Iai, it is spiritual practice."

"Yes, I understand. *Hai, wakarimas.*"

Our blades make the air gasp. We glide in unison, women and men, cutting the empty space that surrounds us. Our swords, synchronized, hack downward on the bias. Halt. We balance steel tips athwart our knees then flip the blades in a single twirl, like drum majorettes with batons, before returning them to the scabbards. Mr. Sato approves.

"The sword is mind. Right-minded is right sword."

Yukie told me that.

SEVEN

KANEGASAKI PROSPERS near the mountainous tip of Japan's main island of Honshu, three hours north of Tokyo by bullet train. The town is one of many speckled along the plain of the Kitakami River between two volcanic ranges. The river, wide and rapid, its shallows traversed by cranes and kites and other riparian birds, swaths through miles of gridded rice fields and isolate groves of larch, red pine and cedar. Beyond Kanegasaki's rice fields lie apple orchards and, ascending toward the Komagatake range, virid cattle pastures reminiscent of Montana grasslands. The loftiest mountain peaks become snow-covered beginning in October.

Kanegasaki began life as a castle village. According to legend, Kyoto's impressive Kiyomizu Temple—propped above its mountain slope on wooden pillars—shared the same builder as Kanegasaki's castle, constructed in 801 CE. Eight centuries later, at the start of the Edo Period, Kanegasaki sustained a precarious existence as a border town, wedged between fiefdoms of rival warlords, the powers of Sendai to the south and Morioka to the north. The castle relied on defensive moats. Homes of royal retainers surrounded it, and cottages of fiercely disciplined samurai. Houses of latter-day samurai, from the nineteenth century, survive today in a neighborhood whose high, distinctive hedges enclose a maze of sharp-angled streets, designed to thwart intruders.

I live here. Through this slowly turning autumn of 1997 I am billeted with a Japanese family, the Tadas. Except for their twenty-eight-year-old daughter Yoko, who is rarely present, they speak no English. Each day they share with me repasts of fish, rice, *miso* soup, pickled vegetables, green tea. Their home occupies the river bluff, part of the original site of Kanegasaki

Castle. The *honmaru*, the main castle building, stood there. Immediately to the east lay riding fields. In centuries past, samurai captains, heads shaven to the topknots, fearsome in skirted armor of leather and steel, galloped their horses and swooped at each other with practice swords.

I'm walking a dike along the Kitakami. The river in its deeper channels moves like wet smoke. Birds convene at exposed shoals of white stones.

A few minutes ago an elderly man bicycled toward me.

"*Konnichiwa!*"

A cheerful torrent of Japanese ensued. I decrypted a few words, including "Amherst."

"*Hai*," I told him, "*Watashi-wa Amherst kara kimashita.*" Yes, I've come from Amherst.

Because I am the first foreigner to practice Zen meditation at Kanegasaki's Taiyō-ji Temple in four centuries, everything I do there, apparently, makes history. One morning I assume my stance near the temple bell and Watanabe whisks from beneath his robes a 35-mm Fuji camera. He snaps photos as if I'm a visiting head of state. Another morning he requests that we take turns seated on rice-straw mats, posing for the camera in changing configurations, rōshi and monk and rōshi's wife and the big American *gaijin*. Watanabe will preserve these photos, I'm amused to learn, in the temple's official archives.

Mondays before daybreak I half-roll from my bed in the Tadas' home. I shut off the kerosene space heater. Swaddled in sweatpants and denim jacket I slide open the garden door. A slap of cold air greets me. Thinning fog in Kanegasaki. Rumors of coming light.

I torque down Kariya on a bicycle, streets of the ancient samurai district freeze-framed at dawn. No one else is out. I cut through a dustlot playground, through hedges, downhill past bluish cedar woods and rice flats. I brake at the temple steps. Ravens begin to stir from rookeries along the Kitakami River.

I nod at a weathered stone Jizō statue, natty in its red bib and kerchief cap. In Japanese folk tradition Jizō serves as protector of children. Also of wayfarers. That's me.

Watanabe rōshi always chuckles when I arrive. Discarding shoes we ascend the bell tower. Till recently Taiyō-ji, built in the 1500s, stood as one of the grand old Zen temples dignifying these remote northern mountains. Then a few years ago it burned to its stone foundation. Lesson in impermanence. The modern replacement temple looks efficacious but lackluster. Its wonderful freestanding bell tower of planed and polished wood restores some of Taiyō-ji's former grandeur.

I've seen photos of Watanabe rōshi building it. Dressed in work robes of a monk the old fellow cut logs in a makeshift sawmill. He stacked lumber. He directed the construction crews, helping with grunt labor. When we stand in the belfry I can see Watanabe's conscientious devotion in every carefully mortised plank. When I sound the bell at sunrise—another, no doubt, of my inadvertently historic deeds—and its wakeup call reverberates through cemetery and temple grounds, my teacher Watanabe bows deeply in gasshō and begins gravely his prayer, as the Buddhist rituals prescribe, to redeem each frail and feeling thing that lives and dies: each insect, human, animal, fish or bird; every single one of us.

☽

A ZEN adage: "Every day is a good day."

Emperor Wu asked Bodhidharma, "What is the holy truth of Buddhism?"

Bodhidharma answered, "Completely full emptiness, no limits. And there's nothing holy about it."

"Our Buddha nature is there from the very beginning," said Ho-Shan. "The sun emerges from behind clouds. A mirror is wiped clean and restored to clarity."

The great Ch'an teacher Lin-Chi: "If you wish to understand the Way, do not be fooled by others. Inwardly, outwardly, destroy all obstacles—right now! If you meet the Buddha on the road, kill him. If you meet the Teacher, kill him. Don't delay. Kill every one of them, now. There is no other way. Don't let anything constrain you. Get past it, move beyond it—become free!"

"One glimpse of the true human being," said Ikkyū, "and we are in love."

Huang-Po said: "Here it is—right now. Start thinking about it and you miss it."

Hakuin: "Just let go."

Before traveling to Japan I bumped into an old acquaintance, a photojournalist, in Amherst.

"So," he asked, "what are you doing these days?"

"Well, I'm spending a lot of time on my Zen practice."

"Hey, that's great! Man, I ought to do something like that. I really need something to help me relax."

I could have apprised him of the old Zen saying: To sit on the zafu means sitting in flames. It means sitting alone, through a creeping half-hour, then another, in silence, the silence of fire.

It resembles the glassmaker's arduous craft. The self is coarse and opaque like sand. Through years of zazen, this self, this rough silica, heats to molten glow, then cools, heats, cools again, till finally it transforms. Till finally it becomes glass. Strong, flexible, shatterproof glass. People unfamiliar with Zen think the practice is meant to create tranquility. What it creates is transparency.

Zazen is not about relaxing or "chilling out." It's about remaining seated in flames, becoming glass; it's about becoming perfectly clear.

☽

MY SEARCH for the true home has led me here. Thousands of miles from Amherst. A lifetime away from Clinton County in the Appalachian Mountains of Pennsylvania.

Fifteen minutes past dawn.

I sit astride the zafu. The monk has struck the rin gong.

Silence.

Knees hurt.
Maybe if I shift like
   ("Thinking.")
Breathe. In hara.
Let go.

Silence.

Hope later I get
   ("Thinking.")
Resume the breath.

Monk beside me, full lotus, car noise outside? How much time until
we—
   ("Thinking.")
Resume the breath.
Silence.
Let go.

☽

DŌGEN: "YOU cannot tell how many layers of misty clouds this sitting
penetrates."

The most tenacious addiction is to the concept of "self." Nothing—
not whiskey, not heroin or nicotine, not the pheromones of sex—can
match the seductively alluring, habituating power of ego.

Think of Zen this way. It is rehab for ego addicts, for self-aholics. A
means for getting clean and sober. Or think of it this way: Zen is jail-
break, a method for busting free of the "me" obsession. Or think of it
this way: Zen accomplishes for each person who practices it a type of

Copernican revolution; each of us ceases to be the center of his or her individual cosmos.

Zen training also helps dispel attachment to the temporal illusion of "yesterday" or "tomorrow," an illusion tugging us so forcefully that we squander the only life endowed us: the life unfolding in this perishable, irrecoverable flicker of time, this miraculous split-second of breath and heartbeat.

Zen training snaps the cognitive abstractions. It shouts, "Look! A cup of tea is a cup of tea! Reality! Taste it!"

Zen training diminishes craving, the incessant yearning that makes us raddled and leaves us perpetually unfulfilled, nagged by desires. "I'd be happy if only I had a loving wife. Or a loving husband. I'd be happy if I could own a Porsche. If I lived in a garden penthouse. If I had a baby. If I could forgive my parents. If I could vacation on Maui this winter. If I lost fifteen pounds. If I could win the Powerball lottery." (Or the trap for Zen students: "I'd be happy if I could find enlightenment.")

Zen teaches delight. Delight in letting go of our thousand little velcro-hooks. Delight in letting go of each rich, ephemeral moment in this world of flux and ceaseless permutation.

Zen nourishes ethical life. In the *jukai* ceremony, students formally becoming Zen Buddhists vow to live by ten precepts. They vow to affirm life, and not to kill. They vow to be giving, and not to steal. They vow to honor the body, not misusing sexuality. They vow to manifest truth, and not to lie. They vow to proceed lucidly, not befogging the mind. They vow to see perfection in others. They vow to realize that self and other are one. They vow to be generous, and not to withhold. They vow to work for harmony. They vow to honor all creatures.

Zen training, if pursued doggedly, can produce human beings whose minds glow with natural sanity; empathetic people; people hospitable to life; unsinkable people who are not afraid. Clear, focused, alert, and balanced.

Buddhas.

Each time I prepare to sit zazen, plumping the zafu and bowing in gasshō, I tell myself, "I'm just sitting on this cushion awhile. No big deal."

No hope of attainment. No striving for anything at all—what's the point of striving? Why bother? The Zen maxim: "Just give up." Nothing to gain. Whatever we need, we already have.

This is not indifference. This is necessary surrender. This is the act of quitting the war, and starting the long walk home.

☽

WHITE SHELL, falcate: last night's moon.

Breathe.
Outside the temple, ravens squall at evergreens. Japanese word for cedar: *sugi*. Word for
     ("Thinking.")
Silence.
For moon: *tsuki*. *Tsuki*; Yukie, her smile; she
     ("Thinking.")

Last Saturday drumming I
     ("Thinking.")
Wonder if
     ("Thinking.")
Breathe.
Silence....

☽

BELL TOWER at Taiyō-ji. Cedars flecked by sunrise. Watanabe rōshi stands beside me. Frigid breeze. Ravens shout "chock-chock!" at the sun's aurora over Komagatake Mountains. Harvested rice fields. Pennants of wind-borne smoke. Cemetery, crowded obelisks of gravestones. We bow. Watanabe shuts his eyes. He drones a prayer-chant. I reach for the log, suspended from the tower ceiling in its roped harness. Pull back then ease it toward the bell's massive iron cone. First of eight strikes: Wake...

Up…. Wake…Up…. Ferruginous sound rolls through pines, rolls over Kanegasaki rooftops.

After sitting zazen I kneel on tatami mats behind Watanabe rōshi, as I do each week. He chants weighted, incantatory syllables of the *Hannya Shingyo*. His wife kneels beside me. The monk pounds his *miyadaiko*, the temple drum, evenly and emphatically as a bass drummer in a Rose Bowl parade. He vocalizes a descant. Vibrating back-of-the-larynx, with deep chest resonance, it blends with the drone of Watanabe rōshi to produce something that sounds like a robot dirge, like androids mourning their dead.

Grapefruit in a bowl. Between chrysanthemums, four tapers burn. Incongruous shiny damask, blue and ivory spattered with flecked gold, drapes the altar. Surmounting it is a tiny gilt statuette, Shakyamuni Buddha.

Incense softens morning chill. Sandalwood fragrance.

Mrs. Watanabe rises. She bows.

I follow, barefoot.

Each week, after prayer-chants and prostrations, after offering pinches of incense at the bronze, redolent bowl stationed on the altar, I join the monk and Watanabe rōshi in ritual breakfast, called *ōryōki*.

We sit on tatami mats at a low table. Watanabe, jocose and moon-faced, leads our chanting in Japanese then zestfully, without comment, gobbles from his bowl of steaming rice, chopsticks flashing. I imitate him. The monk dines intently at my left. When we're finished, Mrs. Watanabe kneels before each of us and refills our bowls.

When we complete the second serving of rice, when we've munched one of the two morsels of pickled *daikon* radish arranged on our white saucers, she fills our emptied rice bowls with scalding water. Into this water we each dunk our remaining sliver of pickle. Then we stir it with our chopsticks. This creates a meager broth, the sort of thing a starveling orphan might have prepared for breakfast in a besieged medieval town. The point, however, is not nourishment but simplicity. We slurp the broth. Watanabe rōshi sighs with satisfaction.

I've noticed the marmoreal smoothness of his hands; impossible to guess his age. He's probably in his sixties, but who knows? His face—its raggedy white eyebrows, mirthful eyes and reliably hearty smile—is smooth like a river-worn pebble.

The real lessons of Zen, it is said, are learned in the presence of a teacher. They are learned by observing how the teacher moves, how he or she acts. Because Watanabe speaks no English I have little choice but to watch him. He seems to live in quiet euphoria. This round, impish man, bald as an infant, bundled in his robes, appears remarkably at ease in the world. His psyche's scales seem balanced. He seems free of all the stormy emotional crap that has buffeted me, that has wasted so much of my life.

When we finish this morning's session Watanabe rōshi glides toward me. He bows and smiles. He looks intently into my eyes. He clasps my hands between his own. His gaze, if I'm reading it correctly, if I can trust it, conveys the purest, most disinterested love.

◯

I lay on my back on the living room couch, its cushions upholstered in gray chamois. It was near suppertime. The TV may have been on, perhaps Quick Draw McGraw or Woody Woodpecker cartoons. I lay with my right leg propped across the left knee, idly twining long decorative fringes of the sofa cushions between my fingers. It was a late afternoon in 1959, our home on Hill Street in Lock Haven, Pennsylvania. I was five.

I don't recall if my eyes were closed or staring at the ceiling. But I began to daydream. I slipped away from earth. I imagined myself floating past the moon, then farther and farther out among the stars—like in "Twinkle the Star," my favorite cartoon story in Children's Digest *magazine—and then I floated farther into blackness of space. As I imagined myself drifting among remote stars, through the outer galaxies, I began to think, "In this whole wide universe that God made, there's only one Steve Ruhl. That's me! I'm the only one! In all the years and years and years of time that'll ever exist forever and ever I'm the only Steve Ruhl that'll ever be alive! Me!"*

An epiphany. It sent my little mind reeling. I rolled off the couch and raced to the kitchen, where I found my mother busy at the ironing board. "Mommy!" *I yelled to her,* "I'm Steve Ruhl! I'm Steve Ruhl!"

The process dubbed "individuation" by developmental psychologists—the splitting of "I" from "Other"—had been occurring, obviously, since infancy. But that epiphany at age five revealed a startling *awareness* of the split, a moment of self-conscious estrangement, of penetrating, undeniable *knowing* that self is separate from the world. Then, it excited me. Now I recognize it as the fall from grace. A banishment from Eden. The triumph of ego.

Thirty-eight years later, a novice Zen practitioner, I'm trying to negate that epiphany.

I try to dissolve it every time I sit on the meditation cushion.

⊃

KANEGASAKI, A town sufficiently small for nearly everyone to share one of three surnames—Oikawa, Chiba, or Sato—and to know intimate, late-breaking developments in neighbors' lives without recourse to the local newspaper, is a sister city of Amherst, Massachusetts. I'm employed as Amherst's director of youth and adult programs for its Supplemental Education department. I've journeyed here officially to study Kanegasaki's innovative "lifelong learning" courses. Weekdays at eight in the morning I speedwalk through narrow streets, passing the windows of drab, tungsten-gray storefronts in Kanegasaki's three-hundred-year-old *chōnin*, or merchant, district. Beyond the fountain plaza of town hall I dodge left at a Shinto shrine with its red *torii*. Then I dash for my office at the Lifelong Learning Center. People often stare at me. Westerners remain curios here. "You may not realize it, Steva-*san*," Yoko has confided, "but you are famous in Kanegasaki."

By eight-thirty sharp on weekdays I'm deskbound with my coworkers, the dutiful Japanese salarymen and the uniformed female secretaries required to serve them tea and cookies twice daily. I review lecture notes. I memorize lists of Japanese verbs. I scribble paragraphs for my report. I fax colleagues in Amherst: "I'll bet you've often wondered what octopus tastes like when it's uncooked. With suckers attached. Having lunched on it, I can tell you it tastes like something B.F. Goodrich might manufacture...." At my desk I wear the obligatory tie and whiteshirt (the Japanese refer to any buttoned shirt with collar as a "whiteshirt." Some days I wear a blue whiteshirt; some days a whiteshirt of teaberry with a faint gray stripe; some days an actual white whiteshirt). Today, however, I mark Saturday in black Levis and a T-shirt. I'm at liberty to wander.

This scudding October afternoon. Deckled edge of cirrus cloud. *Susuki*—an elegant wild grass—seems to canter at the wind, its spikelets plumed like mustangs' tails. Horizon-hugging mountains. Ravens take lookout posts in river trees. They croak. They gargle at each other. Below them wave thickets of fantail leaves, striplings of bamboo. Stalks thin and jointed, it's a plant put together like a Tinkertoy. Red dragonflies with double wings like World War I biplanes are bouncing above the clover. I note this in my journal. I walk the dike in gleeful thanksgiving of solitude.

"If you can't find the truth right where you are, where else do you think you will find it?" Dōgen said that.

Dilatory ravens flap across the river, then settle—black and motionless as taxidermy—atop poles of gathered sheaves. In Kurosawa's film *Throne of Blood,* enemy soldiers disguise themselves in similar sheaves of rice when they steal through croplands to attack the *daimyo*'s castle. I smell a whiff of singed grain, smoke from the charred hectares of Kanegasaki fields. More ravens appear on stubbled earth, on green throw-rugs of grass, screeching and cawing. At the edge of the rice field, a Japanese guy in baseball cap and windbreaker arcs a golf club, practicing chip shots.

THE ANCIENT Ch'an teacher Nanquan took his name from Mount Nanquan in China, where he lived as abbot of a monastery. One day as he raked leaves a wandering monk approached him and asked, "How do I find Nanquan?" The master said, "I bought this rake for a bag of rice." The monk said, "I don't care about your rake; how do I find Nanquan?" The master said, "It feels good when I use it."

—

A monk asked, "Why did Bodhidharma come from the West?"
Chao-Chou replied, "The cypress tree in the yard."

These classic stories, retold over centuries and familiar to every practitioner, comprise an oral "literature" of Zen.

People who study Zen read Mahāyāna sutras, the closest approximation in Zen to "sacred texts," but we also keep a respectful distance. Zen distinguishes itself within Buddhism as "the transmission outside the scriptures"; disdaining written explanations, mocking intellectual pronouncements, Zen insists on being *lived*.

These hand-me-down stories of Zen masters and inquiring monks serve as historical record and pocketsize true-life parables. When I first encountered them I felt drawn to their refreshing quirkiness. Yet they also knocked me off-balance. I found them faintly annoying in their willful inscrutability, like weird jokes in a scarcely translatable tongue. Now that I've begun to understand somewhat, they afford pleasure and instruction:

Pai-Chang placed a large earthen water jug before his disciple Kuei-Shan. "If you can't call this a water jug," he demanded, "what do you call it?"
Kuei-shan kicked the water jug over, then walked away.

A group of traveling monks debated the famous question of whether it is the flag that moves or the wind that moves, and Huineng's equally famous statement: "It is mind that moves." The monks confessed their bafflement in trying to understand the story.

A woman named Miaoxin, an adept of Ch'an, overheard them. She told them, "Listen to me. The flag does not move. The wind does not move. The mind does not move." The monks realized at last.

◯

WE GATHER at a deserted one-room schoolhouse, in leafless autumn woods at the edge of a lake famous locally for its wild swans. A red Shinto *torii* guards the site.

We kick shoes off. From the schoolhouse door we pad in slippers to the rehearsal room, unheated this night in late October. It smells of varnish and mildew. Some nights a mouse steeplechases along the edge of a wall or leaps into a hole between floorboards. Big windows flank the room; tot-sized benches circle a low table. Five miles east of downtown Kanegasaki we meet—a dozen men and women—each Saturday evening and sometimes on Tuesdays. We gather to make these walls shake. We're drummers. Our instruments, lacquered handcrafted taikos with roped sides and studded leather heads, await us on wooden stands.

"*Konban wa!*" We nod when greeting one another. We warm up by improvising beats. White and red stripes on our drumsticks make it appear that we're banging out rhythms with peppermint candies. The drum master, a lean, quick-laughing Kanegasaki architect named Ikeita, hails me boisterously ("Steva-san!") and, lighting the first of many cigarettes, staccatos a bunch of Japanese phrases I can't grab quickly enough to understand. No matter. We're poised to begin.

"Poised" is the right word; choreography governs traditional Japanese drumming, and to begin we half-crouch in expectant power-stances, holding sticks in readiness against the drumheads. Our playing style is called *miyake*. When we perform in public as the Futsukamachi Drummers at an outdoor National Culture Day festival at Iwate Agricultural College, or an arts celebration at a district center, or a hotel party or huge wedding in nearby Morioka, we wear furled white headbands and dark blue tunic-like *haoris*.

Performing, our mission is to create noise and spectacle. The drums include mounted snare-sized *shimedaikos* and formidable cask-sized floor toms and the mighty Mother Drum, the *odaiko*, a scaffold-mounted behemoth that Ikeita wallops with sticks large as whiffle bats. The drums boom. They rumble and retort, the musical equivalent of field howitzers. While playing we bend and sway. We lift and lower our arms in unison like a Motown act. Ikeita, his shirt blotted with sweat, yells commands.

Crowds adore us. In performance, the group honors me by insisting I devise a two-minute solo spot, during which the other drummers kneel and I, the exotic gaijin, improvise a quasi-rock 'n' roll jam on three mounted Japanese barrel drums.

The origins of taiko go back thousands of years. I've seen those origins. At a weekend festival in Kanegasaki I've seen Deer Dancers, surreal drummers with antlers and tumultuous horsehair manes. Their shuffle-hops and potent, hypnotizing drum rhythms recalled Tewa Indian drumming and dancing I once witnessed during a sacred Corn Festival at a pueblo in New Mexico. The Japanese Deer Dancers looked pre-Shinto to me, and certainly shamanic, from an era when hunter tribes in Japan feared and emulated spirits of animals and prayed to those spirits in drum-language.

Much more recently, by 200 CE, Japanese farmers drummed in their rice fields to ensure fine harvests. By the twelfth century drumming had become integral to *dengaku*, the raucous street parades of dancers costumed as dragons and snorting fire-demons and lions. More sedate drumming was incorporated into the conventions of *Noh* drama and *Kabuki*. Drums, of course, are found in all Zen temples. Our drumming, and that of other taiko groups in Japan, crosses elementary but vigorous patterns of beats to create polyrhythms, relying on brute power and on a dynamic control that ranges from shushed tapping of sticks to thunder-blasting crescendo. This can produce shivers in each audience member, as if an ice pack has been applied directly to the spine.

Tonight we're practicing our opening piece. I have no problem with the drumming but tend to mess up the choreographies. Yukie, my attractive friend from iai-dō sword class, stands beside me. To our quiet and undiminishing astonishment Yukie and I have learned we share fascination not only with traditional Japanese sword ritual but with the spiritually transporting rites of Japanese drumming. Yukie always sets up her *shimedaiko* beside my own. She is a drummer of vast inherent gifts and she displays a growing mastery of the instrument. Watching her play it's obvious she teaches Tai Chi: she plants her feet resolutely to the floor, the way a taiko player should, so *qi* energy can flow from the earth through her body. She centers her movements in the hara. Her arms, which I know from experience can heft a sword with lethal precision, swing the drumsticks gracefully, economically. Her gaze remains level, alive and undistracted.

It was Yukie who chauffeured me to taiko practice tonight. Climbing into her car, I announced, "*Konban-wa; josha-no arigato gozaimasu; ogenki deska?*" Good evening; thank you for the ride; how are you?

She laughed and clapped and said in English, "Very good! Oh! You speak very good Japanese now!" Driving out of town past the gate of Taiyō-ji Zen Temple, past the rice fields, she said, "You have lived always in Amherst?"

"No, actually I was born in the state of Pennsylvania. In the Appalachian Mountains. For the past few years I've been wondering where home really is."

"In Japan maybe!"

"Maybe."

"Ah. I am from Japanese island of Kyushu. You know that island? Very far, um, south of here. When I was very little girl, outside my house? We have pond there, many beautiful fish. We were not allowed to swim there. But I would swim anyway. Yes. I was very determined little girl. I love to swim with so many fish, so many colors!" Yukie tuned her car's FM to a Morioka station playing songs from *The Sound of Music* and *West Side Story*. She told me, "Music, it is very—um—very important? To me? To my life? Yes. A very important thing." She explained with one hand steering the car, the other groping at words.

"Ah; so so so. *Hai, hai, hai. Wakarimas*, Yukie-san."

"The taiko drumming, I want to become very good player. Um—yes. It takes much concentration. It takes very much practice. When I was little girl, I did not think so? It was like Zen, it did not interest me. But now is very important, you know? Very important to me. And to you also, yes? May I ask, is it okay, what made you to have the interest in Zen?"

"Well, I felt a need to let go of attachments. To let go of obsessive desire. Do you know that word 'obsessive'? Like 'habit.'"

"Ah, yes. Habit."

"I was in a relationship with a woman in the United States, four years ago. Her name was Corinna." I hesitate, then proceed. "So much burning desire. We were each damaged persons when we entered the relationship. And we hurt each other even more. I see that now. She was in pain. So was I. So much misery. I was so clinging, so needy and so blind. It was like a craziness, wanting her and desiring her so much. Being so attached. The Zen practice has helped a lot."

"Yes, Zen can be very good help for that."

"Like a fish slipping out of the net. Isn't the Japanese word for that *todatsu*? Dōgen used that word to mean liberation, to mean freedom from attachment. Just like a fish escaping the net. Yukie-*san*, I was wondering, how often do you meditate?"

"Every morning I meditate. I center myself, I try to empty the mind. Yes? Some days, I do this better than others. But is important I think to do it, the meditation, every day."

"Yes, I agree. There is a Zen teacher in America, in California, a wonderful woman teacher named Joko Beck. She says that when people complain to her about how hard it is to sit zazen, she tells them the really hard thing is *not* to sit. The hard thing is to live a so-called 'normal' life of clinging and self-centeredness and suffering."

"Yes! That is very true!"

When drumming I try to siphon thoughts into the great encompassing Silence. I try to breathe unhindered. I try to permit drumming to flow from pectorals and biceps, try to allow drumming to feed from energy in my solar plexus.

Eleven years ago I pounded a Slingerland kit in an avant-pop band that included my punkette girlfriend Leslie Staub on electric guitar and another woman, Cheri Knight, on bass. (Cheri later graduated to the national scene, playing and recording for the pioneering alt-country band The Blood Oranges. In a brief but illustrious solo career, her acclaimed album "Northeast Kingdom" was produced by Steve Earle with backing vocals by Emmylou Harris.) We listened to Sonic Youth, Pere Ubu, Hüsker Dü, The Slits, X, The Replacements, The B-52s, Gang of Four, Throwing Muses, XTC, Salem 66, Talking Heads, The Ramones, and our fellow residents in the Amherst area, Dinosaur Jr. And of course James Brown. Our band Pocket Fishermen played in beer-puddled Northampton dance clubs for coked-out girls with chopped, peroxided hair, for black-leather art majors and emaciated scruff boys and musician pals from bands called the Malarians or Beat Therapy or Pie Fight. Leslie and I lived in a rowdy farmhouse that we shared with other punk and post-punk musicians, including John Bechdel, Bruce and Helen's oldest son and Alison's brother; a Hampshire College student and keyboards player, he eventually joined the legendary prog-metal bands Ministry and Prong. Leslie and Cheri and I practiced daily in a studio in the rear of the farmhouse. As a drummer seated among cymbals, snare, toms, and kickdrum I invented rhythms of feet and wrists, tossing raggedy triplets, syncopations and fills off the drumheads. But Japanese drumming is different.

I try to connect with qi energy flowing unreservedly from the earth, as Yukie does. I get distracted. Then I try to recall exact sequences of drum patterns. "Okay, eight-count, now switch, now—damn!" I lose my place or skip a beat.

Too much effort.

Interfering mind syndrome.

After taiko practice, approaching her car, Yukie exclaims, "Oh look! It is very beautiful!" She points to the night sky behind my shoulder. I turn to see the moon—tsuki in Japanese—emerging above the lake, a moon round and shining like the illumined head of the odaiko Mother Drum.

Dōgen: "Gaining enlightenment is like the moon reflecting in the water. The moon does not get wet, nor is the water disturbed."

The Kodō Drummers hone their lives to essentials. Performing they wear merely headbands and knotted, wraparound jockstraps. They're as muscle-cut as triathletes. They dwell communally on Sado Island, a gust-ridden sea outpost off Japan's western coast. They sustain themselves on two activities: drumming and running.

These guys once ran the entire twenty-six-mile Boston Marathon to warm up immediately before a drum concert. When Max Roach visited them on Sado, he departed on a hydrofoil for the mainland and when he looked back he discovered the Kodō Drummers swimming in the wake of the hydrofoil, shouting goodbyes. They seem almost trans-human.

Tonight, in a stylish auditorium in Morioka, I'm seated ten feet from the stage, in the second row; Yukie, in a tailored gray jacket and mini-skirt, sits directly across the aisle with her husband. They look happy and companionable. They and I and hundreds of people watch raptly as four men, led by an indomitable warrior of percussion named Yoshikazu Fujimoto, straddle their gleaming drums—big as oil barrels—and lean backward, grimacing, muscles carved and straining, arms outstretched beseechingly. They gulp air into their abdomens. Laser their concentration at the ceiling.

Then explode: volleys of concussive rhythm shaped with spectacular dexterity and control. They pummel the drums. They thrash the drums in loving, devotional frenzy.

Their arms, hands, sticks blur in flawless synchronization. More drummers take the stage.

These men pounce at the shimedaikos; their beating hands vanish in a high-velocity smudge of air, hands like wings of hummingbirds. The drummers begin to interstitch cross-rhythms. They rev the tempo, they meticulously construct a wild, tribalistic exultation. This controlled intensity does not stop. Even when they hush to diminuendo, a whisper of drumsticks, the intensity does not stop. They resume thundering and it builds for a quarter of an hour. The Kodo Drummers play beyond mortal endurance. When they've hurtled into silence, their opening number finished, they look as if someone has doused them with seltzer bottles.

They pause to acknowledge our roaring ovations. Then they leap into their next drumming feat, naked chests glistering with sweat. Yet these men seem barely winded. They shine joyous smiles. The night has just begun.

An interviewer once asked Fujimoto what he thinks while preparing to strike the odaiko. Fujimoto's reply: "Nothing. I think of nothing. I empty my mind."

Exactly like the Zen swordsmen. These drum warriors of Kodō bequeath *everything*, instant by instant, to the music. Each drummer's body a whirlwind around a mind of perfect stillness.

Watching their drumming, I realize: This is zazen. This is Olympic level, super-fueled, whole-body zazen.

EIGHT

HERE IN Kanegasaki I sometimes have the interesting experience of trying to explain Zen to the Japanese. At a formal banquet my boss, Mr. Inawashiro, a compact, chain-smoking man, bald, with a sly, gnomic face, queries me via our translator: "Why did you start the Zen sitting?" I mentally scan my list of reasons, deciding how to answer.

Because I needed emancipation.

Because I longed to become, finally, an authentic human being.

After a few seconds I choose to keep it simple. "I reached a point in my life where the old ways didn't work anymore. It was a dead end. I needed a new direction."

Because I wanted to flourish in every instant.

Back in Massachusetts, before I left to come here, friends remarked, "You're so calm now. So level-headed." Or: "You look great. You seem really contented. You're just glowing these days."

"Well, it's been hard-won. There's still a long way to go."

Because I thirsted for water iced and clear.

Mr. Inawashiro, whose stated ambition in life is to own a big house and swimming pool like those he saw during a visit to America, asks me through the translator, "What do you think about when you're doing zazen?"

"Well, actually … the purpose is not to think. I focus on breath—on breathing—" I struggle to convey this to the translator, who struggles to convey it to the puzzled Inawashiro, who is squinting at me through a cigarette haze.

I try again. "For most of us? In our daily lives? There is—in the mind much … um … chatter?" I point to my head.

"Hai. Hai."

"And when you sit zazen, you stop that chatter in the mind. You concentrate on breathing. And when the chatter stops, there is silence. And in that silence you can find … um … clarity. Greater clarity. Things become clearer."

"Ah! Hai. Hai."

Because I wanted to live beyond wanting.

Because I wanted to wake up.

Ultimately I started to sit zazen for the same reason Thoreau went to the woods: "Because I wished to live deliberately," he wrote, "to front only the essential facts of life, and see if I could not learn what it had to teach, and not, when I die, discover that I had not lived."

Hour of the white dragon.

Entering Kanegasaki's Zen temple, Taiyō-ji, I shed my boots and socks, then bow like a mendicant, with pressed hands.

Pale light of daybreak. White as facial powders derived from ordure of nightingales, so prized by geishas.

On Saturday mornings Taiyō-ji invites townspeople to participate in zazen. The monk and I find places in a seated row of nine elderly women and men. Each elder is carefully attired and deferential. My bare feet prickle with cold. I settle onto a zafu near closed wooden doors, their glass panels etched with designs of willow leaves.

I remember kneeling on the rice-straw floor at Eikando Temple in Kyoto. I sipped *matcha*, foaming green tea, from a black matte bowl.

Monk taps the *rin* gong.

My hands form the *mudrā*, cupped fingers, thumbs touching. I drift into breathing rhythm. Into the belly. Let the mind hush itself. Hush itself. Hush….

Shikantaza, "just sitting," the pulse of Sōtō Zen.

Words I found on rice paper, displayed on a wall at Daitoku-ji Zen

Temple in Kyoto: "Each day is training. Living each moment equal to anything—ready for anything—I am alive."

○

JUST SOUTH of here lies Bashō country.

Ten miles from Kanegasaki I'm standing before a bronze statue. The man's cloak, his skin, have patinaed to lustrous aquamarine. He leans on his pilgrim's staff. A sculptor has depicted the face of this Zen practitioner and poet as temperate but haggard, visited by the faintest insinuation of a smile—which, while pure speculation, is probably not inaccurate. Devotees have laid one-yen and five-yen coins in a metallic puddle at the statue's feet and, on the afternoon of my visit, a ripe persimmon.

"There is one thing which flows through all great art, and that is a mind to follow nature, and return to nature."

In March of 1689, at age forty-five—two years older than I am now—the Zen poet commemorated by the statue left his hut in Edo. He tramped hundreds of miles into these foreboding realms of the far north. In an age of feudal boundaries and rigid social stratification, he existed as that rare phenomenon: an irrepressibly free soul. Most people seldom wandered from their villages of birth. This man journeyed into unknown hinterlands across the mountains, lands believed by his fearful contemporaries to be inhabited by forest devils and half-savage peasant tribes. Today the bullet train from Tokyo arrives at this place in several hours. It took the Zen poet six weeks. He recorded the trek in his masterpiece, *The Narrow Road to the Deep North.*

It remains a captivating adventure tale. Replete with storms, potentially dangerous border guards, swollen rivers, eerie wilderness trails, and strangers who prove unexpectedly gracious, *The Narrow Road* remains also, across three centuries, a vivid human document of wistful longing, affection, pain, forbearance, and wisely moderated happiness. Best of all, it is liberally spiced with piquant haiku, some written by the man's fellow Zen practitioner and traveling companion, Sora; some written by the man himself, who had revolutionized the art form and become its greatest practitioner. The man, of course, was Bashō.

The northernmost point of Bashō's epic hike brought him close to Kanegasaki, before he decided to swing west and head for the ocean. He reached this Hiraizumi region in springtime and he sojourned here at the wooded hilltop of Chūson-ji Temple, a Tendai Buddhist sanctuary overlooking the Kitakami River valley.

After placing my coin at the statue's feet in homage, I climb Chūson-ji's "moon-viewing path," its gravel trail flanked by three-hundred-year-old cedars, living immensities. When Bashō climbed the same path he'd have glimpsed them as sprigs. I stand before the Konjikido, or Golden Hall, built in 1124 by Lord Kiyohira of the ruling Fujiwara clan. This hall reputedly inflamed the mercenary ardors of Marco Polo, who wrote in his *Tales of the Orient* of luxurious palaces in Zipang, layered with tiles of gold. The Konjikido certainly fits his description. The edifice—from its ornate eaves to its chamber of filigreed entablature and spangled columns—glimmers with gold-leaf and lacquer. Gold peacocks in bas relief dominate the central dais; inlaid with blue and white mother-of-pearl, four golden pillars frame a sarcophagus of gold, surmounted by golden statues of Kannon and Amida Buddha. It's Buddhist Baroque at its most ostentatious, far removed from Zen's austerity. I take notes for my book-in-progress but I do not linger.

When Bashō viewed the Golden Hall at Chūson-ji, exactly five hundred years had passed since the demise of the Fujiwara clan. The once imposing hall had languished in disrepair. In *The Narrow Road* he described how its doors had been bashed in by windstorms, how its pillars had flaked from snow and freezing weather. He appended a haiku in which he remarked upon the ravages suffered by the *hikari-do*, the Hall of Brilliant Lights.

"Every day is a journey," he wrote, "and the journey itself is home."

Bashō demonstrates to me the invigorating possibility of reconciling opposing disciplines of Zen-life and writing-life. At their source, the two share common nourishment in silence, in seclusion and patience and sharp, attentive observation. Both require devotion. Both require endurance. Both require openness to possibility. But in daily practice, how to keep the two from diverging? If Zen-life schools a person to let go of images, of discursive thoughts, of words and feelings as they drift to awareness, and writing-life schools a person to cling? If Zen-life relinquishes the transient and writing-life values its permanent recording? If Zen-life esteems a focused, balanced composure, and writing-life—at least that Western Romantic type inherited by Americans—esteems skewed angles, bright derangement of senses, the mind at rakish tilt? If Zen life instills emotional non-attachment and writing-life savors passion? If Zen-life eschews the self and writing-life decrees an examination of self in all its turbulent discomfiture and glory? If Zen-life seeks to diminish ego and writing-life bolsters ego, in fact requires stupendous, monstrous ego simply to enact its presumptuous rituals of declaiming private truths to the world?

Bashō proves that Zen-life and writing-life may indeed wed happily. It is one reason I laid a yen-coin in tribute at the foot of his statue. The other reason is that his poems delight me.

> *Furuike ya*
> *kawazu   tobikomu*
> *mizu no oto*

This may be the most renowned haiku in Japanese literature. Dozens of English versions exist. I've written a translation:

> ancient pond
> frog — leaps!
> watersplash

That leaping frog, that burst of motion within the poem, startled readers in the late 1600s. Until Bashō, haiku remained corseted by centuries of tightly binding conventions. Elaborate rules produced haiku written as a sedate parlor exercise, with standard allusions to spring snow, or plum blossoms, or the chirp (never the leaping!) of frogs. Bashō snapped the rules. He wrote with untoward exuberance, from immediate experience—a supremely Zen trait. He sketched incisively, in sparest syllables, his direct apprehension of a paulownia leaf, a squid seller's voice, a crow on a dead branch; sketched each incisively, then released it. He practiced, as scholars of Japanese literature have explained, the Zen principle of *muga*, an identification with the object so fervid, so intimate, that self becomes erased. Bashō put it this way: "Learn about a pine tree from a pine tree, and about a bamboo stalk from a bamboo stalk." His haiku crackle. He touches image to insight: sparks flash. He wrote haikus remarkable for their ability to convey a psychic atmosphere of lightness, of buoyancy, of equanimous non-attachment, that Zen-like quality known in Japanese as *karumi*.

The man inspires me. So does my favorite story about Bashō, recounted by D. T. Suzuki in *The Essentials of Zen Buddhism*. It explains the origin of his "leaping frog" haiku:

Bashō and his Zen teacher, Buccho, conversed outdoors.

"How are you getting along these days?" the teacher asked.

Bashō answered, "After a recent rain the moss has grown greener than ever."

"What Buddhism is there prior to the greenness of moss?"

"A frog jumps in the water," said Bashō, "hear the sound!"

つ

AS BASHŌ engaged in his own Zen of daily life, so I engage in mine. My friend Eishi takes me to Geibikei Gorge, where we drift a peaceable river between two-hundred-foot cliffs of limestone, the mid-autumn leafage starting to immolate in flares of orange and crimson. The man poling our flatboat sings tunes his ancestors undoubtedly knew. His tenor echoes through the river canyon. Another Saturday we rove a spot-lit cave, dim and moist as the inside of a rain barrel, murmurous with wings of bats. That night I join fellow taiko drummers for a karaoke revel at a Kanegasaki hotel. There amid hoisted beer seidels and shouts of "*Kanpai!*" I grab the mike for a killer solo rendition of "La Bamba." On a windy afternoon I harvest a rice field for a local farmer, Mr. Oikawa; chaff flying, I drive his racketing combine as it chews a hectare of grain into its three-tined maw.

And I help organize the town's first Halloween bash ("Steva-san," a puzzled coworker asks, "what is purpose of Halloween?").

Each experience affords an occasion to practice Zen's matter-of-fact, diurnal mindfulness. Performing tasks in Kanegasaki's Lifelong Learning Center, Monday through Friday, I use my office duties as a modern equivalent of Zen's "chop wood, carry water." But awareness seems easier, and more fun, on Saturdays and Sundays.

One weekend the Tadas, my host family, squire me into the far northern mountains to a hot-spring resort. We dress in yukata. We dine on iced shrimp plucked from the sea; miso soup; fluffed tempura so light it seems afloat in zero gravity; red slabs of sashimi; minced vegetables; dark, rich-foaming ale. Midway through dinner the ground flexes beneath us. It's a minor earthquake tremor, common in this land of busy geological activity.

Later we retire to the baths. In the men's white-tiled lavatorium I squat naked with the others, lather, scrub, hose to a wet sheen, then ease into the steaming pool. Every muscle seems to smile and whisper, "Yesss...." Opiate for the body. Then I sequester myself with two Japanese men in a sauna of fragrant cedar. We bask in head-numbing heat, dripping, eyes closed. The Saharan air of the sauna, miraculously pine-sweet, parches my nostrils. Cleansed and energized I rush outdoors to air that feels like snowpack. Plunging into a geothermal pool, neck-deep in water, I toss back my head to survey the night sky of Japan. Tiny wings, noctuid, flutter nearby; as I return my gaze skyward the moment incites a Zen poem. Later I write it down:

> Moth near white globe
> of lamp. Look up—
> first star beside the moon.

☽

"ALL THINGS, O priests, are on fire."

Monks sitting zazen. Hushed recesses of a temple. Summer morning in 1945. Birds chittering. Drone of an airplane.

"The eye, O priests, is on fire; forms are on fire; eye-consciousness is on fire; impressions received by the eye are on fire...."

Last breath of silence. Precarious equilibrium. In the temple: teetering universe of silence, poised on tip of silence before the sudden—

Buddhist temples stood at ground zero in Hiroshima. Cloistered for centuries behind white stucco walls in the boisterous Nakajima district, among banks, street-front markets, sake bars and shops, the temples offered oases of quiet and contemplation. Gardens of combed sand. Ponds of irises and goldfish. Monks in the Pure Land temples, the Tendai and Zen temples would have roused before dawn. By eight-fifteen on the morning of August sixth, those in the Zen temples would have completed formal ōryōki breakfast; some may have been raking leaves in courtyards or performing kitchen chores; most had probably resumed sitting on their zafus, in the breathing stillness of zazen. Beyond the walled temple compounds, unsuspecting people of Hiroshima jammed trolley cars, or settled by open windows at their office desks, or queued at vendors' stalls, or along the sunlit thoroughfares beside the Motoyasugawa River. Soldiers flagged trucks through checkpoints. Hundreds of school kids, mobilized to help demolish wooden buildings and widen streets through the city, huddled in work crews as the airplane poised on its tip of silence before the—

Monks in Buddhist temples vaporized instantly. Vanished in a sky wrenched open, a white noise of deafening light.

From the "Fire Sermon" of the Buddha: "The ear is on fire; sounds are on fire ... the nose is on fire; odors are on fire ... the tongue is on fire; tastes are on fire ... the body is on fire; things tangible are on fire—"

A light-flash not of satori; a light-flash of atoms cleaving apart. Enlightenment: hurling shockwave. Bone-melting furnace of exploding light.

"The mind is on fire; ideas are on fire ... mind-consciousness is on fire; impressions received by the mind are on fire—"

In Hiroshima I sit on a bench under maple trees, at the epicenter of the blast, and I look straight up into heaven. That sky is where the God of my childhood Sunday school lessons does not live. That sky is where the sun burst in cataclysmic bloom, unfolding its million lotus petals of thermonuclear fire.

Conspicuously American, I'm sitting in the Peace Park. I'm watching a few Japanese wives and husbands wheel baby strollers. Here where the city lay charred flat, some high school girls consult and giggle then disperse; a jogger passes; pigeons wagtail huffily and peck the sidewalk. Stale mud smell of the river. Traffic and city noises; distant "tongg" of the struck Peace Bell. Women workers sweep ginkgo leaves. A bum grabbles around a trash pail for cigarette butts. Heaped at the wrought iron fence lie tribute wreaths and garlands of folded paper cranes.

I had not originally planned to visit Hiroshima, more than seven hours south of Kanegasaki by bullet train. Then I understood I needed to come here. In 1982, when I joined nearly a million people in a historic march through streets of Manhattan in support of the Nuclear Weapons Freeze, an elderly Japanese woman from a busload of Hiroshima residents handed me a banner. It pictured the bomb-demolished shell of the city's Industrial Promotions Building. Now, seated on this bench, I watch ravens flocking it. This structure, renowned from postwar photographs, has been declared by the United Nations a World Cultural Heritage Site, enshrined forever as a memorial and emphatic warning to future generations. Every person in this building disintegrated in the heat-glare of the Doomsday Bomb. Hundreds of dazed survivors from surrounding neighborhoods, blinded, their skin barbecued, shrieking, ran or fell into the river just a few yards from where I'm sitting, and they drowned.

I watch the ravens. They're black as the black rain that sizzled over Hiroshima after the fireball dissipated. The birds roost at vacant windows of the rubbled brick edifice. They perch on the tortured steel armature of the dome. I have not fortified myself emotionally. Seeing this building has slammed me in the chest. It requires twenty minutes, perhaps longer, to recompose myself once the tears begin.

The unimaginable scope of human suffering.

It's astonishing to realize everything within the range of my vision—buildings, bridges, trees—obliterated in a mere quarter-second. People like these people ambling past me today, smiling, talking....

Later I visit the Atomic Bomb Museum, braving its exhibits. Torn, blood-smeared jackets of children. A cement wall bristling with glass shards hurricaned by the blast. A boy's fingernails that slid off his maimed hands before he died, preserved by his mother. Photos of the flattened city of ash. Photos of comatose victims gasping in hospitals, their bodies torched to carbon. A white wall drabbled by streaks of the radioactive black rain. It looks like an execution wall stained by blood of liquid tar, the blood of humanity's festering heart.... Broken wrist watches stopped at precisely 8:15, the moment when Hiroshima erupted as hell unto the earth.... A bicycle like the mangled skeleton of a prehistoric beast.... A section of a bank's front wall, seared permanently with a human shadow flash-printed by the bomb explosion when it turned the person's flesh to superheated mist.... A full-size tableau of a woman and two children stumbling in the aftermath of the fire-burst and shockwave; live cadavers of singed hair and melted skin plodding through darkness and smoke and pestilential rain, lava-flows of burning debris, the street a conflagration....

A shattered bell from a Buddhist temple.

"And with what are these on fire? ... With the fire of hatred, with the fire of ... death, sorrow, lamentation, misery, grief, and despair are they on fire."

NINE

UNREMITTING SPRING rain in the Catskills, first weekend of May in 1998.

Five o'clock in the morning. Rin gong, wooden clapper: commencement of dawn zazen. Eighty people, including students in gray cassocks and shaven-head monks in black robes, sit in a dark zendo vast as a midsize airliner. One lit candle marks the altar. Night has scarcely lifted from the lancet windows.

I kneel on my zafu, staring at planks of the oak floor. My sole task is to breathe. To watch it happen. I'm residing at Zen Mountain Monastery, a training center secluded in evergreens and hardwood forest at the foot of Tremper Mountain, ten miles west of Woodstock, New York. Two impetuous, boulder-leaping rivers, the Beaverkill and Esopus, border the monastery.

This Catskills terrain is part of the northern Appalachian Plateau. It resembles tangled Adirondack landscapes painted by Winslow Homer a century ago. Earlier during the night I woke in my bunk and heard the rivers' insouciant bucket-sloshing and their stone-rolling as rain continued soaking the pines. Now, in the zendo, I listen to breaths.

It's been five months since my return from Japan.

Arriving in the States, the first thing I observed: everyone goes around starring in his or her own private movie.

The second thing: impatience and surliness, the crabbed meanness of life here.

The third thing I noted—or understood, finally, with enhanced acuity—was how alien I've become in middle adulthood. By the standards of my countrymen I'm scarcely American at all. What matters to me is sitting on a cushion. What matters is a strenuous but invigorating task which has engaged people on the other side of the world for two-and-a-half millennia: the disclosure of authentic Being.

The irony is that when I undertake this odd "foreign" emprise, I become American in the best way, for the person who practices Zen embraces life, liberty, and the pursuit of genuine happiness.

Dharma poem I wrote at Eitoku-ji Temple:

So green,
cedar grove damp with rain.
Where is my life, really?

Two nights before I left Kanegasaki, Yukie invited me to her home. Japanese rarely extend such invitations to foreigners. I splashed there in late-November rain, a magnum of sake cradled in my arm. After dinner she snuggled on the floor beside me. We sat, legs tucked beneath us, at a low table. Her husband, a hipster who had played bass in a Tokyo rock band during his university days, sat across from us, unruffled, sipping wine. Their children finished homework, inking kanji in notebooks.

Yukie said, "Even though you are not Japanese, you do the *iaijutsu* with sword, you do the taiko drumming and the zazen. I think you could have connection here in past life. You understand? I feel that is true of you."

"I've always felt a strong connection to northern Japan."

"Ah. Yes."

She served peach tea in glazed earthenware cups. "I make these! Me!"

"You made these cups?"

"Yes!"

"They're great."

"Thank you." She smiled. Then she produced farewell gifts. She presented me with a handwritten list of aphorisms meant to elucidate our sword practice; she'd translated them painstakingly from Japanese. Her written English flowed with less assurance than her spoken English, but inadvertently she'd achieved beautiful effects: "His mind his mind, sympathetically be silence."

I lingered till nearly eleven. Then Yukie walked me home through the old samurai neighborhoods, past gardens and privacy hedges of unlit houses near the Kitakami River. She chose deserted alleys. Rain clouds had begun to evanesce. They revealed stars, shining in bright patterns I could not understand.

My last morning of zazen at Taiyo-ji Temple in Kanegasaki, the rōshi and the monk and I were joined by an elderly man named Onodera and his son, who spoke passable English. I'd rung the temple bell at sunrise. After a half-hour on the black zafu in seated meditation, after the Heart Sutra, the chants and drumming and incense at the altar, after our formal ōryōki breakfast, we chatted. The elderly man spoke to me as his son translated.

"Foreigners have come to Kanegasaki, but you are the very first one ever to sit zazen with us." He waited. Then he added, "It makes rōshi very happy. He says, 'Now our Buddhism can spread from here even to the corners of the world.' You can take it with you back to your home in America. Rōshi says you make good student."

I bowed. "*Arigato gozaimasu.*" Thank you.

(*My junior-senior high school in Mill Hall, Pennsylvania. I'm fourteen years old. I've scored in the top one percent on a standardized National Scholastic Achievement Test. A teacher takes me aside. Poking me in the chest. "Come here, hot stuff. You think you're pretty smart, don't you? Well, listen up, wise guy. You're no better than anyone else in this school. Got that, Ruhl? Look at me when I'm talking to you...."*)

Turning to the translator, I bowed again and said, "Please tell rōshi I am very grateful. Please tell him how grateful I am to have a real teacher."

For a moment I recalled my other real teacher, Bruce Bechdel, who long ago in that same Appalachian high school had introduced me to canonical Western culture, to history and mythos, splendors of Joyce and Eliot, quest for the Divine in celestial glories of Michelangelo, in the rose windows of Chartres.

Mentor for a vastly different form of education, Watanabe rōshi nodded and smiled. Chuckling, he handed me a gift for my departure: a four-foot temple scroll of linen in shades of ecru, gray, and brown, the midsection imprinted with convoluted stems and blossoms of chrysanthemums. On its gold-bordered central panel of white paper, rōshi had brushed his agile calligraphy and affixed his stamp. The younger man translated the calligraphy. "This is name of temple. Over here, this is name of Watanabe. And here, in middle, this says, 'When I hear the sound of the temple bell, it awakens in my heart the spirit of Zen.'"

Gradually light begins sponging into the zendo. Wind throws rain across the Catskills range of the Appalachian Plateau. Dawn meditation. Here at Zen Mountain Monastery robins wake and twitter, as if cranked on a toy machine. My mind abandons its fixity. It's speeding into action: "Twittering Machine," Paul Klee, Manhattan, the Museum of Modern Art exhibition years ago with my punk girlfriend Leslie, mental image of Klee's painting, its primitive and lucent divinity, its cartoon-like—
I catch myself. "Thinking." Return to silence.
Return to breath.

Franciscan monks quarried this monastery's bluestone granite from Tremper Mountain in the 1930s when they built the main structure as a Catholic retreat center. Near the door extends a Japanese Zen garden of furrowed sand and menhir, like gardens I saw in Kyoto. Still ensconced in a niche within the east façade of this Zen monastery is the Franciscans' huge statue of the risen Christ. Here traditions of Dōgen and Saint Francis of Assisi, spiritual pathfinders of the thirteenth century, meet at last.
Close by is rain-fogged Tremper Mountain, abode of red fox and bald eagle, black bear, whitetail deer. Tucked among the pines, jackleg cabins provide residence for monks or postulants.
My artist friend Jozan lived in one of those cabins for two years. He joined me for dinner last evening in the monastery's busy dining common. "This is an amazing place," he told me as we dug into curried rice, garden salad, slices of hearth-baked wheat bread. "It's so down-to-earth. But what takes place here is really profound."

In the monastery's dining room, while Jozan and I bantered at supper, nearly eighty *sangha* members elbowed the tables, eating, gabbing, drinking herbal tea: a cataract of happy voices.

Many live here for six months or a year. I felt bashful about inquiring, yet I'd like to know what leads people here. What gypsy digression or secret hungering? What impulse? What necessity? What irremeable vision? Eighty people; eighty stories. I know the tortuous route by which I came to this mountain, but what brought that Generation X guy with his shorn head and virginal beard, his subdued grin and aura of bright, protected solitude? What brought that woman of my own middle age, woman of lenitive smile, introspective, a woman defying, perhaps, her own fears in seeking transformation? What brought her? What brought that man, a Baby-Boomer like me, newly intenerated by life's harsh surprises, newly vulnerable at forty-five, reticent, ruffed with fatal gray? That searching man convinced at last that death will not exempt him? And that college girl, so assured in the luck of her youth? What brought them here? How do otherwise normal people make these choices?

In pastures of the world the sangha members work as lawyers, therapists, architects, veterinarians, artists, teachers. Here at the monastery they work on Zen's single-minded query: "What is this self? What is this world? This life? *What is this?*" People must put careers on hold to come here, must temporarily leave spouses, partners, children. They must leave friends, who probably think they've joined a weird cult. What motivates them to rise at four-thirty in the bitter-cold morning? To attempt the radical feat of sitting, hour upon hour upon merciless hour, emptying, watching, emptying, breathing, emptying, alone with others convened for similar purpose in the semi-darkness? Why do this?

(Months from now, when I phone the monastery to register for the intensive retreat called *sesshin*, a monk will grill me with similar questions. "Why do you want to do this? Sesshin is hard work. Why do this? Why not do something fun instead? Why not just go skiing for the weekend?" After I'm accepted for the retreat and I've hung up the phone I'll realize his questions serve as barrier gates, verbal equivalents of the doors at ancient monasteries. Pilgrims knocking on those doors heard a brusque shout from within: "Go away!" A test of the pilgrim's commitment.)

What impels these people to undertake an act so subversive? These pioneers, these sodbusters of the new American Zen? What makes them seek the wild Ox?

Pastures of the world:

On a wall of the dining commons hangs a sequence of ten vigorous brushed-ink sketches with allegorical verses, "The Ox-Herding Series." Over nine hundred years ago, about the time Normans crashed ashore on England, a Ch'an master in China adapted this series from a primordial Taoist text. "In the pastures of the world, I endlessly push aside tall grasses in search of the ox...." This opening line describes a novice Zen seeker's flustered attempts to stalk a wild ox—authentic Being, or Buddha Nature—unaware that the elusive quarry grazes nearby. "The Ox-Herding Series" functions as a "Pilgrim's Progress" of Zen, symbolizing the journey toward Clear Mind. The seeker struggles to lasso the ox, to pacify the rip-snorting bull and lead it home. The series ended originally with the ox and seeker vanished in *ensō*, the slap-brush ink of the Zero, the rounded void and fullness of realized Awareness. When Japanese monks got hold of the series, however, they extended it to a final frame entitled "In the World." Here the seeker—transformed by long effort into a jolly, serene adept, fat-bellied and bald—mingles inconspicuously with folks in the marketplace. No one recognizes him as anything special. Yet his presence makes the trees blossom.

Now, in the zendo as dawn sneaks in, I'm aware of rainlight. I'm aware of light resembling a drift of soft, liquescent soot. Aware of the rainsplashed eaves. Someone coughs. My mind starts to blather blather—

("Thinking.")

Let go. No big deal. Keep letting go.

"Simply to sit," Dōgen affirmed, "is enlightenment."

The monastery operates by ringing bells. When the abbot, John Daido Loori, sounds his handbell for *dokusan*, the private interviews, his formal students display their eagerness by stampeding to his door. This is an old Zen tradition. It seems like they're gate-crashing a concert. The rest of us continue sitting.

Moist intermittent breezes cool the zendo through open slits of arched windows. People are settling into deeper zazen now, our collective energy welling in the room, a shared pulsation, like organ cantatas played at inaudible frequencies—unheard but mysteriously *there*, vibrations felt in the body's every cell.

Inhale. This spiritual practice is based on something so fundamental, so simple: breath, the respiratory loop. Oxygen. Carbon dioxide. Oxygen. The rhythm of life. Exhale.

My mind focuses and grows still. I briefly enter that state where the body dissolves; a blur; quick blaze; presto: gone. Samadhi. "I" have become transparent. Nothing here but the wall, the floor, the quietness. A minute later my body returns, and with it the mind-chatter....

Let go. Let go....

At another bell we start *kinhin*, our barefoot walking meditation. We creep soundlessly as cutpurses. Then we stomp in a rush as if we're urban commuters, the floor quaking. Then we sit again. Silence.

Simone Weil wrote that prayer is attention. If this is so, then to live a Zen life is to live in constant prayer.

Extended sitting. More kinhin. An hour later we offer prostrations and thanksgiving to the ancestors. When we begin the liturgy our chant in New York's Catskills is identical to the chant Watanabe rōshi performed in Japan: "*Ma ka han nya ha ra mi ta shin gyo*...."

Liturgical service completed, Daido welcomes us. At almost seventy, he's an imposing man, brawny, head shaved cleanly as a pro wrestler's. Tattoos on his forearms attest to an earlier period as a sailor in the merchant marine. Years ago, before undertaking lengthy, exacting studies with Japanese rōshi Taizun Maezumi at the Zen Center of Los Angeles, he lived as a highly paid corporate research chemist. He's been a husband and father. He's also an accomplished photographer who studied with Minor White. Addressing the sangha this morning, seated on crossed legs, enfolded in *kesa* and robes, pate glinting in candlelight, Daido offers us a kōan:

"What is the Buddha's teaching of a lifetime?" a student asked a Ch'an master.

"He teaches for one."

"What if he has nothing to say?" the student asked.

"He teaches upside down."

I listen attentively.

The kōan makes no sense to me at all.

When I doze on my bunk later in the afternoon, napping before dinner, a clear, symbol-laden dream comes to me.

I'm driving my car. The land is flat, open, a seacoast.

The car veers at high speed on a snowy road.

Leaving the road my car skims over rocks. Moving fast it rises from the ground. The car soars off the promontory, into the air.

It flies above the ocean. I can see the waves below.

Then the car begins dropping toward those waves, where it soon will crash, and I will be killed—

The instant I snap awake I understand this dream.

Zen is a vehicle for the death of the self.

The word for "novice monk" in Japanese is *unsui*. It means "clouds and water."

People often assume that Zen monks who seclude themselves in monasteries wish to escape the world. Actually the opposite is true. People who piddle away their lives watching TV, or obsessing about cash, or glazing before computer screens, or tethering themselves to careers, or keeping themselves entertained—in other words, most Americans—these are the people evading the world. Zen monks secluded in monasteries engage the world directly, at its most elemental, most sparkling. Monks feast on reality.

Thomas Merton wrote that comparing Christianity and Zen is like comparing mathematics and tennis. Still, in explaining Zen monasticism to Westerners, it's useful to employ Judeo-Christian terminology. To move beyond mere knowledge, to return to innocence and original being, is to return to paradise. This is what monastic life is all about. To move beyond the punishing consequences of the fall from Grace—pain, humiliation, self-consciousness, exile, estrangement from God—is to return to Eden. This, to repeat, is what monastic life is about.

The next day we sit on zafus in the small Buddha Hall listening to a senior monastic, a woman known in the monastery by her dharma name,

Jimon. She instructs us on the relationship between Zen teacher and student. She's an elfin woman of commanding presence. We face her humbly, respectfully; this is Zen etiquette. But it's also a sort of tropism, like that of sunflowers turned to the Earth's star. We listen and watch. We watch her stark economy of gesture. No motion wasted. Lift of her palm. Her wrist. The haiku of her hand. And she, speaking, watches us: a gaze jaunty, regal, and clear. The gaze of a duchess; her domain, Inner Being.

In the years before shaving her head, before taking vows in the monastery's Mountains and Rivers Order, Jimon traveled through life as Joy Hintz, lead soloist and rehearsal director with the internationally feted Nikolais Dance Theatre.

Concluding her address to us, Jimon asks rhetorically, "Why did I become a Zen monastic?" She answers: "I became a monastic so that at the end of each day I could put my head on my pillow and say, 'I have no regrets.'"

☽

ONE YEAR later, 1999:

Storms passed through last night. Surf charges the bluffs.

Foam bursts a green hyaline wave-curl over sunken boulders.

I've come out before breakfast.

Herring gulls volplane the high slopes of wind.

I've walked from a Victorian castle. It's hidden on a wooded cliff surmounting a quarter-mile of rocky ocean beach and forty acres of wild sumac and cedars, just south of Gloucester, Massachusetts, on Cape Ann. The castle is site of a weekend retreat for painters and writers. I'll be revising manuscript drafts of my journeys in Japan. Now, though, I've found a path through blunted, wind-raveled pines to the ocean.

This is Eliot's seascape of "The Dry Salvages." The sea of many voices; of salt on the briar rose. "And right action is freedom / From past and future also."

Breakers luff and surge, explode against the headlands.

Although it's May the early morning air feels sharp. Fog is clearing.

Waves smash two cragged, speck-on-the-map islands, one a half-mile distant as the cormorant flies, the other a mile farther. Instantaneous white spume stacks up, collapsing, booming opposite the lee shores.

Is it the flag that moves? Is it the wind that moves?

"When we view the four directions from a boat on the ocean where no land is in sight, we see only a circle and nothing else. No other aspects are apparent," wrote Dōgen in "Genjōkōan," a fascicle of his masterwork *Shōbōgenzō*. "However, this ocean is neither round nor square, and its qualities are infinite in variety. It is like a palace. It is like a jewel. It just seems circular as far as our eyes can reach at the time. The ten thousand dharmas are likewise like this."

—It is the mind that moves.

I return to this beach at ebb tide. Withdrawing, the swash has exposed cobbles shagged in black kelp. Gulls are beachcombing. Gulls trill in quick descending notes.

Zazen by the ocean. Listen to waves; focus on the ocean's breathing.

Ever-changing. Next day: clouds rip apart before a freshening sky. Percussive under-thump, splash of breakers on granite shelf-rock. Moderate scend and chop to the sea today. Sunlight throws sparks across the waters. It looks as if the surface floats a thousand tinderboxes, myriad of flames striking simultaneously.

Closer to shore, water shifts colors: cobalt to gray, then glass-bottle green, then black. Lobster boats chug south between the islets. Stiff breeze. A wire-mesh trap has washed onto the stones, strung inside like a puzzle box.

Sitting zazen beside the Atlantic.
Breezes flow into deep hara of water, released.
Sea breathing.
Live and liquid body suspiring: *umi, iki o suru, umi….*

—

Day assuming clarity.

Past Dana Island another isle appears, then a lighthouse. More and more is revealed. Farther down the south beach, past blufftop estates and private coves toward Boston, thirty-foot waves geyser upon the tor. Moment by moment, out of the last remaining fogs, a peninsula takes shape to the north, near Gloucester. I descry now its oaks and its preened lawn, its seawall.

Three sailboats on the bay's horizon.

A monarch butterfly skims near my feet, returned from its winter migration to Mexico, a trillion wing-flaps away.

In Zen we say: Every day is a good day.

Vigil at the edge of the New World.

Out beyond these unruly waters of Massachusetts Bay courses the free Atlantic spun with foam, dangerous route of Christian pilgrims ravenous and holy. One hundred and fifty years after the pilgrims' *Mayflower* my paternal great-great-great-great-great-grandparents bound from Deutschland to Penn's Woods with their mute, frail sons accosted that treacherous maritime on a ship named the *Tyger*.

Tyger burning bright.

My maternal great-grandmother followed in the next century from Ireland.

Sitting, I breathe. Animus. Spiritus. Exhaling I imagine my breath carries past the Cape and the clouds' horizon. It carries eastward past four thousand miles of gusting ocean crazed with light, across the northern Iberian peninsula and the Pyrenees, and rounding the globe it crosses the humped peaks of Italy and then the Adriatic Sea, the Balkans and the Black Sea, the Caucasus Mountains and the Caspian. There my breath sails the trans-Ural steppes. It mixes with eastering blasts of wind across thousand-mile Asian deserts and plateaus to sweep down to the littoral of China, across the storied Pacific inlet traveled by Dōgen. Then my breath floats into the night-enclosed islands of Japan, where stars scatter now above the bell tower of Taiyō-ji Zen Temple in Kanegasaki.

Bashō wrote: "Every day is a journey, and the journey itself is home."

In silence I offer gratitude to my lineage. I offer appreciation to those who have brought me here. Thanks to my forebears: to Georg Friedrich Rühle and to the woman he married, Catherine Rühle, scything the summer's ripened grain, working fields of their Pennsylvania farm to murmurs of the brisk reaping blade.... To Elizabeth Ruhl, hushing her babies to sleep in the ragged moonglow and to her husband John, guiding his team of Percherons through the harrows, flinging seed in the promising dawns of April.... To Carrie Bryan, assaying a Celtic ballad at her keyboard.... To my ancestor Dōgen at Eihei-ji, the mountain temple enshrined in snow, writing by lantern: "When you paint spring, do not paint willows, plums, peaches, or apricots—just paint spring".... To my ancestor Ikkyū, practicing Zen by tracing his finger at the nape of a girl's neck, Zen of her shuddering pleasure.... Thanks to my ancestor Takuan, contemplating the Sword of No Mind in his *dojo* at Daitoku-ji, and thanks to all my unrecorded Ruhl ancestors, sowing their lives into the rondelay seasons of an Appalachian homestead, cycle of horses and harvest.... To Bashō, delighted by crickets in the mountains north of Edo.... To the Munsee clan of the Leni-Lenape, their drums a live, dazzling echo across the Susquehanna; and to my ancestor Huineng in ancient China, humble know-nothing genius in his frayed robes; and to my ancestor Lin-Chi at the Monastery Overlooking the Ford, I offer gratitude. To my mother and father, Gene and Jan Ruhl, for their unconditional love—serving as my model for the loving-kindness of *bodhisattvas*, for Avalokiteshvara, exemplar of compassion—I offer deepest gratitude.

In this mere flash of a lifetime one task demands completion: to wake up. In sesshin at Zen Mountain Monastery we've chanted in unison, "Life and death are of supreme importance. Time swiftly passes by, and opportunity is lost. Each of us should strive to awaken. Awaken. Take heed. Do not squander your life."

Letting go. My body is a lightly tied balloon, weightless with helium of joy.

—

Impermanence. Sea swell.

The slow attainment of a life beyond pain, beyond craving. Find the self to lose the self. Let go. Let go of everything.

Opening my eyes, I see the cliff of cedars, the herring gulls. Shoals of wet sand. A crescent-shaped—what is the word? A *tombolo*—extends out to Dana Island. It's not an island anymore at all.

In May of 1999, we approach the vernal season of a new century. At the cusp of forty-five years old I feel rejuvenated, a man in my prime, virile, brimming with that life-force called *ki* in Japanese.

Seven years have passed since my high school reunion in the Appalachian Mountains of Pennsylvania. My homeland of backwoods factory towns, of trouble and hurt, of truck farms, junk lots, neglected bridges of iron trestles. Pasture and greenwood. Homeland of skid-row country motels and cinder-block beer joints. Acres of sweet corn.

May Clinton County lie quiescent inside me. May that killer who has raged within me lie quelled forever.

Slap of whitecaps. Smell of crab rot. Smell of weed slime. Smell of pungent rock and tidal pools and wet, salted air.

Incoming lub and crash, backwash of sea flat-handing against the granite. Squeak of gulls.

Dōgen: "Now if a bird or fish tries to reach the limit of its elements before moving in it, this bird or this fish will not find its way or its place. Attaining this place, one's daily life is the realization of ultimate reality. Attaining this way, one's daily life is the realization of ultimate reality."

Ocean buddha. Rock buddha. Poison ivy buddha. Cedar buddha. Crab-shell buddha. Gull buddha. Wind buddha.

Let go.

How precious to simply be present. To be home.

I am only now beginning.

PART
THREE

ALL IS LOST,
BE OF GOOD CHEER:
ON THE DEATH OF
THE SELF

2003

◠

"A man goes far to find out what he is—
Death of the self in a long, tearless night,
All natural shapes blazing unnatural light."
   – Theodore Roethke, "In a Dark Time"

"It is an uneasy lot at best …
to be present at this great spectacle of life
and never to be liberated from a small, hungry shivering self."
   – George Eliot, *Middlemarch*

"The problem of death is posed most vividly in suicide.
Nowhere else is death so near. If we want to move towards
self-knowledge and the experience of reality, then an enquiry
into suicide becomes the first step."
   – James Hillman, *Suicide and the Soul*

"Few events in life are harder to talk about than suicide."
   – Helen Fitzgerald, *The Mourning Handbook*

TEN

MY SISTER was born on the day that Camus died.

On the day when France's premier existentialist philosopher and winner of the Nobel Prize for Literature died in a car crash—January 4, 1960—my sister Sherry arrived in this world.

Although he did not die by his own hand, Camus had examined the vexing problem of suicide. In *The Myth of Sisyphus* he wrote, "An act like this is prepared within the silence of the heart, as is a great work of art."

When my sister Sherry killed herself at the age of thirty-nine, she had never read Camus, but nonetheless she enacted the deed according to his specifications: in silent and cunning artistry, urged by ruthless inspiration.

"There is but one truly serious philosophical problem," Camus wrote, "and that is suicide. Judging whether life is or is not worth living amounts to answering the fundamental question of philosophy."

Sherry answered that fundamental question with an emphatic "No." She answered it by dying in a car, like Camus, but she died willfully, clamping a hose to the exhaust pipe, sealing the car with duct tape, then slipping into the gathering fumes of monoxide, into oblivion.

Joanne also said "No." A decade-and-a-half earlier, in 1982, my closest companion, my former girlfriend, said "No" in precisely the same manner: Joanne rigged a hose to her car's exhaust pipe, and as the bluish fogs gained toxic density she, too, murmured her final, resounding "No" to life.

I am here to seek the True Home by answering "Yes." Like Camus, who answered in the affirmative, I am here to say "Yes" without illusions, and with scant comfort, yet with a defiant and ferocious and authentic joy.

Zen teaches me to do this. In each moment is the fresh beginning. And so let us start:

Early June of a reluctant summer, breeze-swept and chilled. I'm walking land in upstate New York, a region of lolling hills and pasture, snug between Lake Erie and Lake Ontario. The Finger Lakes shine beyond hills immediately to the east. Seneca Indians, guardians of the Iroquois' "Western Gate," once roamed here.

I'm up in the high meadows before breakfast, savoring that stormlight beloved of Hudson River painters who scouted Catskill valleys two hundred miles to the southeast a century-and-a-half ago. Black cloud hazards a hilltop. It crests like a sea-surge. But here among the feral grasses and the flowers, the timothy, the chickweed and buttercups, among periwinkle at the edge of oak and hickory woods: a brilliant exuberance of sunlight. Maples, sun-blown, enact a frenzied alchemy, transmuting leaves to gold.

This land tops a hillock behind the Springwater Center for Meditative Inquiry, a retreat facility where I have come to dwell for half the summer of 2003. For the past decade I have practiced Zen. I have practiced in Japan, at Taiyo-ji Temple, on the northern plain of the Kitakami, where I became the first foreigner to sit zazen in the temple's four-hundred-year history. I've practiced as a devoted layperson in American Zen monasteries in New York and Pennsylvania. I'm now on summer break from Penn State University, where at the age of forty-eight I'm majoring in religious studies in the university's Honors College, focusing on Asian religions and Buddhism. I've arrived at Springwater on a quest. Supported by a writing grant from the Pennsylvania Council on the Arts, I'm here to sit and to breathe in silence. To write in my notebook. And to drift through these meadows.

In Zen we esteem perception of this living, fleeting instant:

At the pond, frogs high-dive and *plurp*! into mud shallows. Red-winged blackbirds scavenge the air. They rasp and trill. Mingled scents of grasses, of meadow blossom, scent of the windrow maples and the hickories.

This instant: butterfly named "tiger swallowtail." Like a Chou dynasty concubine's miniature paper fan, black and saffron, taken flight.

This instant: leaf blades of the aquatic plant named "sweetflag," upthrust in recent weeks from the pond water, each blade slick, each green, each in fact so piercingly green, so lithe, it seems a rapier honed from jade.

Life in abundance. My quest here at Springwater Meditation Center in the month ahead will involve probing "the Fundamental Matter," as we call it in Zen. The nature of life and the nature of death. "Grappling within the forest of brambles, Zen practitioners the world over probe the question of life and death," writes Daido rōshi of Zen Mountain Monastery, where I studied and trained and where I also lived briefly in the year following Sherry's suicide. Before the question of life and death is realized, Daido continues in his commentary, "it is like a ten-mile-high wall or a bottomless gorge."

This meadow and this pond where I am walking, although they surmount the local terrain, lie for me within Daido's bottomless gorge. My kōan, which I am here to ponder without compromise, without facile consolations, has become the kōan of suicide. Its baffling riddle. I wish to understand how people like Sherry and Joanne, in their trapped desolation, answer Camus' "fundamental question of philosophy" and Zen's "Fundamental Matter" by choosing to murder themselves.

I also wish to understand the choice of my friend Tom, the writer and self-proclaimed "desperado," who introduced me, years ago, to the novels of Márquez, and who later placed a rifle in his mouth and tugged the trigger. The choice of my friend Jim, the big "Pooh Bear," jovial and wry and erudite, who gashed his wrists and died kneeling over his bathtub in Pittsburgh. The choice of my friend Greg, the painter whose dangerous giftedness prompted lengthy paeans in the *New York Times* and whose work graces the collections of the Metropolitan Museum and of prestigious international galleries, and who hanged himself recently in his Amherst studio. I wish to understand also the choice Bruce Bechdel might have made in 1980 when he stepped into the path of an oncoming Sunbeam bread truck, its panels adorned with pictures of golden-tressed Little Miss Sunbeam—*une mort imbecile* worthy of a character in Camus, as his daughter Alison later noted in *Fun Home*.

These are the details of my kōan. But its essence lies, always, in the deeds of my sister Sherry and my lover Joanne: the paradox of choosing annihilation in the midst of the world's insistent presence, its teeming, inexhaustible richness.

My kōan also encompasses America's culture of suicide. Thirty thousand women and men and children kill themselves yearly in the United States. To visualize this, consider that every two years the number of people who snuff their own lives surpasses the total of names on the black granite wall of the Vietnam War Memorial.

While confronting the kōan of suicide I also have come to Springwater to celebrate imperatives of living, the ever-present vitality of this meadow: the pond cattails, the maples, the red-winged blackbirds in ceaseless darting flight, this freshening wind, this chickweed—so white, so fragile, now shaded, now dazzling in the tumult of light—and this promise of early morning and of summer. To answer in each instant, always perishing, always renewing, "yes" then "yes" then "yes."

At daybreak, an hour ago, I sat on my zafu cushion in Springwater's meditation room. I sat amid its white walls. Its windows open to the dew, to the lawn and tangled foliage of the garden, to the brightness of a scattering, windborne sun. Staring at the plank flooring I breathed with deliberation. Slowly. Practicing shikantaza—"just sitting"—I permitted each thought to drift. To vanish. Like steam from a tea-bowl in a Japanese *chadō* ceremony. Breathing, I imbibed *ki*, the life-force. Breathing, I becalmed my own inner stormlight. And, briefly, for successive moments, "I" disappeared: only the sound of crows. Of an airplane. Of bare feet paddering through the corridor near the kitchen. Then "I" returned: "Wonder what's for breakfast, want to stroll in the meadows later, need to phone Jenny tonight, have to get—" Then a disappearance again into silence. Into my breath. Into zazen.

After a Zen practitioner lucidly sees the question of life and death, Daido writes in his kōan commentary, "it is realized that from the beginning the obstructions have always been nothing but the self."

My mission: To attain primal joy, the clarity and fearlessness of undaunted jubilation, by dissolving gradually those obstructions of the ego. It may take years. But Zen adepts have shared this mission for twenty-five centuries, all the way back to the first Zen ancestor and beyond, back to the Indian sage known as "the Awakened One," the Buddha.

My healing mission: to perform what I now call the "controlled sui-cide" of Zen.

My healing mission: to kill my self.

To kill the small, petty, grasping self by allowing it to diminish, thereby opening to All That Is, which exists right here, always: our true home.

Thinking about suicide and Zen, I'm shaping an idea about the psy-chological relationship between these two forms of "ego death"—one pathological, catastrophic, the other numinous and liberating.

I've also come to Springwater to salve the remorse and loss inflicted by suicides of loved ones, to write about it so that readers might learn their own ways of healing.

"An act against the self, suicide is also a violent force in the lives of others," asserts Kay Redfield Jamison in her book *Night Falls Fast: Understanding Suicide.* "No one has ever found a way to heal the hearts or settle the minds of those left behind in its dreadful wake."

And yet a person may achieve the improbable. Twenty-one years after Joanne's suicide I feel that my heart has, defying the odds, stitched itself together. I feel that my mind has settled into composed acceptance of a disaster that, when it occurred, shattered me, seemed utterly beyond sur-viving. In 1982 I cured myself through grieving and seclusion. Through months of talking with a therapist in Amherst. Through confiding in the few friends who didn't desert me in the aftermath of Joanne's self-destruc-tion (a common occurrence after suicide; most people, too frightened, too weak or confused to discuss the horrific, will abandon a person who mourns a suicide victim, wishing it all simply would go away). I cured myself, too, by writing poems. Art serves as willowbark and feverfew and aloe—as natural medicine. I called the poems *Dead Lift* and published them.

But my sister's death....

...Sherry's sitting at a table, looking through a magazine. I place my hand on her shoulder. "I miss you sometimes, Sher." She will not look at me, but her eyes fill with tears. I kiss the top of her head. She turns the pages of the mag-azine, crying. I don't know if she cries because she feels hurt and angry with

me, or because she regrets having killed herself and leaving us. I am close to
tears myself. "I wish I could have been—" and here I begin to half-awaken
from the dream, into dismal blackness of my room, into reality, and as I
awaken fully I hear myself mumble, "—a better brother." It is three-thirty
in the morning and I cannot sleep after that. I lie in bed, exhausted, my
head banging with pain.

My sister's death remains uniquely threatening. Right now I can't look
at her photograph without flinching. Four years after Sherry's suicide I
have yet to venture fully into the perilous terrain of bereavement. I know
that to heal I need to go there.

Through human history the desert has been a place to seek illuminating
fire, the face of God, a blazing wisdom. But the desert needn't be a physical space; it needn't be sky and dunes. The desert may be a person's inner
wasteland. To wander that broken and barren place can lead to revelation.

I've avoided the harshest reaches of my desert. I've delayed my deepest mourning. In the months of anguish immediately following Sherry's
death I did cry sometimes and I did reminisce, painfully, but I owed
an urgent duty to my parents. I needed to guide my dazed father and
mother, emotionally scathed, through a calamity beyond our reckoning.
I succeeded. They're recovering as well as can be expected. But I've postponed the worst of my own grief—and its desert wastes feel endless. I
can't even discern a horizon. But by thinking about suicide, by reviving
memories of Joanne after two decades, I hope to begin thinking about
Sherry (writing these words, "thinking about Sherry," my breath falters,
an inner gasp of alarm) and I hope to journey, at last, more deeply into
the land of grieving. To write about it. To sketch a map, finding a rough
trail in and a trail out.

"Suicide is awful beyond expression for those who have to spend their
lives with its reality," Jamison writes in a later chapter of *Night Falls Fast*.
"Those who are left behind in the wake of suicide are left to deal with
the guilt and anger, to sift the good memories from the bad, and to try
to understand an inexplicable act.... Suicide is a death like no other, and
those who are left behind to struggle with it must confront a pain like no

other. They are left with the shock and the unending 'what ifs'…. Death by suicide is not a gentle deathbed gathering: it rips apart lives and beliefs, and it sets its survivors on a prolonged and devastating journey."

A journey I make alone. Soon after Sherry's funeral, friends—undoubtedly nervous or abashed, for suicide remains a taboo subject in our society, too shameful for conversation—ceased asking about her, ceased to ask how I was coping. Again, a common occurrence.

"How do people survive such impassable grief and rage?" Jamison writes. "How do they keep from being so destroyed by guilt and sorrow that they sacrifice the remainder of their own lives for the one lost earlier to suicide?"

This time, I'm doing it with a precious tool I lacked after Joanne died. I'm surviving through Zen. Not only surviving but flourishing. As I begin to approach my grief, as I begin to allow the pain of Sherry's suicide to penetrate and as I begin to mourn my sister's absence, as I begin to enter that parched, trackless land, I know I can feel sorrow yet maintain stamina and even a measured bliss—no less authentic for being rooted in travail. Zen trains me for this.

To summarize the process I've created a Zen motto for myself.

It occurred to me when I awoke one morning. I jotted it on a notebook page. I repeat it daily. It reminds me of everything I need to know on this journey, or on any journey:

"All is lost. Be of good cheer."

○

WE KNOW about the life force. Indian yogis call it *prana*, the inspiriting breath. Chinese Confucians and Daoists name it qi, meaning "breath, air, vapor," a vital cosmic energy rippling throughout the universe; in a human being, qi surges through the bodymind's meridians. The Confucian sages Mencius and Wang Chong, in particular, emphasized qi's importance and advised carefully nurturing it. The Japanese refer to this life force as ki. In the West, Freud described a "life instinct" and named it "Eros." Jung spoke of "instinctual energy" and borrowed the Freudian term "libido."

Poets describe it more lyrically; Dylan Thomas called it "the force that through the green fuse drives the flower."

But perhaps, as Thomas realized in the same poem, humans also harbor death energy. Thanatos. The pull to extinction. The yearning for annihilation.

Freud, in his daringly speculative monograph "Beyond the Pleasure Principle," published in 1920, writes for the first time of this "death instinct." Groping toward a new understanding of the psyche, he suggests that Eros—with its drives of sex and self-preservation, the biological urgings of life toward unity and complexity—grapples perpetually with an instinct of destruction.

This death instinct, he proposes, may have originated eons ago, in that hour of startling Mystery when inert matter somehow sparked to life, when random chemicals and strands of protein awash in the Earth's primordial seas, zapped by electrical charges, somehow began to flicker, to move, to respond. (Freud puts it more dryly: "The attributes of life were at some time evoked in inanimate matter by the action of a force of whose nature we can form no conception.") However the magic occurred, lifeless clumps of stuff did transform into wriggling organisms. Yet life, Freud says, always seeks return to earlier states. Nature conserves. Thus each time that a batch of insensate carbons changed into a squirmy, living protoplasm it may have caused a tension within the new organism, a tension that only could be "canceled," Freud suggests, "by return to the inanimate state." This urge to resume an earlier quiescence—this urge, in fact, to die—created the death instinct.

Freud initially felt uncomfortable with the notion of a death instinct. He returned to it again, however, in *The Ego and the Id*, the monumental summary of his work published in 1923. By the time he published *Civilization and Its Discontents* in 1930, Hitler's right-wing thugs had gained power in Germany and expanded their lethal influence in Austria, and for Freud these profoundly disturbing situations lent urgent credence to his theory that humans could enslave themselves to the power of a death wish. "The meaning of the evolution of civilization is no longer obscure to us," he declared. "It must present the struggle between Eros and Death, between the instinct of life and the instinct of destruction."

To most of us today—aside from his proponents in the Lacanian camp—much of Freud's revolutionary work seems quaint or wrong-headed or even silly, and it certainly appears sexist. Yet some of his insights retain, more than seventy years after their introduction, their original freshness, audacity, and luster. His theory of the death instinct, still controversial, may qualify as one of those valuable insights.

Curiously, in writing about the death instinct Freud says little of suicide. But when he does he's forceful and intriguing. He suggests that the super-ego—the psyche's guardian of morality, its voice of conscience—may internalize the death instinct, with terrifying results. (Jung believed the anima or animus, if unchecked, might perform this same murderous function.) Writing of suicide, Freud notes, in *The Ego and the Id*, that when a person tumbles into the abyss of melancholia the super-ego "rages against the ego with merciless violence....What is now holding sway in the super-ego is, as it were, a pure culture of the death instinct, and in fact it often enough succeeds in driving the ego into death" through suicide. How? Through relentless harangue. It shrieks at the ego: You're bad, you're stupid, you're ugly, you're worthless, you don't deserve to live. Withering under this barrage from the super-ego, the ego complies. It obeys the command to die.

In his classic book *The Savage God: A Study of Suicide*, A. Alvarez quotes this Freudian passage. He adds darkly, "The death instinct is a moving bass against which all the restless intricacies of desire are patterned."

Here at Springwater as I walk in the high meadows I ponder this "moving bass," this resonant, morbid thrumming of the death instinct.

Freud contended that sublimating Eros—channeling its raw, lusty energies in constructive acts, creating cities, devising art—builds civilizations. But he said little about sublimating the death instinct. Perhaps he saw no means available for leashing this inner blood-slurping thing of fangs and claws, this hidden beast of mayhem.

The brute power of the death instinct horrifies most people. They shun it. They consign it to what Jung called the Shadow, that realm of everything we banish from consciousness and repress. Ignored, the death instinct rises in their nightmares from the moonless dark. It taunts them.

The more they try to hide it, the more powerfully it sneaks out in fantasies of gore, in phobias, in orgiastic violence.

But what if Thanatos can be sublimated, like Eros, to ensure civilization? In fact, what if channeling death-energy is as crucially important as channeling life-energy? Not only for civilization, but for each person? What if each of us, to achieve sanity and wellbeing, to find psychic completeness, must do more than seek healthy release for Eros, for our radiant sex-energy, our vivacity, our shining life-force? What if we also must find a safe outlet for the death instinct?

In my experience, zazen provides this.

Here is my own theory: Offering a method for reaching stillness, for quieting the self, zazen sublimates the psyche's desire for oblivion. It redirects a natural craving for "return to the inanimate state." Zazen and other Buddhist meditation practices transform the death instinct into something benign—they urge its vast, wild energies not toward annihilation, but toward the goal of spiritual freedom.

As art sublimates Eros, so zazen sublimates Thanatos.

In Zen we describe the emancipating "dropping away" of the small self as "the Great Death." This death of the little "me," with its inane chatter and obsessions, reveals the sublime Original Nature—the Buddha in each of us that opens to "everything in the ten thousand directions," to the whirling infinitude of quarks and nebulae, the staggeringly inexhaustible splendor of the cosmos.

The Great Death allows new life. Not only Buddhists recognize this, of course; Saint Francis of Assisi declares that for the soul to know the virtues, the ego must die. The modern Christian mystic Simone Weil writes of this dying as the need for "renouncing everything that goes to make up our ego, without any exception." Trappist monk Thomas Merton speaks of the Great Death as a passage through the "dark night of the soul," an ordeal described eloquently by St. John of the Cross. Merton writes, "There must be a 'death' of…ego-identity or self-consciousness." For Christians, this "dying" of ego awakens the soul to its new life on earth, a life reborn in "the Risen and Deathless Christ in Whom all are fulfilled in One."

Islamic Sufi mystics, such as the poet Rūmī, call the dying of ego *fanā'* and seek it in union with Allah, the Divine Beloved.

Emily Dickinson alludes to something similar:

> A Death blow is a Life blow to Some
> Who till they died, did not alive become—
> Who had they lived—had died but when
> They died, Vitality begun—

We seek this in Zen. "A death-dealing blow to the I is at the same time a life-giving action," avers Zen teacher Philip Kapleau in his book *The Zen of Living and Dying: A Practical and Spiritual Guide.* "To die the Great Death is to transcend life and death and achieve utter freedom. It makes the prospect of physical death secondary and unimportant. Zen master Bunan put it this way: 'Die while alive / And be thoroughly dead. / Then do what you will, / All is good.'"

I propose that, by safely harnessing the energies of Thanatos to accomplish the "self-murder" of the Great Death—to accomplish a mystical suicide—zazen ultimately serves Eros.

It pushes the death instinct toward Enlightenment. The mystical suicide of zazen pushes brilliantly toward life.

When self is gone....

Here is a kōan: A monk asked ninth-century Ch'an teacher Ts'ao-shan, "What are you going to do about yourself?"

The teacher said, "Who can do anything about me?"

"Why don't you kill yourself?" the monk asked.

"No place to lay hold of," the teacher said.

Mid-afternoon I return to the high meadows. This instant: blue skies, fair-weather puffs of cumulus. If you drew a comic strip of a Zen teacher in deep meditative samadhi, if you drew wordless thought-balloons above the teacher's head, they'd look exactly like these clouds: blank and pristine.

Crows report to each other from hickory boughs. At the pond, life-force in abundance: minnows, waterbugs, tadpoles, bullfrogs. The frogs grumble, then make a sound like a twanged bass-string. The tadpoles, bulbous dark torpedoes, flick tails to rudder themselves through submerged cress and algae. Minnows scatter through the pond. Waterbugs, black-carapaced, zip like manic sun sparks, like photons in scanners, leaving traceries, whirls of light, in dazzled concentrics and ellipses as they dart the surface.

At depth, pond water is the color of orange pekoe. A snapping turtle's head periscopes up. Whining of flies. Frogs again: high-pitched tabla, then a slap and quick descending tone.

This instant: an amazing dragonfly appears, as blue as Grace Kelly's eyes.

This instant: smells of pond water and tepid muck, of wildflowers, fields rife with timothy, smell of sweetfern and may apple at the forest's edge.

This instant: commotion that sounds like a skeleton buck-dancing on hollow logs: woodpecker.

This instant: the blue dragonfly perches on my bare knee, live artifact from the Cretaceous. Fascination of the utterly non-human: its tiny onyx of head; the bulged, twin oculae of intricate, silvered, multiple lenses; its hinged bracket of mandible; the ways its odd jaw and that bead of a head pivot and move, so foreign to my own. Yet we share life, share molecules—my knee and this dragonfly's wing of isinglass, no separation.

Fzzp! It's gone.

Aboriginal people in Australia speak of *wangarr*, the ghost image of someone. They speak of *mangi*, both the spirit and physical trace of a person, discernible after he or she has left a camp, a fire circle. For a moment when the dragonfly whirrs away and vanishes I think I see its after-image, its wangarr, and feel the hovering buzz of its mangi—in the same way that I feel memories of the dead, of those who've ended their lives and departed this world.

Out there, beyond the pond and the high meadows and the hills, lies what most people call "civilization."

The manic American version: a wired-televised-downloaded-24/7-postindustrial phantasmagoria of dotcoms and designer drugs and school shootings and junk food and toxic sludge and Weapons of Mass Destruction and virtual reality and trophy homes and S.U.V.s and shopping malls and cell phones and insatiable money lust and pervasive, angry, blank despair.

According to Hindu sages we now dwell in the *Kali Yuga*, a hell-realm of rampant materialism and avarice, warfare, spiritual blindness and delusion. At the start of the twenty-first century our "civilization"—in truth, our technological barbarity—endangers much of life on earth.

This is suicidal.

How long can such barbarism prevail? An astute observer may note that, in fact, it is ending now, in these chaotic decades of our increasingly anxious lives. The age of technological barbarity has been ending, year by year, at first slowly and then with accelerating speed, almost since it began two centuries ago at the dawn of the Industrial Revolution, when Blake decried the "dark satanic mills." It has been ending steadily and irrevocably since its inception because it is driven by greed—a force that eats itself alive—and because it is predicated on vast consumption and unsustainability, on waste and exhaustion.

Indeed we can sense it wearing out, faster and faster, all around us— the sensation registers as apocalyptic dread, that queasy restiveness people feel when they allow themselves to contemplate an unconsoling future. One important question: As the system continues to collapse, how much will it destroy in the process?

As so-called "developing societies" from Uruguay to Uzbekistan, from Chile to China, rush to emulate Western technological barbarity by erecting poison-spewing mega-factories and power grids and by bulldozing forests, how many creatures will perish? Currently we are erasing, yearly, thousands of species of fish, of green plants and lizards, songbirds and mammals, many of them in remote locales. They are cousins of ours in the grand cosmos. Each is irreplaceable.

This is suicidal.

This is the death instinct run amok.

We can speculate on which threat poses the gravest peril to human societies. Is it the dwindling supply of fresh clean water in many regions of the world, leaving millions parched for the essential liquid of life? Is it the quickening conversion of our planet into a smoldering hotbox of droughts, killer storms, malarial plagues and melting ice caps? Is it the risk of thermonuclear combat, now in abeyance but ever capable of resurgence? Is it the grim possibility that genetically tinkered super-microbes, engineered by corporate researchers playing "Sorcerer's Apprentice" with natural forces they dimly fathom and barely control, may accidentally escape the lab to annihilate entire populations lacking any immunity whatsoever? Or is the most dire threat barbarity itself?

A civilization worthy of the name would avoid these suicidal hazards. A civilization worthy of the name would not kill itself. It would provide wondrous technological marvels while ensuring, as indigenous Americans such as the Iroquois who inhabited this land always have urged, that the Earth remains safe and in good stewardship for the next seven generations. A civilization worthy of the name would honor what Buddhists long have called the great web of being, the immense, interrelated network of cities and wild savannas, of winds and farmlands and oceans, of starlight, of people and trees and all sentient creatures—the network of atoms and whirling galaxies linked in dynamic, ever-shifting, vast and inextricable harmonies.

We have the information we need. We have the knowledge we need. What we lack, fatally, is wisdom.

So why live? In *The Myth of Sisyphus* Camus argues that people sleep-walk every day through a mechanical repetition of job-and-meals-and-sleeping, until perhaps for one person the question "Why?" occurs, and he or she momentarily awakens. That moment of "weariness tinged with amazement," when "the chain of daily gestures is broken," strips the mind of illusions—about God, about everything—and in that moment a person feels a stranger in an alien world. A person feels "nostalgia" for lost unity, Camus asserts, feels a longing for coherence. The disjunction between this nostalgia—this "wild longing for clarity in the human heart"—and the reality of a random, senseless universe produces the existential state Camus calls "absurdity."

Awakening to absurdity can lead either to suicide or to recovery. When suicide occurs, it results from the despair of seeing, irrevocably, the meaninglessness of such a life, from experiencing the "divorce" between actor and setting, between self and world. All healthy persons "having thought of their own suicide, it can be seen, without further explanation, that there is a direct connection between this feeling" of absurdity, says Camus, "and the longing for death." But recovery—that is another matter entirely.

Writing in 1940 "amid the French and European disaster," Camus wanders through the rubble of a Western civilization smashed by war, its God vanished, and relies on Western rationalism to find a way out. Nothing avails him. Dispensing first with Socrates ("Know thyself" means nothing, he discovers) and then with Plato, he leaps to moderns—Jaspers and Heidegger, Kierkegaard and Chestou, the phenomenology of Husserl—and finds each limited and flawed. Reaching the distant frontiers of Western philosophy Camus now "stands face to face with the irrational."

In this painful confrontation between "the unreasonable silence of the world" and the human need for happiness and understanding, Camus experiences the absurd. Standing in this confrontation he now asks the "fundamental question" of philosophy. Does a person choose suicide? Or choose life?

"It is essential to know whether one can live" in that state of the absurd, in a universe meaningless and chaotic, he writes, or whether "logic commands one to die of it."

Camus boldly chooses life. He chooses revolt. Suicide is not revolt, he proclaims, it is repudiation—and we must affirm, heroically. *The Myth of Sisyphus* becomes an exhilarating call to insurrection. Revolt! Stand alone to confront a world without order or purpose, do it intrepidly, passionately, and with no illusions. This "restores … majesty" to life. Live without hope, without faith in the future—and live jubilantly. Live, always, with the absurd, with the tension between your aching need for wholeness and your aching awareness of its eternal absence. Do that, Camus says, and discover the hard, clear joy of a defiant life, waged "without appeal," in a universe where "nothing is possible but everything is given."

"To be aware of one's life, one's revolt, one's freedom"—herein lies victory. To do this "to the maximum, is living." The person who commits suicide has quit in desperation, but Camus, an existential hero, stands resolutely in a cold wind and savors every minute of living. "I transform into a rule of life what was an invitation to death—and I refuse suicide.

"The point," he concludes, "is to live."

When Camus urges us to live—to rejoice in the emotional turbulence of existence, to stay with it, to not run away, to face the contradictions and discomforts—he sounds like Zen teachers who urge us to do the same, on the zafu and in our daily lives. When Camus rejects the lure of the death instinct and its temptations to suicide, when he seeks "maximum living": it's pure Zen.

Nearing the end of *The Myth of Sisyphus* Camus writes, "If the descent is thus sometimes performed in sorrow, it can also take place in joy. The word is not too much."

Camus remembers Oedipus, blinded, bereft, tricked by fate, tainted by unspeakable crimes, and remembers too the old man's astonishing declaration: "Despite so many ordeals, my advanced age and the nobility of my soul make me conclude all is well."

Despite so many ordeals, all is well. It could serve as a Zen maxim. "That remark is sacred," Camus affirms. "It echoes in the wild and limited universe" of humanity.

He then invokes the mythological tale of Sisyphus. "One always finds one's burden again. But Sisyphus"—absurdly straining forever to push his boulder up the slope, temporarily free each time it rolls again to the bottom—"teaches the higher fidelity that negates the gods and raises rocks. He too concludes that all is well.

"This universe henceforth without a master seems to him neither sterile nor futile. Each atom of that stone, each mineral flake of that night-filled mountain, in itself forms a world. The struggle itself toward the heights is enough to fill a man's heart. One must imagine Sisyphus happy."

All is lost. Be of good cheer.

And yet my sister Sherry and my former girlfriend Joanne could not live. My friends Tom and Jimmy and Greg and Bruce could not live. I mourn them and regret that, in their torment, they could not find stratagems to survive. Had they even known of Camus' challenge to mount a bracing, fulfilling life against all hazards, they might not have lived. They hurt too much. They had become lost in the black tunnel of suicide, and as Alvarez explains in *The Savage God*, "Suicide is a closed world with its own irresistible logic…. It is like the unanswerable logic of a nightmare."

Returning to the pond the next morning I discover wild iris has bloomed. Each petal a sateen of regal purple, tinted at the stamens with lavender, with white, with dustings of gold.

Fittingly, people have named this flower for Iris, the primordial Greeks' courier of the gods. Iris flitted from earth to sky on a bridge of rainbow, according to the myths. She bore entreaties and solemn prayers.

She also performed another divine task. Iris led souls of dead women to the Elysian fields.

For this reason, ancient Greeks planted purple irises, like this one.

They planted irises on the graves of women.

ELEVEN

"October 27: The color is by. Leaves are mostly brown or yellow now. I DO NOT want the crazies to come. Better to be a timid little corner mouse right now than a raging fury.

Have gone thru papers & notebooks. Am throwing lots away. Will prob. destroy more. Never realized how stupid so much of it is. Real chronicle of a sad, lost, lonely woman. Always managed to keep in touch w/ some sort of reality at least. Some was okay I guess. Depression has always been on the side-line. I've never been able to comprehend how others have stayed clear of it....

What is it that Hamlet says?

This goodly frame, the earth

Appears to me a sterile promontory—"

The day before killing herself, Joanne mailed me her journals. Two spiral-bound notebooks documenting the final months before she died, alone, on November 9, 1982, in the backseat of her car. She died at her parents' summer camp in the woods of the Salmon River Reservoir near Redfield, New York, about eighty miles northeast of where I sit now, at Springwater Meditation Center, on a bench near the pond with its irises and its wild meadows, reading her words:

"I still have yet to be sure I've seen a falling star, wherever I've been. When someone tells me to look quick, I don't think I see it. Maybe I expect too much. Maybe I've been seeing it for years, but couldn't believe that that was all....

Today, at least, I just yearn for a release from this. Death is welcome. Not scary. Just want to sleep.

Not so terrifying—

No edge to it. Feel that peace I've heard about. Joining everything else in the big ball. No more consumption. All too big to fit in my mouth. Tin cans and rusty arrow edges do cut, & then you bleed & you open out in any no. of ways the earth swallows me & I swallow it back. At the same time that its hugeness & complexity overwhelm, you can feel like your own mind could consume it all and obliterate it. 'When I stop, it all stops.'"

Joanne scat-singing round the kitchen in her red terrycloth bathrobe or crooning over the coffee pot, pretending to be all the Supremes at once.

Joanne plunging into the spray on Plum Island. Late summer afternoon, storm clouds boiling up on a blue horizon. Exhilarated by the lunge of surf, thrashing her arms against the gusts, the heaved swell of waves, shouting, "It's great! It's great! Come out here where I am!"

Joanne rocking on her porch at twilight. Humming to herself. Watching heat lightning flicker over Mount Sugarloaf. Letting the phone ring.

Joanne barefoot in her garden, hair tied back, khaki pants rolled to her knees. Gingerly picking cabbage worms. Tamping the soil. Thrilling to the dirt and sun, rhythms of digging, hauling, digging—so pleased when she pulled in her summer tomatoes and green peppers.

"Sometimes, when I look out my window, it amazes me that it's all still going.

Where does all of the energy really come from? Tree moves all of the time, I move around it, day and night keep alternating, the mother feels shame for what she's created.

My father kneels, after another day at the garage, & prays. I saw him by mistake & was ashamed to have been there. And was terrified.

Running away, sinking in & suicide have never been far away. Was sickened by thought of blood, by own physicality. When I thot of it running thru my body, I could not touch myself, but my body was still there & I would try to shake away that knowledge.

I remember my 1st doll, Peggy. Remember how her body exploded—all that rubbery powder came out & I was horrified. I cried at night—parents upset. I kept her head. How do you explain something like that to a small child? Her body was all over the place.

Such a big, exciting world that neighborhood was. 'The boys' roamed far. I realized that my boundaries & the limits of my experience were quite different.

Odd to think back and remember—

So what? That's how it was, is. So here I am. Far away from all that. Who would know that Joanne? Now she's become a suicidal 32 year old woman in the Pioneer Valley in Massachusetts.

We all look so much better as children."

Joanne lolling under the blankets with a mug of steaming cider, snuggling with the cats Souslee or Gaucho on winter nights, clucking and chattering to them in her mocking baby-talk, hugging them, fluffing them.

Joanne propped on her elbows at Delano's in Amherst, stirring a White Russian, wide-eyed and breathless, full of questions, giddy over a Hitchcock movie she'd seen the night before.

Joanne high-stepping and sparkling, peppy in her yellow T-shirt, full of spunk, celebrating the first day of forsythia and spring.

Joanne tussling, her hair flying, collapsing on her bed with laughter.

"Still, I want this to end. Oct. 27. No warm places. The longest month, I think, that I have ever known....

Suicides are willing to take with them those who matter? This spoken in disdain by someone, luckily, well outside the bind. Ques. of will becomes trickier, even, than usual. What shd. I do? Send my folks a letter that says I've gone away for good to search for a gold mine & that most likely they'll never hear from me again, & then go off & drown myself in the coast of Africa somewhere, hoping they'll never find me or identify me?

I don't think I want them to suffer, or at least not like this. This has bothered me for years. At last it just might be possible to center on what I need and want, even if that is suicide. That's a right I must be able to have....

I love Mom & Dad.

Something just went wrong w/ me. It happened. No one is to blame. Things happen to some people. I can shout 'unfair' and 'desist' all I want. It is a fact. I am one of those people. I've been fighting, it seems, forever. It must be okay to admit the weariness, that the battle's become meaningless, you have no idea how it started, & you forgot where you lay your weapons (what do they look like?) You just admit that you're licked. I am no longer strong enuf to maintain this.

The shell is pulling round again."

She grew up Catholic in working-class Syracuse, where girls were expected to marry a high-school linebacker and dutifully raise a brood of children. Joanne was different.

She bicycled with a friend through England, Holland, Germany and France, sleeping in the woods, feasting on black bread and cheese. She roamed to Greenland on an archeological dig, where she unearthed an arrowhead twenty-five centuries old. She learned to throw pots on a wheel and made exquisite earth-hued bowls and vases; she was an unassuming connoisseur of pottery who savored fine, uncluttered lines, and who could stroll into a shop, glance at the shelves, and walk unerringly to the finest piece in the store. She loved theater. She was a sly mimic who observed people closely and had a canny, natural flair for the stage. She enjoyed baking and created exotic breads, delectable, braided and glazed, sprinkled with raisins. She liked sewing. She was so adept at it that when you admired those distinctive pinstripe jackets she wore, or pleated pants, chances are she'd made them herself. She could paint and sketch with a deft hand. She worked as a lab assistant at Harvard.

She had a degree in psychology from Syracuse University and was half-way through a master's in anthropology. She adored Native American and African beadwork, ceramics, painting and sculpture, its clarity, its boldness, its eerie magic; it literally made her shiver, and she'd chat for hours about the Mayan ruins she hoped to explore someday.

She was an outdoors woman, enthralled by peaks and wild, unbroken country, who pitched camp in her beloved White Mountains of New Hampshire and wandered the northern forests by herself, clambering above timberline, above the clouds, on day-long climbs to the summit of Lafayette or Wildcat, a woman alone in the wilderness and enraptured by it.

She loved music, loved Phillip Glass and Nina Simone and Holly Near and Popul Voh. She loved movies, loved Greta Garbo and Ingrid

Bergman, loved any German film by Werner Herzog. In her favorite Herzog film, *Nosferatu*, she was awed by the scene in which Lucy, a pallid girl, a will-o'-the-wisp brushing her raven hair, turns silently, hand to mouth, and sees the vampire—wheezing, pathetic, hideous, white and bald as a termite grub—whispering into Lucy's room, an apparition in the mirror; then the gasp, the erotic pantomime, the shock of discovery. Joanne thought that scene "as riveting and chilling as *Noh* theater," and she saw the film seven times.

She loved Cambridge, the bookshops in Harvard Square, relished searching the shelves for her favorites, for Virginia Woolf or Toni Cade Bambara, for Isak Dinesen, Zora Neale Hurston, Susan Sontag. She loved huddling under blankets on a blustery night reading *Middlemarch* or the radical feminist journal *Heresies* or the food section of the *Village Voice*.

She loved meeting friends for breakfast at Steeplejack's in Sunderland, gabbing cheerily over platters of cheese omelets and blueberry pancakes and morning tea.

And for four years, at a state institution near Amherst, she worked with people labeled "mentally retarded"—teaching them to sort dimes and quarters; teaching them to make a cup of coffee, step-by-patient-step. She spoke to them, teased them and coaxed them with the same forthrightness, the same respect, and the same generosity of spirit that she used with all her friends.

○

MY SECOND week at Springwater Meditation Center in upstate New York. June 2003. I've emerged from a seven-day retreat. Seven days of speechlessness, seven days devoid of human contact. Seven days of sitting on a meditation cushion, staring at the plank floor. Watching morning light sharpen to noon, fade into evening and darken. Watching my grief arise and disappear. Listening to other people shuffle in and out of the meditation hall. Listening to my breaths. To my tangled thoughts. To the *chirr-reep*! of red-winged blackbirds, to the early summer rain. I feel washed and renewed.

This morning I stand in a hemlock grotto a few hundred yards down the dirt lane from Springwater's main building, past meadows where whitetail does and their fawns sample wild grasses. In the hemlock grotto a brook skipjacks over terraced rocks. It whooshes in noisy ovations of whitewater over a twenty-foot fall, then rushes a narrow chute through wet boulders, ferns, and pine. Through treetops the sunlight comes dusting down, sparkling like powdered quartz.

○

IN PHOTOGRAPHS Joanne may look wary—she distrusted cameras—but at thirty years old, at thirty-one and at the final, fatal year of thirty-two, her vivacity and her Gallic beauty, her pallor and dark cloud of tresses, her alert brown eyes, still outshine her apprehension. She looks happiest in wild places. Snapshots of our trips to the Maine coast, to mountains of New Hampshire and Vermont, to Plum Island and the dunes of deserted Cape Cod in late autumn: Joanne on the beach in her black turtleneck and red sweatshirt, beaming, arms outflung in delight; Joanne at the alpine summit of Mount Washington, hair billowed to the wind; Joanne in her beret, scanning the in-rolling surf off Wellfleet, hands on her hips, laughing; Joanne on Cadillac Mountain watching mist unravel off the bay; Joanne lying in sand and beach grass, face to the sun; Joanne on the small boat we rented to seek porpoises and eagles in salt coves off Acadia, turning to gaze at me as I click the camera.

Joanne writing:
"Weds., Oct. 28: November is almost here. It seems like I've waited so long. Days of experience overlaid upon ea. other, it seemed, & only one or two days gone by. Oct. 28. Only three more days left to this month. Tonight I feel a sort of excitement. Things may be reaching a crisis—a decision may be made in this month—one way or the other way. I hope that's the case, at least. If I do kill myself, it will finally end for me. If I do not do it, perhaps I'll return & start a struggle again. As I write that, something in me feels repulsion. I simply am too weary. And yet, to accept that I will carry thru with death is so hard.

I cannot imagine it now—returning to normal & having to face the endless meaninglessness."

"Often, people want both to live and to die," observes Jamison in *Night Falls Fast: Understanding Suicide*. "Ambivalence saturates the suicidal act."

"I do not completely give into the idea of dying. But I cannot see how to live. It weighs heavily on me to even try to imagine coming back and carrying on.

If I were to come back & try to live, I am afraid that it wd. amount to only a temporary reprieve, that it wd. be only a stall while I flounder more for a while. Is living thru a life jail term better than dying? Perhaps the jail term is, but to be the prisoner of forces w/in yourself that won't let you be, that you can't stop or control for very long—

for the confusion to just go on & on....

Listening to some Chopin sonatas now—so satisfying."

We'd met when Joanne was twenty-eight, four years my senior. An older woman. She appealed to me instantly: bohemian, elusive, pale as a woman in a daguerreotype, black hair plunging dramatically below her shoulders in tousled ringlets. She buzzed with intensity. Her entrances, her exits from rooms changed the ozone levels, left the air tingling.

She rented the second floor of a house near Amherst, her rooms awash in cool northern light, their shadows filled with books, Mayan statuary, jazz records, batiks, tendriled plants and foliage, frayed hippie furniture. We sat on her porch after dinner and began confessing our lives.

Two years earlier a man had raped her. If I brushed Joanne's arm with my fingertip she quailed in panic. We embarked on delicate courtship. I needed to learn how to read her moods and hesitations, her conflicted, tentative seductions; needed to discern the vulnerable, flighty creature, profoundly hurt, beneath the formidable woman of independence and fire. Often I misread and bungled everything. Her sudden tears. Her sudden icing-up. Her sudden retreat. Days later we'd try again. A woman who's been raped lives in a twilit realm of muted trauma. We learned patience. For a year I slept in a sleeping bag on the floor beside her bed. We inched toward lovemaking: touch here; okay. Touch here; not okay. Touch here; slowly; not sure; okay. Nice. Yes.

Living together in a two-hundred-year-old house in Sunderland, near tobacco fields and the river—a handsome house with pegged floors and a brick hearth—we slept in separate rooms, an expedient toward healing. If Joanne felt safe she invited me to her bed. After a second year she could relax into sex, could even luxuriate in it, could surrender into orgasms and bask in our newfound pleasures.

We talked interminably. We talked about Bloomsbury, James Baldwin, politics, Truffaut and Fellini. About our families and our friends and our childhoods.

We drove back roads of New England. Camped and hiked. In Maine we climbed a sea cliff. Spidering with tortuous, exacting focus up crevices and rockface, no ropes, our feet and fingers seeking holds in small indentations of stone, the ocean crashing sixty feet beneath us. Though we hazarded that climb a dozen years before I commenced Buddhist practice, we moved on the rock with a minutely pinpointed, live-or-die concentration I now recognize as Zen.

We discovered a sea cave at low tide. A glistering chamber secreted below the cliffs, wet and dripping, bejeweled with starfish and red kelp and anemones. We explored it shouting, "Look! Look!" in a shared euphoria, our voices echoing against the echoes of the sea.

While hiking in Maine together Joanne saved my life. We tiptoed on a trail, no wider than a goat path, upon a high peak. Cliff wall rising immediately to the left and, immediately to the right, nothing but air—a sheer plummet, seven hundred dizzying feet straight down into a glacial lake. I've always felt skittish about heights. But I challenge myself. I had followed Joanne onto the high ledge. At a blind, hairpin turn in the trail Joanne sidled round the corner. I found myself alone in space. I paralyzed. I pressed against the rock wall. Palms sweating. Heart zooming. I knew, with absolute conviction, that any moment the weight of my knapsack would flip me over backward into the void below. Cotton-mouthed, I gasped, "Joanne." I gasped again, "I can't move." She backtracked to me. She expertly took control. "It's okay," she whispered. "Move your right foot toward me. There. Everything's fine. Now your left foot. There. Everything's fine. Touch here, on the rock." Now touch here. Okay. Slowly. Okay. Nice. Yes.

"Why does it have to be so hard to love someone and be loved? Why not be able to get the affection and tenderness and companionship that I need? Why never to get it? Always lonely.... When do I start figuring out how to do it?
  I say Steven. *I say, I am sorry, Steven. I am sorry. I am sorry that it is gone. Everything is gone. I can't remember clearly now what we have had. But gone. Am I crying because I think that the Joanne that was w/ you must be gone now too? Who was that Joanne? That woman doesn't just go down the drain now. And what do I do with the woman who loved to look at you and touch you and enjoyed your excitement and felt that fast mind quicken her? That's what's good to remember. What of all the pain, the silence, all left unsaid—so much we couldn't say to each other."*

We battled like Cossacks, savagely, wielding invective like broadswords. Hours-long screaming tirades. Slammed phones. Slammed doors. Days later, wounded, we'd begin our hesitant apologies, our shy rapprochement. Once amid a gale of words she fled the house, infuriated; I locked the door behind her; she rattled it nearly from the hinges in murderous rage. One memorably dreary afternoon we shouted at each other on a busy Amherst street corner for a half-hour, oblivious, lost in our angry melodrama, as passersby skirted us, appalled.

In those days—years before I started practicing Zen—my anger could splash up like acid. It frightened me. I could not control it. But I also probed that anger, long suppressed, with wary exhilaration. I thrived on its forbidden power, its intensity. Brutalized by experiences in my small Appalachian high school, scarred by the sadistic teachers who ridiculed kids they disliked and hit us with paddles, I seethed with resentment. Remembering how I'd been attacked when a teenager by farmboys and football jocks who scorned me as one of rural Clinton County, Pennsylvania's only "longhair hippies," and as a pacifist who refused to fight back, I lusted in my late twenties for vengeance, and vowed that no one would assault me ever again. By the time I met Joanne in the late

1970s, I often bristled. Abandoning pacifism in disgust, I began listening to the Sex Pistols and the Clash and razor-cut my hair to the bare scalp and wore black leather. I thrilled to the snarling menace of punk.

Joanne's anger festered from the rape. It festered from a stifled girlhood in working-class Syracuse. From growing up submerged in a blue-collar family that maligned her restless aspirations. Her anger also festered in 1980 and '81 and '82, the years immediately before she died, from America's embrace of Reagan and his right-wing ideology. Looking at a newspaper photo of a US-supported death squad soldier in Nicaragua, who had tortured and executed peasants, she hissed, "I could kill him." (But of course Joanne killed no one but herself. She turned her rages inward, as suicides do.)

We lived in Amherst and Northampton in those revolutionary years of the Eighties, era of the feminist revolt, when western Massachusetts became one of the hottest flashpoints in the nation for the radical women's movement.

Earlier, as a seventeen-year-old in Pennsylvania, still choking down my anger in a guise of hippie nonviolence, I had read an article in *Life* magazine about something new called Women's Liberation: photos of women marching with banners and clenched fists. It perplexed me. I understood, in 1971, why the Civil Rights movement and Black Power movement struggled to liberate Black people; I understood why Vietnamese people had battled for decades to liberate Vietnam from foreigners, and still were doing so; I understood why Chicano farm workers were striking on California grape plantations, fighting to liberate their people. But women? Why did women need liberation? Wishing to understand, I lay in bed one night in Cedar Heights. Peering into the dark I devised a thought experiment. I imagined that I was still myself, a teenage guy, but living in an inverted world. What if all the presidents of the United States, all members of Congress, all the Supreme Court justices, had for two centuries been women—and what if my history books, with their accounts of explorers, renowned scientists and philosophers, military leaders and rulers, consisted exclusively of women? What if most of our lauded writers, artists, and composers had been women? And all the business leaders and sports heroes? The astronauts? All the police, the firefighters, soldiers, technicians, doctors, lawyers—what if they all were women? What if God was depicted as a woman? What if I'd been taught in Sunday School that She had sent Her only begotten Daughter to redeem humanity—which was called "Womankind"—and what if religious leaders throughout the world were women? What if I'd been instructed since childhood that boys are weak and inferior? As a male, how would I feel? A shock of revelation: I'd feel born into a world that held no place for me. Then I considered the types of jobs—precisely ten of them—awaiting girls in my high school if they chose careers other than homemaker and mother. They could become secretaries. Or waitresses. Or telephone operators. Elementary or high school teachers. Beauticians and hairdressers. Nurses. Bank tellers. Store clerks. Or, if they dared to move to a city, airline stewardesses. Maybe they could own a small florist shop or bake shop. Those were the options. Then I thought of my own mother, so bright, such an avid reader, so enthralled by music and politics, and how she toiled ceaselessly for us—virtually our slave—cooking our meals, washing our clothes, cleaning our house, and how we took this utterly for granted. Goddamn it! The next day, without comment, I began regularly to vacuum carpets, load and unload the dishwasher, pack laundry into the washing machine, hang clothes and sheets and towels on our outdoor clothesline. Modest efforts, and merely a glimmer of beginning to fathom the true nature of patriarchy. But my mother thanked me.

A decade later, in Massachusetts, Joanne and I felt impassioned about Second Wave feminism, shared its zeal and its hopes. After she died, when I organized a memorial service for her at the Everywoman's Center at the University of Massachusetts, I said in her eulogy, "When Joanne read *Heresies*, when she read *Lesbian Nation* and Adrienne Rich and Mary Daly—with mounting excitement and a growing sense of self-discovery—the writings confirmed what she'd known since she was seven: that things are drastically wrong, and must be drastically changed, and must be changed by drastic women." But increasingly this had left scant room for me in her life. As Joanne, by any definition a drastic woman, threw out her books by male writers, as she abandoned her record albums by male musicians, as she fretted over whether to become a lesbian like so many of our friends, she began to say that living with me meant "fraternizing with the enemy." Our relationship became a barbed-wire zone, out beyond the trenches of the feminist battleground—very literally a "no-man's land."

Baffled, I found myself identified with the patriarchy I deplored. Joanne's attitude toward me became, unnervingly, "guilty until proven guilty." Glaring at me she'd sneer, "You're a fucking man. You own the whole fucking world. Look at what you've done to women, just by being a man."

When I mourned the slaying of the Beatle who'd been an inspirational hero of my youth, she snapped, "So what? Nobody cares about John Lennon except white males."

And with that strike of the match, another argument would ignite.

"I'm sorry that it didn't work for us, Steven. I'm sorry for everything I did that contributed to the mess we ended up with. I'm sorry for the times I upset you. I'm sorry for you because I know you and like you and want you still some and worry about you. And I do still want you and I don't want to. Makes me feel bad about myself. I ain't no superwoman.

So—I'm sorry I wasn't more loving, am not an artist, aren't brighter, am not accomplished or talented, am not more attractive, am not more sociable, not more amusing. I apologize for all of my faults. You had to live with them and often I probably took it out on you.

I apologize for my sexual fears, for taking out my awful anger at men on you, for being too rational, analytical, too emotional, undisciplined, after all, worth what?

And again, for not having faith in my own ideas and beliefs, for being confused and afraid.

Perhaps I'll leave off on naming what you should apologize for until later."

She didn't, in fact, name what I should apologize for. But she could have mentioned my intransigence. My arrogance. My selfishness. My temper and my impatience. My immaturity. My obtuse, fatal stupidity. She could have listed my desertions. My devious and cowardly evasions. My escapes into platonic "friendships" with other women—convivial blonde coworkers, vivacious artists and poets. She could have mentioned my clumsy lies, to her and to myself, about these "friendships"; could have mentioned my habit of disguising randy sexual desire through "innocuous" lunches with one of my "women friends," prolonged into late afternoon; or with tête-à-têtes in cafés; or woodland strolls; or meetings in Amherst nightspots for cocktails. Joanne, with ample justification, resented these "friendships." I never slept with my "women friends," but I wanted to. Few things in nature stink like a rancid chastity. Joanne surely caught the whiff of it each time I told her I planned to meet a "woman friend" downtown "just to talk."

An explosive couple. Each of us high-dosage in those days, callow, mercurial, headstrong, intemperate; each maimed at some crucial, tender place in our psyches; each of us insatiable, each sensitive, each pitiably inept at trusting, at communicating. A couple doomed from the start. Yet we managed to create our own haphazard love. Edgy and raucous but, so often, unexpectedly sweet. Always hard-won. Always genuine.

And of course we relished danger. It felt sexy.

"Sometimes I think our getting together was one large fluke—that it shouldn't have lasted for this long. But sometimes I can see what we've done for each other—why and how it worked for us.

I would love to know what Steven did get out of our relationship. Did it do much for him? What does he feel now?"

LEARNING IT BY HEART

This is the story of how
everything hurt you.

How everything burned itself down
as you dialed long-distance,
weeping with brandy,
sheathed in a final mist
of breath, leaning on winter air.

Hose coiled from exhaust
pipe, the car taped shut
like a Christmas package:
nothing to coax you
from the backseat
where you cuddled yourself
in blankets, begging
sleep, choking
on monoxide
as your brain snuffed itself,
cell by cell, and your heart
fumbled and stopped—

All night an owl wooed
stars home across the hills.
Moon spangled the lake
with broken shards of light.

I slept three hundred miles
from you, still unsuspecting,
still trusting our luck.

This is the story of lives
crumpled like paper
and thrown away.

[1982]

⊃

MY THIRD week at Springwater Meditation Center. Late June of 2003 now, the day after the solstice. Summer weather arrives in this northern lake country and brings welcome sunshine. Ambling through the high meadows after a morning of zazen I note how much has changed.

A hundred-acre bouquet of new wildflowers has emerged among the rippling grasses: oxeye daisies, each one sunny side up; redtop; milkweed, blooming in delicate clusters; purple clover; common fleabane, the daisies' ragamuffin second cousin; yellow hawkweed; devil's paintbrush, each a nova of starburst orange; bird's-foot trefoil; multiflora rose bushes, garlanded with white petals, each a lush natural perfumery; bluets in the mowed trails; wood anemone at the forest's edge.

Last night a man spied, near the center's barn, one of our hulking neighbors: black bear.

This instant: deerflies buzz peevishly. On a trail in windbreak trees I find coyote scat, curled extrusions heaped tidily on a flat rock, dung bristling with bleached fur.

This instant: a monarch butterfly schooners across the breeze.

"Yesterday, as I walked up the hill, some shriveled flowers lined the path—an early frost had snuffed out their delicate lights. Other hardier plants were blooming during the warming day." Toni Packer, writing these words in her book *The Wonder of Presence and the Way of Meditative Inquiry*, describes walking the high meadows at Springwater, the same fields I explore here daily. Addressing a query she has received from a student, Toni continues:

Your question came to mind: "What is it that lives and dies?" We usually ask this question when someone close to us dies or when we ponder our own death. Rarely do we want to know what it is in a flower that has died. We take it for granted that the earth displays constantly appearing, changing, and disappearing colors, forms, and textures.

A moment ago, there was a loud thud against the window. I looked out and saw a beautiful bird lying quietly on the patio, eyes half-open, the white dappled belly and yellow tail feathers freely exposed. The body was still warm but without the lively motion that ended in a crash and fall.

What is it that died? What is it that is born? A bird has died, another one has hatched, an old man has exhaled his last breath, a baby has left the womb, a flower has frozen as another one opened its purple petals. What is it that is born and dies?

—

Toni founded Springwater in 1984. A Zen teacher who broke away from traditional practices at Rochester Zen Center, Toni wished to start a "center for meditative inquiries and retreats," free of rituals, bells, bowing, chanting, and hierarchy. She's succeeded. Springwater provides space for serious, self-disciplined meditators to sit quietly, to roam, to question, to explore—in Toni's words—that "moment of stillness without knowing," whether alone or with others.

Having returned from the meadows I'm seated with four people in Toni's pleasantly spartan, bright little apartment. Toni, white-haired and alert, relaxes on the sofa. At seventy-six, having endured Nazi Germany as a young girl, and having lost her cherished husband Kyle three years ago, Toni knows about death.

We take turns presenting a question. When my turn arrives I explain that I don't have a specific inquiry but wish to share thoughts and feelings—"experiences in the bodymind," as we say at Springwater—that have arisen while I work through issues related to the suicides of my friend Joanne and my sister Sherry. "The death of my friend twenty-one years ago lingers but feels largely resolved, but in some ways my sister's death still feels fresh. I postponed my grieving to provide strength for my parents, who were devastated. I'm only now beginning to emerge from numbness and shock. I know that you've also experienced loss," I tell Toni, "so perhaps you could respond from your own experience. One thing I've been noticing while meditating and practicing here at Springwater is how grief, psychological pain, suffuses the bodymind exactly like physical pain in my legs when I'm sitting zazen for long periods, and how the challenge is to stay with that pain, with no barriers." Toni listens with her usual fastidious attentiveness.

"I'm also noticing an interesting tension and challenge to remember the dead person," I continue, "to hold the person in living memory but to do it without attachment, accepting the death and letting go—yet not forgetting." Toni nods and says, "Yes."

"Another thing is the powerful temptation to find consolation in belief systems," I tell her. "Lately I've been doing some reading in *The Tibetan Book of Living and Dying*. I'm noticing how enticing it feels to be soothed, rather than staying with the uncertainty, with 'don't-know mind.' I find myself wanting to know what happens when a person dies. With a belief system as sophisticated as the Tibetan, it's tempting to embrace the answers it provides rather than to stay with not knowing."

Toni agrees, emphasizing that belief systems function as elaborate schemes to protect ourselves from unsettling encounters with Mystery, with the ineffable. In her tart German accent she speaks candidly, glowingly, of her feelings while her husband died of cancer and Parkinson's disease—the loving care, the inevitable exhaustion—and the vacancy in her life after his death, the pang in her chest, the wish to phone him after a meditation retreat. She speaks of how she learned to relinquish grief. "Know that you did the best you could," she tells me. "You say that your friend died twenty-one years ago, and your sister four years ago. It seems like a long time to be holding on. Perhaps there are feelings of guilt, which are common after suicide. Feelings of guilt, of 'I should have done more,' lead down a blind alley. Let go. Social indoctrination tells us to keep grieving. Do feel the grief," Tony says, her fists trembling at her breast, her eyes clenched shut, "but let go." With those words her body releases, and she looks at me directly with clear blue eyes.

◠

AT THE FUNERAL HOME IN SYRACUSE

They'd filed you away,
lost letter
in an office cabinet,
the coffin beige, massive,
businesslike.

When the box was opened
you looked savage,
angry at one more
disturbance.
Already the flesh sagged

at your chin
like fallen dough,
your hair tugged back
like a samurai's.

The gas had tanned your skin
to saddle leather,
embalmer's
brown powder
sprinkling your face
like cinnamon.
Your brother whispered,
"It doesn't look like her.
It doesn't."

They'd wrapped a mannikin
in your camping shirt,
poised its head
on a satin pillow.
Stroking your hair
my fingers roved
above your eyes, the skin
cool and blank,
a slate wiped clean.
My fingers said:
"We know it now. We know."

I didn't cry again
till the following morning.
One car passing in the street
at 6:30. November rain.
Every tick of the clock
an absence, a heartbeat, an accusation.

[1982]

◯

I'M YANKING weeds from the garlic patch in Springwater's garden. I tug and uproot the stubborn, interloper plants. Unsnag the pea vines, giving the garlic room to breathe. Clear the soil. Barefoot, wearing only my cargo shorts, I kneel in the waning sun. Sweating, working, attentive to my hands and the world around me.

This instant: flies from the compost. Smells of cow shit. Earth. The tepid sweet sapor of green stems and leaves. Food rot from the garbage midden. Each fly, droning past, sounds like a manically bowed violin string.

Early evening, the sky cloudless. A wan blue. A robin, plump as a Flemish burgher, surveys the garden from a gatepost. I pull weeds. Glancing up I notice windbreak oaks and maples still boldly illumined by last rays of sun, greengold trees, trees so bright they seem plugged into electric outlets.

This garden serves as a counterpart, orderly and cultivated, to the feral abundance of the pond's shoreline and the high meadows. Instead of cattails, instead of queen anne's lace and daisies, here I find meticulous plots of tarragon and dill. Sweet basil. Spinach, collards, kale and peppers. "Husky Gold" tomatoes. Asparagus spears. Beans and squash—the latter big-leafed, improbably so, leaves of exotic green.

This garden of life. The life Joanne rejected....

At dusk I see, in the near meadows, women of a Russian corps de ballet, transformed through benign witchery to fleet, tawny animals:

Deer.

I phone Jenny for our evening chat. "Is this my beautiful, wonderful girlfriend?" I envision her on the back porch, cell phone in one hand, cup of tea in the other, her cat Scout beside her. Schooled as a filmmaker, former resident of New York City and Los Angeles and Seattle, at thirty-seven Jenny now lives atop Purdue Mountain in rural Pennsylvania with Scout and her other two cat companions, Oliver and Alice. She works as a homeopath, healing people conventional medicine fails to treat, using natural remedies to revitalize their life-force.

I envision her bright Ukrainian smile, her blue eyes.

"It's my boyfriend! I've been missing you. Much more than I expected! What's been going on up there at Springwater since yesterday? How's the writing project going?"

I envision her hair, the color of a palomino when it turns in mid-gallop and catches the sun.

"I've been working in the garden, pulling weeds. Walking in the meadows. Reading. Later tonight I'll be sitting zazen some more. The writing's going well, I'm getting a decent first draft, but you know, the things I'm writing about are very draining emotionally."

We talk for a half-hour, catching up, voice touching voice. We close with "I love you," the words of Eros.

In the meditation room I watch night arriving. Light withdraws slowly from the floor where I've fixed my gaze. It seeps into darkness. I concentrate on breaths pulling into the hara, the base of the abdomen below the navel, reservoir of qi, of the vital force. A half-remembered quote from Zen teacher Dōgen teases into my awareness. Something about death as a "complete phase in itself." I resolve to look it up later. Return to breathing.

Before bed I find it: "It is a mistake to suppose that birth turns into death. Birth is a phase that is an entire period of itself, with its own past and future. For this reason, in buddha-dharma birth is understood as no-birth. Death is a phase that is an entire period of itself, with its own past and future. For this reason, death is understood as no-death."

No-birth and no-death: I repeat these words twice as I ease into sleep, into cooling breeze, crickets, scents from the garden.

◯

DAMAGE REPORT

The day after the funeral
I rummaged drawers and closets.

Saving her burgundy
sweater. Her nightgown. Yellow
T-shirt with the rainbow, the winged horse.

A baby photo in the desk drawer.
Eight months old, splashing
in the kitchen sink, her fist
clenched tight as a cowrie shell.
Even then, the smile I loved.

Sky erased by clouds.
Her mother snapping the Kodak,
humming "No. Look at me."
The baby named Joanne,
alone at the window.
Thirty-one years to go.

*

Locked car in the woods,
rubber tube
clamped to exhaust
pipe, blue fog
behind the taped
windshield.

*

The day after the funeral
I lay on her bed, my finger
tracing elusive curves
of light. My hand smoothing
her pillow. The hours
it took to do that.

Because it was winter
the light came brittle, cold, and faded
fast.

There is no such thing
as a second chance.

[1982]

◯

[One week before Joanne killed herself:]

"*November 1—Just spent $ on stuff I need* [she means for committing suicide: hose, clamps, duct tape]. *Think will be all right. No real problems. Depends on what happens later. I feel sad....*

I look around me & see so much that still seems good—trees, yellow leaves, leaves on the ground, my big, soft, comfortable bed—all in wrinkled-up sheets & blankets—where I've sat and read & written & thought & cried & made love & sat w/ Steven over good talks and laughs. He doesn't feel like much comfort anymore—rather remote friend—that's all....

Seems to become less & less an open question. Now, really come up against idea of death. Guess it's not death I fear or hate. Hate to leave the good stuff. A nice day, good music, ideas and reading that are exciting—that can make life look good. That is worth living for. But you have to buy *it—must be paid for. And the price is—I can't even read the price.—I don't know what it is.*

Hear the music—Popol Vuh. It sounds so heavy & rich & relaxing. That's what makes me sad. All gone—

I wonder if I'll be able to go thru w/ it once I get away f/ here & to somewhere more neutral and beautiful?"

I don't view sharing Joanne's journal entries as violating her privacy. At this point she's far beyond caring anyway. But I do see her journal writing as providing an intimate, rare, and invaluable glimpse into the psychology affecting horrendous late-stage ideations of suicide. Joanne does this with brilliance and the penetrating ache of honesty. She teaches us. Thus her journal entries comprise one of her final, extraordinary gifts to the world. They preserve her voice. Not sharing them would silence her forever.

At 3:25 in the morning, chilled, I'm treading barefoot into the dew. Standing on a lawn in front of Springwater's main building, I peer at the night sky. A few fireflies still skim the grass, as if stars have drifted down from the blackness to float in our terrestrial sphere.

I look at the lustrous arch of the Milky Way, the distant rim of our galaxy. The Lakota, viewing it from the grasslands of the Plains, believed the Milky Way a celestial path traversed by spirits of the dead, in journeys to another world.

We are within space-time and the dead are beyond space-time. Maybe sitting zazen is a way to momentarily stop space-time, a way to die and live simultaneously.

Timespace stops at the speed of light. Perhaps the dead are a form of light and they move through the universe at light-speed, in the no-time no-space dimension. Perhaps we are matter and the dead are anti-matter, are neutrinos. Perhaps the living and the dead coexist in the no-birth no-death of Zen, beyond dualities. Where stars are fireflies. Where fireflies are stars.

○

TEN WEEKS AFTER JOANNE'S SUICIDE

Zero degrees outside, the light
frozen on the snowcrust.
My hands smell like soap,
because I'm clean.
Not innocent, but clean.
And I feed this green spider plant
because something, after all,
must thrive.

I want to know if this clock
will keep ticking

a few more years, or if it merely
rehearses the passage of time
for its own demise,
its breakdown and decay.
My head is fuzzy inside
because I don't sleep.
I don't sleep because I miss her.

Her skin smelled of spice
but she is dead
this winter. I wonder if the heat
inside this house
can sustain anything so fragile
as a human body.
My hands hold a pen
because, after all,
what else can they do.

Wind makes the sky
frosty and blue,
a color that haunts
the mountains, the snow fields.
She is somewhere
and she can't talk to me.
My crime was to forget
everything, and remember it
too late.

[1982]

ɔ

"Want to stop thinking. Stop.
    Just want to move ahead—No craziness now. Fear of losing control was
unfounded.

Am in control, am not very anxious, for most part.

Am sad.

Should prob. keep myself busy now, so can't think.

Am not so full of self-loathing that self-destruction comes easily. Am full of despair. I do not need to destroy myself. But I need to stop this pain, this endlessness.

I don't feel excited at idea of killing myself. I just want out, want an end, want to just go to sleep."

"To stop thinking." "To sleep." In Zen we pause our thinking—but not so we can sleep. We let go of thinking—that discursive, analytical thinking, that soporific rationalism called "ridiculous reason" by Camus—so that we may awaken.

Would Zen or any Buddhist meditation practice have helped Joanne? I wonder this morning, as I read her notebook passages, here in Springwater's carpeted basement library among books and stacks of cassette tapes and potted ivy. The Buddha found that an ego-bound life of incessant craving causes suffering. He also discovered a way of living that ends suffering. Could Zen have saved Joanne by teaching her to live in such a way? Could it have saved her by teaching her to work through despair? Could it have saved her, as it so often has saved me?

I don't know. She was seeing a psychotherapist each week, but clearly therapy wasn't enough. Could Zen have helped? Could it help any of the thousands of desperate women and men who kill themselves each year?

"This is hard.

If people think killing yourself is easy—that you just accept & welcome it—they're wrong.

This depression, sadness, some remorse, self-absorption, burrowing-in. Collapse.

Still—I wonder where I stand in relation to other people. I'd like to know that. Can others change more easily? How do they define themselves or know who they are? How are they so definite? How do they accept so little?

These questions go on & on, like my writing in here for the past month. On

& on. For some reason, I need to do it. Keep recording myself. Will it make me more real or solid? Same inane questions....

I would like to understand.

If I could understand who I am & what happened, maybe I could die more easily. As it is, I'm still a question mark to myself. Who am I & how did I come here?

I am trying to escape myself. I keep looking, looking, & I don't see any closing. Who the hell am I?"

Joanne unwittingly posed Zen questions, the fundamental self-inquiry of Buddhism: Who am I? What is this self? These profound questions (asked also by Socrates, by anyone seeking wisdom) can provoke turmoil. If the questioner persists undaunted, "Who am I? What is this self?" can trigger the spiritual emergency leading through desperate pain and chaos to the Great Death—to the mystical suicide—and its liberation into new life. Could Zen teachings have helped Joanne to stay with the edgy uncertainty, the "don't-know mind" of her anxious questionings? Could they have helped her navigate what Christian mystics call "the dark night of the soul"? Could Zen teachings have helped her to accept the "moment of stillness without knowing" that Toni Packer describes? When Joanne wrote, "I am trying to escape myself," could Zen teachings have shown her a healthy way to accomplish that? Could they have helped her to realize—with sudden, joyous insight—that the quest to make the self "more real or solid" must always be futile? And could Zen have helped Joanne cope with the "endless meaninglessness" she bewailed in her journals, the "endless meaninglessness" that Camus called "the absurd," and that he insisted must be confronted, daily, while refusing suicide?

I don't know. I don't know.

Could a therapy based in Zen teachings have helped guide Joanne through her spiritual emergency, helped her not only to answer "Who the hell am I?" but to safely channel death-energy, to sublimate Thanatos, and to survive?

◯

SEEING

A northeaster slammed the hills
tumbling half a foot of snow
by morning.   *Joanne*
you should see this. At sunup
the sky is scrubbed clean,
rabbit tracks
sketching an arabesque
through blackberry thickets.
Shadow on the barn roof, penumbra
like a smudge of charcoal
on white quilts: *Look.*
You would have liked this.
This is worth living for.

Tonight at Quabbin, full moon
skidding across an inlet
jammed with ice.
I scrounged the jetty
of boulders, snowpack,
beached timber
where gusts scooped the cove.
Lake beaten to a tintype
by the fading light, sky receding
to deeper blue
over islands
of spruce and white birch: *Look.*
I'm saving this for you Joanne.

I am your eyes now.

[1982]

PRECISELY ONE week before she died Joanne and I blew from the chilled nighttime streets of Amherst into a college pub called Delano's, a congenial place aglow with customers. Surrounded by chatter and busy waitresses we sat in a booth and we gossiped about work, about movies. Light conversation. Joanne smiled. She stirred her White Russian. Suddenly she was weeping.

"Steven, I'm so scared. I think I might kill myself. I've been thinking about it a lot and I've bought the things I need to do it and I think I might really do it."

I fumbled blankly toward comprehending what I'd just heard, what I was seeing: the woman before me, my best friend, hunched over our table, helpless, shoulders in spasms, her face wet with tears. I stared at her. "What—?"

She could not speak.

"What do you mean?" My incomprehension shifting now to alarm.

Joanne, crying, said, "I think I might try to kill myself when I go up to my parents' cabin." It felt like watching her step off a curb into speeding traffic—I grabbed her hand to pull her back.

She sobbed. A waitress approached our table and saw some unexplained disaster unfolding and shied away nervously. I continued holding Joanne's hand, an urgent lifeline. She bowed her head. With her face curtained by her dark hair she cried inconsolably.

"Joanne. Joanne, listen. I'm really worried. If you've bought things, if you've made plans—this is dangerous. Listen. Are you listening?"

How. How do you reach someone. How do you hold someone to this tenuous life. How do you keep her on this side of the void when already she is slipping over. I've wondered now for twenty-one years.

"Joanne, listen. Don't go up there. Don't go up there to the cabin by yourself. I'm really worried about this. Listen. If you really feel you need to get away, if you need to get away from Amherst for a while, I'll go up with you. Okay? We can go up there together. Do you hear me?"

Gradually her tears subsided. She dabbed her cheeks with a napkin, glanced around the restaurant. "I'm so embarrassed."

"It's okay. It's okay. Listen, don't go up there alone. You shouldn't be in a remote place by yourself." The warmth of her fingers, alive in my hand.

Her wan smile. "Oh, Steven, don't worry. You know me. You know how I say things when I get depressed. I didn't mean it. I could never really do that."

I studied her face, still moist with tears, her downcast and evasive eyes, her smile. Her fragile hand. I caressed her arm. Confronting peril, you want to believe. You want to believe. And I knew of Joanne's weekly sessions with her psychotherapist—I trusted that she was being safely held, that she was receiving capable professional care.

"Are you sure?"

"Don't worry. I could never really do that. I'll be fine."

"Are you sure?"

"Did something that is prob. very unfair. Steven and I went out for some drinks; after a couple, I got depressed, morbid, told him abt. what's going on. Now I've ended up by worrying and depressing him. He doesn't want me to go, or wants to go w/ me. He can't help, really. But it was nice to see that he was so concerned. Makes me feel worthwhile....

"November 3 [six days before Joanne killed herself]: *So nervous this morning. Awake early, bad headache from all of that alcohol last night. Feel it all closing in on me. Like I couldn't go back now if I wanted....*

And I should never have told Steven last night. Had no right or reason to upset him like this....

I simply don't know what to do anymore, or I have lost the will *somehow. Therapy is a mess. Last time, especially, felt all wrong....*

People always turn on you. Can't trust anyone. I trust no one. Don't want to accept much from anyone. Always, the sheet is pulled aside & the real, many faces are shown. Nothing remains the same. Nothing is safe. So you go inside & be quiet & watch & wait a lot."

Reading Joanne's tortured words I wonder, again, if her pain could have transformed itself through Zen-based therapy. "Nothing remains the same"—a statement of despair in Joanne's journal, but also the Buddhist truth of impermanence. Seen clearly, it can offer resilience and joy. In Zen we learn to sit with this impermanence. "Nothing is safe." In Zen we learn to live happily on that precipice, with no certainty, no security. We learn—as Camus learned—the exhilaration of life without hope, in a universe of risk, where "nothing is possible but everything is given."

All is lost, be of good cheer.

"So you go inside," Joanne wrote, "& be quiet & watch & wait a lot." Precisely. This is the Zen technique for staying with the despair, sitting with it, instead of submerging into it and drowning in it.

Could this have saved Joanne? If she had known?

I can't stand this walking nightmare—living in suicide. Drawn on, not really living, but not dead. The time is coming. I've planned this for a month now. It's November. I shd. have left on Monday, as planned. This waiting, now, has propelled me into one more phase. It becomes crazier all the time. I make sort of plans with people, w/ no knowledge as to whether I'll be here.

Steven was so warm & concerned & helpful last night. Made me feel good, also guilty. But the warmth & concern—it felt so good.

So hard to get close to people.

It's silly to wait around til after that meeting tomorrow.

If I'm going to die—it makes no difference. If I live, well, it's going to be very hard to start to get on track again anyways. Maybe something too dense has been severed."

☽

THREE MONTHS

Three months ago today
they found your body,
locked tight in the Volkswagen
like a hermit crab
wedged in its shell.

Your father smashing the windshield
to jimmy the door.
Your body hugged in blankets,

a tulip bulb
under permafrost,
pinched by cold
before it could open.

Mouth-to-mouth,
frantic pumping of lungs
dead for twelve hours,
your mother screaming.
Ambulance bouncing into the woods.
The white shroud over you,
a museum statue
draped for storage.

After three months
I sleep late, scuff the kitchen
in a blue bathrobe,
watch the wind honing
snow to its razor edge.
This winter I've invented
a dozen ways to speak the word

"sorry," each one starting
and ending with your name.

[1982]

)

"*November 6* [three days before Joanne's suicide; written in her journal while at her parents' cabin in upstate New York]: ...*Sun setting now. So beautiful. There's the desolate beauty of November here now. No bright colors—various shades of bare trees, green conifers, brown leaves on ground.... Water is shimmering.... Deep woods look eerie in this light....*

Very quiet here now. Feel very alone. Think this is going to work out all right...."

If alive, Joanne would turn fifty-three this August. I wonder sometimes how our friendship might have matured. In my apartment I keep a Japanese-style bowl she made. I keep an earthenware pitcher, shaped and glazed by her hands. I keep a little clay bowl of cerulean and white, of surf colors, its rim undulant, a bowl she gave me as a Christmas present to remind me of the sea. In winter I sleep beneath an afghan she crocheted.

The night before she left on the fatal trip to her parents' hunting cabin at Salmon River Reservoir, eighty miles east of where I'm standing today in these wild meadows, Joanne stayed at my house in Amherst. Lovers no longer, yet each other's closest companion, we slept in separate beds. In the morning she made coffee. Standing in the driveway, she kissed me. My brilliant, vivid, irreplaceable friend.

"I'll see you next Tuesday," she said.

She drove away, and I waved goodbye.

TWELVE

"I remember saying to myself after she died:
'But this is impossible; things aren't, can't be, like this'—
the blow, the second blow of death...."
—**Virginia Woolf, from "A Sketch of the Past"**

○

... I've been sitting on the porch using a typewriter. Taking a break, I step happily into the yard. On the hillside, fields of wild grass and timothy blow in the wind, and a lone tree billows its leaves—a glorious summer day of blue skies and puffed white clouds. Very hot, though. Suddenly I remember that Sherry left early this morning on her bike and she's not back yet. It's been hours. "Where's Sher?" It was cool when she left—she was wearing white jeans and a pink sweatshirt—but now the heat is fierce. Is she okay? Where is she? She's out there somewhere on a country road, all alone. Maybe she's walking her bike, hot and weary. I'm worried. I wonder if I should get in the car and look for her. But which road would I try first? I have no idea where she went....

I recall this dream as I'm driving through farmland on Jacksonville Road: long vistas down the east rim of Nittany Valley, thousands of acres lush with corn and silage, horse pasture, fields of wheat in hues of bleached gold.

I've returned from Springwater Meditation Center in New York to the interior country of Pennsylvania. I'm back among its timber, its hills and Amish farms, its Susquehanna River valley and its Appalachian Mountains. Though I lived in New England for twenty-four years and dwelled briefly in New Mexico and in Japan, this remains my ancestral homeland, its soil hallowed in perpetuity by the grave of my sister Sherry.

In Márquez's *One Hundred Years of Solitude*, José Arcadio Buendía tells his wife, "A person does not belong to a place until there is someone dead under the ground." And so, born here, after nearly fifty years I finally belong to this place—though not in a way I ever desired.

Daylilies throng the roadside. Like orange bells of trombones, of trumpets. Tiers of them, like a floral version of an orchestra's brass section.

Driving I open the car's windows: mid-July fragrances of hillsides rampant with black-eyed Susans, purple asters, clover, ripening blackberries. For a mile southward corn tassels ripple in the wind. They ripple like the surface of a lake when vast schools of fish rush beneath it, all that shimmer, all that energy and restless motion.

I pass Amish farms. Turning onto the narrow lane through Fox Hollow I admire oaks and hickories, the trees intensified in noon's ferocious sunlight. They seem doused with a green kerosene and lit, seem doused with a green fire.

"Not long ago my sister committed suicide." I had knelt, then, in my robe in the vast hall at Zen Mountain Monastery. Eighty monastics and Zen students listened. We had just finished sesshin, a week of grueling meditation. People took turns describing how it felt to live seven days in silence, sitting zazen from four-thirty in the hushed, candlelit morning until late in the dark September evening. "Each day—" Struggling to speak through tears, I said, "Each day I bowed to her photo that I keep in my room, and I dedicated this sesshin to her."

The kōan of my sister's suicide: Where is she? What is this life? What is this death?

During sesshin, in that autumn of the year 2000, the questions hovered. If I rinsed my ōryōki bowls, if I plucked basil from the monastery's garden, if I cleaved red peppers and ripped lettuce apart in the kitchen, the kōan stayed with me: What happened when my sister died? Where did she go? The vital essence of her? When I joined the monastics and the other students in kinhin, our walking meditation, robes swishing our ankles as we stepped with exacting care across that lawn where whitetail deer, grazing, shone russet in the evening sun, the kōan stayed with me: What is death? What is life? What is this?

"Where is my sister?" In the private interview of *daisan* I sat almost knee-to-knee with the senior monk, Shugen. He bundled in his black robes and his beige rakusu, his shaved head glistening. I sat in my gray cassock. Shugen watched as I spoke, his gaze authoritative, direct, alive with Zen's placid intensity. "While I'm living here at the monastery," I said, "it feels like I'm engaged more fully than I ever thought possible in the 'Fundamental Matter' of life and death. Everything seems to center on that question. Where is my sister now?"

"I can't tell you where your sister is. No one can answer that. But as tragic as your sister's suicide was, it was also a great gift. Try to see that. The gift in this painful tragedy is the fundamental question you've identified, the question of 'What is this? What is this?' Stay with that. It's incredibly painful but stay with it. That's the practice."

"Like staying with the pain in my legs during hours of sitting in sesshin. No barriers."

"Exactly. No barriers. Your sister's death has provided you an opportunity to explore a very basic question, one of the most fundamental and amazing questions the universe offers, and that a human being can ask. Use that gift. Enter into the question. Stay with it."

"We vow to save all sentient beings," I said in a near-whisper, contritely. "But I couldn't even save my sister."

"Not all beings can be saved."

We sat for several moments in silence. "I've read a book by a famous American Zen teacher," I said. This book had annoyed and troubled me. "He claims that people who've committed suicide suffer terrible karmic punishments."

"He doesn't know what he's talking about," Shugen said briskly. "Some of these teachers can be very harsh."

Relieved and grateful, I thanked him. He nodded and rang his bell.

People always described Sherry as pretty, but when she fell prey to her mind's affliction it became difficult to see her prettiness because, if she left her trailer at night to go shopping, she hid beneath head scarves and enormous sunglasses, elusive as Garbo. I see her now, in this summer of 2003, as I remove photos from a box. I force myself to look at them:

Sherry as a toddler in her red jumper, seated in a high-chair. Sherry at six, in pigtails, her smile bashful. (I force myself to look. I force myself not to close my eyes. Not to shut down. As I look at these photos I want to put my arm around my little sister, kiss her forehead, tell her how special she is, how cherished by all of us. Immediately I feel morose. Fatigued. Faintly nauseous. I am at the scene of the disaster. I feel the onset of emotional plague, creeping along the nerves, a black death inside me, feel the onset, yet again, of remorse, of loss, of my own shameful failure as a brother.)

Another photo. Sherry in junior high school, jaunty in her white-and-black majorette's uniform, baton in hand, confident and proud. She could fling the baton high in the air—improbably high—and as it descended, whirling, she could snatch it from behind her back, flip it across her wrist, turn, kick, and fling it skyward again.

Another photo: two decades later, seated atop a picnic table in white blouse and jeans—her hair, falling nearly to her waist, of the color called flaxen in Norse sagas; and indeed she could have played onstage the role of a Viking princess, tall and fair. But her face betrays a clouded mind, vexed and unsettled—and here I must stop, I can't look anymore.

"The impact of a suicide on the lives of brothers and sisters has been almost entirely ignored in the clinical research literature, an omission made the more remarkable by the closeness of emotional ties between siblings and the possibility that they may be more likely to kill themselves because of shared genes and environment," writes Jamison in *Night Falls Fast*. "Clinically, siblings experience not only the enormous loss that the death of a brother or sister brings but guilt and a sense of responsibility as well."

—

Cedar Hill Cemetery ascends in knolls of weathered tombstones and sheltering pines. I park the car next to an open lawn of grave markers. My paternal great-grandmother and great-grandfather lie in this cemetery. So do my paternal and maternal grandparents. And my younger sister, whose barren grave has mercifully, and at last, become verdant this summer with clover and wild grass.

Kneeling at her gravestone I experience what I always do: a feeling that she has gone far away, infinitely removed from our world. An empty feeling. Touching the granite, her carved name, the dates of her life's completed span—their terrible finality—I glance at the yellow silk roses my parents have left here. "Be well, Sher. My wonderful sister. Be free of all bad karma. Be happy and at peace. I love you." And, for want of a better place to look, I glance at the sky.

Four years ago my parents and my brother and I stood on this same ground, bleary as patients sapped from long bouts of electroshock. We touched the appalling thing, her coffin. Its heaped bouquets of carnations. Of jonquils and lilies. My parents crumpled and wept that August morning.

The following year I went to Zen Mountain Monastery and when I returned I came here and I read aloud from *The Tibetan Book of the Dead*: "Deliver her from the dangerous straits of the between, / And carry her to perfect Buddhahood!" I recited the text as a precaution. Perhaps these venerable words from Tibet still could guide and safeguard the essence of Sherry's spirit, her wandering, injured spirit, if such a thing as spirit exists. Perhaps these translated Tibetan words could escort her essential being through its inconceivable passage between dimensions of time and cosmos. In one of our last phone conversations, a week before she died, she'd told me of watching *Kundun* on TV, Martin Scorsese's film about the youthful Dalai Lama. "The Tibetan people look so beautiful," she marveled. "Their faces are so radiant."

"May Buddhas mild and fierce exert the force of their compassion/ And clear the dense fog of darkness and misknowledge," I chanted in the cemetery. "Now that she wanders alone, apart from her loved ones, / And all her visions are but empty mirages, / May the Buddhas exert the force of their compassion...."

And guide her homeward.

How do we survive the fact that someone in the faltering care of our kinship and love could not survive this world? How do we survive?

I came here on a different day in June, a mere ten months after Sherry's suicide, and discovered, near a copse of trees at the edge of fields above this graveyard, wild strawberries. I plucked six. I placed them like garnets on the broken dirt where my sister lay buried. Then I returned to the upper ridge.

I'd walked those same fields above Cedar Hill Cemetery as a teenager, thirty years before. I'd walked them almost daily, on a deserted tractor path that divided orderly regiments of corn from the unkempt meadows. I never saw anyone. Walking these fields as a teenager I would smile and fantasize about my future life: the adventures, the vistas, all the vast, exhilarating spectacle of adulthood waiting for me, the beckoning lovers, the books, the champagne, the triumphs, the delights beyond these narrow Appalachian hills.

On that June day, ten months after Sherry's funeral, after finding the strawberries I walked the tractor path again, a man of forty-six now, all of that future behind me. So little had worked out as planned. And now, unimaginably, my sister lay dead in this ground. I felt the crush of three decades of disappointment, their culmination in the final, irrevocable catastrophe of Sherry's death. I closed my hand in a fist. With the back of the fist I dabbed at tears.

I walked to the edge of woods. There the tractor path turns a corner before it vanishes into the forest. At this corner has always stood a cluster of eastern hop-hornbeam trees, also known as ironwoods. I always loved the spot. Thirty years ago I pushed my bike through the dust, among sportive butterflies, and these ironwood trees seemed to welcome me in the morning sun.

I dabbed again at my wet eyes. I gazed at the ironwoods and thought of all I had lost. I remembered myself as a teenage boy, so bright and eager for the world's bounty, its infinitude of promise. I looked at the trees and said aloud, "It's me. I'm back. Do you remember me?"

A becalmed day. Windless.

Yet from the topmost bough of the highest tree, a single leaf detached. I watched as it spiraled down.

The ironwood leaf slowly wafted to me, and it came to rest on my shirt, near the breast pocket. Where the heart beats.

⊃

"THERE'S NO God." My father said it in a voice sanded raw from grief, in the days after Sherry's funeral. "There's no God. If there was a God, why would He allow all the suffering you see in the world?" In disgust, his anger mounting, he said, "I don't want to hear any more of that religious crap from churches. It's all a lie. If there was a God, how could He let that poor girl"—his cherished daughter—"just lie there in that car and not do anything to help?"

My mother said grimly, "I don't believe in God anymore. I don't." And yet she wept at the thought that Sherry might roast eternally with other suicides, damned to a Christian hell. Confused, sharing my father's newfound, heart-shattered atheism, yet lacking his steeled conviction, she wavered and doubted.

"That minister who spoke at Sherry's funeral was a buffoon," my father said with quiet fury. "He just talked in cliches that didn't mean anything. Don't let anyone tell me there's a God. I don't want to hear that garbage anymore."

My parents felt, hour upon excruciating hour, the painful disjunction between a chaotic universe and the human need for order and meaning: Camus' existential Absurd. They had entered the Void. At this desolate extreme Christianity only can demand faith. My parents' faith had vanished.

But Zen thrives in the Void. "Recovering from my sister's suicide is the most difficult challenge I've ever faced in my life," I told Shugen at Zen Mountain Monastery. "And Zen is allowing me to do that. If anyone ever asks if this Zen stuff actually works, you can use me as an example. I'm field-testing it right here, every day. I'm living proof."

Five months before Sherry killed herself she told me of voices and hallucinations.

She didn't call them "hallucinations," though. The fiends, utterly without mercy, who crept into her room at night were real to her, as real as the telephone she held in her hand as she described these terror-stricken encounters to me. She confided from her trailer in Hubbard, Ohio, during three nights in March of 1999 as I sat on my bed in Massachusetts and listened in alarm.

She told me how these creatures might have placed an implant in her brain to control her. She told me how they transported her through the walls of her bedroom, through the walls' lattice-like molecular structure, into the hallway. Or how they entered the locked bedroom to hurt her or whisked her away to remote secret locations for nightlong experiments in torture. "It hurts so much. The pain is excruciating, and they don't care." Powerless against them, living in dread, she slept with a knife. Or she forced herself to go without sleep.

Her husband Ron, a kindly man, a long-distance truck driver, worked nights. He often needed to stay on the road for most of the week. He knew nothing of Sherry's lone nocturnal battles with these monsters. No one did. She told me the incidents had occurred periodically over the past twenty years. And the voices:

"I remember when I was about twelve, everyone went to the store and I was alone in the house but I heard a low murmur of voices, people talking. I thought maybe someone had left a radio on. I walked all over the house trying to find out where these voices were coming from, but I couldn't find them."

My God. My poor sister. I needed to do—what? What could I do?

She said, "I'm telling you because you won't think I'm crazy."

"Schizophrenia is the most severe and frightening of the psychiatric illnesses," Jamison writes. "Left untreated, it usually gets worse over time. Alienation from family and friends is the rule rather than the exception. Suicide, though less common than in the mood disorders, is still common enough to make it a very lethal disease." In fact, a schizophrenic person is eight times more likely to commit suicide. I knew nothing of this statistic as I listened to Sherry. I only knew that my scalp prickled and my skin chilled as I listened to her revelations. I felt an urgent need to help. But how? We were treading on such a delicate catwalk, over such a vast abyss. The merest suggestion of therapy or of antipsychotic drugs and I'd lose her. She was skittish about doctors. "I'm telling you because you won't think I'm crazy...."

The next morning I talked secretly to a friend in Amherst who works as a therapist, seeking advice. I thought that if Sherry continued to trust me and confide in me I could bargain for time and devise a solution.

"Hallucinations, the perception of something where nothing exists, and delusions, false beliefs that persist in spite of incontrovertible evidence to the contrary, are only part of the terror of schizophrenia," Jamison continues. "Often the entire visual and emotional world is transformed into a dark, mapless horror. Auditory hallucinations, especially hearing voices, are common. The voices threaten, condemn and demand....

"The gradual disintegration of a mind is almost incomprehensible. To observe its unwinding from within is surely intolerable. To be frightened of the world; to be walled off from it and harangued by voices; to see life as distorted faces and shapes and colors; to lose constancy and trust in one's brain: for most the pain is beyond conveying."

Zen practitioners in sesshin often experience fleeting hallucinations called *makyō*. Hours of intense meditation, of silence, of sleeplessness and hunger can push the mind into strange corners. I've seen the floor ripple. I've seen the wall dissolve in light. I've seen woodgrain in floor boards arrange itself in patterns of cartoon animals or leering faces—extremely common occurrences, trivial and harmless incidents of the type mentioned in Zen literature and reported by hundreds of meditators. Once during a sesshin at Zen Mountain Monastery, sitting on my zafu since long before dawn and half-starving, I momentarily forgot the prohibition against eye contact. I looked at the woman ladling oatmeal into my ōryōki bowl. Instantly the room around us disappeared. I saw her face, its eyeless, gaping sockets; her skin striated with wriggly orange lines; her mouth an open maw of pain—a macabre parody of Munch's *The Scream*. I blinked and everything returned to normal. "Makyō," I told myself.

Some meditators experience more grandiose visions. A golden Buddha. Clouds unveiling brilliances of sunlight. When meditators report hallucinations, sublime or otherwise, Zen teachers chuckle. "No big deal," they tell us. "Transient illusions, like all thoughts." They admonish us to simply observe these waking dreams and let them go.

Tibetan Buddhists train to encounter similar "hallucinations" of rainbow colors or threatening demons in the *bardo* after death; such training, they believe, will help them in the afterlife to see these phenomena—whether enticing or horrifying—as nothing more than mind-projections.

Brain anomalies similar to epileptic misfirings, or prompted by imbalances of serotonin and other neurotransmitters, may have triggered Sherry's hallucinations. Researchers have begun to realize that zazen and similar Buddhist meditation techniques slowly "rewire" the brain, actually changing its circuitry to make it more tranquil and alert. Could Zen have helped to reconfigure the chemical and neural imbalances in Sherry's brain? If she had been able to try it? If she had been able to meditate? Could Zen have helped her to see the menacing creatures that tormented her—literally to death—as makyō? Or was her illness too crippling?

She never mentioned suicide. According to Jamison, many never do.

Five months before she killed herself Sherry told me on the phone that, during the past year, her small trailer in Ohio had not been invaded and the evil creatures had not menaced her. She said, "I hope they never come back."

"I hope so too, Sher."

She often sounded cheerful. In the last weeks of her life, in that summer of 1999, she and Ron invested in their first computer. It thrilled Sherry to whoosh e-mails and go vagabonding across the Internet, easing her isolation in the trailer. In those final days she became intrigued by classical music. She wanted to buy a CD of Mozart, and she phoned me happily: "Which symphony do you think I should buy? What are some of the best orchestras and conductors?" When I mentioned that I planned to drive to Pennsylvania to see our parents in August, she told me blithely that she'd drive in, too, and visit me—something she rarely did.

"Great!" I told her. "We can hang out and talk. It'll be really nice to see you."

What I saw that August, as it turned out, was her casket in a Pennsylvania funeral parlor.

I think her monsters must have returned abruptly. I think they must have come screeching through the walls again. I think Sherry must have escaped in the only way she had left.

If Freud is right, the death instinct seized her and it won.

In one of our last phone conversations some of the old strangeness had returned. Sherry told me she'd been reading an apocalyptic bestseller called *The Bible Code*. She said she believed the world would end in four more years. She said, "I'm worried about demons."

Tired and exasperated, I said, "Oh, Sher. You don't really believe all that, do you?"

"What?" Her voice tensing.

"You know, demons and the end of the world and all that."

Her voice scorched the phone line: "I know demons exist."

If her psychotic symptoms did flare that summer after a long quiescence, it may have felt unendurable. Jamison writes that people who've struggled through schizophrenia's waking nightmares, and who then enjoyed a reprieve, live with a "terrible anxiety" that the horrors will come back. These fears "play a decisive role in many suicides." She mentions Virginia Woolf. Realizing that her own demons had returned, Woolf, a survivor of past assaults, wrote, "I shan't recover this time. I begin to hear voices, and I can't concentrate. So I am doing what seems the best thing to do."

The thing that seemed best? To die. Virginia Woolf, as we all know, loaded a ballast of stones in her pocket. She walked to the river Ouse. Then she walked into it and disappeared.

ↄ

HOW TO restore in language the life of a person who refused that life, who said "yes" with less and less conviction, then finally said "no"? How to convey the gifts she bestowed?

The tangible ones: candles and sachets, formed lovingly by Sherry's own hand. Her letters, written on thick rag paper marbled pink and saffron, paper she'd made laboriously herself. Ginger snaps, baked from ginger she'd dried and ground. A fading Christmas tree ornament, memento from our childhood, rescued by Sherry and boxed with ribbons.

She gave me an antique bowl of cranberry glass, with her handwritten note: "This is to commemorate the first foreign-language film I ever saw, and my first visit to an 'art-house cinema.' The movie was Werner Herzog's *Heart of Glass*, in German, with the subtitles in English, and you took me to see it at Pleasant Street Theatre when I visited you in Northampton. The movie was so mesmerizing and beautiful. I'll never forget it. Over the years you have introduced me to so many new experiences that I would not have known otherwise. I am so grateful. And so this bowl of antique cranberry glass is in memory of *Heart of Glass*. I hope you like it."

She gave me, as a wedding present, two tickets for a hot-air balloon ride above the canyons of New Mexico, the tickets nestled in a scroll she'd calligraphied: "For Steve and Catherine, as you begin the journey of your lives together."

Each spring she assembled "May baskets" of cut daffodils, iris, and tulips and she gave them as gifts to elderly neighbors. In fall she gave them scarlet carnations, the state flower of Ohio, because Sherry in her guileless and indefatigable good-heartedness thought people might appreciate the significance. That summer before Sherry killed herself the trailer park blistered in a heatwave. Sherry walked from door to sizzling door of each trailer carrying her picnic cooler, a carton of vanilla ice cream, a scoop, and a box of wafer cones, surprising each shrunken old widow or desiccated old man, living alone, with an impromptu treat to cool and cheer and refresh them. "I thought you might like this," she announced, then she lingered to chat, relieving their loneliness, and of course that was her true gift to them—her companionship—on that hot day.

So many gifts....

Her volunteer work in a nursing home. The gift of her intelligence, of her initiative and zest: at sixteen she quit high school and won a job as a newspaper reporter and created front-page stories notable for their breezy, engaging leads, their smartness and aplomb.

She took a correspondence course to learn Greek. She taught herself to play the flute.

The intangible gifts: Her laughter, the giggle with the sharp little falsetto squeak on the intake of breath, a giggle of delight that burst when she described a *Far Side* cartoon or a Tracey Ullman skit she'd seen on TV, or Woody Allen, or Mel Brooks' *Young Frankenstein*. The gifts of her caring and concern. Her sensitivity. Her inquisitiveness. Her ardor for books, for funky jazz and Tina Turner and Celtic folk music, for classic Hollywood flicks like *Gone with the Wind*, the gift of her bubbling enthusiasm.

Once in late September she led me through meadows to a knoll in the Amish hayfields, one of her favorite places, to show me the view of Appalachian foothills visible through Lick Run Gap. From there she led me through ragtag cornfields to the woods. As we neared the trees the air of Indian summer began to sweeten, heavy with cider. "Look," Sherry said. Her prize discovery: a mammoth apple tree, gnarled matriarch from the era when everybody around here—not only the Amish—rode in buggies drawn by trotters. The tree's branches drooped with pippins burnished red and bronze. At the tree's roots lay a mash of fallen apples, a perfumed, sun-fermented pulp, and yellowjackets flying woozily, drunk on the nectar of applejack. "This tree must be two hundred years old, at least," she marveled. "Isn't it beautiful?"

When owners of an abandoned limestone quarry down the hill from the apple tree threatened to resume their mining operation, gouging the meadows and destroying the land, Sherry protested to a state official. She didn't make an irate phone call. Instead she mailed him a heart-shaped pillow she'd crocheted herself, filled with milkweed and cattail fluff she'd gathered. She enclosed a letter:

"I live in the Foothills development and have walked the nearby fields and roads, including the quarries. On my travels I have seen: deer, a fox, rabbits,

skunk, groundhogs, opossum, and a black bear on the Ridge Road. The sky has contained hawks, goldfinches, hummingbirds, black-capped chickadees, bluebirds, mourning doves, owls, cardinals, robins, red-winged blackbirds and others.

"At night in the summer the fireflies cover the fields thickly, creating quite a display. I love to see the mist rolling in from the gap and along the base of the range. I am particularly proud that there is not one light blemishing the mountainface, like you see elsewhere.

"The whole area is surrounded by Amish families and their farms. They travel the roads here often....

"Lick Run is a little brook that now runs crystal clear. I have often seen men fishing from it. There is a large stand of cattail and milkweed.

"Monarch butterflies will lay eggs only on milkweed plants. The caterpillars then feed on the plants.

"Scientists have only recently discovered Mexico's secret valley to which the butterflies migrate. So many cluster on the trees that the trees look like an autumn tree in North America....

"In the fall, milkweed pods yield a downy fluff which can be used for stuffing material.

"Just some of the many beautiful plants growing here are: wild lilac   day lilies   blackberries   daisies   shamrocks   black-eyed susans   sumac ferns   yarrow   pokeweed*

(* - legend has it that the Declaration of Independence was signed with pokeberry juice)

toadflax   teasels   hedge bindweed   clover   new england asters northeastern yucca   and a magnificent wild apple tree

"Across from the quarry entrance is a lot of wild purple and white phlox— which smell as good as they look. I have also gathered much goldenrod and Queen Anne's lace to use for dried arrangements. Another precious find was a patch of wild strawberries.

"I think that our little corner of paradise has paid our dues already by the two huge quarries that have already been dug here.

"Please use your influence to avert a potential tragedy...."

I always expected that someday Sherry and I would stroll those fields again. On the day of her funeral, I drove my sobbing parents in their car, following the hearse. En route to Cedar Hill Cemetery we rode past those same fields Sherry loved, where she had meandered for hours picking armfuls of milkweed, watching for hawks.

I made so many mistakes. In the final days of her life, I'd hear her messages on my answering machine when I'd dragged myself wearily home from work, her voice obviously disappointed: "I guess you're not there. Okay. I'll try later." When the phone rang in those last days sometimes I told her, in my busy self-involvement, "Sher, I'm too tired to talk right now," and again I'd hear her disappointment: "Oh, alright," she sighed. "I'll talk to you later." We think we always have time. If I had recognized those phone calls as the last ones before Sherry fell into the blackness forever, I would have said so many things. I would have said, "I love you." I've said those words to half-a-dozen women who later drifted out of my life but I never spoke them to my own sister. Of course I signed my letters to her with "love"—my rushed, infrequent letters—but I felt too shy to speak the three crucial words aloud. Now I say them every time I visit her grave.

On August 10, 1999, the day she killed herself, Sherry arranged her husband Ron's dress shoes neatly on the floor of a bedroom closet. Above the shoes she hung his suit jacket on a hanger, and a new tie she'd purchased, so he could wear them to her funeral.

She had already done laundry and vacuumed and cleaned the trailer to make it immaculate. She'd paid the bills and deleted files from the computer. She'd stocked the refrigerator with groceries so her husband might embark with minimal inconvenience on a life without her. She'd set out his coffee cup with a carefully measured spoon of decaf.

Did she perform these acts in cold and barely constrained rage? Or in a stuporous, misguided goodness of heart? Or in a daze of mental illness?

She drove to a storage locker facility beside the highway in Hubbard. She paid cash to rent a locker, a remote one at the edge of the lot. The locker, the size of a one-car garage, had a metal door that yanked up and down. Undetected, Sherry drove the car into the storage locker. She tugged the locker's door down behind her. The locker became her tomb.

She attached a hose to the car's exhaust pipe, as my girlfriend Joanne had done seventeen years before.

An Ohio detective told me later, over the phone, that in Sherry's trailer he'd found a hardware store receipt for the hose. She'd purchased it in May, four months earlier. Apparently she'd kept the hose in readiness all summer, in case the hallucinatory creatures returned at night to terrorize her.

After Sherry attached the hose she ran it through the car's rear passenger window, got inside the car, sealed it with duct tape, and lay down on the back seat. The detective told me she'd done a thorough job.

Did she lie there with her eyes open or closed? Did her life—a life of greater distress, of greater extremity than we ever supposed—flash before her in those terminal moments, as we are told to believe? If so, what did she see as carbon monoxide began to smother her brain, as the sleep engulfed her?

She lay dead in the car for two days. A storage lot attendant heard the muffled hum of the engine. He flung open the locker's metal door.

The day steamed. On August 13, 1999, in Northampton, Massachusetts, the leaves dripped, the air was dense as Singapore's or Manila's, the sun oozed through that density in a vague delirium of light. Trying to breathe felt like trying to suck oxygen through a hot, wet rag. Miserable in that sultry humidity I made lunch. Prepared to shower. The phone rang.

When I answered I heard a tentative, "Steve?" Then wailing: "Steve?"

"Mom," I said. "What's wrong?"

◯

TWO-AND-A-HALF YEARS after Sherry's suicide, at a First Night celebration on New Year's Eve, my girlfriend Jenny and I listened to a recital performed on a glass harmonica. "Have you ever heard of it?" Sherry asked me once on the phone. "It's not what you might think. It's not a harmonica like a mouth organ. A glass harmonica is an eighteenth-century musical instrument invented by Benjamin Franklin. I saw a man play it on TV this morning. It sounds so beautiful, it's breathtaking."

I went to the concert, in a Presbyterian church in downtown State College, Pennsylvania, as a personal memorial to my sister.

A glass harmonica makes music in precisely the same way that a moist fingertip produces ringing tones when it circles the rim of a crystal goblet. To play a glass harmonica the musician operates a foot treadle, which spins a row of gold-rimmed glass bowls arranged in descending sizes on a silver rod; applying wet fingers to the moving glass produces shimmering tones, ethereal, like bells whistling through a pipe organ. As Jenny and I watched the glass harmonica's spinning chrysalis of bowls, as we listened to celestial harmonies produced from its glistening spindle of gold and silver, I remembered what Sherry had said:

"Oh, Steve. Oh, Steve. I wish you could hear it. It's so beautiful. It's the most beautiful thing I've ever heard. I think it must be what you hear when your soul is floating up to heaven."

WHEN THIS summer began, ten weeks ago, irises—those flowers placed by Greeks at the tombs of women—and wild buttercups graced the pond and high meadows of Springwater Meditation Center. Red-winged blackbirds announced early June through fields of rural New York, across hills west of the Finger Lakes, their impeccable black plumage smeared at the shoulders with crimson and yellow as if they'd brushed against fresh paint—as if they'd brushed against the colors, still moist, of the dawning world.

Now, a humid evening in the Appalachian ridges of Pennsylvania, mist rising from Amish cornfields. Sweet, heavy perfume of mid-August. When summer began these fields looked barren. But if an Amish horse were to canter into one of the fields now it would instantly vanish: the corn is that high.

Finishing my evening's zazen, I step outdoors. Moon rising at dusk in a deepening blue sky. Last night Jenny and I dined at an Indian restaurant in State College and for dessert I ordered mango ice cream; the moon is that color now, that same creamy orange.

—

Next day the air feels swampy. At ninety degrees the thermometer seems to wilt. Late in the afternoon I watch a duo of white butterflies, twirling as they ascend on thermals. I'm walking among trees and wildflower thickets at a nature preserve a few miles from Shingletown Gap. Tussey Mountain hulks to the south. To the west a livid sun burns its last embers.

I move among Queen Anne's lace. Goldenrod. Daisy fleabane. Eros, the life instinct, abounds in this ripened summer. But within weeks Thanatos will reign, the autumnal kingdom of death. Life and mortality entwined in flight like these two butterflies.

Purple thistle gone to seed, silken whisks, white as spun fiberglass.

I snatch a fistful of the summer's final blackberries, tart on my tongue.

This instant: peppery scents, like dried potpourri, of the unmown flower meadows basked in daylong sun.

Nested in grass, corpse of a robin, its eye hole plucked clean.

Bumblebees and sweat-bees work remaining blossoms with their fervid, single-minded concentration. In Zen we call such concentration *joriki.*

I find baneberry, its bright red fruits like latex to the touch, each berry a morsel of poison. Nearby grow clumps of touch-me-not with its orange bell-cups; it's a medicinal plant, good for soothing poison ivy. Around a bend in the trail I find Joe Pye weed, easily seven feet high with its pink cockade, a plant that cures fevers. The poison and the medicinals, death and life, flourishing side by side.

FOUR YEARS AFTER SHERRY'S SUICIDE

crows, all my life crows
escort me,
crows in black chitons,
crows in livery

black
as chauffeurs

of hearses, crows blackly
insistent in raw flatted
corn, companions

hoarse with news
of season's terminus, of summer
fatally

succumbing –
all my life
crows escort me
to hillocks, wheeling home
blank skies and the skies' encroaching
winds, each a herald
of coming storm,
squalor of ice

in raucous voices, choir
of black wings and vanishing

light: crows today
fling past me,
call   where's your sister
where's your sister?

[2003]

◡

"ALL FAMILIES of suicides are alike. They wear a kind of permanent letter
'S' on their chests," Janet Malcolm has written, invoking both Tolstoy
and Hawthorne. "Their guilt is never assuaged. Their anxiety never lifts.

They are freaks among families in the way prodigies are freaks among individuals."

This weekend marks the fourth anniversary of Sherry's funeral.

Four years ago we arrived at the small funeral parlor in the broken-down hamlet of Howard, Pennsylvania, as if chloroformed, walking in a haze of disbelieving sadness. My parents wept without relief. Sherry, so kind-hearted and generous through so much of her life, had secretly endured a harrowing schizophrenia without benefit of friends, and so not a single friend existed to attend her funeral. My parents caressed her coffin. My aunt and two cousins flew in from Ohio, bearing wreaths of lilies, and Sherry's husband Ron, stricken, pale with distress, arrived with his own supportive clan. My brother and I had jetted from New England the night before, sleepless and numb. I stayed awake and scrawled a four-page eulogy for Sherry's funeral. It is the hardest task I have ever accomplished.

"So now we say goodbye.... She loved us so much. If, in the end, her private struggles overcame her, it's not because she didn't love us with all her heart." Reading the eulogy aloud my voice threatened to snap. Tears began to well. Because in Japan I had practiced iaidō, the meditative martial art of drawing the sword, to steady myself while delivering the speech at Sherry's funeral I thought repeatedly, "Bushidō. Bushidō." The samurai warrior code of strength and valor. "Bushidō," I urged myself, struggling not to cry. I needed to remain strong for my parents, who were near collapse. "It's important to remember how heroic she was, how she managed to remain loving and good despite her secret tortures, and she fought heroically—with all her soul, hour by hour—to enjoy her life, all the way to the age of thirty-nine."

We emerged into a peerless summer day. Blue skies and euphoria of sunshine clashed obscenely with our grief. We followed the hearse. If I remember that blurred, infamous day correctly, I drove my parents in their station wagon; but maybe not, maybe someone from the funeral parlor drove us. We rode for seven miles to Cedar Hill Cemetery, passing the meadows Sherry loved, the places she'd walked in search of Queen Anne's lace and milkweed pods for her dried-flower arrangements. At the cemetery we stood in stunned farewell. We gazed at the heaped bouquets, at the green carpet provided by the mortician to hide, discreetly, the raw gouge in the clay where her coffin would soon repose. My parents sobbed as if they might die with Sherry. My brother put his arm on their shoulders and I did the same. We stared at the coffin in horror.

Today we go back. Of course we go back often. On this Sunday afternoon, four years since the burial, we place a basket of red portulaca on Sherry's gravestone. My mother brushes mown grass clippings from the granite marker with her hand, tenderly. I tidy a vase of silk yellow roses my parents brought to the grave last spring. My father cries. He shakes his head, still faintly incredulous. How can this have happened? My mother cries and touches her palm to the gravestone, whispering, "I love you, darling." My parents have aged markedly in the past four years, trauma scraping away at them with its heedless blade, leaving them wizened and hobbled and frail. It seems an appalling violation of nature, I think, as I watch my elderly parents tend the grave of their young daughter. How can this happen? What kind of world is this?

Yet as I look beyond Cedar Hill Cemetery to the green meadows, to the ridge of corn, lush in the sun, then to clouds and pines and open sky beyond, I know it's all inviolate, all of nature simply existing as it must: the earth holding my sister's body; the lilting, eternal waltz of living and dying, of no-birth and no-death, nothing created and nothing destroyed; the breaths I watch in Zen and the breaths that cease at the moment we enter the vast Unknowable—realm where Joanne has ventured, perished by her own hand, and now my sister Sherry. All of it interconnecting, all of it sacred in Mystery.

All of it meriting joy. Not shallow happiness but, as Camus proclaimed in *The Myth of Sisyphus*, joy: hard-tested, a joy unvanquished, a fierce and resolute joy.

As we turn to leave the cemetery in this haunting place, my Appalachian homeland, I look again beyond the cornfields to the far ridge of woodlands, where I asked the ironwood trees, "Do you remember me?" Where in answer, on a windless day, they sent one leaf from topmost branches and it spiraled down to touch my shirt at the center. At my breastbone.

Where the heart beats.

PART
FOUR

ERRANT PILGRIM:
ON ZEN BUDDHIST
MINISTRY

2005–2011

◯

"Here in America we cannot define Zen Buddhists the same way we do in Japan…. You are on your way to discovering some appropriate way of life."
– **Shunryu Suzuki,** *Zen Mind, Beginner's Mind*

THIRTEEN

I FIRST read Ralph Waldo Emerson's "An Address" the way, I assume, many of my fellow Harvard Divinity School students have read it: in the Divinity Hall chapel, in the very room where Emerson first spoke the words aloud. I read it there to get the tang of it, the original zing and tartness.

I sat by myself in a pew on a late afternoon in September 2005. Though hushed, the chapel soon began to ring in my imagination with the brisk appeal of Emerson's voice, with his clarion sentences as I encountered them, moment by moment, on the page. I envisioned him in the pulpit. I envisioned the Harvard students who had invited this amiable renegade. I envisioned their elders—the glowering men with their muttonchop whiskers and starched cravats, who would shun the "Sage of Concord" for thirty years following this address—as they began to squirm. I envisioned the students again. I saw them listening, at first politely, then saw one or two of them jolted into a sort of incredulous, astonished joy as they began to grasp the possibilities Emerson dared to offer them.

And then I was jolted myself: the fire bell in Divinity Hall began to blast. As I closed my book, as I joined staffers and professors evacuating the building in an unannounced drill, I thought: how appropriate. A sermon by Emerson can still set off alarms.

When he delivered that startling Divinity School address in 1838, Emerson had renounced his preaching vocation, but the address remains every inch a sermon. It cajoles, it reasons, it provokes. It seeks to awaken the reader, or the listener, from a perilous slumber, from a torpor of the soul, from that sluggish death-in-life that afflicts as many now as in

Emerson's time. Like all good sermons it speaks urgently, from the intellect, from the spirit, from the heart. It speaks so urgently that, minutes before the fire alarm sounded in Divinity Hall, I had already, by the ninth page of Emerson's address, bolted upright in my pew, fervid with excitement, clenching my fist and whispering, "Yes. Yes."

How does Emerson do it? He begins with the immediate, the tangible; he begins with what he loves, with the natural world, "this refulgent summer," the sweet "breath of the pine," the "new hay." Emerson brings the countryside of Concord into the Cambridge chapel. He, in effect, flings open the windows of the chapel so that his audience may luxuriate in the miracle of summer—a miracle, he implies, that they have probably taken for granted lately.

Soon Emerson starts to risk danger. Halfway through his address the scandal begins, as he boldly identifies two errors of "historical Christianity." First, Emerson declares, traditional Christianity not only concerns itself exclusively with a distorted image of Jesus but denies us the chance to truly seek and discover the divine in ourselves. And second, it fails to recognize that the Moral Law can speak directly to the infinite soul in each of us.

Then this man who has renounced his own conventional ministry warns the audience that they face an emergency. (The chapel in Divinity Hall is tiny. Emerson would have been able to feel his audience—clergymen and young divinity students—bristle.) The address, impassioned now, turns to the issue of preaching.

Magnificent with scorn and conviction, with earnest pleading, it issues directly from Emerson's deepest core. You can tell he has brooded about this during long walks by the Concord River and through long nights in his study. You can tell he is obsessed. You can discern, immediately, that *this* is what he cares about, that *this* is what impelled him to accept the Divinity School invitation, to stand before these people and talk. He speaks from his own experience, precisely as he urges ministers to do:

> I once heard a preacher who sorely tempted me to say I would
> go to church no more. Men go, thought I, where they are wont
> to go, else had no soul entered the temple in the afternoon. A

snow-storm was falling all around us. The snow-storm was real, the preacher merely spectral, and the eye felt the sad contrast in looking at him, and then out of the window behind him into the beautiful meteor of the snow. He had lived in vain. He had no one word intimating that he had laughed or wept, was married or in love, had been commended, or cheated, or chagrined. If he had ever lived and acted, we were none the wiser for it. The capital secret of his profession, namely, to convert life into truth, he had not learned. Not one fact in all his experience had he yet imported into his doctrine.... Not a line did he draw out of real history. The true preacher can be known by this, that he deals out to the people his life—life passed through the fire of thought.

To convert life into truth.... Life passed through the fire of thought. Reading these words, I imagined the stress Emerson would have placed on each syllable, his forefinger jabbing the lectern.

"You're pioneers." At Harvard, in the spring of 2006, six months after reading the Emerson address, I sit each Wednesday morning at a long table in a seminar room on the first floor of Divinity Hall with seven or eight fellow students in the "Colloquium for Buddhist Ministry." Since 1636, Harvard has trained a learned ministry. Most of my classmates in the Master of Divinity program study in preparation for careers as Christian ministers—Lutheran, Unitarian, Baptist, Pentecostal, Methodist. We in the Buddhist Colloquium rank among the very few, and also among the very first, to train for Buddhist ministry—we're discovering this new landfall and mapping it as we go. We're explorers. Our advisor, Janet Gyatso, the Hershey Professor of Buddhist Studies here and an internationally renowned scholar of Tibetan Buddhism, told us on the first day: "You're pioneers. Your karma brought you here, and so did mine. You're the first students to train in the Buddhist ministry track in the new curriculum here. Given what Harvard is in American culture, and indeed in the world, this is a historic moment for Buddhism. It really is."

It's a moment within more than a century of haphazard Buddhist transmission in North America. Buddhism initially came here about the time of Emerson's address in Divinity Hall, with the arrival of Chinese workers in California, and it "officially" arrived in 1893, with an Asian Buddhist delegation to the Congress of World Religions at the Chicago Exposition. Asian immigrants, particularly on the West Coast, established temples and strong Buddhist communities. Among non-Asians in the US, Buddhism gained some hip notoriety in the Fifties, with the Beats. It started to flourish more rapidly on this continent in the fabulous 1960s and '70s, in my own lucky lifetime. Thus we who now practice Buddhism in the United States belong to the first generations to see it begin to prosper on a widening scale. It offers an exciting opportunity, like being among the first communities of Christians established by Paul in Corinth, in Galatia, in Philippi.

Here at Harvard we try to imagine—as students at Naropa, the Buddhist university in Colorado, or as students in Buddhist Studies programs throughout the country try to imagine—what Buddhism will look like in America during the twenty-first century. (Or perhaps we should say: try to imagine what "Buddhisms" will look like. The practices vary dramatically, from Vipassana to Soka Gakkai, from Shingon to Pure Land, from Tibetan Vajrayana sects to Sōtō and Rinzai Zen.) We work to make our visions happen, in all their freshness and vitality.

Harvard's Divinity Hall stands an improbable distance from that trailer in the Appalachian hills of Pennsylvania where my family lived through most of my childhood. It stands an improbable distance from the smokestacks of the paper mill in Lock Haven, from the busted luck of the withered farms, from surly hangdog men with guns in the backwoods hunting camps of Bald Eagle Mountain, from the waters of the Susquehanna. It stands a great distance, too, from our house in Cedar Heights. From Bruce Bechdel's classroom in Bald Eagle-Nittany High School. From the Amish boys in April plowing with their horses. A great distance, finally, from the banks of Fishing Creek, where as a teenager I lounged beneath oaks, thrilling to ecstatic incantations from *Leaves of Grass*, pausing to watch the flicker of trout in shaded water, or to gaze at kingfishers and herons. Yet all of that led me to Harvard Yard.

FOURTEEN

NEARLY NINE years have passed, now, since I lived through an autumn in Kanegasaki, Japan, sitting zazen in the frosted dawn light of Taiyo-ji Temple with Watanabe rōshi, or flashing my sword in iai-dō practice, or rapping brisk cadences on the shimedaiko with Yukie and my fellow taiko drummers. Nearly nine years since I wandered alleys and temple grounds of Kyoto, since I ventured to Hiroshima, to the shrines and pagodas and forested deer park at Nara, to the northern mountains. Increasingly, Zen practice becomes my true home. Life itself becomes my home.

Zen practice has engaged me in the vast hall of Zen Mountain Monastery, amid silence of solemn candles, chirrup of sparrows, dawn rain. (A haiku I jotted there: "This 'self' a lens cap / on a telescope—lose it, / see a thousand miles.") It has engaged me in the intimate zendo of Mount Equity Monastery in rural Pennsylvania, the former Quaker homestead where Dai-En Bennage, one of the first American women ordained as a Sōtō Zen priest in Japan, presides. There roving peacocks slash the evening hush of zazen with their squeals. Appaloosas graze a fenced paddock. (A haiku after walking with others in silent kinhin meditation at Mount Equity: "Good silent Buddhas / we pass white and purple phlox— / horse couldn't care less.") Zen practice has engaged me, too, in the meditation room at Springwater.

Through working with kōans ("How do you stop the sound of a distant temple bell?" or "Take a five-storied pagoda from a teapot" or "Draw Mount Fuji from your breast pocket") I'm discovering a different way of knowing, one beyond the cerebral functions I use here at Harvard. When I sit with a kōan it feels like I'm falling in slow motion down an elevator shaft from the brain in my head to the brain in my belly, into the hara, where a lucent, intuitive "gut wisdom" resides.

My practice continues ripening. I scarcely recognize the person I used to be. Who was that conflicted, surly, mixed-up person, the one in fading memory who shares my name and a younger version of my face, but who seems almost a stranger now? At this stage of practice I let go more readily. I succeed more often in keeping my psychic doors open and receptive. Anger bursts less frequently. When it comes, it comes in a flash, lightning in a desert sky—instantaneous then gone, hurting neither myself nor anyone else. I learn and make blunders ("one continuous mistake," as Dōgen says) and grow on the path.

Errant pilgrim.

Errant in the sense of "fallible."

Errant in the sense of "traveling or given to traveling; straying outside the proper path or bounds; moving about aimlessly or irregularly; deviating from a standard."

Far from my origins in the hills of Appalachia.

○

IMPROBABLE HISTORIES. Almost no one in my small rural high school in Mill Hall, Pennsylvania, went directly to college after graduating in the late 1960s and early 1970s. In addition to its "General Academic," "Business," "Vocational," and "Agriculture" tracks, my school did keep the fanciful pretense of something called a "College Prep" curriculum, but it remained nearly meaningless; in my own class of '72 only two or three kids in "College Prep" actually went straight to college after graduating; another enrolled in a Bible institute in Texas. A handful of "College Prep" kids might have trickled later into Lock Haven State. A few eventually tried several of the other tiny colleges scattered among the region's mountains—Clarion State, Mansfield State—or made it into Penn State, and a very rare few gradually ventured to colleges outside Pennsylvania, perhaps leaving Clinton County on extended sojourns for the first time in their lives. It's different now, of course. I've heard of young people in Mill Hall and Lock Haven going to Stanford and Cornell. And I'm told that some of the kids who played among us in Cedar Heights even became adults who earned doctorates. But in the early Seventies, many of my classmates did what their families and the local culture urged them to do: They stayed close to home in those Appalachian hills and found jobs in construction, nursing, farming, retail clerking, trucking, or signed up with the army or navy. Bruce and Helen Bechdel's fervent efforts to engage them in Eliot, Joyce, and Faulkner were, for most, the last formal education they would receive.

But some eventually did find their ways out. Now I've joined them. Before arriving at Harvard I became—in May of 2005, at the age of fifty, at Penn State University—one of the few in my high school class, and the first person in my family, since the arrival of the Rühle clan of German peasant farmers upon the American coast in 1771, to graduate from college with a bachelor's degree.

In midlife, people often take care of unfinished business. More profoundly, at midlife the lost possibilities—truly, the lost selves—that we've forsaken, that we've famished for so many years, demand their long-belated feast. At nineteen I had yearned to study the world's great religions, but I starved this deep need. I chose art and literature instead. (Like so many aesthetes, I eventually crashed hard against the limitations of artistic life, of literary life. Yet unlike those people I did not end up drunk, embittered or dead.) As I neared the half-century mark of my life, the delayed task of earning my college diploma at Penn State and of studying religion—not so much to find answers, but to seek new questions—felt urgent.

Had a soothsayer told me when I was a teenager that someday I'd become a graying, middle-aged, undergraduate honors major in religious studies, I'd have guffawed in derision. Me? Yet at Penn State that's what I did. I savored a course on Islamic civilization, reading *hadith* as well as *sūrahs* from the Qur'an; and a course on Second Temple Judaism, reading the bold entreaties of prophets from throughout the Hebrew Bible; and on Hinduism, selecting from the *Rig Veda* and the *Upanishads* and the *Bhagavad Gita*. I splurged on a course called "Early Christianity," inching not only through canonical Gospel texts and the odd, disturbing commentaries of orthodox "Church fathers" such as Tertullian, Origen,

Clement, Ireneus, and Justin, but discovering with elation the non-ca-
nonical teachings of Jesus—including my favorite, the richly provocative
"Jesus kōans" of the Gospel of Thomas.

I wandered under Penn State's campus elms musing on Essene monks
of two millennia ago, praying in their desert refuge at Qumran near the
Dead Sea. I scrunched into study carrels at Pattee Library to research my
papers on Hindu Tantra. On Kierkegaard. On Confucianism and Taoism.

In classrooms, finding a vacant seat in front rows and plopping my
shoulder-bag stuffed with notebooks and textbooks, I'd settle in among
students thirty years younger. It felt peculiar being conspicuous and invisible at the same time. Conspicuous, as an out-of-place adult among kids
scarcely done with high school, and invisible, as someone irrelevant to
their social networks of dorms and parties.

Most Penn State professors greeted me with relief, glad to have an
attentive pupil. One or two were suspicious, or even dismissive. I realized
that if a woman returns to college at midlife, she's applauded—people
assume she's lived as a homemaker, raised her children, and now she's fulfilling herself, winning her long-postponed college diploma. Wonderful!
But if a man returns as a nearly fifty-year-old undergrad, people assume
he must have screwed up royally out in the world, botched a career, and
has finally admitted defeat by slouching back to school with the young-
sters. What kind of real man would do that? One university official asked
me if I was in college at my age because I'd served prison time.

I persevered. Daily I sat in meditation. I watched emotions arise from
stillness and quietness, solidify and waft like plumes of colored smoke in
a magician's act, then dissipate into quiet and stillness.

I didn't study religions exclusively. I added courses in Earth sciences,
symbolic logic, African art, positive psychology, Japanese language, mathematics, astronomy and lab, biology, Chinese art, Native American cultures, jūdō. I won straight "A"s, which provoked pleasant bafflement in
my science professors, who considered religious studies majors to be sim-
pletons. They invited me to lunch.

Meanwhile I drafted a massive honors thesis, exploring mystical paths
of Saint Francis, Dōgen, and Rūmī in the thirteenth-century worlds
of Christianity, Buddhism, and Islam. In final weeks before the thesis

deadline I sat at my computer like an anchorite within a cell of books and notes. I typed nonstop. Each day the sun rose. Its light wandered the room. It shifted into darkness. It returned at dawn. I continued typing. During that week I slept for a total of three hours. It felt like the sesshins I've done when living in Zen monasteries—those week-long marathons of meditation, in silence and without eye contact, when I sat in the candlelit zendo at four in the morning and observed breathing, the drifting thoughts, the sensations in the bodymind until nine at night, sitting, getting up to walk in meditative kinhin, working quietly, sitting again in zazen, hour after hour, day after day. The breakthrough into hyper-clarity, vibrant and buzzing and fiercely alive.

Three decades earlier, when I had enacted my "self-education" program, alone in Appalachia, scorching my way through books, I had craved power. Now, at Penn State, I studied simply to learn. And I had so much to learn. It was like the *World Book Encyclopedia* of my childhood springing to life.

As a working-class person, to augment my scholarships and my hefty school loans—tens of thousands of dollars—I labored one semester in the overnight shift at a group home in town, a few blocks from campus. It housed adults, some of them violent, suffering from profound physical and mental impairments. Between bouts of leading them back to their beds when alarms rang and I found them roaming the halls, I stayed up and did homework. One night I got to the group home late because I'd been visiting my parents and found my father perched on the edge of his bed speaking gibberish, and I realized his brain was short-circuiting in a mini-stroke. I rushed him to the hospital and, sitting beside him in the emergency room, I studied for exams.

It all paid off—Phi Beta Kappa, a diploma with high honors, selection as college marshal, delivering a graduation address at commencement—but academic success also provided my family a joyful counterpoint to Sherry's funeral, six years before. From the podium at the Penn State graduation ceremony in that spring of 2005, where I stood in my indigo cap and gown to deliver my speech, I saw, among the crowd of five thousand people in the packed tiers of the hall, my brother, my girlfriend Jenny, and my parents, beaming. And thus our slow healing continues.

Even so, a working-class person who becomes first in the family to graduate from college often feels ambivalent and conflicted, grappling with commingled emotions of victory, validation, shame, guilt. Though my parents glowed with pride, I also felt acutely how my lofty collegiate triumphs distanced us from each other—making my parents feel quietly self-conscious and inadequate; making me feel traitorous in rising above my social class.

Here at Harvard I'm engaged in a three-year master's program; when I graduate, I'll receive a degree naming me a Master of Divinity. I grin at the phrase. What does a master of divinity do? What does it mean to have mastered the divine?

Months after arriving I'm still making adjustments. The Divinity School seems a fortress of Christianity, in which some of us exist as a token Muslim or Hindu or Jew, or as a forlorn Buddhist. My Christian class-mates don't see it that way. "We have so much diversity here!" one of them exclaims. "We have Lutherans, Methodists, Presbyterians, Episcopalians, Catholics—" When our miniscule coterie of Buddhist students com-plains about biases in the required general classes taught by Christian theologians, a dean informs us that we live in a Christian culture and need to accept it. That's the deal: we're tolerated as long as we acquiesce, and the school can point to us and pride itself on its religious pluralism.

In the meantime I study. Because Zen has existed for centuries as a "transmission beyond words and scriptures," because it urges direct tast-ing of reality—here, now—people assume Zen ignores books and aca-demic study. Yet Dōgen proved himself a formidable scholar. And during the autumn of 2000 when I'd returned from Japan and lived in gray robes at Zen Mountain Monastery, we practiced "book learning" as one of the "Eight Gates" of Zen training, reading and discussing methodically the *Vimalakīrti Sutra*. Here at Harvard I sit in the neo-Gothic stone bastion of Andover Hall, or across the street in the Center for the Study of World Religions, or across the Harvard campus in Sever Hall near the Yard, lis-tening intently to lectures and writing slapdash in notebooks. Or I rush through the marble foyer of Widener Library, then descend three floors into labyrinthine stacks to ferret a volume of commentaries on poems by Chinese Buddhist nuns.

Most people probably don't realize the arduous toil undertaken by ministers in training at Harvard. At the Divinity School we're assigned four books to read, in their entirety, each week. It's like the vow we make each day in Zen: "sentient beings are numberless, I vow to save them"; at Harvard, it's "books are numberless, I vow to read them all." We read French philosopher Pierre Hadot on Socrates and Marcus Aurelius, we read Catherine Bell on ritual theory, we read Dietrich Bonhoeffer, we read Judith Butler and Luce Irigaray and Julia Kristeva, applying their postmod feminist theories to Buddhist scriptures. Studying with some of the foremost Biblical scholars in the world, we read the New Testament, we read from the Didache, we read Athanasius on Saint Anthony. We read from translations of the Nag Hammadi scrolls. We quench ourselves with texts. For my "Buddhism in China to the Sixth Century" course we read Hsi Ch'ao and Seng Chao, we read the *Lotus Sutra* and the Sutra in Forty-Two Sections. For "Tibetan Buddhism" we read the biography of Milarepa and wondrous first-person accounts of feral visionary yogis in caves; we read of Jigme Lingpa who gets zapped with Treasure teachings from *dakinis*; we read Orgyan Chokyi, a questing, indefatigable hermitess of the Himalayas. For "Women in Taoism" we read poems by Yu Xuanxi. For "Intro to Ministry" we read essays by Foucault. We read books about the Black church in America, about a woman rabbi in New York, about a Hindu sacred city in Nepal, about Bloods and Crips in L.A., about Mennonites, about the post-September 11 Muslim world. We study theological languages. As a Zen practitioner, mine is the lexicon of Japan, so I labor to translate the squiggles of a Sōtō Zen manual into English and I study for intensive written exams in Japanese.

And we write academic papers. Hunching at my PC keyboard I compose dozens of them, with pedantic-sounding titles such as "Beyond the Broken Mirror: Applying Theories of Performative Mimesis Constructed by Gadamer, Ricoeur, and Derrida to the Northern Thai *Buddhabhiseka* Ritual," or "Buddhist Monastics, Sexless *Sannyasins*, and Finding a Middle Path for Nuns: The *Cullavaga* and *Suttavibhangha* in the Context of Late First Century BCE / Early First Century CE Hindu and Jain Attitudes Regarding the Status of Women." Writing these papers doesn't feel like pedantry, though. My mind goes supersonic with excitement. It's hard labor, but it's fun.

Of course this comprises merely the intellectual part of our work. We Master of Divinity students also learn pastoral care and counseling, training in deep listening and offering spiritual guidance to one another in supervised practice sessions. We learn techniques for attending to people who are nearing death and for consoling their families. We learn the mechanics of ministry and how to work with members of congregations. We learn the psychological dynamics of transference and counter-transference, and the necessity of maintaining proper boundaries (critical especially in contemporary American Buddhism, with its burden of sex scandals and its power-trips by dharma stars and unscrupulous so-called "masters.") We learn ministry, too, through our field placements: in Cambridge hospital wards and rape crisis centers, in Boston homeless shelters and food banks, in street churches and hospices. As co-chair of the Harvard Buddhist Community, I also help to lead a Zen meditation group on Monday nights—which eases us out of the cerebral life and back into the somatic dimension of the body-mind, back into breath and silence and sanity.

By nature a rebel, conforming to the standards of an elite institution like Harvard challenges me sometimes—the Zen I love most is Bodhidharma's and Ikkyū's and Lin-Chi's and Yun-men's, irreverent, earthy, iconoclastic. (A monk piously asked Master Yun-men, "I heard a teaching that speaks of the purity of all-encompassing wisdom. What is that purity like?" Yun-men spat at him. Still not getting it, the monk continued, "Please explain to me a teaching of the old masters." Yun-men said, "Come here! Cut off your feet, replace your skull, take the chopsticks from your bowl! Now, lift your nose up from the floor!" The monk asked, "Where would one find such teachings?" Yun-men said, "You windbag!" and hit him with his stick.) As always I find my own way.

And each time I saunter through Harvard Yard, I laugh in astonishment. "I'm at Harvard. I'm actually at Harvard." My suffering in that distant Appalachian high school in Mill Hall, Pennsylvania feels redeemed.

—

Meanwhile I also enjoy Cambridge, the heedless, headlong vivacity of it. I'm accompanied by a friend named Patricia, who has eased into my life as a surprise blessing of nurturance and knowing, mellowed laughter. An insatiable and savvy bibliophile with a master's in theater, she's working on a novel and also vets manuscripts for a Boston literary agent. Patricia thrives in yoga studios and loves to jog along the Charles. She rents rooms in a posh neighborhood near Radcliffe and the old Tory mansions on Brattle Street.

I love the bookstores. I love the Bernini terra-cottas and the Jackson Pollock canvas in the Fogg Museum and the bronze Chinese bodhisattvas in the Sackler. I love *Jules and Jim* and *Children of Paradise* at the Brattle Theater and up-to-the-minute indie flicks in Harvard Square. I also love the resonance of history—slate tombstones from the era of Hester Prynne, askew in grass of the Old Burying Ground; brick sidewalks; colonial manses on the street to Mount Auburn. I love the green leafiness of Cambridge in May, accented with dogwood and redbud. I love black sculls in silhouette against the late morning sparkle of the Charles River, the rowers lithe and lean like Eakins' on the Schuylkill.

But I see *samsara*, too. I scrimp so I can give dollars to haggard panhandlers in Harvard Square. (At first I walked hurriedly past those homeless beggars, averting my gaze and feeling guilty, musing, "I'm a grad student, I have no money to give, what am I supposed to do?" Then I did a street retreat with members of the Zen Peacemakers Order. Grungy and unshaven I stood alone on a sidewalk in Springfield, Massachusetts with a Styrofoam cup in my hand. Of each person who passed by I asked, "Spare some change, please?" I felt their disgust and contempt. My question transformed me from a Harvard graduate student to a piece of dogshit on the sidewalk. When I returned to Cambridge after the street retreat I began taking dollar bills out of my bank account each week so I could give them to local homeless people. Now I always look them in the eyes and say, "How are you?" and "Take care of yourself, okay?" as I hand them the money. They always say, "God bless you."). I see the destitute asleep in corners beside their duffels and shopping carts. I hear about robberies and shootings in Central Square. I see the contradictions.

I live in a protected two-story stucco building in a Harvard residential complex ("like a British barracks in colonial India" a classmate has said), the windows of my private apartment overlooking a courtyard of clipped grass and park benches and flowering crabapple. One prosperous, sedate block away stands the house where William James lived when he delivered the monumental lectures at Harvard that later became *The Varieties of Religious Experience*, a book I read at Penn State in an honors tutorial. Little did I then suspect, reading James on mystical experience, that two years later I'd become his neighbor—our homes separated by a three-minute stroll, even if a century divides our lives. (But what are centuries among friends?)

Though ostensibly privileged, I live here very simply, as I always have, a sort of scholar-monk: no TV, no cell phone, only a bare hardwood floor with a zafu for meditation. Books. Some CDs. A barbell. Running shoes for jogging. A table and some chairs. A refrigerator stocked with organic Gala apples and fresh romaine, some yogurt, some tempeh and veggies and pita bread. A serviceable computer, a machine so old I'm surprised it's not hand-cranked and powered by steam. A futon bed. That's all. Often even this seems too much. Though I entertain no illusions about the harsh lives of panhandlers in Harvard Square, I do wish I could live like a Zen vagabond, like Bashō, with just a change of clothes and a begging bowl. Perhaps someday I will.

At school I'm struggling toward defining this new thing, Buddhist ministry. In American Buddhism, in the early light of the twenty-first century, we have several types of clergy: We have priests, who basically serve temple functions of ritual and liturgy; we have chaplains, who serve in hospitals, prisons, hospices, the military; and we have dharma teachers, who offer meditation instruction and talks and formal training. Increasingly these roles overlap. It seems to me, though, as I ponder it in our Buddhist ministry colloquium, that in addition to these essential types of Buddhist clergy we need a new one. A Buddhist minister could perform the duties of priest, chaplain, and dharma teacher, and also provide pastoral care and counseling in a Buddhist context—something sangha members want, but that most Buddhist clergy lack sufficient training to provide. Couldn't this become a vital spiritual vocation?

I'm beginning to think so. Buddhist ministry could mean helping people awaken to an understanding that we can work with our calamities, with the inevitable afflictions of our lives. A marriage starting to fester. A promotion denied. A friend's melanoma. A father's sudden collapse. We can feel the ache, the distress, the rage, we can abide with those emotions, neither acting upon them nor fleeing them. We can sit with the anguish. Observe its nuanced shadings. Its burning. Its subsidence. Its renewed burning. Not evading it with vodka or with Paxil. By staying with the pain, by watching it, then letting it go—minute by minute, month after month—we slowly build personal resilience and valor, and we grow strong.

Continuing to ponder through my first semesters, I decide that Buddhist ministry also involves helping people reawaken to their fundamental kindness. Helping them see the hurt and fear in which so many of their neighbors live, and the crises of hunger and plague, of poison and bloodshed, that imperil, each day, our beleaguered planet.

Perhaps it can mean, too, helping people awaken to the richness of silence, the treasure of solitude. So many distract themselves with babble of cell phones and iPods. So many clutter their lives with appointments, crowding their "to-do" lists with daily tasks in desperate haste to avoid spending time alone. "I keep busy," they shout over the din, "otherwise I wouldn't know what to do with myself." But the sacred speaks in whispers. People need to hush and listen. The sacred visits those who sit unattended. "But if I didn't keep myself busy," people shout, "I'd feel completely lost." Can a Buddhist minister teach them that the sacred visits precisely those who dare to become lost, those who dare to lose their habitual lives?

Can ministry in a Buddhist context also mean teaching people to open their eyes, to open all their senses in awakening: to a coffee cup, a blue jay, a wisp of jazz, a yellow Checker cab, a zest of cinnamon? To perceive each "ordinary" thing as splendor? To perceive each sublime thing as gloriously mundane? Can the art of ministry in a Buddhist context mean, moreover, teaching people to wake up in another way—to become aware of vast, intricate networks of kinship pulsing throughout the cosmos, the coffee cup and the blue jay joined across the merest fraction of an instant by whirling electrons, and linked across light-years to the wheeling stars? Can it mean teaching people to awaken in thanksgiving to Mystery? To bow before it? Not in supplication but in awe?

Could Buddhist ministry be the art of serving people in their process of awakening, of assisting a person in waking to that glow of stillness and clarity? To help people experience that bright attentiveness, that gleam of wonder obscured, all too soon, by a dark stupor of ego, with its selfish cravings, its resentments and delusions?

"I know no speck," wrote George Eliot in *Middlemarch*, "so troublesome as self."

When I did meditation retreats at Springwater Center in upstate New York, in hills and farmland west of the Finger Lakes, I often left the meditation room to rove outdoors into the high meadows. I loved the open meditation room, clean and austere with its blue immaculate cushions. But I loved as ardently the open meadows with their maples disheveled by wind and their darting red-winged blackbirds and their unkempt acres of ragweed, daisy fleabane, and clover.

I walked in those meadows hourly. Gazing toward the slope of a distant field I could often discern cattle. Each dairy cow in the herd roamed without pause, feeding on the bounty of early June.

"Meditation," writes Chögyam Trungpa in *The Myth of Freedom*, is precisely that: "giving a huge, luscious meadow to a restless cow."

Meditation, in other words, can give spaciousness and calm to the mind by providing ample and nurturing pasturage. And this act of giving pasturage to the mind, or to the spirit, lies in turn—or so the *Oxford English Dictionary* informs us—at the heart of what clergy do. For the word "pastor" derives from the Latin *pastorem* and means literally "feeder, giver of pasture." To offer pastoral care, then, implies offering abundant meadows of mind and spirit where congregants may find easeful sustenance.

Indeed, the *OED* defines "pastor," in part, as "a shepherd of souls," as "one who has the spiritual oversight over a company or body of Christians

... with particular reference to the spiritual care of his 'flock.'" We have switched here from Trungpa's metaphor of the cow and its meadow and meditation, of course, to one of sheep and pasture and stewardship, but I think of both as I wonder how to adapt the Christian model of pastoral care to Buddhist ministry.

It seems a potent challenge. At Harvard in this spring of 2006 as I recall the life I knew at Springwater Center, at American Zen monasteries and in Japan, I wonder how I might combine a life of contemplative practice with the intellectual rigor and commitment to service espoused at the Divinity School. I wonder, too, how to shape such a combination into a uniquely innovative form of Zen-influenced pastoral ministry that will benefit my future sangha. What kind of feeding, what kind of pasturage will I offer my "flock"? Particularly when Zen practice makes each person responsible for his or her own spiritual journey, for his or her own spiritual nourishment—so that my "flock" will not be one of restless sheep, but of shepherds? How will I serve as shepherd to a flock of shepherds?

When I read Emerson's Divinity School address, in the chapel where he delivered it in the summer of 1838, riling his small audience of ministry students and clergymen, I felt electrified by his demand that those who preach sermons should "convert life into truth." I realized from Emerson's address that, when "preaching" in my dharma talks as a Buddhist minister, I will need to share with listeners the intimate testimony of my own life, "passed through the fire of thought."

I can heed Emerson's instruction. Does someone feel crushed by loss? I remember how, at the age of twenty-eight, stupefied by incomprehension and grief, I helped shoulder Joanne's coffin; how at the age of forty-five I steeled myself before the coffin of my sister Sherry and, bereft, choked back tears to intone my eulogy of devastation and bewilderment, of futile contrition. I know what mourning feels like. I know how it hollows a chilled vacancy beneath the ribs. A place that feels empty in perpetuity. I know how painfully it scoops—from that intangible, deeper place no anatomist will ever locate—an eternal void in the psyche. I can speak from that feeling. I can offer consolation and healing.

Does someone feel a seething anger? I know that feeling. I remember how, wounded by those I derided as loutish backwoods neighbors and sneering teachers in a hick Appalachian high school, I stifled my anger. Wounded by years of insult and ambush I stifled it through my mid-twenties. I stifled it until it began to corrode me from the inside. When I could allow myself to feel that seething anger I wore it outwardly as a threat and a provocation, the way I wore my punk-rocker black leather jacket in the Seventies and Eighties and the glare on my face and the spark in my eyes: don't touch me. Beneath the rage, however, I felt injured and scared. (But I realize now that those who assailed me in my hard Appalachian homeland had been wounded, too.) I can speak from those feelings. I can offer consolation and healing.

Does someone feel dazed and frail? Or tricked in love? Or frazzled? Or stripped of hope? Like everyone, I've known those feelings. Does someone tend an aging parent? Struggle with working-class poverty? I know those experiences. I can offer, too, this assurance, having earned it: We survive our most grievous hurts, and if we persist we grow dauntless and plucky, impervious to fear, and yet we also grow tender in commiseration with others. Life restores itself in moments of blessings and laughter.

I can tell people this, straight from the heart. The way Emerson would have.

FIFTEEN

NOW, IN the spring of 2009, I come full circle. Last year on a budding June day I stood onstage during commencement ceremonies in Harvard's Memorial Church, clad in doctoral robes of black and crimson. (Because the Master of Divinity degree is a terminal degree, M.Div. grads wear the same robes as those receiving doctorates, and, like Ph.D.s, can teach in universities.) As the culmination of three years' study I took my diploma as the first graduate in the Divinity School's new Buddhist ministry ordination-track. Today I'm driving again in my homeland of central Appalachia, among Pennsylvania's mountains and the greening farmland of early April. Errant pilgrim.

Throughout my journeys in quest of true home Zen has challenged and sustained me. This extraordinary practice of attention, of agility in the fleeting instant, this practice of open eyes and open heart, of utmost exertion, of fearless joy.

Appalachian Zen.

Driving south in Bald Eagle Valley on Routes 150 and 220, beyond the hamlets of Beech Creek and Wingate, edging the village of Unionville, I pass a rural slum-house with a Confederate banner festooning the porch. Scrapyard of junked semis and mobile homes, rusted hulks of panel vans. A trailer park near the freight tracks. "Jesus" graffito daubed on a utility box. Pinto mares grazing in fenced pasture. A mile down the highway, a glider port. Careworn houses. The far creek secluded in maples and sycamores at the base of mountains. The mountains a rampart of forest pitched against the horizon. Reaped fields glow an hour before dusk, the light penetrating and strong.

Full circle. In Zen we value Japanese scrolls adorned with the *ensō*, the ragtag zero brushed in *sumi* ink, emblem of wholeness and emptiness, dabbed on paper in the span of a single breath. "Round and perfect like vast space, / Nothing lacking, nothing in excess": spoken by a Chinese Buddhist teacher.

Having come full circle in my journey, knowing that true home exists in every place and every hour, I return now to my natal home in this Appalachian valley, at the age of fifty-four ready to claim my life's work. I see it anew. I see it freshly. Eliot said it best in the "Four Quartets": We return to the place where we began and know it for the first time.

For much of the past year I've lived at Montague Farm Zendo in western Massachusetts, studying with a handful of fellow trainees in a seminary affiliated with the Zen Peacemakers Order. We've dwelled communally in a nineteenth-century farmhouse, sat zazen each morning and taken classes in the gloriously refurbished two-hundred-year-old barn with its bamboo floors and cathedral ceiling, and in afternoons we've enjoyed liberty to stroll the meadows of wild grasses and Russian olive or the woodlands bordering the Sawmill River.

Recently I've taken another step. In the barn at Montague Farm Zendo I knelt on the floor to receive my new name during the formal rite of *jukai*, of taking Precepts vows. The word *ju* means "to leap," and *kai* means "to be held"—*jukai* means jumping into the unknown, trusting that the universe will hold you.

"I've given you the dharma name of Kanji," intoned my Zen Peacemakers teacher, Sensei Eve Myonen Marko, who has been leading me through rigorous kōan training and precepts instruction. I held the *rakasu*—"five-striped robe" of the Buddha, worn by Zen practitioners— that I'd stitched in preparation for the ceremony. I held the scroll tracing my Precepts bloodline through all our Zen ancestors, from Shakyamuni Buddha to Bodhidharma to Hui-neng to Dōgen and all the dozens of illustrious names in-between, and through all the more recent names up to the current era of Sensei Eve. Four of my dharma brothers, also taking *jukai* vows, knelt with me.

To receive a dharma name means recognizing that an old self has died and a new identity is born. "Kanji," Sensei Eve repeated, with her wry smile. "Your dharma name means 'the Will to Accomplish,' or 'Indomitable Spirit.' That's what you'll need," she said, "when you go to work in Appalachia."

So here I am, back on my home turf of Pennsylvania. As my year-long field assignment for the Zen Peacemakers seminary I'm here to establish an "Appalachian Zen House"—a loose-knit assortment of projects to help ease suffering of the rural poor and to address the endangering of this land's fragile eco-systems.

"Steve Kanji Ruhl is the ideal person to start a Zen house," proclaims an article in the national Buddhist magazine *Tricycle*. I can only hope so. I feel overwhelmed. Who will help me in this fledgling ministry? Where will the money come from? Where do I start? I maintain "don't-know" mind, as the Korean Zen teacher Seung Sahn always advised. I trust the process.

The oft-cited truism about Pennsylvania: "There's Philadelphia in the eastern part of the state. There's Pittsburgh in the western part of the state. Everything in between is Arkansas."

In America's neglected farm-and-forest hinterlands, people of all ages contend with dire hardship, lacking even basic services taken for granted by the urban poor. If you live on a remote farm, you can't rely on a bus to a doctor's appointment—no buses exist. If you barely survive on Social Security and a retirement pension in a ramshackle house in the mountains, you can't walk to a soup kitchen for a free lunch when you feel hungry. Those who live in poverty in rural America suffer alone, and in silence.

In Bald Eagle Valley, I feel empathy for people I fiercely denounced years ago as "hicks" and "rubes," "as rednecks" and "hillbillies." I spoke from hurt. Now I feel community. True, it helps if we avoid discussing politics or religion. I rediscover how much I love the easygoing friendliness of these familiar people, their lack of pretense, their cheerful neighborly spirit.

They express it in willingness to help the sick or grieving by toting home-baked casseroles, by aiding with chores. They express it also in forms I remember from my childhood, still flourishing today: church socials, 4-H Clubs, firemen's carnivals, the Grange Fair, small-town Memorial Day parades and high school football games. Families here remain proud of their heritage.

Some of it I can't share. Buck hunting. Ford pickups. Twangy Top-40 country-and-western music. Fundamentalist, trust-your-Bible Christianity. It's a heritage that values tradition, the wisdom of the "good old days." Red-white-and-blue patriotism.

But much of it feels imprinted deep inside me: folksy affability; working-class humor; a knowing reticence; the dignity of sweat and muscle; hearty personal independence, yet with refuge in neighbors and kinship. I felt none of this in Cambridge. I loved the elegant neighborhoods near Harvard Square and the venerable mansions of Brattle Street, loved the heady seminars in paneled classrooms of Andover Hall, but now that I'm home in Bald Eagle Valley I realize how lonely I felt in Cambridge. How cold it felt. How much I missed the "howdy neighbor" and "take 'er easy" cordiality of my native people, of my rural terrain. How I missed nodding and waving to strangers. Missed the languid front-porch visits. I've noticed that when socio-economically privileged people—the ones who refer to themselves as "people of means"—get together, they share information; when working-class people get together, they share stories. Riffing off each other, tale-spinning, chuckling: "Well, ya know, that reminds me of the time…." I've missed hearing the stories.

Returning to these hills, these people, their stories, continues my journey of forgiveness.

I hold the contradictions.

Much of this Appalachian Mountain region of central Pennsylvania wilts from crises typical of the American heartland. Working-class penury. Squalls of violence. A pandemic of corrupted health, of soaring blood sugar and plugged hearts and waddling obesity, caused by trash diets. People sapped by constant scutwork for minimum wage at Walmart. People languishing in stagnant pools of hopelessness, squirming on hooks of booze or crystal meth. Isolated elderly people. Aimless, disaffected young people. Iraq War vets from local National Guard units, forever singed in body and spirit by combat. A chronic dearth of funding and resources. And streams killed by acid rain—stretches of Fishing Creek that teemed with rainbow trout and crayfish and blue herons in my youth now roll lifeless water over lifeless stones.

Here in Centre County, where the Appalachians rise at the rim of the Allegheny Front, nearly one-in-five people live below the poverty line. Some of them live here in the narrow lowland of Bald Eagle Creek, in drab houses clustered near the mountains.

On the other side of those mountains, by contrast, lie rolling, fertile Amish farmlands of Nittany Valley and the Victorian town of Bellefonte, close to Interstates 80 and 99, a community of stately homes and bed-and-breakfasts with mansard roofs and Queen Anne turrets. In that other valley, too, lies the rapidly growing town of State College, its affluent, immaculate, tree-lined streets bordering Penn State's University Park— the campus a small city in itself, the sporting den of the fabled Nittany Lions, residence of forty-five-thousand students. Measured by the norms of Appalachian Pennsylvania, the town of State College seems liberal, cosmopolitan, multi-culturally vibrant, and awash in cash.

Over here in Centre County's stretch of Bald Eagle Valley it's starkly different. With no major towns, with land too crimped and with soil too meager to attract large-scale farmers, and where the collapse of a nine-teenth-century timber industry meant the collapse of the local economy, those managing to stay above the federal poverty line eke out an existence through laboring at menial jobs, while those below it subsist as best they can. In Bald Eagle Valley's extension into Clinton County, the heavily forested region where I grew up, it's no better. In my hometown of Lock Haven, where the Hammermill paper factory has closed, many people struggle on welfare. Some sleep in their cars. Others have found mainte-nance or clerical jobs at Lock Haven's small university, but hardship stalks the county. It's a tough row to hoe, as they say here.

What can my Zen seminary project hope to achieve in these indigent hills of Appalachia? In these hamlets battered by decades of systemic eco-nomic injustice?

—

Dōgen said, "The mountains belong to those who love them."

Full circle. Returning where I began, to know it for the first time....

This April the robins, too, return, and the red-winged blackbirds, and the finches, a season of nest building as the maples begin to bud. From a distance their branches appear dipped in claret. Willows don a haze of freshening green.

In boyhood, among my *How-and-Why Wonder Books* of dinosaurs, my *Little Golden Books*, and my *Highlights for Children* magazines, I kept a book called *God's World and Johnny*, which depicted a boy like me wandering on his grandparents' farm after an April shower, reveling in the presence of God among newborn chicks, pussy willows, and mud puddles. This was theology a child could understand and savor.

As Easter approaches my mother prepares roses to place at the gravestone of my sister Sherry, dead now a full decade. At seventy-five, white-haired and shrunken yet with a ready smile, my mother copes with arthritis, with worsening deafness, and with cancer, the slow attrition of non-Hodgkins lymphoma. She's endured a hard life. A tightly circumscribed existence in these vales and ridges of Pennsylvania; she's never traveled west of Ohio, south of Tennessee, north of Massachusetts. Yet within the narrow range of these geographical constraints she's ventured far intellectually, reading widely and avidly. She has her Tolstoy, her Steinbeck, her *Angela's Ashes*, a biography of Anna Pavlova, *A Tree Grows in Brooklyn*, her *New York Times*. She's identified herself as a progressive working-class Democrat ever since John F. Kennedy and the vanished days of Camelot. She's helped elderly people by working as director of a senior center. Elderly now herself, she tends daffodils and feeds backyard sparrows. She's selflessly kind. Tender-hearted. Concerned about the world and unfailingly, sweetly generous. Though my mother knows little of Buddhism, she's more enlightened than most of the spiritual celebrities I've met.

My father at eighty-five shuffles along gamely in his Navy cap, suffering from diabetes, incontinent from prostate surgery, weakened from cardiac disease, his maimed heart cobbled together with the surgical equivalent of rubber bands and Scotch tape, and kept running with six stents. "I tell ya, Pal," he rasps. "Growing old is not for sissies."

As he ascended in his career to become chief planning engineer in factories near Nashville, Tennessee, and Wilmington, Delaware, transferring from state to state, my parents moved also into the middle class. My dad retired early and they returned home to these cornfields and mountain forests of central Pennsylvania; they've managed to maintain a small, attractive Cape-style house near the village of Howard—barely. Meanwhile they've reverted to peonage. It's easy to fall from financial grace in America. Living on pensions and Medicaid and Social Security, my parents survive here as members of the region's hard-working poor. I help them as best I can.

Teaming with local Christian ministers—those progressive enough to welcome a Zen Buddhist—I help gather piles of castoff clothes, furniture, and bedding to distribute to families living at the dire margins of a Dickensian pauperdom. We also create the first Pennsylvania chapter of Interfaith Power and Light, the nationwide consortium of religious groups and congregations working to engage directly with urgent crises of environmental destruction. At a scrappy little farm in Bald Eagle Valley called Ahimsa Village I partner with the homesteaders, Kelly and Bob, and their friend Sunny in a visionary effort to create spiritual refuge on their fertile bottomland, abundant with herbs and salad crops. I'm joined from Massachusetts by a fellow Zen Peacemakers seminarian named Jiko. Sunday mornings we offer meditation, dharma talks, and shared lunch to a handful of local Buddhist aspirants with connections to Penn State. Birdsong accompanies the dharma talks.

Full circle.

"Do not ask me where I am going, / As I travel in this limitless world," wrote Dōgen. "Every step I take is my home."

ɔ

MY SPIRITUAL practice has evolved from many sources. It has grown from Bible stories of my childhood: God strolling gardens in the cool of the evening, savoring the splendors of all He'd wrought. Jesus, His vagabond son, temperate sage, coaxing kids like me onto his knee to receive placid instructions, or summoning loaves and fishes from the air to nourish revelers, or luring corpses out of their graves into stunned renewal of life. Jesus, who began his own life as a baby in a trough of hay among ewes and lambs and lowing cattle, then was raised as a youth by a carpenter and his wife—Jesus, a working-class boy like me. Jesus who finished terrestrial life weeping and abandoned, mocked and tortured, as I saw when I lay on the carpet of our trailer on Easter Sundays, viewing the annual TV drama. Jesus who rose from a tomb and strode the dusty byway to Emmaus a final time—earthly yet no longer so; near yet distant; transfigured eerily by his passage through death—a mysterious revenant in a white robe, bidding farewell before his ascent skyward.

Yet Christianity couldn't hold me, any more than my Appalachian roots could hold me. Though I loved Jesus (and still do), even as a child much of what I learned in Sunday School seemed implausible.

When I was ten, on a morning in January as my mother drove us to school on a Lock Haven street, our station wagon slid on a patch of ice. It began spinning like an Olympic skater, and as I watched the broad, blue prow of an oncoming sedan approach in slow-motion I repeated the words, "God won't let this happen." Seconds later, when shards of window glass and twisting metal crashed down on me, my already skeptical faith in a caring and omnipotent God began to crash, too. My last prayer to that God occurred four years later, the night Bobby Kennedy lay pooled in blood on the kitchen floor of a Los Angeles hotel. I knelt by my bed. "Please let him live and somehow be well."

It's a specious understanding of prayer, I realize now. By then I was a teenager in the late Sixties and felt estranged from my Christian culture—even if the incongruous sight of three young nuns in wimples and black habits in the *Woodstock* movie, stepping among gala tribes of fringed-and-tie-dyed hippies at that carnival of music and its impromptu, loving community, enthralled me. The trio of nuns looked jubilant. One smiled into the camera, and the movie freeze-framed her, flashing two fingers in the "V" sign for peace, at a time when that political gesture meant something daring and important. It impressed me. As a younger kid, my viewing of TV news footage or up-to-the-minute photos in *Life* magazine of clergy marching in protest with Reverend Martin Luther King also had stirred me. Seeing that young nun at Woodstock, and seeing ministers, priests, and rabbis closing ranks with people in the Civil Rights Movement, taught me the vital need for clergy, for people of conscience, to walk at the vanguard of social change.

But I was moving in other directions. George Harrison and John Lennon had opened my mind to exotic possibilities of meditation and Eastern religion during the Beatles' pilgrimage in India. Listening to "Within You, Without You," "The Inner Light," or "Tomorrow Never Knows" or "Across the Universe" on our hi-fi I began to perceive new vistas. I never did mind-expanding drugs. I let the Beatles drop acid, and then I listened to the Beatles—that was trippy enough. Besides, I was congenitally ultra-sensitive to nuanced richness of color, luminosity, and sound, seeming to lack the normal sensory filters. To me the world already appeared vivid and spellbinding.

It made sense, therefore, that my mystic spiritual practice evolved also from a lifelong nature pantheism. It first seized me as a teenager, though even before, when very young, I loved the cycling of scarlet and gold leaves and hoarfrost to snowfall, then to forsythia and robins, then to luscious green depths of summer, my birthday season. I felt a placid connection within those cycles, embraced and happy. But as a teen I went further. After watching a PBS documentary on Van Gogh, seeing him wander the meadows of Arles, peering intently at wildflowers, I did the same, and discovered I could penetrate in vision to the inner glow of chicory and asters, of cedars, and see them enveloped in a charged halo, silent, in stillness, but piercingly, radiantly alive. "Speak to me," I'd whisper, and they would, in brilliance. The summer I turned nineteen I lived each day outdoors. Sun-bronzed, naked except for a pair of cutoff denim shorts, my waist-length hair flying behind me, I glided on my bike as if its frame and blurring wheels had fused with my body, this machine/me a single entity of balance, impulse, and speed flitting through trees light chorusing birds shadow purling waters along Fishing Creek Road in a spiritual *ekstasis* of Oneness. Of course I couldn't have described it that way. I only could experience the feeling, a sensory onrush of wonderment and awe.

In my early twenties I continued exploring Jung, in-depth studies which had commenced during my two years of self-education following high school. I scribbled woozily each morning into a dream notebook. Seeking, I also read *Seth Speaks* and related volumes, their spirit-channeled séances, their revelations of multiple worlds, layered dimensions of spacetime, forays into the afterlife, an earthly carousel of transmigrating souls. I wondered about UFOs. I read the Castaneda books, too, wily teachings of Don Juan in the desert hills.

I grew enamored of Tarot, the Rider deck with its acid blues and yellows, its medieval symbology of knights and falling towers, of maidens and crescent moons, images throughout the Major and Minor Arcana plumbing chthonic depths in the psyche. Weekly I'd fan out the cards in a Celtic cross.

Investigating books of post-Einsteinian astrophysics fed my spiritual growth as well—my spirit expanding as I read of an expanding cosmos, from the Big Bang through neutron stars and black holes. Or reading, at the micro end of the scale, of quantum physics, where material solidity dissolves into subatomic flashes of energy.

My spiritual practice evolved further in my late twenties after experiencing an obscure movie called *Resurrection*, starring Ellen Burstyn, based on the true story of a woman who technically "dies" in a brutal car wreck, floats toward a celestial light, then zooms back into her mangled physical body as she's resuscitated by EMTs. After lengthy recuperation in a hospital she discovers she has access to a healing energy innate in each of us. By touching or holding people suffering from illness, she can make them well. It fascinated me. I hadn't heard yet of scientific research into mind-body healing, or of Reiki, the Japanese technique similar to "laying on of hands," developed by Mikao Usui at the turn of the twentieth century to direct salutary qi energy outward from the palms and fingers. Soon, however, I began to experiment with mind-body healing.

○

THERE ARE other kinds of healing. As my spiritual practice deepens I feel called to places of suffering, to stand in presence and walk in prayer. In the late fall of 2010, thirteen years after venturing to Hiroshima, I participate in a weeklong retreat at Auschwitz-Birkenau, the former concentration camp in Poland where Nazis murdered more than a million people. I've journeyed here as a pilgrim on a bearing-witness retreat sponsored by Zen Peacemakers. Accompanying a somber retinue of Jews, Christians, Muslims, and other Buddhists, I'm traveling with a woman I recently dated, Myoki, most of whose extended family perished in the Shoah. We're all staying in a hostel on the grounds of the death camp. I've opted to create a solo retreat, wandering alone, not speaking.

At Auschwitz and, a mile distant, at Birkenau, among the barracks and guard towers and barbed wire, I walk for days in hushed pilgrimage.

I soak up death. At Hiroshima, when I wandered alone I felt the gray fog of a despairing grief in my chest, the horrors of human cruelty. At Auschwitz it happens again. I stand in a dimly lit gas chamber. In that solitude I look at scratchings of fingernails on the wall, raked by the hands of the doomed in their final moments. I see and touch ovens where people burned to ash and smoke. I see the shooting wall. Nazi soldiers shot forty thousand people there. Guards led or dragged them naked to the wall, some so weak from starvation that chains held the victims upright to make better targets. One of those forty thousand shot was a ten-year-old Polish girl.

I see the Gestapo's torture cells. I walk through the facility where guards shaved incoming prisoners' heads and tattooed their arms with numbers. I walk beneath the infamous *Arbeit Macht Frei* sign—in German, the language of my ancestors, of Georg Friedrich and Catherine Rühle. Walk past the gallows. Walk down corridors lined with countless photos of the dead and gaze into their eyes. One woman looks like my mother. I walk through the museum room heaped with thousands of suitcases emblazoned with the yellow Star of David. The fatal yellow star. Walk through a museum room with its endless piles of human hair, bleached white by the Zyklon B gas. I walk alone at Birkenau among the imprisoning fences and birches to ponds where capos dumped cinders—the remains of people, hundreds of thousands of people. Walk in the drear fields, the colorless sky above. The disarming odors of smoke, even now. Walk in deserted bunkhouses where people had lain hungry and freezing. Walk into the silent children's barracks and see the mural: trees and a white school building with red roof and inviting, open doors, and its parade of boys and girls, one with a drum, one wearing a folded paper hat and riding a stick-pony, one in pigtails with a doll, one pulling a toy horse on wheels, the mural on cracked plaster that charmed small children before Mengele experimented on them in his nightmare "medical lab," or before the Nazis gassed them.

Each day prior to walking alone I silently rejoin the interfaith group. We sit at the selection site, beside the railroad track where locomotives had chugged through the massive archway, pulling boxcars crammed with people. Jewish mothers clutching babies, Jewish grandfathers, men in dress coats, grandmothers in kerchiefs, kids toting satchels had been chosen by SS officers either for slave labor or immediate gassing in the "showers." We sit in zazen meditation, in cold winds that whip the barbed wire. We recite names of the dead. We light candles. A friend, Rob, blows the ram's horn of the *shofar*. We chant *Kaddish*.

Dōgen, in the *Uji*, or "Being-Time," fascicle of his Shōbōgenzō writes that time can flow backward. I wonder if, in ways foreign to the rational mind, our sympathy and concern in this November of 2010 might communicate telepathically, as a sort of retro-message, back to 1942 or 1943 to soothe, in an inscrutable way, a cadaverous woman with bald head, wheezing on her bunk, or a man with a number etched into his forearm, or a child led to the lethal brick chamber—might communicate as a single moment of inexplicable warmth amid tumbling ash and snow, or as a flicker of light in the barracks' gloom, or as an unaccountable instant of solace in the midst of despair.

In Kraków we walk untrafficked streets of the former Jewish quarter and sit in a synagogue desecrated by Nazis. We tour the factory of Oskar Schindler, now a museum, where I see a wallet crafted of human skin. At the beginning of the week, when I saw such things I felt rage. I wished that I could have been a member of the Polish Resistance so I could have killed Nazis. At the end of the week, after days of walking alone in silent pilgrimage, after taking in so much suffering, my heart opens. Without excusing in any way their monstrous atrocities, I see that when those men in the firing squad shot the little ten-year-old Polish girl, something vital inside each of them died, too. They killed their souls. I feel compassion for all of them—the girl, the millions of people like her, the executioners. All of them.

◯

IN A narrow, carpeted room above a gym on Main Street in Greenfield, Massachusetts, its Venetian blinds pulled tight against traffic noise and evening glare in the spring of 2011, I stand amid wafting incense. I'm chanting my vows.

Master of Divinity degree, then seminary, and now ordination in Zen Buddhist ministry: an elementary but highly formal ceremony, replete with processional and bows and purifying ritual. I've drawn a colorful Life Mandala, arranged according to the Five Buddha Families of Wisdom Energies, and a Gate of Sweet Nectar Mandala. These lie displayed on a table beside me. Friends in my Green River Zen Center sangha (formerly Montague Farm Zendo) sit on black zafus. Garbed in a fresh *samu-e* jacket of royal-blue denim, cinched at my waist, and a new bib-like rakusu draped at my neck, I receive from Rōshi Bernie Glassman—founder of the Zen Peacemakers and a trailblazer of American Buddhism—my charge to go forth in ministry to serve all beings.

The first person to graduate from Harvard's innovative Buddhist M.Div. ministry track three years ago, I'm now the first Buddhist minister ordained in the Zen Peacemakers. In fact, as far as we know, I'm the first anywhere.

The true work commences.

Awakening, the path of transformation, unfolds throughout a lifetime. It never ceases. It beckons each of us. And who, in this unending process, do we each become? Our truest self. The shining, alert presence that's been our authentic ground of being since birth—often obscured, but always there.

And where, in this unending process of transformation, do we end up? Do we arrive at some magical, transcendent place?

We arrive here. Now. Home.

PART
FIVE

GONE BEYOND:
ON THE PATH
OF HEARTLAND

2012–2022

○

"What is homing? It is the instinct to return, to go
to the place we remember. It is the ability to find,
whether in darkness or daylight, one's home place. We
all know how to return home. No matter how long it's
been, we find our way. We go through the night, over
strange land, through tribes of strangers, without maps
and asking of the odd personages we meet along the
road, 'What is the way?'"
– **Clarissa Pinkola Estes,** ***Women Who Run with the Wolves***

"Home, is where I want to be,
But I guess I'm already there."
– **Talking Heads**

"Who needs anything more? Away — away
into this hundred year life and beyond,
my story and I vanish together like this."
– **T'ao Ch'ien (fifth-century China)**

SIXTEEN

THE GREAT Mystery.

I shake some of my father's cremated ashes from a small box into the Susquehanna River where he swam in his childhood. The ashes sift the undercurrent. They flow the riffles like a white scarf unraveling.

Less than a week ago, in mid-June of 2012, the man who fathered me died before my eyes in a Pennsylvania hospital bed. The man whose own father had died when he was five years old, and who therefore as an adult had no role models for fatherhood, and who was forced to improvise from his own resources of devotion and love. The man who had doted on me. The man who had hurried home from work to revel in our playtime together, who in the black-and-white baby photos from 1954 and 1955 beams down at me as I lie on the carpet and chortle in our game of "Hold Daddy Up," my pudgy arms and legs like small Doric pillars supporting him. "I couldn't wait to be with you, Pal," he always smiled, looking at those photos. "You and me, we really bonded in those days." The man who had read me bedtime stories, who had sat with me at the kitchen table in Lock Haven to draw a picture together of an eagle in flight, who had cut and stained authentic maple handles to fit my toy cowboy pistols, who accompanied me to archery classes near McGhee elementary school. The man who built elaborate cantilevered bunk-beds for my brother Larry and me. The man who took me kite flying on the hilltop cemetery across our street, the flutter of that surrogate, tethered bird of balsa and cellophane transmitted from the high winds down the whipping line to my fingers, as if I held something live. The thrill of that at the age of six. My dad who escorted me on hikes up the shale cliffs of Peter's Steps where he'd romped in the legends of his boyhood. Who tossed the football and softball with me, who showed me how to totter around the backyard on stilts for a Cub Scout project and helped me contrive a "Floating Egg" exhibit for a science fair, who brought home huge blow-ups of our coloring-book pages that he'd made on blueprint paper at the factory where he worked as a drafting engineer, pages large as tablecloths and cool to the touch and scented with that wonderful scent of blueprint ink, pages with giant images of wranglers in Stetsons galloping over the range wielding six-shooters and Winchesters, or feathered warriors careening on ponies as they bore down on a stagecoach, images we converted to Technicolor with our Crayolas. The dad who taught me to walk quietly on moss Indian-style. Who read "T'was the Night Before Christmas" to us every Christmas Eve. The man who assisted me patiently with my bedraggled stamp collection and my coin collection, who did number flash-cards with me and wildflower cards and animal cards and Famous Americans cards. The man who piloted our station wagon singing "cool, clear water" and "all day, all night, Marianne" and "Tom Dooley" and "Anchors Aweigh" and "The Caissons Go Rolling Along."

The man who had sat eagerly in the hall of Lock Haven Hospital as my mother gave birth to me, who rejoiced when the nurse summoned him, who ran to hold me for the first time, had died, six decades later, in June of 2012, in a hospital bed, before my eyes.

What is this?

An ancient Buddhist tale from India:

Seven wise sisters planned a spring journey. One of them said, "Sisters, instead of going to a park to enjoy the spring flowers, let's go together to see the charnel grounds."

The others said, "That place is full of decaying corpses. What is such a place good for?"

The first woman replied, "Let's just go. Very good things are there."

When they arrived, one of them pointed to a corpse and said, "There is a person's body. Where has the person gone?"

"What?" another said. "What did you say?" And all seven sisters were immediately enlightened.

Where has the person gone.

The dad who played chess with me. Who took us camping in our canvas tent in rain-drenched forests of Halfway Dam and on a vacation to the Finger Lakes where we saw, for the first time, fireworks—like parasols in the night sky, bursting into flames of phosphor and bright pastels. The dad who taught me to pedal a bike. Who built elegant wooden drafting tables for us, like the one he used at his job. Who took me ice-skating in the frozen marshes of Great Island. Who dropped me off at dances and parties in junior high school. Who taught me to steer the Rambler on empty miles of newly built Interstate 80 before it opened. Who rafted the whitewater of Fishing Creek with me. Who Sunday night after Sunday night sat beside me on the couch to share installments of *War and Peace* on "Masterpiece Theater." Who came to all the boisterous high school plays I starred in. Who waved hello to Amish kids in their buggies. Who explored deserted beaches of Martha's Vineyard and Plum Island with me, off-season, ambling at the edge of Atlantic surfs. Who often relaxed with a book of Emily Dickinson poems and who toured her homestead in Amherst with me. Who hiked Civil War battlefields in Virginia with me and helped me locate the spot where Rebels shot a distant ancestor, Captain Edgar Ruhl, from his horse as he tried to rally Union troops during the dawn attack at Cedar Creek. The dad who liked to stargaze with me on August nights when I visited and to watch for the Perseids.

The dad who quit his high-level management job at a factory in Delaware in disillusionment, when I was in my thirties, declaring that "corporations don't care about people at all; the only thing they care about is money." A piercing revelation for him. Who then devoted the last decades of his life to designing and creating classic wooden toys for children—biplanes with spinning propellers, antique roadsters, puffer-belly trains, dump trucks, farm tractors—aesthetically pleasing and expertly crafted, in bright nursery-school colors. He sold these cheaply at local crafts fairs with my mom. When an Appalachian child would gaze longingly at a toy log truck or a crayon truck and hear from gruff parents that they couldn't afford the fifteen dollars it cost, he always smiled and handed it to the child as a gift.

The dad who visits me now frequently in dreams.

When he embarked on the Pacific War at the age of eighteen, he had little idea what to expect. When he embarked on raising our family twelve years later, after a failed attempt with a first wife and after their divorce, unwittingly he began a journey fraught with equally jarring surprises. He must have assumed that he would raise normal American children, a trio of kids who would play Little League, grow up with the usual scrapes and smiles, eventually make it to the prom and then to the marriage altar, and finally devote themselves to conventional careers and raise families of their own. But instead—

Instead he got a smart, generous, good-hearted, schizophrenic daughter who killed herself. He got a son chosen by life to pursue the erratic vocation of a musician. He got a renegade elder son selected by life to write words on paper and to sit for hours on a cushion as a member of an odd Asian religious sect.

Throughout, our dad remained genial and benign, even-tempered toward us, wholly accepting, and he made no secret of the fact that he cherished us. A miraculous father.

Among my friends, each person without exception suffered a malignant relationship with The Father. The bullying, tyrannical father. Or the aloof, inscrutable father. Or the demanding, impossible-to-please father. The silent father. The scary, abusive father. The self-obsessed, unpredictable, yelling father. The meek, failed father. The churlish, dismissive, know-it-all father. The cold, businesslike father. The pushy, egomaniacal father. The missing-in-action father. The clueless, out-of-touch father. The embarrassing father.

My father was none of these. I'm the only person I know who had a salutary relationship with a dad who was available and engaged. I know my good fortune.

Of course, it gets complicated between sons and fathers. We survived skirmishes when I became a precocious thirteen-year-old in 1967 during the kaleidoscopic Summer of Love. We clashed on the battlegrounds of long hair and rock music. (For girls, the teenage fights with fathers swirled around issues of makeup and miniskirts.) Once my dad tricked me during a stroll on Lock Haven's Main Street, shoving me into a barbershop and ordering the barber to administer a close shearing. I scalded with outrage. Back home in Cedar Heights, in a Freudian act that's embarrassingly obvious now, I grabbed an ax from the garage, stormed through the meadow into the woods, and to vent my white-hot wrath began assailing the largest tree in the forest. That day marked the nadir of our worst conflict. Soon after, he relented. In subsequent years as I grew my hair to Prince Valiant length and then to extremes farther and farther below my shoulders, he gallantly defended me. He even learned to enjoy the Beatles.

Now, four days after I kept vigil in his hospital room and saw him die, we're driving his ashes to his boyhood home of Lockport, across the broad river from Lock Haven, on a day buffed by June sun to a high sheen.

I'm in the driver's seat. My mother's beside me. My father's ashes repose in a box. It reminds me of the lacquered receptacle for incense ashes on the altar of a zendo. I carry the box in my lap as I wheel the car into Cedar Heights, the rural neighborhood of my adolescence. "Here we are, Dad," I whisper. We pass our former house where the Japanese maple and white birch saplings my father planted have grown to mature shade trees. I drive into Cedar Springs Cemetery, past the pines sheltering his mother's and father's gravestones—where, as a little boy, I saw for the first time my father kneel and cry—then past my sister Sherry's grave, past those of his grandparents, as my brother Larry and his passengers follow in a car behind. We're a funeral cortege paying homage to places meaningful in our dad's life.

In Lock Haven we drive his streets. Our two-vehicle procession rolls along a dappled, nearly deserted East Water Street, where, during my own childhood, this town seemed stuck in the decade of my father's youth. On Sunday mornings he and I would drive into Lock Haven from our family's trailer and buy the *Grit* paper from a newsboy in a cap, like a kid in a Mickey Rooney flick, tugging his wagon down the middle of the road beneath the horse chestnut trees. A vanished America.

"When summer came, you put your shoes away. Because you knew they had to stay in good shape to last through the next winter. Then we went barefoot, all us kids. The only time we put on shoes in summer was to cross the bridge over the river into Lock Haven. To us, that was going into the big city. And that didn't happen very often."

My dad told me this one winter. Each Christmas during the Depression, he said, the Roxy Theater in Lock Haven—movie house with gaudy Art Deco marquee—offered free newsreels, cartoon, and a Hollywood feature to local kids, and gave away handfuls of ribbon candy. "That was a big thing, free candy. A really big thing," he told me, his voice husky, nostalgic and not yet, after six decades, fully estranged from the sadness. He shook his head slowly. "My Uncle Charlie would go to the dump and get the throw-aways, fix 'em up. I got a little red wagon for Christmas one year that way.

"The doctors and the lawyers, the bankers in Lock Haven, of course, they ate well and had cars and so on. But other people—I remember people coming to our back door, over in Lockport, and we didn't have much, but my mother would make them sandwiches. Down at the railyards in Lock Haven you'd often see hoboes, on the trains—and it was an odd thing to stand there and see men in the open doorways of the boxcars going by, looking out at you. In fact, my other uncle, William, was a hobo, somewhere out in America, riding the rails...."

"There was a place in Lock Haven where they'd give you free food. Some cornmeal to make mush and so on. Sometimes my mother would send me over there to get something for us. We had a schoolteacher, Mrs. Grover, who lived next door and one of her chickens got into our cellar. We didn't say anything to her. My brother Ralph chopped its head off and we ate the chicken for lunch. That was the first meat we had in a long time.... Those were hard times. Not just in Clinton County, this here Appalachian Mountain region, but all over the United States. A lot of us were in the same situation."

Now we drive my dad's ashes past the abandoned Lock Haven High School and its vacant windows. "The teachers knew most of us couldn't afford college, so I s'pose they figured why waste time on us," he told me once. "But I did well anyway." He ranked second out of all students in the county in scholastic test scores.

We swing around to cross the Jay Street Bridge to Lockport. Today it's a riverside park, its former houses, including my dad's boyhood home, razed and converted to lawn and picnic tables as part of a Susquehanna River flood-control project. Here my dad and his young friends Chip and Tommy and Dutch had scamped through the woods, leaping and whooping like Leni-Lenape warriors atop the bluffs of Peter's Steps, which was used as a lookout perch in the French and Indian War, its bare ledge affording sweeping vistas of Bald Eagle Mountain and the river. Down in the fields they played cops-and-robbers, each vying for the honor of impersonating Pretty Boy Floyd, or Prince Farrington, the real-life Robin Hood who pulled bank-heisting capers over in Sugar Valley. They played baseball and football. They swam the Susquehanna. On Halloween they tipped outhouses. They had fistfights and swearing contests. They played poker, betting matchsticks. Some mornings they waved at cavalrymen in Sam Brown hats, trotting through Lockport from the armory. In winter they walked out on the river, shoveled snow from the ice till they'd cleared a rink, then they played "shinny on your own side," a hockey game in which they used a crushed tin can for a puck and, for sticks, curved tree saplings which they'd cut from the riverbank.

The Ruhls' house in Lockport had a coal-fed heater in the kitchen. The cast-iron cooking stove, with griddles on top, burned coal and wood. A tank at one end of this stove heated water; to bathe, young Gene or one of his siblings hauled pails of steaming water from the stove upstairs to a washtub. On chilly nights they'd heat bricks and slide them under bed sheets to warm their toes. Every morning, kids in Lockport carried ashes from the stoves and dumped them over the riverbank. To earn pennies, from May through September they cut grass with rickety hand-pushed mowers. The rest of the year they raked leaves or sharpened knife blades on grindstones or shoveled neighbors' snowy gate paths. Older brothers worked in Lock Haven at the paper mill.

"We walked everywhere," my dad told me. "Our family couldn't afford to own a car. The only means in or out of the Lock Haven area was on a bus. That was expensive, too. We walked for miles. We walked to our schoolhouse, a one-room cabin down by the riverside, every day—it was a three-mile round trip."

At a pavilion near where that schoolhouse had stood, we look at photos in an album Larry has compiled—Dad as a young gunner's mate in his white sailor's cap, Dad hugging our mom, Dad hammering together a sun deck, Dad cavorting with his grandkids. Larry strums guitar chords and sings a popular tune from the '40s, "Heart of My Heart," that always moved Dad, a romantic softie, to tears.

I sift some of his ashes into the grass at the schoolhouse site, where he'd learned to pen the alphabet and read *Last of the Mohicans* or *Treasure Island* next to the woodstove. I sprinkle more ashes on the green esplanade between the riverbank and the cliffs of Peter's Steps. Finally, as my mother and Larry and his wife Ellen watch alongside my Aunt Cil and cousin Mike and his wife Carol, all of whom had driven in from Ohio, and my friend Jenny, I pour some of Dad's ashes into the Susquehanna, the river where he'd ice-skated as a boy in the raw winters and on summer afternoons had dived and splashed—and the same river where he'd dumped the stove ashes as a household chore. Now his own ashes ease into the river's southward flow. I recall momentarily the ash ponds at Auschwitz-Birkenau. There, the remains of incinerated people were dumped as trash. How differently, how reverently, we hold and honor my father's ashes and release them into the water.

Early followers of the Buddha Way often sat among bones and decaying bodies in the public charnel fields to meditate, in stench and buzzing flies, and to reflect on the transience of life. Letting go of my dad's ashes I feel reconciled to that transience. I feel at home, as if gliding on the porch swing my dad built years ago, watching the cycle of generations: relinquishing the elder into death, heralding the younger as it arises to replenish the Earth.

Part of my father's legacy remains his example of protecting those who can't defend themselves.

In Navy sparring bouts, when boxing matches on ship decks entertained swabbies and their cheering officers, Gene Ruhl won a reputation as a champion light-heavyweight boxer nicknamed "Bazooka" for the lethal power of his fists. As a teenager he'd struggled through half-orphaned love, inarticulate fury. Nightly in the cellar he'd lifted a barbell made of a broomstick and cement blocks; nightly he drilled on a sparring bag made of a sand-filled gunnysack. Practicing moves. Combining punches. His older brothers were a rough-and-tumble bunch of scrappers. They'd gained notoriety in Lock Haven as barroom fighters. By the time my father reached the Navy, he often said, "I was lean and mean."

He could put his pugilistic skills to commendable use outside the ring. "This one white guy on our LST was from the South—one day on shipboard he pulled a knife on one of the Blacks. Said he was gonna carve the Black guy up and use him for shark bait. Called him a 'nigger.' The Black guy, he was just—he just looked so scared. Well, I calmed that situation down in a hurry. I came up behind the white guy. I grabbed his arms. I made him drop the knife. I threw that ignorant S.O.B. in the brig."

Bazooka Ruhl. Yet he remained true also to his other nickname, "Golden" Ruhl—a pun on the Biblical injunction to do unto others as you would have them do unto you.

Several years after his departure from the Navy, he and my mother began dating, and they loved jitterbugging to Glenn Miller hits. They left a dance one night in South Williamsport, Pennsylvania, a riverside town. Strolling past a hotel in a tough neighborhood, they encountered two thugs accosting a woman, trying to grab her purse. My dad threw off his suit jacket. "Leave her alone!" The hoodlums ran at him. My dad took his boxing stance. He smashed the first one with a left jab and right hook. The brute toppled to the sidewalk, knocked-out cold. The second one snatched a broken beer bottle. He lunged at my dad, who disarmed him then pounded the thug till he staggered back against a wall and fled.

A few months later, as my father walked my mom back to her room at the YWCA, a convertible passed them. My mom was a nineteen-year-old secretary at Bell Telephone, and gorgeous. Two men in the convertible wolf-whistled at her—in the early 1950s, a brash insult to a respectable young woman escorted by her date. Unfortunately for the two men, half-a-block later they came to a stop at a red light. My dad raced to the car. When the two men leaped from the convertible to confront him, he fought them both, and he won. Bazooka Ruhl.

A little over a decade later, when I was in fourth grade and attending a Cub Scout picnic for boys and their fathers on the open lawns of Price Park in Lock Haven, a softball game commenced after we'd finished our Cokes and hamburgers. The boys played against the fathers. The men on the fathers' team—hulking guys who worked at the paper mill—soon turned it into a macho contest, competing to hit the ball hardest and farthest. The boys began to vie with each other on behalf of their dads. Each time a man swaggered to the batter's plate, his son in center field or right field would brag to the other boys, "My dad's gonna really slam it!" and moments later, at the pitch, the man would blast the ball, scorching the air inches above our heads.

When my father's turn at bat finally arrived, I shouted to my team-mates, "Move back! Move back! He's really gonna hit it!" The boys in the outfield trotted backward in readiness. Grinning, I watched the pitch. My dad took a mild swing at the ball. It wobbled upward in a languid arc. The ball plopped to the grass and dribbled toward the pitcher's mound. Red-faced with shame and shock I watched my father lope to first base as the pitcher jogged toward the ball.

After the game I sulked. I refused to look at him. He put his hand on my shoulder. "What's the matter, Pal?"

Moments of resentful silence. Glancing away, I muttered, "I thought you were really gonna hit it."

My father studied me. Then he said quietly, "I don't need to prove to all those loudmouths that I'm some kind of tough guy. Listen, Pal. I wasn't going to slam that ball as hard as I could. It might have hit one of you kids. Do you understand? It might have hurt somebody."

⊃

TRADITIONALLY, BUDDHISM contends that the components of "self"— form, sensation, perception, mental constituents, and consciousness (also called the five aggregates, or *skandhas* in Sanskrit)—arise and subside in ceaseless flux moment by moment, until the final dispersal of these "self"-components at the instant of physical death. This leaves the universal field of pure awareness, of luminous Mind, of no-self, which has been present all along, and which we can directly access and experience during life through meditation.

Because pure awareness is always here, it is also called the Unborn and Undying, realm of the Absolute, of Oneness, beyond dualities of birth and death, beyond arising and subsiding, beyond going and coming.

In other words, "self" is like the ephemera of weather. The pure awareness of no-self is like the bright vast sky through which it passes.

In life, most people mistakenly assume that the passing weather of "self," of "me," is solid and real, the totality of all we can experience; they never realize the spacious clarity of the open sky. Clinging to this mistaken assumption is a root source of suffering.

In regard to what exactly happens in a dispersing of the aggregates of "self" at the instant of physical death, Zen maintains noble silence. It disdains such speculative, unanswerable questions, focusing instead on the here, the now. (Several kōans featuring death as a theme also feature this refusal to respond.) If I ask, "Where is my father now, where is his 'self,' the person I knew?" there is no Zen answer. Or, if I ask myself this question while watching a dragonfly as it pauses at a daylily in my backyard, the Zen answer might be, "insect hovering at speckled orange-and-black petal"—not in a pantheistic sense of "my father's spirit or essence now pervades that small creature and that flower," but simply to draw my attention away from unanswerable metaphysical queries and back to the living here-and-now.

Is what Zen proposes about life and death really true? I don't know. Zen training encourages me to forego spiritual ideology, to eschew attachment to dogma. It encourages me to question. What Zen proposes seems confirmed through my direct experience in meditation, but how could I ever be certain?

Watching my dad in the hospital room as he lay in a coma for two days, and as I held his hand through the final night at his bedside, I saw that his "self" had vanished. But what remained aside from the vast universal consciousness? Anything? And what happened when I saw him draw that last breath and his heart stopped?

Perhaps the practitioners of other Buddhisms are correct: the Tibetans who tell me Dad is in the bardo, readying for the next round of reincarnation; or the Chinese and Japanese Buddhists with their family altars, who would tell me that he's now a buddha who has joined our ancestors, or that he has entered a Pure Land. Or maybe Hindus are correct in their eschatological beliefs. I know that a Christian might tell me that Dad is in paradise with our loved ones in everlasting life. I know that a Jew might tell me that Dad enjoyed a fulfilling, generous existence and raised a family and did what he could to heal this broken world, and that he endures in our treasured memories, and in his progeny. Or maybe the pantheists are right, or the numerous Native American clans with their spirit-realms—the Lakota, for example, with their ghosts, *wanagi*, who walk the celestial Ghost Road, the Milky Way. Or the African spiritualists who posit a spiraling of ancestral energies through generations. Or aboriginal Australians with their presences of the vanished dead. Or practitioners of other traditions. Maybe the nihilists, the secular materialists, are right—maybe my father simply has lapsed into a black nothingness. Again, I don't know. It's not confusion or ignorance. It's the mind of not-knowing. The freedom in that.

Perhaps at death the "self" leaves a vestigial imprint, a sort of electromagnetic resonance, in the quantum field—and later we still can feel that resonance. I do feel my dad when he appears in dreams or when I remember him in the daytime. An energetic or vibrational buzz in those moments of recollection.

Or perhaps the instant of a person's dying resembles the collapse of a star in a black hole: the "self" dissolving in something like a spacetime singularity, and a finite personality subsumed into infinities. Perhaps at the event horizon of death, karmic information and consciousness radiate outward at the quantum level as a wave function, the karmic bits coalescing for rebirth while the consciousness expands as pure awareness throughout the cosmos.

And what of the Vikings' Valhalla? What of the Greeks and their River Styx and posthumous journeys to the underworld? Those people believed in their conceptions of death and its aftermath—conceptions that now seem so archaic and quaint—with as much commitment as we in the twenty-first century believe in our quantum fields and energies and space-time singularities.

The fact that the human community has experienced the death of loved ones for untold millennia and yet has no consensus on what the phenomenon actually is, and the fact that we offer radically contrasting interpretations of it, prove how inscrutable death remains to us.

That's why I call it the Great Mystery. Ultimately I'll find out for sure when I cross over the threshold that my sister and countless others have crossed, and which my father now has joined her in crossing.

And yet he remains present to me. Indeed, when has he ever flown away?

A Zen kōan called "Pai Chang's Wild Ducks" from the ancient *Blue Cliff Record* compendium:

Once when Great Master Ma and Pai Chang were walking together they saw some wild ducks fly by. The Great Master asked, "What is that?" Chang said, "Wild ducks." The Great Master said, "Where have they gone?" Chang said, "They've flown away." The Great Master then twisted Pai Chang's nose. Chang cried out in pain. The Great Master said, "When have they ever flown away?"

Dōgen in the *Eihei Kōroku*: "So it is said, although there is arising and perishing, there is no coming and going."

My father's ashes sift the undercurrents of the Susquehanna. They flow the riffles like a white scarf unraveling. They disperse into the river, and I feel him close at hand.

SEVENTEEN

FOR CENTURIES, Buddhists have referred to monks as "home-leavers."
Monks forsake their loved ones. For this reason I never can become a
monk, not while I'm blessed with living family. It's not a matter of clinging in attachment; it's a matter of thriving freely and doing so within a
realm of profound affections. If assayed by standards of the world's valuation, my two surviving family members—mother, brother—are worth
more to me than bullion. They're apprized in love, inestimable.

My mother, who at the age of eight trekked daily through woods to
her Appalachian schoolhouse, a two-mile journey, now in 2013 at the
age of eighty remains hale, traipsing two miles each day in the streets
of her new community of Manchester, Connecticut. She keeps a small
apartment, resplendent with Degas prints, tropical plants, magazines and
books. Recently, at her Tuesday morning senior-center gathering, the
young facilitator proposed a game: "Let's see if we can find smaller words
hidden within a larger word. Okay? Let's start with 'therapeutic.'" The
woman chalked it on the blackboard. "Can anyone find a word concealed
within it?" One elder offered, "Cat." Another said, "Hat." Another, "Pet."
The facilitator burbled, "Wonderful! That's very good! Anyone else? Are
there any other smaller words hidden in 'therapeutic'?" My mother, who
had wished fervently as a young woman to go to college but could not—
there was no possible way to afford it; for a working-class girl it was out of
the question—raised her hand. "Yes, Mrs. Ruhl?" My mother glanced at
the blackboard then said, "Heretic. Taupe. Petite. Ratchet. Puce. Capture.
Pathetic…." Not bad for an octogenarian.

I visit her, staying overnight when I catch the train to Yale to lead

Buddhist dharma discussions. Larry and Ellen live nearby, frequently dropping in, helping with errands, whisking her off to films or dinners or recitals. Married sixty years, she sometimes feels uneasy with her new-found solitude in the apartment. She also frets with unspoken anxieties, the legacy of a childhood marred by drunken hillbilly violence. She still mourns Sherry's suicide. Occasionally she wakes in the night, having heard my father's voice calling "Jan!" or glimpsing him standing for a moment, indistinct in the darkness, with my sister. It rattles her.

But she's won new friends, enjoys a Scrabble club and a library up the street, outdoor concerts, and the Methodist church next door, where she pitches in on food drives for impoverished people or sews pillow cases to make dainty dresses that the congregation sends to young girls in India. A devoted Obama supporter, she scans newspapers avidly, sympathetic to plights of African-Americans and gay people and jittery about wars and the destruction of eco-systems—political positions that she hid from her Tea Party neighbors in central Pennsylvania. Nonetheless she misses those mountains, the Appalachian forests and creeks of the "Pennsylvania wilds." Sometimes she cries, remembering them. I used to drive her into the majestic north country of Big Pine Creek on Mother's Day, and she and I would picnic beside pristine waters among the mountain pines. We'd watch great blue herons fish the shallows. Bald eagles sheared across the sky. "It's so beautiful," my mother would say in a near-whisper, her eyes moist. "Thank you, God, for creating all this." Those days are over. Destitute local families in that region of Pennsylvania have sold their land, their birthright, to oil and gas corporations from Texas that have invaded the Appalachians and rampaged through those once-glorious lands, fracking the Marcellus Shale in an orgy of greed and noise and pollution.

Decades ago, when my mother was a girl of thirteen, she left those mountains for the first time. Rescued by a cultivated, well-to-do foster family named Robinson, she moved to their lavish home in the small Lycoming County city of Williamsport.

"One day Mrs. Robinson took me to New York when I was in seventh grade; my God, what a day that was for me. Here I was, this little hick from the country—do you believe it, I didn't even know how to answer the telephone. The Robinsons took me in, they taught me so much, they were so good to me. Mr. Robinson owned Lowry and Robinson Electronics in Williamsport, he had a business trip to New York and they took me, it was just before Easter around 1944, 1945. Mrs. Robinson told me, 'Now dearie, you'll leave school early today. After lunch we'll pick you up and go to the airport.' My God, the whole day—it was practically overwhelming—we flew in an airplane, out of Montoursville, it was my first time on a plane. I was so excited I got airsick.

"We took a taxi into New York City—I just couldn't get over it. So many people. I loved just being on the street. I wore my new Easter bonnet and we made plans to go to the Easter parade on Fifth Avenue. We went to Schwabb's, the famous drugstore with the soda counter. And Mrs. Robinson took me to Radio City Music Hall and we saw the movie *Showboat*—I'll never forget it. I'll never forget it. Paul Robeson, that big Black man, singing 'Old Man River'—I'll never forget it. What a day that was for me."

As a bobbysoxer in the late 1940s she dated and she ran around Williamsport's department stores and malt shops with her new girlfriends. I've seen a photo of her: slender, brunette, with wavy Rita Hayworth hair, wearing a jacket and pedal-pushers and saddle shoes, sitting on a curb on a September day, petting a kitten.

Everything seemed unprecedented and thrilling to her. She jitterbugged at socials. She went to Williamsport Millionaires high school football games. Williamsport in those days still retained an aura of its Gilded Age glory, when timber barons spent fortunes there. Jan loved the little city's elegant homes and parks, its traffic and its tumult.

One Saturday morning in the summer of 1951, when Gene Ruhl was a full-time student in a two-year engineering program at Lycoming Tech, courtesy of the G.I. Bill, and also working daily eight-hour shifts at a Williamsport factory, he hurried into a corner sandwich shop. He noticed a striking girl of eighteen seated in a booth, sipping coffee and smoking a cigarette.

"I used to run in there on Saturdays," he told me once, "and they'd pack me a lunch for my job later, and I always saw her. The first time, I'd been sitting there eating breakfast with one of my buddies from work, and she came through the front door and I spied her right away—she was so pretty! So this one Saturday I finally went over to her booth and introduced myself, said I'd seen her there a lot—I don't think she'd ever noticed me before. I asked if I could call her sometime."

Jan had just broken up with her boyfriend. She said yes.

☽

VIEWED FROM the Zen perspective of Oneness, of the Absolute, social class—like race, like gender—is an illusion, a construct. Seen from the simultaneous Zen vantage of differentiation, of the Relative, social class—again like race and gender—exists in actuality as part of our phenomenal world, with tangible consequences.

I'm not attaching to a firm identity as a working-class person; my Zen practice disavows such attachments and such belief in fixed ideas of self-hood. But living in the United States, a country which has long insisted on the lie that this is a classless society, I do acknowledge how social class has shaped my life.

Nor am I claiming victimhood. That would be a gross misunderstanding. I'm simply describing facts of American life that too often remain ignored.

Being raised working-class in America means you go forward with few material resources. No trust fund. No savings for college. No high school experiences that include swim teams, private SAT coaching, French Club trips to Giverny. No assumptions that the world lies waiting breathlessly for you, abundant, ready, in welcome. You go forward with almost nothing. You go forward with nothing except a fury of purpose; knowledge seized as rightfully yours; a capacity for dauntless toil and sacrifice; natural, indefatigable resilience; a questing, skeptical, independent spirit; sly, mordant humor; and—if you're lucky—an unassailable love bequeathed you by life-battered parents, those masters of survival whose love will safeguard you long after they've vanished from a world that, without a moment's hesitation, would demolish you.

That's my experience. Yet coming to Buddhism in America means also coming to a liberating discovery. In the unbounded expanse of each instant exists an opening of heartmind, of tender wisdom and unsullied awareness, where inner and outer, stillness and focused movement, converge. This, too, is my experience.

I grew up working-class in the American heartland. But a realm of natural benevolence and lucidity exists within me: the Buddhist *heartland*.

It exists, beyond class, beyond social constructs, within each of us.

○

THE BUDDHIST heartland nurtures my Zen ministry.

As I drove through Connecticut to visit my mother in Pennsylvania for Christmas in 2013, shortly before she moved, an exit sign on I-91 startled me: "Newtown." I jerked the steering wheel and took the ramp off the highway. One week earlier, a gunman had slaughtered children and teachers there, at Sandy Hook Elementary School. The gunman, a kid himself, had been an untreated schizophrenic like my sister Sherry but, being male, had taken his violent inner nightmare to others before turning it on himself. Still reeling from what happened to all those children, I knew that I needed to pay homage.

Others felt the same way. I joined a solemn procession of cars inching, bumper to bumper, into Newtown. We passed police cruisers. We passed TV news crews outside a Catholic church, filming one of the funerals. On Newtown's main street of trim nineteenth-century clapboard houses, a flag bristled at half-mast. The December afternoon was sunny but staggeringly cold. I parked and walked to the makeshift shrine, one of the many that have come to mark sites of American tragedies. Eyes misting, I stared at hundreds of teddy bears. Christmas trees. Toys. Dolls. Photos. Stockings with names of the slain children. Letters sent by bereaved strangers from throughout the world. Heaped like a rubbish pile in a landfill, yet each object carefully chosen and laden with emotion. I looked at other bystanders. We shared sorrowful glances or wan, sad smiles of momentary comfort. In the town hall, grief counselors offered free sessions to console people still distraught a week after the massacre.

Then I drove that long mile into the village of Sandy Hook, inching again in traffic past homes with improvised memorials—paper angels, banners proclaiming loss and grief—and parked behind a row of shops. Police watched from motorcycles, from patrol cars, or huddled on corners. Again, the silent, dazed crowds, somber glances of communion, the pall of mourning. Townspeople hugged each other. Strangers nodded, in tears. Again, there were shrines overflowing the sidewalks—lit candles, pictures of Jesus, wreaths and cards and more teddy bears, more tinseled Christmas trees, more toys and dolls, more snapshots, more letters heaped by the thousands. I joined people trudging uphill on a street toward the massacre site of the elementary school. Access to the school itself was blocked. At the fire station, where a field hospital had been set up hurriedly the week before to handle an expected inflow of the wounded—but there had been, in fact, no wounded, because how can a first-grader survive being hit multiple times by automatic weapons fire at close range?—I faced the trees that screened the school from us, and as a police officer stared from his cruiser I performed a brief ceremony as a Zen Buddhist minister. Closing my eyes, I bowed in gasshō and prayed, "May they be in peace. The children. The teachers. The gunman. His slain mother. The broken survivors. May they be in peace."

Buddhism doesn't posit a force of active evil in the world. It explains harmful karma caused by greed, anger, and ignorance and manifested in deeds of body, thought, or speech as the result of our conditioning, not of intrinsic evil. But at Auschwitz-Birkenau and now in Sandy Hook and Newtown I've wondered, as I wondered at Hiroshima: Is there some behavior born of conditioning so vile, so destructive, so reprehensible, that we may call it evil? And although Buddhism rarely uses the word "evil," one of the Three Pure Precepts is "Refrain from evil"—so what does that mean? Does it mean to refrain from participating in a culture of Thanatos, of death?

I wondered as I walked downhill, bracing against a bitter wind.

Returning to the village I saw signs in cafés and store windows: "We are Sandy Hook, and we choose love."

I bear witness, as well, to the suffering of planet Earth in this age of impending environmental apocalypse. In the fall of 2014, I join more than 400,000 impassioned citizens at the People's Climate March in New York, a city I relish as fervently as Kyoto. On a day of overcast skies and mild, intermittent sun we gather on Eighth Avenue between lavish high-rises and the greensward of Central Park, a surging, ebullient crowd wielding banners and placards. We convene en masse to halt the ravaging of our only home, this tiny, perfect blue-and-white living sapphire of a planet in the black immensities of space. Marching, I wear my Zen Buddhist *rakasu* and *samu-e* and tote a handmade sign: "One Earth, One Chance."

Two or three times during the fall and spring semesters I teach Buddhism and meditation among the groomed lawns and quads and colonial manors of Deerfield Academy, about twenty minutes from my apartment in the western Massachusetts woods. One of the most prestigious boarding schools in America, six US presidents have sent their children there. The King of Jordan is a Deerfield alum.

As a Buddhist adviser at Yale University, I catch a train to New Haven every few weeks to give dharma talks and facilitate discussions about karma, or enlightened relationships, or the *brahmaviras*, or other topics chosen by students in the Yale Buddhist Sangha. We sit on zafu cushions beneath high, vaulted ceilings in the Gothic stone chamber of the Harkness Tower's Buddha shrine on campus.

Another journey far from my Appalachian heritage. As far away as Harvard. As I teach the *crème de la crème* in America's elite educational institutions, I recall the ancient Ch'an teacher Lin-chi and his admonition: become a true person of no rank.

I've come to a time in life when I harbor no regrets. My childhood prepared me admirably for a Zen life of simplicity, of flourishing within austerities, lacking in material wealth but abundant in spiritual richness.

I've seen that those with pampered upbringings are good people but they live with pressures—to get into the best college, get the best career, get the best status symbols; pressures that warp their values and their views of reality. They become flustered when life challenges them unexpectedly and their entitlements fail them. Despite their veneer of assurance they tend toward anxieties; they fall apart. They worry. My upbringing, by contrast, has made me fearless.

I see, too, how they ensnare themselves in a social realm of prestige, competition, flashy accoutrements and appearances, a realm that's ultimately shallow and based on nothing. The American Dream promises that, born working-class, I can aspire to that rarefied realm, can rise to win it for myself. But Zen calls that "the world of wind and dust." The Buddha, born a prince, walked away from it. He became free. Little by little, I, too, am becoming free. I have no regrets at all.

Mentors, not Zen masters.

This seems mild, but in the context of Zen tradition it's revolutionary.

If I see young members of the Yale Buddhist Sangha treating me with exaggerated deference or trying to hand their power over to me, I cut it off. I don't allow that. As I explain to them, "I'm not a rōshi or a sensei. I'm a minister. But really I'm here as a mentor, as a trail guide on the path. What do I guide you toward? I guide you back to yourself. Instead of being a 'master' who dispenses answers to you, while you sit obediently as a passive receptacle, as a mere consumer, I dispense questions, and guide you back to your own resources so that you can uncover the solutions yourself, within. Why? Because you have original Buddha nature, and the wisdom lies inside you. You only need to find it, buried beneath your conditioned habits and opinions, beneath your superficial layers of anxieties and confusion. I'll try to help guide you into your still, deep place of inner clarity. When we do that together, as a sangha, we engage in a process of collective awakening. Sure, I'll give you information to help you along, and clarify any misunderstandings you may have about doctrine, and help you see where you get stuck. But when it comes to exploring the dharma, we're in this together."

Many Zen traditionalists claim that it's vital for a student to submit to a "Zen master" so that he or she or they can learn spiritual humility. True, learning humility remains essential in spiritual training. But the best way to learn it? Simply to love, putting others before yourself. My message to Zen traditionalists: try it and see.

No gurus. Toni Packer reached this transformative insight and it prompted her to found the Springwater Center in upstate New York, where I practiced a dozen years ago. I appreciate her insight now more than ever.

One of my favorite Zen mentors, though I never met her directly, is Charlotte Joko Beck. I've repeatedly read her book *Everyday Zen*, the best written in America on the subject, and its follow-up, *Nothing Special*. She wrote, "I'll tell you how far I'd walk to see a new teacher: maybe across the room, no farther! ... What is needed is a guide who will make it clear to you that the authority in your life, your true teacher, is you—and we practice to realize this 'you.' There is only one teacher. What is that teacher? Life itself." When Joko asserts that "your true teacher is you," she's not endorsing a facile egotism. Precisely the opposite. She's espousing surrender of the self to *what is*; she's espousing openness to the dynamic process of living.

I also believe that Zen's male monastic samurai heritage needs to reconnect with Zen's female domestic heritage in order to become whole.

When Ch'an returned to Japan through Eisai at the end of the twelfth century, after a brief flourishing in the ninth century under Empress Kachiko, and when it became established as Zen, it soon allied itself with the warrior class. That alliance persisted for centuries, particularly with the Rinzai school. As a result, Japan emphasized a masculine, monastery-based, militarized Zen (even as it accommodated nuns willing to conform to its standards, as in Dōgen's Eihei-ji). Of course, beneath the gruff swagger of Ch'an and Zen we catch glimpses of what's called "grandmotherly kindness." But much of Zen's heart-practice of Buddhist loving compassion was muted and—like anything discounted in a patriarchal culture—relegated to the women's sphere, which comprised household and family.

This split remains today. In Japan, the tradition of male monastic samurai Zen lives on, and "Zen masters" have transmitted it to us in the West; women's domestic Zen also continues in Japan, but in America, except in homes of Japanese immigrants, it remains virtually unknown. Paula Arai, in her important but woefully under-recognized book *Bringing Zen*

Home: The Healing Heart of Japanese Women's Rituals, does a terrific job of trying to correct that. Reading her book helped me develop the insights that I'm sharing here.

As I see it, the split between male monastic samurai Zen and women's domestic Zen creates two distinct paths:

Male monastic samurai Zen values a dharma transmission lineage of masters and students, honoring ancestral teachers at the zendo's altar. Women's domestic Zen values a family lineage of grandparents, mothers and fathers, and children, honoring familial ancestors at the *tokonoma*, the home altar.

Male monastic samurai Zen emphasizes kōan work and meditation. Women's domestic Zen tends to focus on mantras (particularly the *nembutsu*); on medicine, including magical spells written as mandalas on rice paper and ingested for good health; and on ceremonial rituals that have healing power.

Male monastic samurai Zen stresses hierarchy. Women's domestic Zen respects the authority of head priests in local temples, but it's also more egalitarian. Any woman, no matter how humble her role in the sangha or the larger society, can go into ritual trance in the *hyakumamben* ceremony and channel the voice of the Buddha. While she's in trance and channeling, she has as much authority as the temple priest, or even more.

Male monastic samurai Zen historically has emphasized a narrow doctrinal focus. It's often sectarian and aggressive. Women's domestic Zen, looser, more fluid and ecumenical, happily includes elements of Pure Land Buddhism, Shingon Buddhism, and other traditions.

Male monastic samurai Zen relies on *jiriki*, or self-power. It relies on the faith that, through your own strenuous discipline and effort, you can awaken and realize your Buddha nature. Pure Land Buddhism and other Japanese Buddhisms have always criticized Zen for this, or at least they've criticized monastic male samurai Zen. But the other half of Zen—that of women householders—relies, as Pure Land Buddhism does, on *tariki*, or other-power. This is the path of surrendering effort. It's the path of saying, "I need help. I can't do this by myself." It's the path of relinquishing yourself to a Higher Power. In women's domestic Zen, that Higher Power is

Kannon, the female bodhisattva of compassion, and Amida Buddha, the Buddha of Light, who offers salvation to everyone mired in karmic sins who will trust his salvific vow.

I contend that here in the West, because we've received exclusively the male monastic samurai Zen, we're getting only half the story. We're suffering grievously as a result. Yes, we do need the rigor of male samurai Zen. We need its daring and grit. We need its beautiful, unsparing simplicity. I love all of that. But we also need the missing half that women's domestic Zen provides, the half that focuses on children and family, on spirits, on healing, on ritual, on open-heartedness, on tolerant exploration and eclecticism, on surrender of self to other-power, to energies of the universe, to the rippling flow of life.

The Reverend Ralph Waldo Emerson, after delivering his Divinity School address at Harvard, left the Unitarian Church to create a truer, more essential ministry. He followed his conscience. In working outside standard perimeters of the "church" of institutionalized Zen, I'm doing the same.

I keep my distance not merely because of American Buddhism's scandals of power abuses and the sexual improprieties of "masters" involved with women students, and not merely because by temperament I'm an iconoclast, but because in honoring the ancient traditions while questioning the institutions I remain faithful to Ch'an's wild spirit and to Zen's insistence on seeking truth no matter where it leads.

○

ONE OF those truths, elemental to Buddhism: the fact of impermanence and its corollary, the Great Matter of life and death.

Many of my high school classmates have died since our twentieth reunion in 1992, scythed clean from the fields of this earthly realm by tumors, strokes, heart seizures, vanished in the prime of midlife. Those of us who survive approach a fiftieth reunion. I recall how on the last day of tenth grade I skipped school, and on that sun-blessed morning of early

June I hung out in Price Park in Lock Haven with four guys in my class named John, Mike, Joe, and Chip. They're all dead now. I'm the last one.

Helen Bechdel, too, is gone—dead recently of cancer, as her son John informed me by email. Helen Bechdel who, prior to becoming a schoolteacher in Mill Hall, Pennsylvania, yearned for life as an actress in New York. Now she's played by one on Broadway.

And Bruce Bechdel is long gone, too, of course. The small-town charms of neighborliness and community in Mill Hall, in Beech Creek, in Lock Haven were enclosed within tight confines of bigotry and conformity, and Bruce felt trapped there. In those viciously conservative, violent, and homophobic Appalachian backwater towns, he was as boldly and courageously himself as he dared to be, and he inspired those of us who were seeking a way, as teenagers, to discover and realize our own authentic selves. He did this in the classroom with good-hearted humor and charismatic aplomb, much of the time, and sometimes he did it with understandable weariness, resentment, and peevish exasperation. He was complex. The many former students who love him remember his wit and generosity and his gifts as a teacher—none of these evident in *Fun Home*—and his bravery in enduring daily the sneers of other high school faculty members, who envied his popularity and mocked him for not fitting Mill Hall's standards of manhood. In a school where nothing really mattered but football and deer hunting, Bruce was a "sissy" as far as they were concerned. Yet he remained defiantly and triumphantly true to himself, and many of his students were heartened by it. I was. My mentor Bruce and I eased into a unique camaraderie. We could laugh and talk for hours about books and movies and politics and gossip, or sit comfortably together in silence, Bruce grading papers and me reading. We each intuited how the other thought, could finish each other's sentences with a knowing glance, anticipate each other's responses. It was a close and special friendship. The brilliant gay man and the intellectually ravenous straight kid. We developed an intimacy befitting the traditional ideal recommended for a Zen teacher and a student. That nurturing bond. Remembering it, after more than forty years, I begin to miss him. Had he lived, had he not succumbed to probable suicide, it would have been fun to have stayed in contact. It jolts me to realize that Bruce Bechdel would have turned eighty next year.

Gone, too: Bruce's and Helen's acquaintance Mrs. Greiner, a brittle-looking but spry *grande dame* when I met her as a teenager, lady of whimsy and sparkle who loved her greenhouse and gardens, her Book-of-the-Month Club, her four o'clock tea served with Pepperidge Farm cookies. She lived with Mr. Greiner, a reticent, pipe-smoking colonel, at Willow Dell Farm, in a large clapboard manse that might have inspired a Currier and Ives lithograph. Their son George, a year younger than I and, like me, an erudite hippie and aspiring writer, became my friend the year after I escaped high school. While George read Milton and Donne at Antioch College (years later he earned a doctorate at the University of Massachusetts and became a dean), I lived with Mrs. and Mr. Greiner after quitting academia. I labored on my first chapbook of poems. From one of my bedroom windows I could rejuvenate myself with the view of an ancient millpond and a brick springhouse with its languid waterwheel, the pond bordered by whitewashed buckets of red geraniums. From another window I could watch Judy the horse grazing in her pasture.

Willow Dell Farm lay only fifteen minutes from my teenage home of Cedar Heights but, like the Victorian home of the Bechdels, seemed vastly different. In that genteel farmhouse—appointed with leather-bound books, antique sofas, breakfronts, grandfather clocks, lace and china, with a framed map in the hallway of ancestral lands in an Irish county—I joined Mrs. and Mr. Greiner at dinner each evening. She sighed over her day's experiences as a caseworker in the county's child welfare department, tending to indigent Appalachian families. Somehow she managed to arrive home from that worthy, earnest, heart-bruising job and conjure a pot roast and green beans and russet potatoes, or broiled haddock and steamed squash, for me and "Mr. G," as she jovially called her husband, who managed a chemical plant on the river flats outside Lock Haven. We ate using the family's heirloom silverware which was—I marveled—actual silver. Over dessert Mrs. Greiner, one of the rare people in Clinton County who had gone to college, regaled us with accounts of her current progress in reading *Tristram Shandy*, delighted by one of Sterne's lead characters, that bumblesome wit Uncle Toby.

As much as her friends Bruce and Helen Bechdel, Mrs. Greiner offered me a crucial formative model of a person who graced a milieu of Clinton County far estranged from the pickup-truck-and-deer-shooting hillbilly culture that surrounded us. Willow Dell Farm, with its eponymous trees drooping to shade the wild sedge and riffles of Duck Run and its adjacent meadows, with its home devoted to literature and flowers, to daily ceremonies of tea and conversation, suggested to me that rural life could be soothed by civilized enjoyments and—more important—savored in a world I could actually inhabit, not merely watch in a British drama on PBS.

Mrs. Greiner and her husband also didn't object to my hair. Though I had trimmed its waist-length glory, it still hung past my shoulders. Nor did they mock my sartorial dandyism (in those days I paired my floral hippie shirts and bell-bottom jeans with vests and scarves in bird-of-paradise colors, and vintage fedoras, and 1930s wide-lapeled pinstriped suit jackets, salvaged from thrift shops. I looked like a denizen of Haight-Ashbury staging a one-man revival of *Guys and Dolls*). They respected not only my eccentric tastes and talents but my outlandish aspirations as a poet. My local notoriety, given that a few years earlier, in adolescence, I'd practically had a bounty on my head, never fazed them. My later transformation into a Zen Buddhist minister might have seemed more freakish, had they lived to see it, but I'm certain they'd have indulged me.

My own loving family had moved to Tennessee in those years of the mid-Seventies, following my dad to his new job near Nashville, and Mrs. and Mr. Greiner gave me a surrogate home of kindness and warmth.

George and I remain friends. He's director of operations and systems at Jacob's Pillow. I run into him occasionally on July and August evenings when I'm there to watch dance festivals, realizing my teenage dream from those days when I would spread the Sunday *New York Times' Arts & Leisure* section across the kitchen table, read about Jacob's Pillow and the Straw Hat Trail of the summer Berkshires, and vow to go there someday.

Back in Pennsylvania, with Mrs. and Mr. Greiner both gone, Willow

Dell Farm has been sold. The current owners, I'd be willing to bet, do not serve tea and scones at four.

⊃

MEMORY IS selective; memoir, even more so. Organized artfully by themes, memoir chooses from within this world of flux a few sketches from life, stabilizes and holds them, and excludes a trove of others. Excluded from this memoir:

My junior-high buddies Kurt and Roy, neighbors in Cedar Heights. "Watch when a man's face really comes to life," a woman once said. "It's when he's talking about his buddies." Butch and Sundance. Robin Hood and Little John. Huck and Jim. The Three Musketeers and d'Artagnan: All for one and one for all.

Kurt and Roy and I, fourteen and fifteen years old, comprised a trio of daredevils, hitchhikers, hell-raisers, and goof-offs. Shooting pool. Sneaking gulps of homemade hootch in Kurt's basement. Hurling a football. Messing with firecrackers. Wrestling on the lawns, testing each other. Kurt and Roy were a year older, but I could pin Roy and could almost pin Kurt, so I held my status in the hierarchy.

Coltish, devil-may-care, each chewing a stem of wild garlic. Pummeling each other and laughing. Me: a withy kid in eighth grade, all surfer bangs and swagger. Still trying to make the Panthers wrestling squad. Roy: thatch-blond, muscled like a dock-walloper. Kurt: dark-haired, compact, athletic, a smirk hiding his bashfulness. Like Roy he reveled in buck hunting, squirrel shooting, casting for brownies with salmon eggs and crawlers, grease-monkeying with chains and derailleurs on his ten-speed.

Force of memory:

Kurt and Roy and I would skid bikes outside Dotterer's country store, across the road from the tractor dealer. Lean the bikes against hand-cranked Esso pumps. Cowboy inside, letting a screen door whack shut. Flip open the Coke cooler. Slosh hands into wrist-numbing ice water to flush out bottles, tossing dimes on the counter where old Mr. Dotterer eyed us suspiciously in his gray coveralls. If he turned, we'd shoplift beef jerky. Hostess Cupcakes. Peel out on our bikes, whooping. We'd loll on one of the open-strutted bridges over Fishing Creek built in the 1930s. Watch the water slurry underneath. Watch trout torpedo through the shadows. Daring each other. Double-daring.

"Betcha can't balance an' walk all way 'cross that damn beam up there."

"Hell, what beam?"

"Right up there, squirrel-bait. Dare ya."

Evenings we might thumb rides into Mill Hall, puffing cigars called Swisher Sweets. We'd scale the fence at Starlite Drive-In and toss cherry bombs at parked cars then run. Hell-raisers. Hoods. "That Cedar Heights gang."

On July nights we slept in meadows beneath a halved moon, stars turning slow, barely perceptible reels through the firmament. Woke at dawn, sleeping bags moist with dew. We tramped through alfalfa fields. Flushed cottontails. Heard gabble of starlings. Grasshoppers whirred, helicoptering through the air, landing on our knees. We nailed together tree forts down in the woods. Gaped at *Penthouse* centerfolds swiped from outdoor wood-boxes of hunting cabins. Watched heat lightning over the Nittany Mountains, like a tin sheet rippling, sky black as melanite. We'd sneak through apple trees on late September afternoons. Orchards belonged to a man who kept his shotgun loaded with rock salt. He'd snipe at trespassers. Alert to this danger we swayed surreptitiously in upper boughs, legs dangling, munching forbidden fruit: Northern Spy. Cortland. Winesap. Macintosh.

Our lives as yet unused and unencumbered....

On winter afternoons, sledding snowbound trails high in the mountains. On summer nights, building campfires and tenting in pine hollows. Wary of rattlesnakes and copperheads. Lashing together lean-tos in the woods. Dining on "surp samwiches"—Appalachian argot for Aunt Jemima syrup drizzled on slices of Sunbeam white bread. Sharp shooting at bottles and cans with a .22 or blasting skeet from the sky with a shotgun. Rafting Fishing Creek on stolen motorcycle crates. At Halloween, garbed in black, sneaking at night into the hamlet of Salona like a commando team of vandals to smash jack o' lanterns, soap windshields, spatter houses with hurled eggs, throw mini-bombs. On spring mornings, pedaling our clunky bikes over dirt roads on forested ridges and into the open farm valleys on daylong sixty-mile jaunts. Tanned and brash and fit. Hanging out over cans of Fresca, shoving each other, confiding about girls, politics and Vietnam, our families, the existence of God, life on other planets, how we wanted to live someday. Buddies. Our motto: "The gang sticks together."

Until I turned fifteen. Until I realized my fate: to become a different person—a reader of books (Roy boasted that he'd never read one in his life), a writer of poems, a hippie kid obsessed with the transistor radio and its new oracles: "Light My Fire, "Purple Haze," "Jumpin' Jack Flash," "Pinball Wizard," "Strawberry Fields Forever." As I began to realize this about myself, I asserted it in ways cowardly and mean. Kurt and Roy would jostle up our driveway spinning a football in the air. Knock at the door. "Tell 'em I'm not here," I'd order my mother. This happened half-a-dozen times. Kurt and Roy stopped coming.

I'd begun moving in a direction of my own—ruthlessly—for the first time. Like Huck, I was lighting out alone for the territories. And I didn't glance back.

Also excluded from this memoir: my wild forays into hazard and discovery. At sixteen, as a longhair kid seated in a room watching three wraiths—two guys and a girl, each a junkie—snare rubber tubing round their arms and jab the needle primed with smack into their wasted veins. Watching them slide open a window to squirt blood from the syringe. Watching and knowing, then and there, I never would do that, no matter how crushing life became. The rough-and-tumble years of my twenties and thirties: work and write by day; hit the streets at night, sometimes with other flamboyant, debauching *artistes*, sometimes by myself. Malodorous barrooms scuzzed with cigarette smoke and Chicago blues and stale Budweiser. The strip joints where contemptuous, dead-eyed vixens strutted naked on tables. The late-night hustlers and bullshit artists and dope dealers and ex-cons and sleaze dudes under streetlights, the easy pickup girls with their slurred lipstick. Era of the sexual revolution; after I'd had sex with twenty of those girls I stopped counting. *The road of excess leads to the palace of wisdom.—William Blake.* Waking up next to the toilet. Jailhouse drifters and tramps and the muttering, misplaced fuckups—as

I thought of them then—encountered in Greyhound bus stations. In the food stamps office. The scut-work jobs. Graffitied piss-alleys at three in the morning. Cop blinding me with the spotlight on his cruiser, barking, "Put your hands where I can see them—show me your hands!" as I realized, my god, he might blow me away at any second.

Bleary incoherent women and their scarface boyfriends. On the make. On the prowl. Raised working-class, it's easy to fall one step lower, into the demimonde. Into the ranks of the doomed.

Me, accepted always and without effort into those fraternities of the American underclass, the Preterite, the passed-over. Or, as I've come to see it, the Buddhist realm of samsara, of suffering.

Me, observing. Talking. Hanging out. Alert to threat. Listening. Getting street-smart. Avoiding the traps, the lethal pitfalls.

Learning to fend and improvise. Living for art, the bohemian squalor, choosing liberty over lucre. Writing poems through all of it. One can of Campbell's soup in the kitchen cupboard. Scrounging pennies from a fountain in a park to make a call from a pay phone.

In the mid-Eighties, months of homelessness in a drear fall and winter, after breaking up unexpectedly with a girlfriend and vacating our shared house in a cyclone of hurt feelings and dislocation, sleeping furtively on a stack of newspapers in the *Amherst Bulletin* office where I worked, sleeping on friends' floors or couches, spooning cold beef stew from cans, each day a new conundrum of subsistence to puzzle out—where to shower, where to sleep that night—in weariness and uncertainties.

◯

MEMOIR IS a willful glancing back. In Zen training, by contrast, I focus on whatever presents itself. Everything brings me to this instant. This instant brings me to everything.

In the Heart Sutra we chant, "*Gate, gate, paragate, parasamgate, bodhi svaha.*" This can be translated roughly as, "Gone, gone, gone beyond, gone completely beyond—awake! So be it." When you've gone completely beyond, where do you arrive? Here.

When I sit zazen and the convenient fiction of an "I" briefly drops away, that "I" cannot be located; it's nowhere (which is also everywhere). At the same time that the "I" is *nowhere*, there's an experiencing of complete presence: *now here.*

Cartier-Bresson spoke of "the decisive moment." Fifteen years ago at Zen Mountain Monastery I practiced *kyūdō*, Zen archery, under the tutelage of Shibata XX, twentieth-generation bow-maker to the emperor of Japan. Clutching the long bow, I aimed at the target and waited for the decisive moment. "Release!" Shibata's assistant urged me. "Release!" It didn't feel like the perfect moment. Minutes passed. Finally, I gave up and let go. The arrow streaked to the target. And I realized: every moment is the decisive moment.

Presence is an unbroken series of present moments, the seamless now; it's alertness to presents—and presents are gifts. But I don't open these gifts. I open *to* them.

And who is this "me"?

Sit on the zafu. Meditate each day. Face the white wall. Inhale into the belly, into the hara. Exhale. Watch that. Watch images, notions, memories arise in consciousness and evaporate. Back to silence, back to the breathing silence.

Daily, read and practice with the kōan collections. I love working with these quandaries, these succinct, enigmatic exchanges between ancient adepts, pithy stories engineered to slap the rational mind into a state of blank incomprehension, then slowly reveal their truths outside our habits of discursive thinking. *A monk asked Pa Ling, "What is the Blown Hair Sword?" Pa Ling said, "Each branch of coral supports the moon."* You realize a kōan through the hara. No one told me this; I learned it myself, through effort. In Zen you also must present the kōan by demonstrating how it has penetrated your life. At this stage I've presented a couple of hundred kōans to my Zen mentors—not that the numbers matter—and passed them. (It's hard work, though. Sometimes passing a kōan can feel like passing a kidney stone.) I've labored through the preliminary kōans and *The Gateless Barrier* and *Blue Cliff Record*, through the Precepts kōans and the *Book of Five Rings* and the *Book of Serenity*. Each day I review one of the kōans, studying anew, uncovering fresh angles and unforeseen vantage points. The centuries-old kōan anthologies stand among the

supreme achievements of human spirituality and the world's literature—
intricate in their baffling simplicity, insightful, sometimes funny, often
poetic, earthy, touching, challenging, and stocked with interesting characters—though most people remain unaware of them. Kōans keep the
bodymind's clarity focused and sharp.

Most importantly, I live the kōan of daily life.

In 2015, Zen, a path of personal transformation, also offers one of
the most subversive ways to exist in our contemporary world. Instead of
fixating on a smart phone in your hand, instead of posting trite ephemera
on Facebook, instead of staring at NFL highlights on a flat-screen TV
or staffing an office cubicle and helping the firm meet its production
quotas for the third quarter, instead of ogling the Kardashians, instead of
munching a Big Mac as you floor the Chevy down the interstate, spewing
noxious fumes into the atmosphere, instead of participating in the vast
social dementia of twenty-first century America, you're sitting on a cushion. Gradually you're becoming lucid, empowered, and sane.

You're undermining the System. When I see kids attired as "punks,"
with the hackneyed pink Mohawks and ripped T-shirts and jeans and
black Converse high-tops that safely signify "rebellion," slavishly imitat-
ing what my friends and I wore nearly forty years ago in 1977 when it was
original and exhilarating (I think of such kids on today's streets as "punk
reenactors," like Civil War reenactors), I feel inclined to tell them, "Hey.
You want to be really subversive? Sit on a cushion and watch your breath."

Most people from my home area of Appalachian Pennsylvania never
write their personal histories. Those who hail from my childhood working-class environs of trailer parks and paper mills and hunting cabins
certainly do not.

Even Alison Bechdel, who draws pictures and writes about our native
region, does so from a middle-class viewing point. Not me. After my
dad advanced from blue-collar draftsman to white-collar engineer and
manager, and our family arrived shakily in middle-class Cedar Heights,
my sensibility remained, forever more, that of my struggling proletarian
youth. It's indelible. As nature imprints a hatchling bird with intimate,

lasting bond to the first thing it sees, so I'm imprinted with the experience of working-class Clinton County.

I've wanted to bring that experience to literature. Southern Appalachia has the dark folk balladry of "The Daemon Lover," "Pretty Peggy-O," "The Wagoner's Lad," or "Edwin in the Lowlands Low." The northern Appalachia of New England farms has the stark lyricism and flint of Robert Frost. But the central Appalachia of Pennsylvania has no song, no poetry. In this book I've hoped to remedy that.

A half century ago, an outsider to my region driving Route 220 past our Pine Acres Mobile Home Court would have seen me playing at the edge of scrub woods behind our trailer and thought, "Hillbilly white trash." For me to become a writer, a Harvard alum, a speaker at Yale, a pioneering minister in an esoteric Asian spiritual tradition—who could have predicted such an astonishment?

The likelihood that someone of my origins would become a Zen Buddhist minister is so preposterous that I've wanted to share the story. Yet, just as the act of looking backward in memoir tugs against my Zen practice of remaining in the moment, so this autobiographical focus on self—on the illusion of a fixed identity—pulls against my Zen realizations of selflessness and my wish for anonymity, for leaving no traces.

Is it even possible to write a memoir without a riotous indulgence of ego?

Pursuing this question further, how might a Zen practitioner write an autobiography without the taint of narcissistic self-promotion?

Or without taking part in contemporary pop-Buddhism? For one of the greatest threats to Western Buddhism remains its accommodation to an American celebrity-worshiping and consumer culture.

This fact dismays, but it needn't surprise. After all, Buddhism has a long history of adapting to the cultures it enters. Arriving in China from India around 70 CE, it began a slow, dramatic process of acclimating to Taoism and Confucianism. Arriving in Japan around 550 CE, it began adjusting to pre-Shinto nature pantheism. In Tibet during the seventh century CE. it clashed with some aspects of the native Bon shamanism and assimilated others. These were healthy accommodations. But arriving in

America full-force in the mid-twentieth century it speedily began a toxic adaptation to the culture here—one of money, mass media, and celebrity idols.

The result? Among the genuine teachers, the humble ones, often obscure or unknown, we're inundated with a plethora of dharma stars, brand-name Buddhist hotshots, self-advertising Enlightenment hustlers, fame-seeking gurus lording over retreats in posh *nirvana* resorts, their faces beaming from glossy pop-Buddhist magazines and catalogs, with affluent mobs of craven fans rushing after their teacher-idols. These disciples nurture rampant projections and fantasies about the attainments of their chosen "masters," eager to surrender their innate wisdom and power (and, of course, their Visa card numbers) to Buddhist celebrities. How to write a Zen memoir without participating in this hoopla of clowns and monkey-trainers in the garish Ringling Brothers-Barnum and Bailey tent that is contemporary pop-Buddhism?

Because of these concerns, crafting an autobiography feels odd.

Particularly over so many long, patient years. *A wild patience has taken me this far.—Adrienne Rich.* There's a point at which patience becomes passion, as in writing, and passion becomes patience, as in Zen training. In Buddhism, patience is one of the *paramita* virtues. When I patiently began writing this book in 1992, near the start of my Zen training, I clung more tenaciously to memory and to self. Decades of practice not only have taught me to flourish mostly in the present, but have worn away and reshaped much of that "me," like water transforming limestone in my native Appalachian hills.

"Self" comes and goes. Frequently goes. Like thoughts. How to write about it?

And, of course, each word, each act of speech, is a blaspheming against the ineffable. Yet we need to speak. To write.

⊃

SPRINGTIME IN the Berkshire foothills. Moments ago at the mill pond, cedar waxwings banked and power-dived in sorties against black flies. I wended through a meadow at the base of Mount Adams. White flowerlets of wild strawberry interwove acres of grasses and clover. I spotted a box turtle. Hunkered beneath her six-inch carapace she sat flush on a nest scooped from turf and topsoil. Now I'm tarrying on a woodland path. It's a five-minute jaunt from my door. Maples, pines, sweetfern. From a brackish pond a stream crickles over palisades of a beaver dam. A fly loops delirious circles. Moist vernal air, scented with hemlocks. Trillium, its white trefoil petals emblazoned at the center with regal purple, adorns the trailside like tiny floral replicas of heraldic shields, ornately medieval. Geese returned from their seasonal northward migration wing overhead toward Pelham Lake. They navigate by magnetic channels in the Earth and by reading celestial signs. Calling to each other in flight, they sound like French horns warming up in an orchestra pit.

I follow the trail to dry masonry walls of stacked glacial rocks encrusted with lichen, the flat capstones shrouded in moss. Big earth-cobbles and boulders heaved and piled by farmhands more than a century past. The walls formed a pen for grazing sheep or dairy herds when these New England forests were pasturage. Now the trail carves its narrow passage over leaf loam, rubble of twigs, roots upraised and sinuous like veins in a crone's hand. Mother Earth. Neurobotanists tell us that roots of trees in a forest such as this intertwine with mycelia to share nutrients and chemical information, the entire system interconnected. In a woodland, each tree exists as part of the networked whole, and the whole manifests itself in each tree. It's differentiation in Oneness, Oneness in differentiation, as we say in Zen.

I make my way along the trail through beech and ash and bracken, through bricolage of cherry and maple, deadfall logs, evergreen and spars, jack-in-the-pulpit glade and wild apple, the trail an open airway of filtering light tunneling through foliage.

It leads homeward, and each footstep is home.

I know my path.

EIGHTEEN

THE ATLANTIC shores of Ireland: sea, lush pasture, stone walls, and open sky. Sounds of wind, surf, and gulls. Piercing smells of kelp in the tide pools. May of 2017: I put the clock away and live in sacred time. My only companions, the grazing cattle. Mostly I sit on the rock beach fronting the remote farm cottage where I'm staying. I watch the tide surge in, whitecaps smashing at the headlands, and watch the tide seep out later, the ocean vast and churning. I watch the light shifting on the Cliffs of Moher to the north.

Or I walk atop those cliffs: grandeur of seven-hundred-foot crags, bulwark of stone against crashing Atlantic surfs. Rough-hewn, wind-chiseled strata. Crevices of wildflowers, of yellow gorse and sea-pinks, of sea-grass, niches for nesting birds, the puffins. Gulls. Choughs....Sea-stacks, isolated pillars of rock upthrust at the cliff base, lashed by foaming waves.... Gulls drifting chasms of air between the cliffs. I stand on summits and peer down into dizzying voids, seabirds wafting far below and, even farther beneath me, the pounding breakers. Vast blue ocean. Aryan Islands on the horizon. Smiling as tears come to my eyes, I whisper, "I'm not in Mill Hall, Pennsylvania. I always knew I'd travel to a place like this someday." Another working-class triumph.

I explore downcoast. Magnificent and wild. Towering crags and pummeling breakers.

The tiny Gaelic villages in my motherland of County Clare, their bungalows of painted stucco—red or purple, saffron or blue—their shops and pubs, the wafting odors of burning peat. My Irish great-grandmother Carrie Bryan would have known that scent as a young girl.

I hear cuckoos in the woods of the Burren. I stand beside a five-thousand-year-old Neolithic tomb.

Back at the cottage I stroll the clifftop meadows. I return to the beach to sit for hours on the rocks, or to scavenge for shells, for polished sea stones and fossils. The sun setting. The moon rising. The lingering twilight. Day after day. Ocean medicine, indeed. True home.

And the following week, London! The West End. Throngs of people, palatial art museums—Botticelli, Rembrandt, Velázquez, Van Gogh—literary shrines, cathedrals, hidden parks and fountains, grandeur of architecture, street buskers, magicians, lights on the Thames, and *Twelfth Night* at Shakespeare's Globe. Bedazzlement and urban flair and fun. I love it. Two years ago, with my artist girlfriend at the time, Ulanda, I romped through Paris, my dream since I read Proust in the treehouse behind my Appalachian home. Ulanda and I rented a Latin Quarter apartment in the Boulevard Saint-Michel. Narrow alleyways and gleam of cafés, watching the Seine from the Musée d'Orsay, gardens in the rain, echoing clamor of bells at Notre-Dame.

Redeeming my vow to escape the provincial land of my youth. Redeeming my vow to discover the grander, far-flung carnival of this beckoning world.

I return from Ireland and London to an America in which Donald Trump has occupied the White House for the past four months. Pennsylvania helped push Trump to victory on election night. My homeland of Clinton County voted overwhelmingly for him, so in a very real sense I can say that my rural, ultra-conservative, white working-class region of Appalachian Pennsylvania proved instrumental in putting Trump in the White House. I know, too, that political pundits scramble now to fathom the grievances and resentments of the white working-class voters among whom I grew up, and with whom I experience such complicated bonds of kinship and estrangement.

Growing up in Clinton County in the late Fifties, the Sixties, the early Seventies, though we budgeted and scrimped, though we made do, lived modestly, we seldom felt deprived. I felt no stigma when our family lived for weeks in a motel waiting for our new trailer to arrive from the factory. The motel boasted colored spotlights playing across a small pool, which I loved. At night, after school, we huddled on the beds of our motel room to watch TV and read Dr. Seuss books. It felt like living in perpetual holiday. Nor did I feel stigmatized when we moved into our trailer. It felt snug and cozy, like living in a trim houseboat, everything compact and shipshape. It felt special. My friends lived in ordinary houses, but we inhabited something unique and, to a child's mind, worthy of pride: a mobile home. My dad built a rose trellis and my mom brightened the patio with marigolds. I felt lucky.

In the postwar American heartland we and our neighbors lived in a realm of rough economic parity. The incomes of a veteran unionized Hammermill factory worker and a professor at Lock Haven State lay in approximate alignment. We saw the broken farms around us and the hillbilly shacks in the mountains and the unkempt ridge-runner people who dwelled there—skittish around schooling and shakily employed—but we consoled ourselves on our good fortune and left them alone. At the other end of the economic scale, we knew nothing of lavish wealth except as fantasies in television and movies. Thus class resentments barely arose.

For me, direct encounter with material wealth and the awakening of class consciousness—that epiphany—occurred when I left Clinton County and arrived in the magic kingdom of Massachusetts where, to cite one example, an acquaintance invited me to a weekend writers' retreat at her family estate in the town of Manchester-by-the-Sea. There I discovered, hidden discreetly behind a wooded ridge at the end of a long gravel driveway, a fabulous compound, as if conjured from the lamp of a genie: Victorian castle with porte-cochère, where my room looked out on a moonlit ocean; half-an-acre away, the family's Mediterranean-style villa; nearby, their sleek Modernist mansion among pines; all of it secluded along a quarter-mile of head-spinning, majestic private beachfront.

That Victorian castle stood as testament to the opulence of what Mark Twain and Charles Dudley Warner contemptuously dubbed the Gilded Age. Today in America we inhabit a second Gilded Age. A chasm divides scrabbling, nerve-frayed working-class people and those in the vanishing middle class from the lordly one-percent of multimillionaires and billionaires at the financial peak, who bask in godlike realms of splendor.

Resentment seethes. But working-class people persist in believing that with luck, or with God's favor, if they toil diligently, or scratch the right Powerball ticket, they, too, may live in the gilded palaces. They envy the rich. They hope to emulate them. If they're white, they may adore the flashy Trump class of the nouveau-riche and direct their resentments toward people within their own social stratum, perceived as vying against them for the few available scraps; and toward cultural overlords ensconced in New York and Hollywood and on Ivy League campuses; and toward denizens of an "undeserving" class of Blacks and immigrants below them, scorned for supposedly prospering from what's imagined as "welfare handouts" and "unfair" preferential treatment.

Trump's election dismayed me but did not surprise me. I know the American heartland because I grew up there, and I know that the heart of the heartland is clotted with a sclerotic rage that is tenacious and dangerous. In final weeks before the presidential election I could detect that rage, and the possibility of Trump's victory, abroad in the heartland, though I continue to live outside of it in the wealthy liberal-progressive enclave of western Massachusetts. Election night stunned people around me. Artists, co-op farmers, college professors and students, therapists, hipster baristas, Buddhists, goddess devotees, vegans, queer and trans activists, social justice crusaders, all staggered in numb disbelief. But my disappointment was tempered. I'd been prepared, for one thing, by listening on a recent afternoon to six songs on a country-western radio station. I almost never listen to Nashville music when driving; my radio stays tuned to our local college station with its playlist of indie alt-rock, Afro-pop and world-beat music, funk and contemporary R&B, or I listen to our classical music station: Dvořák, Beethoven, Haydn, Borodin, Schubert, Mozart, Mendelssohn, Stravinsky. But sometimes when I'm out of range I'll tune into a country-western station for a few minutes to eavesdrop on what one of the other Americas—the white working-class one—is thinking. What I heard before the election concerned me. Six songs in a row, each drawling the same theme: They make fun of our pickup trucks, they make fun of our cowboy hats, our love of huntin' and fishin', our work, our play, our music, our churches, but *we're proud to be Country!* "They" of course meaning me and my associates. Listening to the songs I thought, "Trump could win this thing."

The people who listen to those songs in their Ford F-150s or Chevy 4x4s, the people for whom those songs serve as tribal chants and rallying cries, work double shifts at Costco or Walmart. They do roofing or lay pipe or drywall or fix heating ducts. They waitress at Cracker Barrel, serve onion rings and sirloin at Appleby's. They wear green scrubs in hospital corridors and push the food carts. They're firefighters. Receptionists. Postal clerks. They deliver propane or fix carburetors or sit in cubicles answering phones. Or they listen to those country-western songs on headphones as they perch in the cabs of their tractors, spraying fields of soybeans. They flock to their kids' Little League games and baton-twirling pageants. They chat on Skype with their brother or sister or son or daughter who is clad in desert camo on a base in Iraq or Afghanistan. They haul pans of lasagna to PTA bazaars. They steer around potholes in their gutted downtowns, past the blighted storefronts of hairdressers and quick-loan joints and Chinese take-out, past the junk shops and corner stores hawking cigarettes and beer. They motor past factories with shuttered windows. Past the struggling malls. They worry about their cousin who's hooked on heroin. They scratch Megabucks tickets. They come home tired. Many sing to Jesus in evangelical worship halls on Sunday mornings. If they ever glance at a news report, it's on Fox.

They feel beleaguered and betrayed. I understand. I know those people. They feel scared and angry because they know that for all their unrelenting labor and monthly strain in paying the bills and for all their stalwart upholding of their treasured patriotic values, they're becoming outnumbered and irrelevant in a rapidly transforming, multicultural world (a world that people like me welcome). Political commentators recognize this now that Trump has won the presidency, and assert that he triumphed because he voices in his snarling racism and misogyny and his incitements to violence and in his unbridled demagoguery the crude, inchoate wrath of a desperate white working-class—a group feeling the estrangement that Black Americans, Native Americans, Latino

Americans, Asian Americans, and other marginalized groups have experienced for years. The power base is shifting.

There's truth in this. And yet.

Consider my father, born in rural Appalachia in the 1920s. By the time he died he belonged to the political demographic of pale, choleric, elderly white males courted by Republicans. But he defied them and remained a traditional Democrat. In part this happened because years earlier he'd been promoted at his factory job to chief planning engineer, donning suit jacket and tie, moving us from our trailer into the lower middle class and our impressive stone chalet in Cedar Heights. When he excelled at his job—he was featured in articles in national tool-and-die trade magazines—the company sent him to management seminars at Penn State and on business trips to Cleveland and Chicago. Later he transferred to suburban Delaware. Therefore he knew something about life outside of Clinton County. When he and my mother returned to central Pennsylvania after his retirement, he deplored the local rubes and ruffians. He called them "bubbas" and, sardonically, "good ole boys." Dad—unlike his brothers, my uncles Ralph and Dick, and unlike many of our neighbors in Lock Haven and Mill Hall—never spoke the word "nigger" or guffawed at "nigger jokes." Such language disgusted him. Unlike one of his distant acquaintances, an erstwhile Lock Haven High School assistant football coach, Dad never joshed that an enjoyable event was "more fun than killin' niggers." He never emulated the racists who surrounded us. The year he died, he mentioned that he planned to vote for Obama.

So how do political pundits explain that my dad was a white working-class Appalachian guy, but that he would have loathed Trump and the travesty of the Trump presidency? That he would have despised the loudmouth braggadocio, the lies, the buffoonery, the cheapening of the Executive Office? The bullying stupidity and ineptitude? Would have detested the truculence, the bellicosity and bluster of a soft-bellied, cowardly chicken-hawk who never faced combat but who delights in provoking Americans to fight each other in the streets? How do pundits explain that my father would have abhorred the vulgarity and the divisive rhetoric? Would have been repelled by Trump's glitzy life of privilege, the unearned millionaire inheritance, the gold-plated towers, the narcissism, the moral rot and corruption? "Oh, your dad would have hated Trump," my mom affirms—my eighty-four-year-old mother who also is white working-class Appalachian, and who adored Bernie Sanders during the primaries and voted for Hillary Clinton in the final presidential race, and who watched TV with me in her Connecticut apartment, tears in her eyes, as voting results oozed in from our native Pennsylvania on election night, putting our home state in the Republican red column and sealing the disaster.

So how might the political experts account for this? How might they explain the aberration of my white working-class Appalachian parents? My parents who seem to be the last remnants of the early Sixties social bedrock of working-class Kennedy Democrats? Who wanted to share the Norman Rockwell America they thought they knew, wanted to share it with everybody decent and law-abiding, regardless of skin color or creed or national origin? My parents who also saw their hearts broken and their faith shattered?

These questions come in 2017 amid increased publicity of lethal attacks against Black people, especially Black men—attacks that have persisted since the dawn of the Republic, and even before, with the enslavement of Black people in Florida by the Spanish in 1565 and then by English colonists and their descendants throughout the South. Black slaves, unlike my indentured German ancestors, almost never could buy their way out of servitude; furthermore, Black people, unlike my German forbearers or my Irish ancestors—members of a group initially despised and discriminated against—could not win a free pass of eventual assimilation into a racist society's constructed hierarchies of whiteness. The traumas persist.

Our current racial struggles in America perpetuate the nauseating chronicle of injustices against Black people accumulated over centuries: forced unrequited toil, from shipyards to cotton fields, of kidnapped Africans and their progeny; rapes; whippings; terror; beatings; murders; mutilations; savage lynchings. Redlining. Theft of farms. Rampaging mobs looting and burning Black neighborhoods and businesses. Jim Crow. Thwarting of voting rights. Entrapment in rat-infested urban ghettos. Wretched schools. Segregated bathrooms and lunch counters and swimming pools. Poverty and degradation. Broken promises. Police harassment. Systemic domestic terrorism and white supremacy. Bombings, shootings, cross burnings. Assassinations. Mass incarcerations and plantation prisons. (And not only in the South: as a kid I saw chain gangs of Black men in striped prison uniforms working the fields at Rockview Penitentiary outside the town of State College.) Humiliation, mockery, blackface shows, exploitation, insult, dehumanizing caricatures. And throughout all of this brutal American apartheid, the extraordinary resilience, artistry, brilliance, and soul-redemption of Black people, who have bequeathed this nation so much of its vibrant culture and character.

Four years ago, in 2013, the Black Lives Matter movement sprang to life with marches and demonstrations. It highlighted the vulnerability of Black people to ongoing violence, entrenched racism, and the toxins of white domination. A vicious backlash has ensued, and Trump encourages it. Hardcore extremists on the far right agitate for white power and white Christian nationalism and vow that "we will not be replaced" as America grows ever more vividly multicultural.

Press reports tend to conflate this dangerous but comparatively small lunatic fringe of Trump-voting racist militiamen and hatemongers with his massive base of white working-class supporters. But those supporters, the type of people who were my neighbors in Appalachian Pennsylvania, bristle at the association. "We're not racists," they insist. To liberals and progressives this seems disingenuous at best, and a self-deluding lie at worst. Yet, pressed to explain, my former Appalachian neighbors (and people like them who live here in western Massachusetts and elsewhere nationwide) try to make the point that, in effect, they still believe in Martin Luther King's dream of equality for all, and they wonder bitterly why—from their perspective—Black people win so much sympathy when white working-class folks struggle miserably, too. "What about us?" they ask. "Don't all lives matter?" If they hear the phrase "white privilege" it stymies them. Unfamiliar with lethal hazards Black people face daily, in routine traffic stops and other threatening incidents that they, as white people, take for granted, they only know that they seem left behind in a country hurtling forward without them. "Privilege?" they demand, struggling to pay the mortgage. "How the hell am I privileged?" Feeling hurt, ignored, and unheard, they rally around Trump, the demagogue who gleefully spews their frustrations and stokes their resentments. They resent what they view as a betrayal of equal rights for all Americans in the growth of what, to them, appears a "Black supremacy" movement. They resent a mainstream media that, in their eyes, coddles this movement, and so they turn to Fox News. They feverishly resent the elite classes of the American cultural aristocracy, who—again in their view—glance down at them occasionally, from Olympian heights, with sneering disdain. They resent Hollywood. They resent with undisguised loathing the professors in the most prestigious enclaves of academia, professors they consider effete, pampered, and cloistered propagators of outlandish, unworldly theories that, when enacted on streets and job sites and in town halls via social justice movements, attack everything these people cherish and believe in—values shared, in fact, by working-class people across racial and ethnic lines, white, Black, Latino, indigenous, Asian: the dignity of hard physical work, service to country, basic fairness, and devotion to God and family.

The resentment has brewed for a long time. In the mid-1990s, when I worked as coordinator of youth and adult education programs for Amherst's Department of Leisure Services and Supplemental Education, I hired a part-time building supervisor for evening workshops at the junior high school. I took him to the site, oriented him, and handed him the keys. During the day he worked at a Mobil station in town. Driving him back to his gas station, I asked him, "So, how do you like Amherst?"

"Oh, I like it okay. It's a pretty good place, you know."

"I don't like it so much," I told him, turning a corner. "I come from a working-class family back in Pennsylvania. I think there are a lot of wealthy people here who take their privileges for granted."

"Really?" He paused. He studied me closely. "Okay, then," he said. "Let me tell you what I really think." He stared at the road ahead. "I hate this fucking town. I fucking hate it." He began to boil. "At the gas station, I get a call to take the tow truck out and rescue some fucking college professor, and these professors treat me like I'm some kind of fucking grease monkey." He shook his head. "Me and my buddies, we go down to the

NASCAR races down in North Carolina and we feel right at home. But then we come back up here, and—man, I fucking hate this place."

I don't know what's happened to him since then; we've lost touch. It wouldn't surprise me if now, twenty years later, he votes for Trump. What could I tell him if I met him today? That for my ancestors the price of entry into this country was indentured servitude; that they later struggled as farmers; that in the Appalachian hills and valleys of central Pennsylvania my paternal grandfather, a man I never met, worked at an ax factory; my maternal step-grandfather, also never met, was a hillbilly moonshiner who operated a corn-whiskey still at his shack in the woods; that my uncles, of whom I was fond, were World War II combat vets and barroom fighters and deer hunters and trout fishermen and worked at the paper mill; that my dad, a Navy combat vet, worked in tool-and-die factories; and I am a Zen Buddhist minister who circulates at Harvard, Deerfield Academy, and Yale; and that I try to hold it all, lightly and loosely, and observe it with freedom and curiosity? Is that what I could tell him?

Unlike that tow truck operator at the gas station, I've never hated Amherst, despite my qualms, and because of Zen practice I've ceased to resent the fact that I've never met anyone in the Amherst area who grew up like me or who has lived for years in heartland America. I do marvel, with mild amusement and incredulity, that they have no awareness of class issues. I do marvel that they've been so sheltered. I do marvel that they're blithely ignorant of the lifelong advantages they've enjoyed.

The Dalai Lama declares, "As far as social economy is concerned, I am a Marxist." I don't go that far—I dislike ideologies or manifestos of any stripe—but I do see his point.

"Between two worlds," wrote Byron, "life hovers like a star." Much of my life I've hovered between dual worlds of my people—my working-class people and my academic elite people. I hover between the world of Appalachia and the world of Harvard and Yale, where I'm still returning as a guest speaker and to teach.

Sometimes it requires code-switching. Knowing when a homey, folksy idiom in my relaxed Pennsylvania drawl helps to facilitate easeful conversation; knowing when multisyllabic words, scholarly allusions, and crisp enunciation are appropriate. I do it by choice and try to accomplish it in a way that employs what Buddhists call "skillful means," a way that's responsive to the situation at hand, in a fluid shifting between "selves," yet also authentic and sincere—not posturing, not a false persona.

Still, it presents challenges. A Zen kōan from the ancient *Gateless Barrier* collection: "Sen-jo and her soul are separated; which is the true one?"

If I resort to code-switching, I try to do it in a manner that's not condescending, on the one hand, or craven or ingratiating, on the other, but that serves as a simple expedient for establishing mutual comfort and a smooth flow of talking between diverse people. Nevertheless, code-switching as a means of navigating between two very different cultures always feels awkward. I'm conscious of its unwieldiness when I do it.

Two cultures, two worlds....

When I studied as a grad student in Buddhist ministry at Harvard Divinity School, I won grants and merit scholarships and borrowed thousands of dollars in school loans, but as a working-class person one of the ways I also financed my education was through jobs during the summers. And so, eleven years ago, in the bright estival season of 2006, I secured a three-month position through Harvard student employment, serving as caregiver for a frail, eighty-year-old Harvard Law alum who'd suffered a stroke. He was a retired Boston attorney. My job was at his million-dollar summer home on Georgetown Island off the coast of Maine.

His wife picked me up in Bath. We crossed to the island on a narrow bridge, then drove for twenty minutes through rustic landscape till we reached a gate tucked in the pines. The gate opened onto two miles of private dirt lane through the family's acres of forest and wild blueberry. We reached their vacation home, three stories of varnished wood and wraparound glass with panoramic views of a wilderness shoreline and the saltwater of Robin Hood Cove. No other houses were visible. The wife dropped me off and returned to Boston. My employment consisted mostly of taking the elderly man to restaurants in Bath, which he paid for, and lounging on the dock of the summer home as he regaled me with nautical lore. During time off I kayaked the cove. Ospreys winged overhead. Seals popped from the waves to survey me. Four-foot sturgeon leaped from the water in flashes of silver, twisting in mid-air spumes of dazzling spray and plunging back to the depths. Sometimes the man's wife, thirty years younger, visited, or his two children. Sometimes the wife's secret lover joined her. At those times it felt like we inhabited a Chekhov play, the wealthy family and the paramour idling with their servant in the countryside amid lethargy and strained decorum. The wife, incidentally, had never in her life possessed a Social Security number, because she had never worked a job.

Recently I jotted a list of the more than twenty-five jobs I've held over forty years. Dishwasher in a Lock Haven steakhouse (the sweltering night I quit, the boss, feet on his desk, informed me, "You can't do what you want in life"—and there it was again, my hometown motto). Door-to-door canvasser. General laborer. Babysitter. Direct care provider in group homes. Newspaper reporter and editor. School van driver. Drummer in a rock band. Bookstore clerk. Clothing model. Art class model. Test designer. Movie reviewer. Gym attendant. Ad proofreader. Program direc-tor. Classroom teacher. (This is why working-class people seldom write books. Drudging for paychecks consumes too much vigor, too much day-light, too much precious life. There's little time or energy left for writing anything.)

One day during my summer in Maine I accompanied the elderly man's wife on an outing to a hardware store to stock up on household supplies, and I noted how nonchalantly she tossed whatever she fancied into her cart. She didn't pause to consider prices. She didn't scan the shelves for bargains. Whatever she glanced at—into the cart it went. (I do this, too, sometimes, but not as an act of unconscious entitlement; I do it as an act of insouciant rebellion against the bleak penny-pinching I witnessed in my hard-pressed mother and father their entire lives.) I also noted how oblivious she was to the muted hostility of the locals. Their families ran the lobster trawlers and seafood shacks and tourist shops. They identified her instantly as a rich summer person.

Working-class people in America don't lack merely this privileged woman's easy-going freedom with money. What they lack, crucially, is social capital. This is the most valuable point that J.D. Vance makes at the end of his book *Hillbilly Elegy*. Working-class people—and I know this from my own experience—don't understand how the world really functions. Working-class people think that to get a job you scour advertisements and send out dozens of résumés and sit and wait and hope for a call; people with social capital know that to get a job you meet your father's friend at the Harvard Club or have lunch in Manhattan with your college roommate's cousin. You network. You use your connections. I see this at Harvard and Yale all the time. Henry Adams, in his vaunted autobiography, declared it explicitly: even in the mid-nineteenth century he observed that Harvard exists so that students can make social contacts that will advantage them throughout their ennobled lives.

Furthermore, working-class people believe—the sentiment is almost touching in its childlike innocence—that to become financially successful means that you work for money. Privileged people of the American elite know that, as the truism asserts, financial success means making your money work for you.

People from my white working-class world, people who voted for Trump, the self-professed "rednecks" who inscribe "Redneck Pride" on mudflaps of their pickups, and the white laborers, tradespeople, and lower-tier office professionals who subsist as hapless, forlorn members of the disappearing American middle class, believe indignantly that the people of my elite Ivy League world have abandoned them in favor of "upstart Blacks and immigrants." How little they know. America's elite class hasn't abandoned them; in truth, America's elite barely knows they exist, because working-class people don't circulate in the exclusive, self-perpetuating, rarefied networks of those who possess social capital. They're irrelevant. Or irrelevant until there's a plumbing problem in the sauna, or landscaping to be done, or a necessary repair to the Lexus. Then the peasants are summoned to the manor houses.

I feel camaraderie with the peasants; I feel kinship with the lords of the manors; I feel compassion for both. As a Buddhist practitioner I know suffering visits both poor and rich, sparing neither the deprived nor the lavishly entitled.

And yet I observe how I chafe against both. I notice how I chafe against what I perceive to be the provincial ignorance and kitsch and stolid right-wing ideologies of my fellow working-class folks in the heartland; I notice how I chafe against what I perceive to be the insularity, arrogance, smugness, privilege, thought-policing and rigid left-wing ideologies of my companions within the exclusive halls of the academic elite. My challenging practice edge in Zen is to let go. To not judge. To maintain don't-know mind.

Within America's plutocratic state and its centuries-old war between the underclass and the ruling class, I'm taking the Buddhist option. I'm following the Middle Way. Maneuvering in the median zone that divides Appalachia and Ivy League. Between two worlds....

I navigate what we call in Buddhism the world of Relative phenomena, our conventional world of individuation and differences, where distinctions of class and race assume momentous significance. Simultaneously I hold a view of what Buddhists experience as the ultimate world of the Absolute, of Oneness, beyond facile dualisms of working-class and elite, conservative and progressive, Republican and Democrat, red state and blue state, binaries of male and female, and beyond categories of white people and Black people, Native American people and Pacific Island people, Latino people and Asian people. The realm of connectedness and interbeing. Heartland.

The forces that produced Trump will not abate soon. But if we transcend divisions of race and class and gender, of politics, of religion, we abide, at last, by an ancient maxim so elementary that it's often forgotten:

Live and let live.

◯

MY BROTHER Larry has died, shortly after my return from Ireland. Again I'm ushered into the bleak dungeon of grieving.

My younger brother. To lose a younger sibling upends the natural order, like watching a blood moon emerge through a clear sky at noon.

Death ambushed him. Showering after mowing the lawn on a summer afternoon, he collapsed from a brain aneurysm, then lay in a coma in Hartford Hospital for eighteen days. Doctors informed us that he would stay in a brain-destroyed vegetative state forever. In shock and sorrow, we gave permission to turn off his life-support machines.

How to explain him? A sumptuously blessed musician, he lured music out of acoustic and electric guitars, out of drum kits and congas and steel drums, out of harmonicas, out of piano keyboards, out of trumpets and alto saxophones. He penned hundreds of songs. An amateur musicologist, he filed in his formidable memory an encyclopedic knowledge of American composers and songcraft. Larry was the person I talked to about pop music esoterica. How to explain him? He loved people. He loved parties, loved good cuisine, loved classic movies, loved his wife Ellen and his two adult children, loved nature, loved Manhattan and Spain and London and Puerto Rico, loved theater, loved life, loved love itself.

A wry comedian of spontaneous wit, my younger brother often reduced me to gasps and tears of helpless laughter. I phoned him when I needed an urgent shot of hilarity. Most important, Larry was the sole person who knew how it felt for the two of us to endure the vicious working-class milieu of Appalachian Pennsylvania in the late Sixties and early Seventies; how it felt to have survived as lone teenage longhair pariahs, as rebels and budding artists. We drove across America together when I was eighteen and he was fifteen. Back home we perused the gritty little hippie tabloid *Rolling Stone*; we listened to the Beatles' *White Album* and the Mothers of Invention and Led Zeppelin and Dylan's *John Wesley Harding* album and Santana and the Stones' *Sticky Fingers* and Joni Mitchell's *Blue* on the stereo in his bedroom, lying on the floor next to the speakers, analyzing the lyrics and instrumental tracks together. We flipped through *Zap Comix* and sketched cartoons. We hitchhiked together, explored mountain glens and pine forests, sought girls together, shared cheap apartments and starving-artist poverty when we were young. Like many close siblings, we signaled in a private jargon of coded words, mannerisms, and jokes that we comprehended with a knowing glance, a nod, a wry smile. We'd banter for hours. He and I shared a bottomless trove of reminiscences.

Yet it took merely the bursting of a tiny blood vessel in the brain—the aneurysm—to obliterate all of that in a microsecond. Utterly gone. What we cling to so ardently as our "self" is no more solid or perduring than a champagne bubble.

When he died I placed my hand on his heart, then on his forehead. I said, "I love you, Lar. We're brothers always. You fought the good fight these past two-and-a-half weeks. Your struggle is over. You're free. There's nothing to fear. Go for the light. Go for the light and the joy and the love."

A week after watching Larry die in the summer of 2017 I receive medical news following an exam: a sinister mass lurks in my groin. Stage II intermediate-level prostate cancer.

Old age, sickness, and death: the "three inevitables" in Buddhism.

My goal has become radical remission. I'm refusing surgery, radiation, and hormonal therapy, with their dire side effects. I intend to heal by ramping up my body's natural immunity, bolstering it through a medicinal vegan diet and herbal supplements prescribed by my naturopathic oncologist. I'm gulping dozens of pills and capsules each day. I'm committing to energy work, to Reiki, tai chi, and healing white-light visualizations, supporting my health on every level. Life force whooshing through my body's tissues and cells. Potent qi.

Twenty-three years of Zen practice afford me a fierce discipline required for this.

A close friend supports me with money for expensive natural treatments that insurance refuses to cover. Others buoy me with affectionate care and concern. They're jewels in my personal sangha. Two former girlfriends prove especially solicitous—Jenny, busy with her homeopathic clients in Pennsylvania, and Myoki, training here for ordination as a *Kohenet*, a Hebrew priestess, phone me nearly every day to check in. It helps immeasurably.

A Zen saying: "An old buddha remarked, 'I have a very strong power. When the wind blows, I bend gracefully.'"

Not that it doesn't hurt to bend sometimes. It does.

ɔ

FALLING SNOW tufts the oaks and streetlights outside my mother's apartment windows on Christmas Eve of 2018. We're mere days past the winter solstice of a hard year. Now amid darkness the light, keeping its age-old promise, begins its annual return.

As a Buddhist I mostly ignore Christmas. I do savor the carols and the *Nutcracker Suite*, and I'm moved by a religion telling us that the Supreme Creator of the cosmos incarnated on Earth as a helpless infant lain by his humble parents in straw of a feeding trough meant for barn animals. But I'm glad to be free of the holiday's glitz and shopping sprees. For my mother, though, Christmas remains a cherished time of sentiment and memories. So I've come here to Connecticut to be with her—the last two survivors of our demolished family, together on the couch as snow sweeps across the night.

I tell her I remember the Christmas Eves of my childhood in our trailer outside Lock Haven. How after midnight I'd tiptoe from bed into the living room to gape in awe at the evergreen tree, tinseled and strung with parti-colored lights and festooned with orbs of sparkling glass. The air charged with a lingering spell, a thrill of magic. The astonishment of seeing that the cookie we'd left for Santa had vanished, the glass of milk had emptied—proof that the enchanted Being from the polar North, in his tour of millions of homes throughout the world on that frigid night, had not forgotten us. His actual sleigh and reindeer had parked outside. Our trailer had no chimney—a worrisome fact at Christmastime when I was seven—but somehow he'd found his way inside, a burglar in reverse, breaking into our home to leave us improbable piles of gifts. The grandest astonishment of all: those ribboned boxes wrapped in candy-cane paper and Frosty the Snowman paper and paper of midnight blue spangled with snowflakes, heaped beneath the miraculous tree, each one tagged "For Sherry from Santa Claus," "For Larry from Santa," "For Steve from Santa Claus." In our Appalachian world of scrimping and careful working-class budgeting, this night of largesse, of delightful, unfathomable abundance, of dreams come true, staggered me.

"I don't remember you and Dad opening presents for yourselves on Christmas morning," I tell my mother. "I remember the kids, the three of us, ripping open our presents in this total delirium of excitement at five in the morning and the two of you beaming at us, really happy, but I don't remember you or Dad getting anything. As usual you sacrificed everything for us. It's one more example of what extraordinary parents you were."

"Well, it was just so great to be able to give you most of what you wanted. And we always thought we had the most extraordinary kids."

"But I don't know how you did it. You were so busy, running our household, taking care of us, volunteering as the Den Mother for my Cub Scout pack, volunteering as president of the school PTA. And Dad, too, busy at work, busy on the Salona school board —those wonderful Christmases for us, how did you manage it all?"

"Oh, I don't know, honey. We enjoyed it."

The supernatural mystery of those Christmas Eves, the flurrying pixie-dust of wonder, ended when I grew skeptical. Still seven, I began to admit heretical doubts about the Magical Night. I began subjecting it to rational inquiry. Could someone really dwell in the Arctic with elves and make toys and soar through the skies in a reindeer-propelled sleigh and visit the house of every slumbering child in a single nighttime? Even though my parents, my school teachers, the whole world insisted it was true? I felt troubled, perplexed, guilty for questioning what society urged me to believe. And I fervently wanted to believe. I opened volume "S" of our *World Book Encyclopedia* and looked up "Santa Claus," expecting to find my doubts dispelled—and recoiled in shock from the opening words: "Santa Claus is a mythical being...." My discovery served as prelude to realizing, a few years later, that the white-bearded God of Sunday school must exist only in fantasy as well. But by then, at ten, I had become hardened.

I share these reminiscences with my mother then ask, "What was Christmas Eve like for you in your farmhouse in the woods? Christmas back in those Appalachian Mountains of Pennsylvania in the 1940s? Did you have a tree?"

"Oh yes. My sisters and I decorated it with paper ornaments we made and that we colored ourselves with crayons. There were no electric lights on the tree; electricity came when I was seven or eight; before then we lit with kerosene lamps. There was no running water, either; we had to go to a pump outside."

"Did you sneak out in the middle of the night to see the tree and the presents, like I did?"

"No, we were excited on Christmas Eve but it was too cold to get out of bed—there was ice on the windows. But there was a nook between the woodstove and the wall and during the day I liked to sit there and see the tree in the corner."

"What kind of presents did you get?"

"Oh, we got paper dolls and coloring books and books of stories like *Black Beauty*. And I got my doll Betty, which I still have here in the closet all these years later."

Earlier today I found her crying. "I miss everyone. I miss the family. I miss Sherry and Larry and your dad." If I were to inform my mom of Buddhism's First Noble Truth, "Life is suffering," she would need no persuading. Yet she's also quick to laughter, generosity, joy, and love. Her resilience through a lifetime of heartbreak and losses is the true miracle, at Christmas or anytime. At this moment, though, she's enjoying our foray into the distant past, and so I coax her back to recollections of her childhood.

"What did you do on Christmas Day?"

"We went to church in the morning. Remember that little church in the woods that I showed you when we drove up past Pine Creek a few years ago? That one. And in the afternoon we might go sledding. We always had to hope that my drunken stepfather wouldn't show up. But my mother always made sure that we had a nice day. Maybe she couldn't get us a music box we wanted, but she made cornbread for us, and pies, and ham, and pickles."

"I remember how Dad read *The Night Before Christmas* to us on Christmas Eve in the trailer, before we went to bed. I always liked those lines, 'The moon on the breast of the new-fallen snow / Gave the luster of midday to objects below.'"

"You remember that, Steve R.? I'm so glad, honey."

We fade into silence as the snow falls. On the radio, turned low, a Christmas choir sings "peace on Earth and mercy mild...." A noble sentiment, but peace on Earth feels elusive. In recent weeks my mother and I have watched installments of a Ken Burns documentary airing on public TV, a riveting series on the Vietnam War. Now my thoughts veer toward it.

"That episode about the antiwar protests and marches and demonstrations brings back a lot of memories. It was pretty hard to be antiwar in Mill Hall."

"I remember that day you and I took a ride out around the East End of the valley," she says. A secluded rim of Nittany Valley—tenacious farms, waste pasture overgrown with sumac and honey locust, wooded mountain foothills. "I was driving and you were in the passenger seat and we were talking. You were probably a senior in high school and had your really long hair. Suddenly you spotted some hillbilly farmer sitting in a rocking chair on his porch with a shotgun in his lap. And you immediately—my God, you immediately ducked down on the floor of the car as we rode past. I've never forgotten that." My mother shakes her head. "I was stunned. It was my first clue of how hard it was there for you."

"I just ducked down automatically—it was pretty instinctive by that time. Survival instinct. I mean, he was probably just getting ready to go out into the fields and shoot crows or something, but I didn't even think about it. It was just—get down. Not taking any chances. Pure survival. You know, the danger everywhere, living in that place. The constant threat."

I tell my mother that I remember the draft lottery held the year after I graduated. I walked down our driveway in Cedar Heights to get the *Lock Haven Express*. Returning to our living room I spread the newspaper on the floor in solemn anticipation. I began tracing my finger down the printed table. Seeking my birthday. Learning my fate. I'd been starting the process of registering as a conscientious objector. Approval by our region's hardcore conservative draft board seemed unlikely. As I scanned the chart for my date of birth I wondered if it would auger my date of death—would I draw a low number and be shipped immediately to firefights in Vietnam's fetid jungles? Would I draw a mid-range number and wait in limbo? Or would I draw a high number and be safe? My future swayed in the balance scales. I found July 14. My number: 324. A high one. Safe.

"It was an intense experience at age eighteen," I tell my mother.

"Your dad wanted you to go to Canada if you got drafted," she tells me.

I've never heard this before. At eighteen I'd indulged heroic fantasies of going to prison for my beliefs; later, as an adult, I realized how naive I'd been; a callow, longhaired peacenik kid, I wouldn't have survived the first night in my cell. "Really? To Canada? Did the two of you talk about it? Were you worried?"

"Oh, God yes. We talked about it a lot. We were worried for both you and Larry. Your dad, because of his own combat experience in the most hideous place of World War II, in the Pacific, wanted you to go to Canada if you got a bad draft number."

I mull this is silence. An alternative life begins to unscroll in my mind. I imagine my dad and I driving in the Rambler through winter grayness and grit and snow squalls to the leaden Canadian border. I'm eighteen. At customs we improvise a story, say we're visiting a friend of mine at a Canadian college somewhere. In Montreal my dad helps me find an apartment. "I love you, Pal," he says, tears streaming, as he turns to leave. And I begin my exile. Those first Christmases alone. Over the years I learn some French. Maybe I wrangle a job at a newspaper. Ideally I meet a woman—a photographer, let's say. We marry. We move from Montreal to the Canadian prairies. I publish a novel. It's successful. Why not? Stranger things have happened. We have a daughter, then a son. I teach. Years later, when the US grants pardons to "draft dodgers," I return to the Appalachians in Pennsylvania and my graying parents hug their grandchildren for the first time.... An alternate life that easily could have happened, given a slight turn of fate.... The memoir I'm completing now could have turned out differently.

But I didn't go to Canada. I stayed. Now, decades later, on this night of snowfall, I hold my mother's shriveled hand. I rejoice in its warmth.

And if I had left Appalachia for Canada, would I have found Zen? More likely, Zen would have found me, wherever I roamed.

◯

MY MOTHER died four months after that Christmas Eve. Four months after I wrote those words. My friend. My companion. Bestower of my life. Never-emptied fount of unquestioning love. My most cherished spiritual teacher. After a torturous two weeks of induced coma during a bout of pneumonia, as her kidneys faltered and then failed, I kept vigil at her bedside in the Manchester hospital. When my sister-in-law Ellen and I consented to switch off Mom's life support, I placed my hand over my mother's heart. She left this Earth within seconds. And once again I entered the dungeon of grieving. But that is a tale for another book.

I'm the last survivor in my family.

Now, with Mom gone, I think of the words from Job 1:15. "*And I only am escaped alone to tell thee.*"

I orbit death and Eros, Eros and death.

Issa, eighteenth-century Japanese haiku poet, after the deaths of every person in his family, wrote: "This world / Is a dewdrop world, / And yet, and yet...."

My Zen ministry, quiet and unassuming, focuses on pastoral care and guidance. It's how I can best enact the Bodhisattva vow and engage the suffering of the world: one on one, a single person at a time. This ministry makes me available to anybody groping his, her, or their own way through pain and confusion. It excites me to see each one discover a brilliant, inborn clarity. And when I minister to individual people, woman or man or non-gendered, the effect becomes cumulative. It helps relieve, in a small way, this world's burden of misery.

Sometimes I conduct a funeral or a wedding, the ceremonial passages that bind us together, that honor our transitions, that hold us in affectionate community. This, too, becomes a gift of Zen Buddhist ministry to our American sanghas.

Meanwhile I've moved from the high, forested gateway of the Berkshire Mountains to the Connecticut River Valley of western Massachusetts, where I'm dwelling alone in a tranquil garden paradise amid brooks and woodlands. I live in a single room, a studio apartment with a kitchenette. I've come here to heal. I continue to emulate the ancient Chinese literati and wild Ch'an monks who wandered the hills while inscribing poetry, studying, teaching a few students, observing nature, and meditating, living simply while forsaking "the world of wind and dust." I'm here to get well. In doing so, I distill my Zen practice, as always, to six words: Be clear. Be kind. Be present.

By miracle I seem to have survived into this life of contentments, stripping away, giving up, letting go, while gaining immeasurably at every step. I've found a life spare in its delineations, yet rich in amplitude. My life's as elemental, as darkly luminous, as the Rothko black-on-maroon murals I saw at the Tate Modern in London.

Two-and-a-half years into my cancer journey and my intensive natural healing regimen, in January of 2020, an MRI reveals that the tumor has vanished. My approach is working. But that, too, is a tale for another book, one I'm calling *The Whole Earth Is Medicine*.

I continue my path of awakening.

This very instant: monarch butterfly sups at milkweed in evening sun. Wind scavenges topmost pine boughs. Alone at the garden's edge I murmur, "I love you, Mom. And Dad. And Lar and Sher."

This realm of suffering and death is, inescapably, the realm of awakening and life. This is it. There is no other paradise but this broken, bedazzling world. We relinquish the people we love. And our love sustains us.

At night I step outside and the stars are so close I can walk right into them.

One of the classic Zen kōans: At the place of the Third Ancestor, Jianzhi Sengcan, the novice Daoxin at age fourteen said, "I entreat the teacher with your compassion to give me the Dharma gate of release and liberation."

The teacher said, "Who has bound you?"

The novice Daoxin said, "Nobody bound me."

The teacher said, "Then why are you seeking for liberation?" Daoxin, hearing these words, had a great realization.

—

How free are you willing to be?

I have no idea what comes next. I trust life. Or, as I sometimes phrase it, I throw myself on the mercy of the court. We'll see what happens.

Words that came to me once in a dream: "All is lost, be of good cheer."

Words that also came to me once in a dream: "Come on! Life is inviting you to play! The hero is nimble and lives by his wits."

Years ago I rode out of Taos Pueblo in New Mexico with a young Tewa Indian guide, across the scrub plain into the high mountain trails of the Sangre de Christos. I rode a buckskin stallion. On the open flatland we galloped and I floated in the saddle, feet pressed to the stirrups, a half ton of charging muscle and mane and hooves churning beneath me. Life feels that way to me now: something powerful carries me. My hands loose on the reins, I roll with it. It hurls me forward into the sun.

☽

NEVERTHELESS, I don't hide from the samsaric world of wind and dust. I observe it avidly. In early 2021, Trump has skulked away from the White House in defeat, but as he departed, a mob of his most extremist shock troops, incited by lies and QAnon delusions bordering on psychosis, stormed the US Capitol in a tempest of mayhem and destruction. We continue to feel the after-tremors. The worst are full of passionate intensity, as Yeats wrote during a different apocalyptic era.

The ignorance and suffering of these people are profound. I pity them. I pity Trump, too, lost in his hell-realm of rancor, preposterous fantasies, and perpetual complaint. But I don't let my pity blind me. Letting my pity blind me would be what Zen calls "foolish compassion," compassion devoid of wisdom. I see the danger. Having experienced firsthand as a teenager in Appalachian Pennsylvania the violent prejudices of right-wing people, I'm aware of what they can do. Granted, the more reasonable members of Trump's working-class base stayed home on that day of insurrectionary rioting, working hard at their jobs as they always do, raising their families, regardless of their bitter feelings about the election. I see, however, the peril that Trump's other base, the extremist faction of America Firsters and Christian nationalists and white supremacists, poses to the country.

I also see the crisis, worsening by the minute, of our global environmental catastrophe. Drought and searing heat and wildfires, mega-hurricanes, torrential deluges and floods, melting ice caps, rising seas, and the vanishing, forever, of vast species of plants, insects, fish, birds, animals. I hide from none of it.

We need a mass transformation of human consciousness. We need it urgently. We need to change how we think, how we live, how we perceive reality. To survive, we need to wake up. Now.

In my modest way, as a Zen minister and a lay dharma teacher, I'm doing my small part in trying to make that happen.

〇

NOW, AS I approach the year 2022 and the elderhood age of sixty-eight, much of the former "Steve," the person who trekked home to the Appalachian heartland for his reunion thirty years ago in 1992, has quietly, gradually dimmed in abeyance. The person known as "Kanji" finds home in a heartland of union with each moment, quietly, gradually brightening in abundance.

Dōgen, from the *Eihei Kōroku*: "Nobody knows how many straw sandals I have worn through. Returning to my home mountain, I just rest."

As you finish reading, you know what has happened to me so far in this lifetime—or at least you know how for three decades I've constructed a narrative, artfully, employing both the foggy imprecisions and the vivid certainties of memory, trying sincerely to match subjective experience with objective facts of a personal and social history, and hoping with earnest desire to get it at least partially right. It's a narrative about a self by a Zen minister who teaches kōans and meditation for realizing no-self. It's a narrative in written language by a Zen minister who works in a spiritual tradition that skeptically refers to language as "going into the weeds and brambles." It's a story narrative by a Zen minister who often tells his students to give up clinging to their stories and be free—right now, right here.

Yet our stories are important.

This has been mine. How a scion of indentured servants, farmers, soldiers, and factory workers discovers fulfillment in a life he never could have predicted. How he grew up in a culture of violence and is finding peace; in a culture of hardship and is finding treasure. How he lost those he loves and finds solace. How, living between contrasting worlds, he seeks the dharma and finds his way home.

Now you tell yours.

NOTES

Because this is a memoir and not a work of academic scholarship, the sources for quotations, lines from poems, and so on usually are provided directly in the text. Sources that are not given can often be found quickly and easily through a Google search.

However, for sources that are not provided in the text or are not likely to be located conveniently through an online search, information is provided below.

INTRODUCTION: PRACTICE AS IF YOUR HEAD IS ON FIRE

— The Dōgen quote is a famous passage from the "Genjōkōan" ("Actualizing the Fundamental Point") chapter of the *Shōbōgenzō*. The translation I've used is in Kazuaki Tanahashi, ed., *Treasury of the True Dharma Eye: Zen Master Dogen's Shobo Genzo* (Boston and London: Shambala, 2012).
— The Merton quote is from his essay "Zen Buddhist Monasticism," included in Thomas Merton, *Mystics and Zen Masters* (New York: Farrar, Straus and Giroux, 1967).

PART ONE: IN PENN'S WOODS

— The Thich Nhat Hanh quotes throughout this section are from his book *Going Home: Jesus and Buddha as Brothers* (New York: Riverhead/Penguin Putnam, 1999).
— The British map is reproduced in Robert Secor, ed., *Pennsylvania 1776* (University Park, PA: Pennsylvania State University Press, 1976).

— Information regarding hardships of eighteenth-century German immigrants voyaging to America derives from Lavern Rippley, *Of German Ways* (Minneapolis: Dillon Press, 1970), and from personal research in the Genealogical Room of the Centre County Library, Bellefonte, PA.

— The Leo Held massacre is extensively documented in the *Lock Haven Express* throughout October 1967.

— The Thoreau paraphrase about "best books" is from his classic *Walden*.

— The Yuan-Wu quote is from Thomas Merton's "Zen Buddhist Monasticism" chapter in *Mystics and Zen Masters*, cited above.

— The Bashō quote is from Lucien Stryk's introduction to *On Love and Barley: Haiku of Basho* (London: Penguin Books, 1988).

— The future US Poet Laureate who called the poems "beautiful" was William Meredith; his quotation is from the blurb he wrote for my chapbook of poems, *No Bread Without the Dance,* and is reproduced as well in my book *The Constant Yes of Things: Selected Poems 1973-2018* (Amherst, MA: Off the Common Books, 2018).

— The Yantou quote is from Dōgen's *Eihei Kōroku*, Volume 9, #15 (Boston: Wisdom House, 2010).

PART TWO: NARROW ROAD TO THE RISING SUN

— The Zen stories and adages throughout this section can be found in Paul Reps and Nyogen Senzaki, *Zen Flesh, Zen Bones* (Boston and London: Shambhala, 1994) and Timothy Freke, *Zen Wisdom: Daily Teachings from the Zen Masters* (New York: Sterling Publishing), among many other sources.

— The Alice Walker quote is from her essay "This Was Not an Area of Large Plantations," in *Turning Wheel: The Journal of Socially Engaged Buddhism,* Summer 2003.

— The Tanzakis essay is included in Philip Lopate, ed., *The Art of the Personal Essay* (New York: Anchor Books, 1995).

— The Dōgen quote regarding practice-realization is from his *Eihei Kōroku,* Volume 7, #526.

— Information about Ikkyū derives from Stephen Berg, ed., *Crow with No Mouth: Ikkyū, Fifteenth Century Zen Master* (Port Townsend, WA: Copper Canyon Press, 2000); Nelson Foster and Jack Shoemaker, ed., *The Roaring Stream: A New Zen*

Reader (Hopewell, NJ: The Ecco Press, 1996); Freke, *Zen Wisdom*, cited above; and John Stevens, ed., *Wild Ways: Ikkyū* (Buffalo, NY: White Pine Press, 2003). The Ikkyū "attention" anecdote is from Philip Kapleau, *The Three Pillars of Zen* (New York: Anchor Books, 1989).

— Information about the history of Japanese swordsmanship derives from Darrell Craig, *Iai: The Art of Drawing the Sword* (Boston: Tuttle Publishing, 1988), in addition to King's book, cited in the text.

— Information about the history of Japanese drumming is from Mark Coutts-Smith, *Children of the Drum: The Life of Japan's Kodo Drummers* (Hong Kong: Lightworks Press, 1997).

— Information about Bashō derives from Stryk's introduction to *On Love and Barley*, cited above, and also from Nobuyuki Yuasa's introduction to Bashō's *The Narrow Road to the Deep North and Other Travel Sketches* (New York: Penguin Books, 1966).

— The Ox-Herding Series is discussed in John Daido Loori, *The Eight Gates of Zen: Spiritual Training in an American Zen Monastery* (Mt. Tremper, NY: Dharma Communications, 1992).

— Simone Weil says that prayer is attention in her essay "Reflections on the Right Use of School Studies with a View to the Love of God," included in the collection of her work *Waiting for God* (New York: Perennial Classics, 2001).

— The Thomas Merton quote about comparing Zen and Christianity is from his book *Zen and the Birds of Appetite* (New York: New Directions, 1968).

— The Dōgen quote "Now if a bird or a fish..." is from "Genjōkōan," cited above.

PART THREE: ALL IS LOST, BE OF GOOD CHEER

— The John Daido Loori quotes are from *Mountain Record: The Zen Practitioner's Journal*, Summer 1998.

— The statistic of 30,000 annual suicide deaths is from Kay Redfield Jamison, *Night Falls Fast: Understanding Suicide* (New York: Alfred A. Knopf, 1999).

— Regarding the Thanatos discussion: As I discovered after drafting my manuscript, James Hillman anticipated some of my ideas regarding spiritual crisis, ego-death, and suicide in the original 1965 edition of his book *Suicide and the Soul*, although he did not do so in a Buddhist context, and he does not mention zazen as a means of sublimating the death-wish (Woodstock, CT: Spring Publications, 1965, new edition 1997).

— The Francis of Assisi reference is to his poem "The Praise of the Virtues," *Saint Francis of Assisi: Writings and Early Biographies* (Chicago: Franciscan Herald Press, 1971).

— The Simone Weil quotation is from her essay "Concerning the Our Father," collected in *Waiting for God*, cited above.

— The Merton quote is from his essay "The Zen Koan," collected in *Mystics and Zen Masters*, cited above.

— The Dickinson poem is #966 in R.W. Franklin, ed., *The Poems of Emily Dickinson* (Cambridge: Belknap Press, 1999).

— The excerpt from the Ts'ao-shan koan is from Foster and Shoemaker, ed., *The Roaring Stream,* cited above.

— The Dōgen quote is from his essay "Birth and Death" (*Shoji*), included in Tanahashi, ed., *Treasury of the True Dharma Eye*, cited above.

— The translation is from Robert A.F. Thurman's *The Tibetan Book of the Dead* (New York: Quality Paperback Book Club, 1994).

— The Janet Malcolm quote is from *The New York Review of Books*, June 21, 2001.

PART FOUR: ERRANT PILGRIM

— The anecdote about Yun-Men and the monk is included in *The Roaring Stream,* cited above.

— The Chinese Buddhist teacher who said "Round and perfect like vast space…" was Chien-chih Seng-ts'an; Taikan Monju quotes him in Audrey Yoshiko Seo, *Enso: Zen Circles of Enlightenment* (Boston and London: Weatherhill, 2007).

— The statement about Pennsylvania as Arkansas reputedly originated with James Carville during the first Bill Clinton presidential campaign in Pennsylvania.

— Poverty statistics of one-in-five for Centre County are from the 2000 US Census, available online through the US Census Bureau website.

— The Dōgen quote about mountains belonging to the people who love them is from his "Mountains and Rivers Sutra," included in Tanahashi, ed., *Treasury of the True Dharma Eye*, cited above.

— The quote from the Dōgen poem "Do not ask me…" is from a translation by Heine in *Zen Poetry of Dōgen*, cited above.

PART FIVE: GONE BEYOND

— The Talking Heads quote is from their song "This Must Be the Place (Naïve Melody)."

— The Indian tale of the Seven Wise Sisters is included in Florence Caplow and Susan Moon, ed., *The Hidden Lamp: Stories from Twenty-Five Centuries of Awakened Women* (Boston: Wisdom Publications, 2013).

— The Dōgen passage from *Eihei Kōroku* is #380.

— The Dalai Lama has made the "Marxist" statement in numerous interviews and says something similar in his books *Beyond Religion: Ethics for a Whole World* (Boston: Mariner Books, 2012) and *A Call for Revolution: A Vision for the Future* (New York: William Morrow, 2018).

— The Henry Adams reference is from the "Harvard College" chapter of his classic *The Education of Henry Adams*. (New York: The Modern Library, 1999).

— The George Gordon, Lord Byron quote is from *Don Juan*, Canto XV, Stanza 99.

— The Pa Ling koan is from the classic koan collection *The Blue Cliff Record*. This translation is Thomas Cleary and J.C. Cleary, *The Blue Cliff Record* (Boston and London: Shambhala, 2005).

— The quote from the Book of Job is from the King James version.

— The Adrienne Rich phrase "wild patience has taken me this far" is from her poetry collection of the same name.

ACKNOWLEDGMENTS

I offer deep gratitude and bows to my beloved family and to my friends—I won't list names, concerned that I might leave someone out by mistake, but you know who you are. Lots of appreciation and love.

I am grateful to my teachers and my students, in zendos and in classrooms.

I give thanks to the writers, artists, musicians, actors, dancers, and film directors, my intimate companions, the kindred spirits whose work sustains me and whose lives, coming to me across centuries and into the present, support my own. Though I've never met most of them in person, I know them well.

I give thanks to my spiritual mentors, alive in Buddhist sutras and Bible scriptures, in Native American tales and Sufi poems, in arcane Celtic legends and Zen kōans, providing support and inspiration through millennia.

I'm grateful to the Pennsylvania Council on the Arts for a writing grant in creative nonfiction, awarded in 2004 on the basis of the opening chapter of *Appalachian Zen.*

I'm also grateful to *Tricycle: The Buddhist Review* for publishing in its online edition, August 2022, a modified version of the Hiroshima section.

I couldn't squeeze every significant person into the narrative of this spiritual memoir. One deserves mention here. John Balaban, remarkable poet—winner of the Academy of American Poets' Lamont Prize, the Williams Carlos Williams Award from the Poetry Society of America, and other honors, and twice nominated for the National Book Award—grew up in a tough working-class neighborhood of Philadelphia. Like me, he graduated with high honors from Penn State and went on to Harvard. A conscientious objector during the Vietnam War, he served there as a medical volunteer, helping to treat injured children. In the decades following the war he has translated Vietnamese *ca dao* poetry and established the extraordinary nonprofit Vietnamese Nôm Preservation Foundation to rescue Vietnam's ancient literary heritage from oblivion.

Years ago, in 1975, after I returned from the summer writers' conference at Bread Loaf in Vermont, I enrolled in a fall-semester poetry workshop that John was teaching at Penn State—the only poetry workshop I've ever taken. John encouraged me, and we remain friends half a century later.

More significantly: In 1977, after I dropped out of college, John encouraged me to move to Amherst, where he'd recently given a poetry reading at Amherst College. He thought I'd like it here. His suggestion changed the trajectory of my life. Aside from brief sojourns of living in Santa Fe, Japan, Cambridge, and back in central Pennsylvania, I've lived in the Amherst area ever since. Much of what has happened in the past five decades of my spiritual journey occurred because John Balaban urged me to leave Pennsylvania for western Massachusetts.

From small suggestions in our lives, enormous consequences.

I'm grateful to Dr. Charles Prebish, professor of Buddhist Studies and my honors advisor during my second stint at Penn State in the early 2000s, who provided instruction, advocacy, and friendship.

A person who also deserves mention is Dr. Anne Monius, professor of South Asian Religions at Harvard Divinity School. Brilliant and warmly personable, Anne came from a working-class background and, like me, was the first person in her family to graduate from college. She understood that first-generation college students need extra information to navigate an unfamiliar system, and extra encouragement and support. She gave that to me, unstintingly, during her office hours in Harvard's Center for World Religions. "We need more students here like you, from your background," she told me. She supervised my graduate thesis on Francis of Assisi, Dōgen, and Rūmī, and critiqued it and praised it. When I felt overburdened she told me stories and jokes and laughed with me and helped me persevere. She ignored the clock and gave me a sanctuary.

Anne died recently. I wish she could have read this spiritual memoir. I offer many thanks.

I close here by offering deep thanks to the magnificent team at Monkfish: publisher Paul Cohen, editor Susan Piperato, proofreader Dory Mayo, cover designer Colin Rolfe, and publicist Ginger Price. It's been a tremendous privilege and a pleasure to work with them.

I devoted thirty years to writing *Appalachian Zen*, beginning in 1992. I worked on it, through countless revisions, during evenings and weekends while toiling in full-time jobs. I'm grateful to Monkfish for bringing my book to you, and I appreciate Paul, Susan, Dory, Colin, and Ginger for making its publication such a smooth and joyful process. Many bows.